"In the summer of 1992, I drive us to their home in Medici Elmer as his writings had been so to articulate my educational miss as I was sat in the front of the car and subjected to an interrogation far more demanding than my recent viva. That journey was the beginning of an enriching philosophical and theological conversation spanning a friendship of nearly thirty years now. Elmer's autobiography is a privilege to read as it gives a window on the man who helped shape my academic career. And I was so glad to read that it seems we now agree on the way forward for Christians to fulfil their vocation in education!"

Trevor Cooling, *Emeritus Professor of Christian Education, Canterbury Christ Church University, UK*

"Elmer writes as Elmer is. Serious. Intense. And so much more! If you already know Elmer as a friend, or have been taught in one of his classes, you will know about the serious and intense part, but in this book you will find the "so much more." This book is about a life lived very deliberately, conscientiously, and purposefully, and usually successfully. Deeply personal. Ever thoughtful. Philosophical. *Stumbling Heavenward* is an education in itself, and an amazing journey with the author.

Martha Pauls, *a friend of 50 years*

"I now realize why Elmer and I connected so well. We both had German-speaking grandparents who emigrated to the Canadian Prairies, we both grew up in rural Saskatchewan and we each had a false start at the University of Saskatchewan. However, our connection was much deeper than that. His teaching prepared me for law school, my legal practice and a career on the bench. But more importantly, his integration of faith and academia provided an example and encouragement for my own vocational path. I was able to take every course he taught during the two years I was at Medicine Hat College (MHC 1979-1981), not because they were easy grades but because they were enriching and enjoyable experiences which made one think and re-think one's presuppositions. He influenced thousands of students over his career at MHC but also impacted scholars around the world through his research and sabbaticals – from Belgium and former Soviet countries, to Oxford and University of Toronto. It was a privilege to be his student, an honour to be his friend, and a pleasure to read his life story. Elmer's life and career is one reason why "small beginnings" should not be despised! Those in the world of philosophy and those in the church would benefit from Elmer's writings (and need to read them!) but a great place to start is this engaging autobiography."

The Honourable Dallas K. Miller, *Justice of the Court of Queen's Bench, Lethbridge, Alberta*

"Elmer Thiessen's collection of memories feels like a visit with an old friend. His work covers all the highlights of a full and well-rounded life while answering many of the questions one might pose while seeking to understand the context of those highlights. It is precise, honest, and filled with enough relevant detail to consistently take us back to the central passion of the author's life. It was a real encouragement!"

Alvin Penner, *Pastor & former student*

"To read *Stumbling Heavenward: One Philosopher's Journey* is to take a thoughtful, thought-provoking ramble with a Christian philosopher across the ranges of his rich and varied life in his family, the church, and academia. Throughout a decade of annual Christmastime meet-ups for coffee and conversation, I've had the pleasure of coming to know Elmer Thiessen as a philosopher, a colleague, and a fellow Mennonite (a rare combination!). Through Elmer's memoirs – part autobiography, part spiritual diary, part curriculum vitae – I've enjoyed coming to know him also as a son and student, a husband and father, a teacher and scholar, a preacher and leader – and in each of these aspects of his life, as a disciple of Jesus."

Darrin W. Snyder Belousek, *Visiting Assistant Professor of Philosophy at Ohio Northern University*

"What a life! What an adventure! Both spiritually and academically. No wonder Elmer Thiessen is recognized as one of the best writers on the subject of integrating knowledge and faith. The many battles he fought in the fields of theology, education, evangelism, ethics, and humanities have been a great encouragement and inspiration to many of us. In Europe we consider Elmer to be the authority on the problem of indoctrination. Not a trivial subject to anyone who wants to raise his children well. Thank you, Elmer!

Jan Hábl, *Hradec Králové University, Department of Pedagogy and Psychology, Czech Republic*

Anonymous course evaluations by students:
"This was a great class, Dr. Thiessen. Unfortunately you opened up my conscience; is there another class I could take so I can shut it off!" (Introductory ethics course at Medicine Hat College)

"I appreciated Elmer's honesty about his beliefs and the fact that I did not have to share them to enjoy this course. I felt comfortable disagreeing, and never felt my grade would suffer because I had a different opinion." (Introductory ethics course at the Brooks Campus of Medicine Hat College)

"The most enjoyable aspect of this course was that the instructor *demanded* that we think for ourselves. He offered positive reinforcement at all times of everyone's ideas. . . . His courses, better than any I have ever taken – *educate*. They fulfill the role of this institution so well that I believe his courses should be required by every discipline taught here. His courses are not comforting. They demand that students actually think, that students learn how to learn. Consequently, they are not easy but they are invaluable." (Philosophy of science course at Medicine Hat College)

"Dr. Thiessen is a cool old man!!!! A cool course, and my most challenging one." (Worldview studies seminar at Emmanuel Bible College)

"Best class I have EVER taken! Elmer Thiessen is the best. Pay him lots of money to stay here." (Worldview studies seminar at Emmanuel Bible College)

"Still did not solve all the problems of the world." (Course on Plato's *Republic* in the life-long learning program at Wilfrid Laurier University)

STUMBLING HEAVENWARD

One Philosopher's Journey

Elmer John Thiessen

Mill Lake Books

Published by:
Mill Lake Books
Chilliwack, BC, Canada
https://jamescoggins.wordpress.com/mill-lake-books

Cover design and layout:
Gregory Thiessen, Thiessen Visual
thiessenvisual.com

BISAC Codes:
BIO026000 Biography & Autobiography/Personal Memoirs
BIO009000 Biography & Autobiography/Philosophers
REL051000 Religion/Philosophy

Audience:
01-General Trade
Of interest to adults, thoughtful laypersons, philosophers,
Christian philosophers, educators, Christian educators

ISBN: 978-1-7771926-5-5

To Maggie,
our children and their spouses,
Audrey and Geoff, Andrew and Rachel, Gregory and Laura,
our grandchildren,
Madeleine, Sylvie, Ariane, Beatrice, Josiah and Lauren,
and
my sisters Alvina and Lottie.

In memory of
my brother Ted,
my sister Ruth,
and
my parents
John and Justina Thiessen.

CONTENTS

PREFACE

In the fall of 2018 I found myself with nothing to do. Perhaps I should qualify this statement just a little. I had no major project on hand. I had written my "last" book – *The Scandal of Evangelism* had come out at the end of May in 2018. I had given a talk, "On Writing Books," at our vibrant seniors group at Waterloo North Mennonite Church at the end of June of the same year. Here I publicly announced that I had written my last book and I even suggested to the seniors group that they could hold me accountable to keep this vow. My wife, Maggie, had her heart surgery that fall and after her remarkably quick recovery I started to do some culling of my research library in the field of education, given that I would never use these books again. I then reviewed, organized, and tabulated all my academic articles, religious articles, book reviews, and newspaper articles, collecting them into four binders. And then the urge came.

Changes were also occurring in the cycle of teaching that I had been enjoying for nearly a decade – in the fall semester, a life-long learning course at Wilfrid Laurier University, and a worldview course at Emmanuel Bible College each winter semester. I discovered that I would not be teaching at EBC in the winter semester of 2019 and so again I needed something to do. Why not begin writing my memoirs, starting with a chapter describing the research and writing I had done in my academic career. So it was that on January 8, 2019, I started writing Chapter 10 of these memoirs. I began writing this chapter because it dealt with my research and writing, the results of which I had just organized, and so these details were fresh in my mind. I finished the first draft of this autobiography just over one year from that date.

The moral of this story is, don't make any rash promises. But I have come to realize that writing is in my blood. I just can't stop. Indeed, upon completing the first draft of these memoirs, I already had an idea for another book, dealing with a fascinating topic on which I had been researching and giving lectures – intellectual virtues and vices.

Rudy Wiebe, in the introductory essay of one of his recent books has called the urge to keep writing a "Terminal Disease."[1] After panicking upon discovering he had this disease, he talked to people in whom he had recognized similar symptoms, and they laughingly told him "there were no known practitioners who specialized in treating such cases, no medicines, and there certainly were no institutions, anywhere where one could go for a cure." They also told him that he would die of it – "The deadly Writeritis."[2] That pretty well describes my problem, though I am certainly not as prolific or as good a writer as Rudy Wiebe.

So this explains why I am writing my memoirs. I really shouldn't. I am not a celebrity, and I am neither rich nor famous, having taught at a small secular college in the Canadian prairies for most of my life. But I find myself at a loss as to what I should do right now. So, why not write a book about my life. I won't promise that this is the last one, because I will probably keep writing until death do us part.

But what is it that I am writing? I did some research in trying to answer this question and discovered that there is a difference between writing an autobiography and writing one's memoirs. An autobiography is more chronological and descriptive in nature, with a minimum of interpretation. Memoirs tell a story and involve reflection on the events of one's life. I am told that one should write either an autobiography or a memoir, and not try to do both at the same time. I am not going to heed this advice. I am writing both an autobiography and a memoir at the same time, and will therefore use either of these terms to describe this book. Some chapters and some parts of the following chapters are more autobiographical in nature, while other chapters and parts of chapters will be more reflective in nature and hence feel more like a memoir.

Who am I writing for? Mainly for my children and grandchildren, siblings, and close friends. That is another reason why this book is in part autobiographical in nature. My children and grandchildren want to know what happened and when it happened. Of course, sometimes I will also address the question of why something happened and then what I have to say will be more like a memoir. Readers beyond my family might want to skim chapters and parts of chapters that are more autobiographical in nature and focus on those parts where I do more reflection on the events of my life. Readers should also be forewarned that because this book is a mixture of autobiography and memoir, some duplication is inevitable, though I have tried hard to keep this to a minimum.

My story intersects with that of other people. Most often these intersections have been positive and so there is no problem in identifying the people involved by name. Then, as might be expected because life is complicated, there are also painful interactions with people. How does one describe these in an autobiography? I have tried to be as gracious and loving as possible. I will also be telling stories about my interactions with students. Here I will in most cases use altered first names in order to protect identities.

An explanation might be in order about the detailed descriptions I provide of some of the exchanges with my students as well as some of the events of my life. No, I am not producing these from memory. I have from the start of my career made it a practice to write up the more significant interactions with students. It has been fun to review these in preparation for writing these memoirs. Since my twentieth birthday I have also kept a yearly journal. Sometimes these yearly diaries were only a few pages long, but at other times, especially during difficult times, they would reach chapter length. In writing these memoirs I reviewed my yearly journals and found the exercise enlightening though sometimes painful, but also therapeutic. So these yearly journals have provided some of the detail that is found in these memoirs.

A final warning. This is a religious autobiography. My Christian faith is an integral part of who I am and what I have done. I have belonged to a religious community and this too has shaped me. So I cannot avoid the religious dimension of my life in these memoirs. However, I want to write about this in such a way that those who are not religious, or whose religious convictions are different from my own, will not be put off. Again, some readers might just want to skim parts that are too religious for them!

A final feature of these memoirs should be noted. This is also an intellectual autobiography. I am after all a philosopher and so I will also be describing my intellectual journey. To avoid dealing with the ideas I have been wrestling with throughout my life would lead to a distorted picture of who I am and what has transpired in my life. So the reader should be prepared for some philosophical musings.

And finally, some acknowledgements. I would like to thank my wife, Maggie, for her encouragement in this writing project and for reading several drafts of this manuscript. I am also delighted to have my son, Greg, design the cover and do the typesetting and interior layout. Thanks also to Jim Coggins for steering this project through the publication process.

Elmer Thiessen
November 16, 2020
ejthiessen@sympatico.ca
elmerjohnthiessen.wordpress.com

NOTES

1. Rudy Wiebe, *Where the Truth Lies: Selected Essays* (Edmonton: NeWest Press, 2016).
2. Ibid., p. 3.

"The LORD delights in the way of the man
whose steps he has made firm;
though he stumble, he will not fall,
for the LORD upholds him with his hand."
(Psalm 37:23-24)

"Not that I have already obtained all this,
or have already been made perfect, but I press
on to take hold of that for which Christ Jesus
took hold of me. Brothers (and Sisters) I do
not consider myself yet to have taken hold
of it. But one thing I do: Forgetting what is
behind and straining toward what is ahead,
I press on towards the goal to win the
prize for which God has called me
heavenward in Christ Jesus."
(Philippians 3:12-14)

Chapter 1
EARLY LIFE

I was born in 1942. Who else was born in that momentous year? I limit myself to names I recognize. Stephen Hawking; Ehud Barak, later prime minister of Israel; Kim Jong-il who eventually became the leader of North Korea in 1994; Barbra Streisand; Daniel Dennett, American philosopher; Muammar Gaddafi, Libyan revolutionary; Paul McCartney; Joe Biden, who became the forty-sixth U.S. President in 2021; and Preston Manning, founder of the Reform Party of Canada that eventually evolved into today's Conservative Party of Canada.

What was happening in the world in the year that I was born? I move from broader to more specific categories. We were in the middle of World War 2. In January of 1942, Nazi officials held the notorious Wannsee conference in Berlin to organize the "final solution" – the extermination of Europe's Jews. In June, Major General Dwight Eisenhower was appointed commander of the U.S. forces in Europe. This year also marked the beginning of the "Manhattan Project," code name for the American effort to develop and test nuclear weapons which sadly were used three years later when they were dropped on Hiroshima and Nagasaki. Also in June, Anne Frank began her diary on her 13th. birthday. The horrendous events of this year led twenty-six countries to form the United Nations.

Who were the important world leaders in 1942? Germany: Chancellor Adolf Hitler; Italy: Prime Minister Benito Mussolini; Soviet Union: General Secretary of the Central Committee, Joseph Stalin; U.S.A.: President Franklin D. Roosevelt; United Kingdom: King George VI and Prime Minister Winston Churchill. China: Premier Chaig Kai-shek.

What was happening in Canada in 1942? The population of Canada was 11, 654,000. Our Prime Minister was William Lyon Mackenzie King. World War 2 dominated Canadian news. Japanese Canadians were interned and moved further inland starting February 26. Mennonites with German names and backgrounds were often viewed with suspicion. In the spring of 1942, German U-boats operated in the approaches to Newfoundland and Nova Scotia, even penetrating the Gulf of St. Lawrence where they sank over twenty merchant vessels and warships. Some Germans even landed in Canada. All this prompted Ottawa to close the Gulf of St. Lawrence to ocean shipping. While the 1930s were dominated by the Great Depression, the outbreak of the war spurred the greatest growth the country had ever known, what with factories being retooled to manufacture war equipment and munitions and agriculture expanding to help feed Great Britain.

What was happening in the province of my birth, Saskatchewan? The premier of Saskatchewan was William John Patterson, but his tenure was soon to end, what with the growing influence of the Cooperative Commonwealth Federation (CCF) which in its 1933 manifesto actually promised to eradicate capitalism! Just two years after my birth, Tommy Douglas, a Baptist pastor with a working class background, led the CCF to power and kept it in power until 1961. Douglas headed the first socialist government elected in Canada, and is recognized as the father of socialized medicine and the leader who put democratic socialism in the mainstream of Canadian politics. My father was a loyal supporter of the CCF – this might explain my leftist leanings!

Narrowing the field still further we come to Chortitz, Saskatchewan, where I was born. Chortitz is located twenty-five kilometers south of Swift Current, and six kilometres east of Wymark. A Google search reveals that the village of Chortitz was founded in 1905. It will have been a typical Old Colony Mennonite village, a main street with yards on either side of the street, most of them with houses attached to barns. (One barn at the south end of the village was separated from its house and relocated to the Mennonite Heritage Village in Swift Current.) There will have been an

Old Colony Mennonite Church (Sommerfeld) in the village, as well as the Chortitz Rudnerweider Church, which eventually was renamed the Evangelical Mennonite Church. My Google search also informs me that in 2006, Chortitz had a population of twenty-six, living in ten dwellings, a 62.5% increase from 2001.

The final step in locating my birth involves a description of the family into which I was born. My father, John Jacob Thiessen, was born in the village of Ferstenwerder in the Molotchna Mennonite Colony in the Ukraine in 1898. He suffered much as a young man, being conscripted into the White Army, nearly dying of typhoid fever and starvation. He emigrated to Canada in 1923 when he was twenty-five years old. After some high school education in Saskatoon, Saskatchewan, my Dad began teaching.

My mother, Justina Siemens, was born in Main Centre Saskatchewan in 1906. Her parents had emigrated to Canada from the Ukraine in 1904, first settling in Manitoba for a brief time after which they homesteaded and farmed in Main Centre, Saskatchewan. My mother only completed Grade 6 in school because she was needed on the farm. She worked hard as a young woman, helping her mother with household duties in addition to doing outdoor chores even though there were many boys in the family.

My parents were married on July 16, 1931 in Main Centre. My Dad continued teaching at the Main Centre School for another two years. It is here where their first son, Theodore Arthur, was born on April 15, 1932. Teaching positions were not very secure in those days, and so after a total of four years in Main Centre, they moved to Mennon, near Dalmeny, Saskatchewan, for a one-year teaching stint, after which they moved to Lowfarm for another one-year teaching stint. Then on to Blumenhof where they stayed for two years (1935-7). It was here that a second child, a daughter, Alvina Lenora, was born on April 2, 1935. After Blumenhof, my Dad took on two more brief teaching stints, one in Main Centre and then Chortitz, followed by a painful one-year experiment in farming in Sardis, B.C. Fortunately, Dad was able to return to teaching, given an invitation from the school board at Versailles to come back to Chortitz, where he remained for three more years (1941-4). And here I enter the picture.

Chortitz school and teacherage

MY BIRTH

It was in a small teacherage just outside the village of Chortitz that I was born. My father was forty-four years old and my mother thirty-six at my birth. My older brother, Ted, was nearly ten years old, and my sister, Alvina, nearly seven at the time. The lengthy gap between my sister and my birth was due to my mother having had some miscarriages.

I, Elmer John Thiessen, was born on January 18, 1942, at 1 a.m. (8 pounds, 21 ½ inches). Dr. Irwin helped my mother with the delivery. The family diary records, "Baby boy born, healthy, but harelip and cleft palate." Accepting a less-than-perfect child must not have been easy for my parents. In my own yearly diary which I began writing when I was twenty years old, I recorded that my Dad left the room and cried when he first saw me. My mother, after first seeing me, thought it would be better if I would die, but this thought was quickly replaced with a commitment to love me and care for me. Many years later, I was told by a former student at the Chortitz school, that my Dad had announced my birth to the students the following day, tearfully expressing his concerns about the challenges his little boy would face in life.[1]

The page describing my birth in the family diary is therefore a little fuller, recording what was done in light of my birth defects.[2] After a few days at home struggling with how to feed me and afraid of my being malnourished, my parents brought me to the Swift Current Hospital where I stayed for six days as they fed me carnation milk using a Brecht-feeder. I returned home for a while but was brought back to the hospital on February

4 and stayed there for twenty-six days. On July 18, just six months after my birth, my mother took me to the Winnipeg Children's Hospital where I stayed until the first day of September. Mom stayed at the Mary and Martha home in Winnipeg during my 1 ½ month stay in the hospital. On August 13, I had my first surgery to repair my harelip and cleft palate. Dad joined Mom in Winnipeg a few days later. The family diary records that the Red Cross paid for these expenses.

I am indeed very thankful for all that my parents did for me given my deformities at birth. In those days, treatments for my condition were still very crude, but Mom and Dad did everything they could to get me the best possible medical help available. They weren't happy with the surgery done by Dr. McGinnes in Winnipeg, and so a year later, I was again taken to a hospital, this time in British Columbia (B.C.), where a Dr. Neufeld operated on my cleft palate on July 13, 1943. A few days later I had a second operation for lip repair. I was taken out of the hospital on August 11. Hospital bill – $133.50; Doctor's bill – $100.00. Tickets – $133.50. At a salary of $65 a month, Mom and Dad were obviously sacrificing a lot to give me the best in medical care.

My being born with a harelip and cleft palate merits further reflection as I believe this has had a profound effect on my life. There is first of all a very practical question that arises when one is born with certain deformities. What does one do about them? Obviously this question was initially answered by my parents, and as I have already mentioned, I am grateful to them for all they did to repair my harelip and cleft palate. But I had to face this practical question myself as I matured into an adult. Orthodontic care was in its infancy in those days and thus nothing was initially done with my cross-bite and very crooked teeth. It was only after I was at university that I received orthodontic treatment. I agonized over the decision to get my teeth straightened. Should one not accept what God had ordained? I still recall discussing this question with my roommate at the time, Len Pauls. He maintained that with this kind of an argument it would mean that all medical help would be precluded, and obviously we did not practice this, nor should we. Then why not do as much as I could to improve the aesthetics of my mouth and teeth?

I began orthodontic treatment during my undergraduate studies at the University of Saskatchewan (U of S) in 1964. I still remember the orthodontist, Dr. Schachter, expressing his dismay that something had not been done with my teeth earlier. When I explained the financial situation of my parents, he empathized and then gave me several years of orthodontic care for a minimal fee. On my 23rd birthday, I had an appointment with a plastic surgeon in Saskatoon, Dr. Knight, to discuss plastic surgery to do some further repairs on my cleft palate and also on my nose.

In April of 1966, I went to City Hospital in Saskatoon for my first surgery, a bone graft to repair the split in my gums. After a week in the hospital I drove home with my mother's car, only to sideswipe a runaway horse on the highway ten miles from home. My mouth hit the steering wheel of the car and as a result there was considerable bleeding and I was in despair thinking that my bone graft had been undermined. However, a visit to the dentist the following day was reassuring. He informed me that the damage was mitigated because I still had braces. That fall I had another surgery to improve the shape of my nose. Here I recall Dr. Knight sitting on my bed before the surgery trying to persuade me to let him also redo the earlier repair on my harelip because current techniques in plastic surgery had improved considerably since the time I had first had this repair. I gave him permission to repair both my nose and my harelip. The final step in repairing my teeth was a bridge which I had done much later while teaching at Medicine Hat College. It was a long journey, but one that I believe was right for me, as it helped me to cope with another dimension of being born with deformities – its psychological impact.

PSYCHOLOGICAL REFLECTIONS

Dealing with the practical question of what to do about birth defects is only a small part of the implications of being born with a harelip and cleft palate. The bigger issue for me was psychological in nature. Analysing this is of course subjective, but I trust my reflections will carry some validity given that I am writing this in my mature years! What is perhaps most difficult to analyse is the effects of the initial responses to discovering that I was born with some significant birth defects. How did my mother's initial reaction to seeing me and wondering whether it would be better for me to die affect me? Did my father's weeping as he announced my birth in the school where he was teaching somehow have some long-term effects on my life? How did my mother's blaming herself for my birth defects affect me? I was obviously a "problem" as soon as I was born.

When in 2019, I questioned my older sister, Alvina, about what she remembered about my birth, she recalled "a heaviness" in the home after I was born. Mom and Dad were at a loss as to how to care for me. How do you feed a baby who can't suck because of a harelip? Further questions arise. How did immediate hospitalization affect me? How did months away from home, the time spent in hospitals having surgery and being cared for by nurses, affect me? These are questions I really can't answer. But I suspect the answers to these questions would provide some clues as to my eventual development as a person.

I am more confident, however, about addressing issues of self-esteem that I faced as I was growing up. In my yearly diary that I began writing when I was attending the Mennonite Brethren Bible College (MBBC), I reflected briefly on "the stigma of realizing that I was born defective." Throughout my teen-age years I was very self-conscious about my physical defects, not helped at all by the fact that I also had large ears and severe acne. My college and university years were marked by an ongoing struggle with an inferiority complex. I addressed the problem of an inferiority complex in a "Psychological Autobiography" that I wrote as a term paper for Dr. F.C. Peters in a psychology class I was taking from him during my first year at MBBC (March, 1961). Dr. Peters wrote the following comments at the end of the essay: "Keep up the good 'honest' work and do not become too introspective. God bless you!" In retrospect, I realize that my psychology professor was gently suggesting that feelings of inferiority are largely self-imposed. So don't do too much introspection.

What were the accompaniments of this problem of a low self-esteem? Self-absorption, introspection, painful shyness, feeling sorry for myself, taking life too seriously, being too sensitive to criticisms, perfectionism, desperate efforts to be noticed (e.g. pranks while at MBBC), preoccupation with excelling in school as a way of proving my self-worth, a defensiveness when anything seemed to undermine my self-worth, and difficulties in developing good social skills.

What is more difficult to determine is whether the problem of low self-esteem and its accompaniments were due only or mainly to my being born with a harelip and cleft palate. Perhaps my inferiority complex was simply an expression of the fragility that we all feel and the desire we all have to be loved and appreciated for who we are. Perhaps I am introspective by nature. Perhaps my wanting to excel in academics was simply due to the fact that I was blessed with a fairly good mind. Perhaps I am shy or serious by nature. Perhaps my social backwardness was due to my growing up in the context of Old-Colony Mennonite villages. Yet, I cannot help but believe that my being born with birth defects was a significant if not the main causal factor in the difficulties I faced in growing up. But not all the accompaniments of this struggle were negative. I learned that life is at times a battle. I excelled in school and I learned survival skills.

It took a long time for me to accept myself as God had created me. My parents certainly loved me, but I think I would have been helped if they would have had some frank conversations with me about my unique physical make-up. Instead, I recall overhearing my Dad evaluating my appearance after I had closed the door on my way to Sunday School while we lived in Gouldtown – "Elmer doesn't look too bad when he is dressed up for church." A personal conversation with me would have been more helpful. Perhaps my parents did initiate some conversations, but I have forgotten these. I think I also would have benefited from some professional counselling. I recall a conversation with a family friend of my parents, Mr. Shapinsky, a middle-aged man, who also had a harelip. On one occasion my parents showed him my unusual chest formation, another accompaniment of a harelip and cleft palate, I believe. He reassured my parents and me that as I grew older, this would become less visible. But of more help to me was the fact that here was a mature man who had the same deformities as I, and yet was well-adjusted and happy. All of us need models to help us understand and cope with what we view as liabilities in our own lives.

Of particular significance in helping me to accept myself was a conversation I had with my Uncle Jake Thiessen while I was at U of S. I shared with him my worries about ever finding a wife, given my deformities. My dear uncle wisely reassured me that girls were able to overlook these sorts of things in men. Besides there are a lot of men who really aren't that handsome and yet they seem to get married.[3] Well, eventually I did find a girl who loved me. The security of love in marriage certainly played a significant role in overcoming my inferiority complex. My deepest thanks to Maggie for marrying a not-so-handsome husband, and for loving me the way I am. Other factors helping me to overcome my inferiority complex included some significant friendships, success in my studies, and then eventually the confidence that comes with professional accomplishments.

THEOLOGICAL REFLECTIONS

Ultimately there were some theological issues that I needed to work through in order to overcome my inferiority complex due to my having been born with a harelip and cleft palate. One of the toughest bible passages for me has been Paul's words found in a discussion of God's sovereign choice in the destiny of individuals: "But who are you, O man, to talk back to God? Shall what is formed say to him who formed it, 'Why did you make me like this?' Does not the potter have the right to make out of the same lump of clay some pottery for noble purposes and some for common use?" (Rom 9:19-21). This sounds terribly harsh and unfair.[4]

What does one do with a passage like this? First of all, one needs to accept it as true. God is sovereign, and there are any number of other affirmations of this truth in the bible.[5] But, how does a one deal with this at an existential level? By submission, plain and simple. I needed to submit to God's sovereign choice for me. God had created me with some birth defects. Therefore I needed to accept these as God's will for me. I have sometimes appealed to the notion of a "divine lottery" which I think can be supported by Scripture.[6] God asks each of us to submit to the lot that he has assigned to each one. Here I have been helped by a statement made by Epictetus, a Stoic, which I have often used in my introductory philosophy classes when talking about the meaning of life. Epictetus was born into slavery in 50 B.C. and lived in Asia Minor. "Remember that you are an actor in a drama such as the playwright wishes it to be. If he wants it short, it will be short, if long, long. If he wants you to play a beggar, play even that capably. For this is yours, to play the assigned role well. Casting is the business of another."[7] I believe this statement is very much in keeping with a Christian worldview and captures the heart of how a Christian needs to respond to God's sovereign choice for each person.

The appropriateness of this response is further reinforced when one focusses on the unfairness of the divine lottery. Some people are born handsome, while others are born with disfigurements. How unfair! While Jesus' parable of the talents will have reminded his audience of the unjust economic realities of the day, Jesus was also forcing them to think about their relationship to what they had been given by their Creator (Matt 25:14-30; Luke 19:11-27). Each person in this parable is arbitrarily given a different amount of talents/minas. It seems terribly unfair, and yet God is depicted as a judge before whom individuals and groups of high and low standing will need to give account as to what they did with the treasure with which they were entrusted.[8] There is no point in being envious about the person who was given more talents/minas or who was born as a normal human being without any defects. Indeed, envy is sin.[9] The proper response is again submission and doing one's best with what one has been allotted.

There is another biblical theme that relates to the issue at hand – the fall of Adam and Eve, which affected all of creation. Birth defects need to be understood as resulting from the fall of Adam and Eve. There is a flaw in everything. Indeed, recognizing the comprehensiveness of the effects of the fall helped me to deal with my inferiority complex. All people are flawed. My birth defects were physical in nature and therefore more visible. But every human being is deformed in many ways. So I was not as unique as I had assumed.

How does one reconcile the interpretation of physical and psychological defects as resulting from the fall, with the language Paul uses when he describes these as part of God's sovereign choice? I think this is ultimately a mystery. But I for one needed to submit to God's sovereign choice for me. God had created me with some birth defects. Therefore I needed to accept these as God's will for me. God doesn't make mistakes.[10] I find it significant that during a day of prayer and fasting in 1964, when I was reflecting on "the stigma of realizing that I was born defective," I went right on to quote Paul's words in Romans 8: "all things work together for good" (vs. 28). In fact these words of Paul occur within the context of a brilliant analysis of all creation being "subjected to frustration" and "groaning" and waiting for "redemption," including "the redemption of our bodies" (Rom 8:18-25). Already at the age of twenty-two I was getting my theology right. God could work good even out of birth defects. Indeed, I now realize that because of my being born with deformities I am more sensitive to the hurt and pain of others, though when I was younger, I tended to shy away from anyone with visible handicaps.

One final theological point needs to be made here. God is not only a sovereign God who elects some people (me) to be born with defects. God also loves me unconditionally just as I am. In fact, even the hairs of my head are numbered. "Don't be afraid; you are worth more than many sparrows" (Luke 12:7). Indeed, our dignity and worth comes from the fact that we are created in God's own image. I find it significant that I recalled this truth on the day I spent in prayer and fasting mentioned earlier, when I recorded as one of my objectives, "to find God's answer to my terrible inferiority complex." Other verses I noted that day in relation to this problem included a reference to Romans 8:37-9 where Paul says that nothing can separate us from the love of God that is in Christ Jesus our Lord. I paraphrased: "even an inferiority complex cannot separate us from the love of God." I also made reference to Jesus' beautiful words in Matthew 11:28: "Come to me, all you who are weary and burdened, and I will give you rest." I paraphrased the verse in this way: "Come to Christ and find rest from all your self-striving."[11]

Now, many years later, I can wholeheartedly say, "I praise you [God] because I am fearfully and wonderfully made" (Ps 139:14). It has been a long journey, but I am grateful for the struggles I have faced due to my being born with a harelip and cleft palate. It has made me a better person.[12] I am also very thankful that I was able to practice a satisfying career in teaching despite the deformities surrounding my mouth, lips, and teeth.

EARLY LIFE

The first two years of my life were spent in Chortitz where my father was a teacher. Alvina remembers the teacherage as consisting of a living room, one bedroom, and a kitchen located in a lean-to addition to the house. We all slept in the one bedroom with Ted and Alvina in a bunk bed with straw mattresses. When I came along, they added a crib to the already crowded bedroom.

Apart from some lengthy stays at hospitals, the only other event of note concerning my life in Chortitz, as recorded in the family diary, is that on May 25, 1944, I recited the prayer, "Ach lieber Heiland, mache mich fromme, das ich in den Himmel komme" (Oh loving Saviour, make me holy that I might arrive in heaven). Some interesting theology here that I find rather problematic today! What were the other challenges faced by my parents in addition to caring for me and the rest of their family? Teaching in Saskatchewan in the 1940s had its unique challenges. Salaries were low, sometimes paid in goods and services. The family diary describes some quarrels Dad had with the local school board in Chortitz about having the Christmas program during the day and without a tree. Thus it was time for Mom and Dad to move once again.

There followed two short teaching stints, the first, a one year stay at the Iris School in Rheinfeld (1944-45). The family diary records that I began to sing in the fall of 1944 (2 years, 9 months old). My Dad also wrote that I began to construct decent sentences in October of that year. Alvina remembers that I fell down a long set of stairs in the school, amazingly unhurt. Another memory of hers is that she and Ted earned some money in the summer spreading gopher poison in the fields surrounding the village. That fall, another sister was added to the family. Ruth Irene, was born on November 12, 1944, in the Swift Current hospital.

The next short teaching stint for my Dad was at the Maharg School in Schoenfeld (1945-46). Living in Schoenfeld was not pleasant for our family. A large group of delinquent youth from Old-Colony Mennonites families would be out on the streets at night. They would also sometimes disturb our family by peeking into our windows. There were so many of them that it was difficult to get home from church at times. Hence the short time spent in Schoenfeld.

We then moved to Rhineland where Dad taught in the Flora West School for a grand total of six years (1946-52). My childhood memories begin here. Rhineland was again a one-street Mennonite village located about fifteen kilometers south of Swift Current. The population consisted mainly of farmers who had house and barn attached in their yards in the village.[13] We lived on the large school yard in the village. I still remember the three-room teacherage which was "conveniently" attached to the school.

The door separating these two parts of the same building had a small peep-hole which allowed for monitoring of the classroom from the teacherage during times when Dad was out for one reason or another (e.g. coffee-breaks with Mom). The above arrangement also

allowed Mom to become very involved with students, especially in the music program. This arrangement also made it possible for us as children to use the school room as a play area. The aisles were ideal for driving tricycles. Also, one or two wide aisles were used for floor curling, a game that my Dad introduced in the school with specially made round, hardwood blocks that were used instead of the regular curling stones used for outdoor curling. (I still have a set of these curling blocks.) Great fun on a cold winter day.

The stairs to the attic in our small teacherage played a significant role in my life. Many were the hours when I would be playing under the stairs. Often I would also be sitting on the stairs badgering my mother with questions. This questioning eventually led to my conversion in 1951 when I was nine years old. I describe this in more detail in Chapter 11. I also recall times of playing games as a family – blind-man's buff was a favourite. There was a piano in our teacherage and my diary records that Alvina would often be practicing the piano while I was already in bed.

The family attended the Mennonite Brethren church in the nearby village of Rheinfeld. I still have a faint memory of preacher C.C. Penner's booming voice. And when I hear a similar voice in church today, it still evokes the awe I came to connect with the sacred. In inclement weather we would attend the local Mennonite church in Rhineland, pastored by a Mr. Friesen.

In the spring of 1948 my Mom spent two months attending to her dying mother in Long Beach, California. Not knowing what to do with me while my mother was away, it was decided that I start attending school. The following year my Dad felt I was ready to start Grade 2. This meant I was only six years old when I started Grade 2, and thus I was always one school-year ahead of others my own age. No doubt this contributed to my often feeling somewhat isolated in school. Another contributing factor was no doubt the fact that my Dad was my teacher. Fortunately I did well in school. My final average at the end of Grade 2 was 83.3%. My lowest mark was in Art where I got a 70%. In his comments on my report card my Dad also commented on my poor penmanship. Looking at my report card now I cannot help but sense the difficulties my Dad had in commenting on my academic progress. In the second quarter of the year, he wrote, "improved in penmanship." In the third quarter, simply "Will pass." And then no comment in the fourth quarter.

I can still picture the school room – rows and rows of desks, with the outside aisles wider to allow for floor curling. In the early years Dad will have been teaching about 60 students, ranging all the way from Grades 1-10. Each school day began with a Bible story, followed by the Lord's prayer. Each day there would be a schedule written on the top-left side of the blackboard indicating what each grade should be doing in each segment of the day. Dad would slip from one grade to the next, teaching and giving students some help with their homework. He also used the senior students to tutor those in the lower grades. How Dad kept up with these demands, I don't know, but he was a very disciplined person. But this had a toll on family life. Evenings he would often be back in the school room, preparing for the next day. Mom and Dad were also the custodians of the school, as a way of supplementing their meagre teacher's salary.

I can still recall the winters with lots of snow and blizzards. Dad would build huge snow slides on the school yard – great fun with sleds and toboggans. Most of the time students were expected to play outside during recesses, no matter how cold it was. Another memory I have of winters in Rhineland is of cars having a heavy board tied to the rear bumper which was then dragged along the street to help pack down the snow. Spring was wonderful, as deep trenches had to be dug on each side of the street to drain the water from the melting snow.

A highlight of each school year was the annual Field Day where all the schools of the area met for an all-day competition in a variety of athletic activities. The afternoon was devoted to ball games where competition was stiff and enthusiasm high. A particularly memorable field day was in the year 1949, when our school took the cup in the Field Day events. Flora West had been on a winning streak for several years and thus all the other schools were out to beat the Rhineland School. However, Flora West, with a team consisting mainly of girls and equipped with only two gloves for the entire team, won all fifteen games in soft ball, thus gaining first place both in junior and senior softball. My brother Ted played a major role as pitcher in these wins.

One feature of my schooling deserves to be highlighted. I, along with my older siblings, had our Dad as teacher for many of our early years of schooling. It is difficult for a child to have one's father as a teacher, especially given that my Dad was a strict disciplinarian. When Dad would discipline students, they would sometimes take it out on his children. I still have a memory of one girl abusing me because I was the teacher's son. Our Dad was also very careful not to give even the appearance of playing favourites with his children. His expectations of us were also very high.

Having one's Dad as a teacher creates another dilemma for a child. There is an ambiguity surrounding your father. Is he your teacher, or is he your Dad? I remember Dad more as a teacher than as a father. I'm not sure whether this is simply my own perception or whether this was due to the fact that teaching was so demanding, and so our Dad had difficulty switching roles from being a teacher to being a father. Here is another puzzle that remains from my childhood.

Moving beyond school-related events, during these years our family made annual summer pilgrimages to British Columbia where we had many relatives. Our times here were filled with picking raspberries for my Uncle George Siemens. In part this was done to supplement Dad's rather meagre salary and to pay for the expenses of these yearly excursions. I hated picking raspberries, but remember that one summer I was given a tricycle for my efforts. The family diary records that the 1940 Chevrolet we were driving at the time was causing all kinds of trouble. This led eventually to the purchase of a brand new 1948 green Plymouth in June of 1948, for a price tag of $2,450. This car, Dad writes, gave us "no trouble," on the annual trip to B.C. We drove this car for many years, and I can still picture this rather clumsy looking green hump-backed car.

Another member was added to our family on October 24, 1949, a sister for me – Lottie Florence. She became the darling of the family, providing

Family on Uncle Henry's farm, about 1952

entertainment during every meal – there are literally pages and pages in the family diary describing her antics. No wonder we siblings thought she was somewhat spoiled! Unfortunately, Lottie became very ill two months after her birth, as a result of a cyst growing on her bladder, which had reached the size of a grapefruit. She was brought to the hospital shortly before Christmas, had surgery to remove the cyst, but was very near death for a couple of days following the surgery. I can still remember the pastor, Rev. Friesen, coming to our house and praying with those of us children who were at home while Mom and Dad were at the hospital keeping vigil all night. Lottie did finally recover and came home after a month's stay in the hospital.

It was in Rhineland, after some twenty-three years of teaching that Dad missed his first day of school because of illness. He had always managed to get sick on weekends, and then on Monday he would be back in shape for teaching again. However, in 1952 he got very sick and had to miss an entire week of school – the problem was "Gesichtsrose," a swollen and twisted face. As if in sympathy, Lottie got sick as well (eczema and problems with her molars), and was in the hospital with Dad.

After six years at Flora West School in Rhineland, the longest my Dad ever taught at one place, it was time for a move. This was probably not a forced resignation, though there was a Christmas program that created difficulties – one family made a fuss when their children were not given prominent parts in a Christmas play and as a result pulled their children from the program. These six years in Rhineland were the years of my early schooling. In the final year I was in Grade five, and for the first time did not have my Dad as my teacher. Another schoolroom was added to the school yard to house the elementary grades and so I had a Mrs. Kruse as my teacher. This is the only year out of nine or ten years of schooling that I didn't have my father as my teacher. As I result, I was never keen to teach my own children in churches that we attended or at the college where I taught.

ADOLESCENCE

Our next move was to Pambrun, a town 61 kilometers southeast of the city of Swift Current, where my Dad taught for another three years (1952-55). Here I completed Grades 6-8 and celebrated my eleventh, twelfth, and thirteenth birthdays. During our first year in Pambrun Alvina took her Grade 12 in Vanguard, after which she left home to continue her schooling.

Ted had by this time already left home and was living in Moose Jaw. So our immediate family was getting smaller. Sadly, I didn't get to know my older brother and sister very well.[14] One other event of note in Pambrun – I have a vague memory of our getting electricity in our teacherage.

Ted and Alvina at the Pambrun teacherage

Pambrun is the home of the Millar Memorial Bible Institute, and our family attended the church associated with the school. Sunday school classes were a highlight for me in this church. I even won a memory verse contest. Of significance also is that in my yearly diary I made mention of two close friendships with Darcy Yerex and David Pieler, who I believe was the son of the Bible Institute principal. Developing friendships was difficult for me, what with the family moving so often. In my yearly diary I also noted that I started doing chores at home during our time in Pambrun. We had a cow at the time and it was my job to get the cow from a distant pasture each day. What better excuse for a good walk in nature, though I am sure I didn't see it that way at the time. Interestingly, I also took up trapping in winter. We had a neighbour who was into trapping and selling pelts, and he was kind enough to teach me the tricks of the trade. I remember setting a trap at the village dump, and discovering one day as I was checking my line that I had in fact trapped a skunk. What to do? My neighbour came to my rescue and shot the skunk and advised me not to skin it. Instead, we buried it in our garden.

Another item of some significance was my entry into sports. I was never good at sports – always the last to be chosen for a ball team when young people got together to play ball. In part this might have been due to the fact that I was small for my age.[15] One day the juvenile hockey coach put me on the ice – no doubt catering to me because I was the school principal's son. I could hardly skate at the time, but I started participating in hockey practices. I remember when I was put on the ice at an actual game and the coach praised me for an aggressive move to get the puck out of a corner. I think this was the first and last time that I was ever praised for participation in sports.

Our extended family experienced some tragedies that year. Aunt Annie, my Mom's sister lost her husband in an accident just outside their home in B.C. He was hit by a car as he was getting the mail from the mailbox on the road at the end of their driveway. Alvina, who had just finished high school went to B.C. after the accident in order to be with Aunt Annie – a not exactly pleasant experience for a young girl. Then our favourite uncle, Henry Siemens, a farmer in Main Centre, had an accident on his way to visit us in Pambrun. The visit was prompted in part by their wanting a report from Alvina regarding Aunt Annie. Upon getting news of the accident, our family drove to the scene of the accident which occurred some twenty miles away from Pambrun. I can still remember the accident scene, a police car, an ambulance carrying our uncle to the hospital, my Dad crawling under a car to verify the identity of Aunt Tina who was killed, and three very frightened boys, my cousins, Art, Alvin, and Glen. It was a horrifying scene, and I am not sure that I should have been taken along to witness the tragedy. It was my first experience with tragedy and death. Fortunately, my uncle eventually recovered after a long stay at the Swift Current hospital.

After three years in Pambrun, Mom and Dad moved to Gouldtown, where Dad taught another three years (1955-58). Gouldtown is located six miles from Main Centre and twenty miles north of Herbert. It is now a prairie ghost town, boasting a population of ten people, with a post-office

Gouldtown teacherage

and a well. When we lived there it was a thriving little town with a post office, store, grain elevators, a Mennonite church (now relocated to the Mennonite Heritage Village in Swift Current), and a school yard with a teacherage and two school buildings. I completed my grades 9 and 10 here, again with my Dad as my teacher. I recall my Grade 10 class being very competitive, with Allan Giesbrecht, Henry Harder, and I competing for the best mark in mathematics. Interestingly, I played piano for the school's Christmas program that same year.

It was here in Gouldtown that I got my first part-time job, working at the local store after school. I recall this job making me feel quite important. These were the days when customers of a local store did not pay cash for every item they bought, but would have accounts which they paid at the end of the month. The store had all the customer accounts pinned to a board behind the front counter. I recall being frustrated about the difficulty of finding the appropriate location for each customer's account because these were not listed in alphabetical order. So I took it upon myself to rearrange the accounts and put them in alphabetical order. The store owner had to gently ask me to stop indulging in my penchant for order. Here I thought I was being a good employee by taking some initiative! Another job I had during the summers was working on the farm of my uncle, Jake Siemens. I spent many hours on the tractor, doing summer-fallow.

One other vivid memory I have of Gouldtown and also earlier in Pambrun, is that of spending hours and hours playing alone with my Meccano set. I seemed to relish the painstaking work of putting together parts with little bolts and nuts. Each Christmas my parents would add a supplement to my Meccano set. A memorable addition was a set of gears and chains which made it possible to build even more complicated creations. Somehow, my children never took up this hobby. Lego took the place of Meccano. Too bad!

In the meantime my parents bought a house in Swift Current, in the beautiful Riverdene area near the Swift Current Creek, complete with a huge fenced garden across the back-alley (635 – 9th. Ave. N.E). They were also able to rent the land beside the creek for additional garden space. An irrigation system was installed for the gardens. This was to be the ideal retirement home for my parents. In part, the reason for buying this house at this stage was to provide accommodation for Alvina who was teaching in Swift Current at the time, and also for me so that I could get a good high-school education. While Mom and Dad and the girls (Ruth and Lottie) were still in Gouldtown, Alvina, I, and a cousin, Art Siemens, lived in the Swift Current house. Part of the house was rented to the pastor couple of our church, Ed Lautermilchs. Alvina and I had bedrooms on the main floor, the Lautermilchs took the upstairs bedrooms, the kitchen, and the living room, and Art lived in the basement.

I completed my Grades 11 and 12 at the Swift Current Collegiate Institute (1957-59). For me this involved a big adjustment – attending a large city school, not having my Dad as my teacher, and being away from home for the first time. Art and I would walk to school each day – Art, tall and athletic, and Elmer, small and academic – we were known as Mutt and Jeff. I joined the Inter-School Christian Fellowship and thus developed friendships with some Christians, including my first close friend, Arnold Dyck. Towards

High school graduation

the end of my Grade 11, I had a severe case of appendicitis, which led to surgery. Unfortunately, my appendix had burst and so inflammation set in again after the surgery and thus a second surgery was required. So I missed the last month of school but was granted my Grade 11 certificate on the basis of my academic work during the year.

There is one incident in high school that bears telling. Mr. Dyer, a former army officer, was my chemistry teacher and also my home room teacher. One day he had a group of us students at the blackboard doing some problems, when all of a sudden I heard a loud crack. Mr. Dyer was not pleased with the attitude of one of us at the blackboard so he took his big chemistry text and smacked it on the back of the head of one of the students. Now Mr. Dyer was a small man and the student he was disciplining was big and strong. The student turned around and angrily confronted Mr. Dyer as to what on earth he thought he was doing. Meanwhile, I was terrified at this confrontation and peed my pants. Amazingly, the student and Mr. Dyer resolved their differences over time. I can't imagine such disciplinary techniques being used in today's schools.

MY FATHER'S DEATH

In the fall of 1958 the remaining family moved to Swift Current, while Dad commuted to Rush Lake where he had taken a position as Principal. In the spring of the following year, Dad got sick and spent a few weeks in the hospital. During the Easter holidays he went to Regina for some tests but the doctors were unable to diagnose the problem. A return visit a few months later showed that he had cancer at the entrance of his stomach, and therefore was vomiting frequently. He taught school until the last week in June despite feeling very weak. That summer, in a last desperate attempt to find a cure, Dad went to the Taylor Clinic in Texas which offered special medical treatment for cancer patients. Alvina accompanied Dad because Mom was struggling with menopause and didn't feel well enough to go with him. The trip was very strenuous, and in the end, despite the medicines from the Taylor Clinic, Dad was admitted to the hospital in Swift Current in July where he stayed for three weeks until his death.

I recall spending time with Dad while he was in the hospital and finding it very awkward. What does a seventeen-year-old boy do in a hospital room in which your father is quietly waiting to die. I read books, and felt guilty doing so. Lottie recalls one of the few visits she made to the hospital together with Grandpa Thiessen, and after he had said a prayer, she heard Dad say a loud "Amen." Mother describes Dad as struggling with doubts. She would often read from the devotional, *Streams in the Desert,* late into the evenings and Dad would always conclude with a prayer. My grandparents read Scripture and prayed with Dad, and sang old hymns.

My Dad died on the evening of August 14, 1959, while Grandpa, Mom, Uncle John Voth, and I, and perhaps a few others, were at his bedside. Ruth and Lottie were babysitting at the neighbours at the time, and someone from the hospital called to tell them that Dad had died. How much better it would have been for someone to do that personally! But in that era little attention was paid to children and their sense of loss and need to grieve.[16] However, it was good to have Grandpa and Grandma present during this time. The funeral was held in the large Herbert Mennonite Brethren Auditorium on August 20, with Dave Nickel and Mr. Klassen officiating. I can only imagine how hard it was for my Grandpa to give the sermon at his eldest son's funeral. Many of Dad's former students attended, paying their last respects to their beloved teacher. He was buried in the Mount Pleasant Cemetery in Swift Current, Saskatchewan.

This chapter of my life ends on a rather sad note – the death of my father. I was only seventeen years old and immature for my age. My Dad was only sixty-one years old when he died. How terribly unfair! I missed my Dad terribly in the years that immediately followed, and I'm sure in addition to my grief there was anger at God for taking my father away from me so soon. I still miss him, and there are times even now when I feel sorry for myself for not having had a father in the years that followed. After my Dad died I recall my Grandpa pointing out some verses in the Psalms which describe God as being a father especially to the widow and the fatherless (Pss 10:14; 68:5; 146:9). I often reminded myself of this truth in the years that followed. I also regret not having the privilege of developing an adult relationship with my father. Then there were the added responsibilities I had to take on without a father in the home. I was reminded by Alvina that after the funeral while we as family were standing at the graveside, and after I broke down and cried, my Uncle Dave came to me and told me, "You are the man of the house now." While he may have been suggesting that I shouldn't be crying, he may also have been reminding me of the role I would now have to play in the family, given that my older brother, Ted, was no longer at home. But I was far too young to take on the role of being the man of the house.

My Dad died shortly after I had graduated with my Grade 12 diploma. During the last part of this school year we were of course preoccupied with my Dad's health. But I do remember my Dad being very excited about a phone call he received before my graduation informing him that I would be receiving a $250 scholarship from the Kinsmen Club. I am not sure whether he attended the awards ceremony but I am sure he was extremely proud of his son that day. But life had to go on. I was working part-time at

Smith's Flower Shop and Greenhouse towards the end of that school year, and then during the summer I had a job as a gas attendant at Whitley's Esso Service on the highway.

How did the death of my father affect my life, given that I was just a teenager when he died? Profoundly. The death of my father "changed the trajectory of my life. I am a different person than I feel like I was meant to be."[17] In some ways the death of my father made me more mature – I felt I had to care for my mother. But it also contributed to a delayed maturity because I simply could not mature in a normal fashion. Another writer describes my situation so well: " Teenagers have to balance the typical tasks of adolescence with the extraordinary demands of mourning. If overwhelmed by both, they may push one aside for a while, only to revisit it 10 years down the road. Or 20. Or more. This is how childhood grief becomes protracted over a lifetime."[18] But there is more. "One's entire worldview is shaped by such a tragedy. One becomes a catastrophist".[19] "For a fatherless child, all things are possible but nothing is safe."[20] I have often described myself as a pessimist and I think in part this is due to my having lost my father so early. Thankfully, God enters the picture. "We are called to accept the world God gives us and to accept it with love. . . . . [T]he world and all that is in it is an expression of God's love, and we have to accept it. There is no other option."[21] This is not easy to do as I have found out.

We made a trip from Ontario to Alberta and Saskatchewan in August of 2019 to visit our children, relatives, friends, and of course the beloved Rocky Mountains. On our way from Regina to Medicine Hat we stopped in at Swift Current to visit the Mount Pleasant Cemetery where both of my parents are buried. It took some time for us to find the gravesites of my

parents – they are unfortunately not buried in the same location. It should also be noted that there is an error on my Dad's gravestone – he died in 1959 not 1958. How that happened, who knows. I read a portion of 1 Corinthians 15 on the hope of the resurrection and prayed over each grave. It is probably the last time that I will pay my respects to my parents in this way.

Perhaps a few reflections are in order here about my Mom and Dad and their life together as a married couple. They worked as a team. Mom was always helping Dad with teaching, especially with music and the preparation of Christmas programs. Even at the end, before he accepted his last teaching position at the Rush Lake School, Dad asked Mom to promise to come to school with him one day a week. Their life must, I think, be described as a difficult one, having lived through the depression, and Dad beginning his teaching career at a time when teachers had very little security. Dad was a good teacher, but had to work very hard at it, given the large multi-grade schools he taught in for most of his career.

I do recall that as a child I was aware of what I thought were serious flare-ups between Mom and Dad which I heard while I was lying awake in bed in the evenings. How serious these were, I really can't tell. Children's perceptions are not always accurate. Among the happy times as a family were the games we as children would play with Mom and Dad. The whole family would be involved in playing blind-man's buff, climbing onto chairs and other furniture, just to keep out of the way of the person trying to get you. Mom and Dad also liked to get together often with the Siemens relatives, and I remember good times playing with my cousins. Unfortunately, Mom always felt inferior among the Thiessen relatives, and as a result did not join Dad in attending a major Thiessen reunion in B.C. held in 1955. All in all, I'm sure both of them saw their life together as good.

Mom missed Dad a lot after he died. She needed him, as he needed her. Dad asked Mom before she died whether she would remarry. She interpreted this as a request not to remarry, and promised the same. Her reply, in German, "You are the man I love and the only man I will love." My mother never did remarry.

As I look over this account of my childhood and adolescence, I cannot help but see my early life as difficult. It began in crisis mode with me barely surviving, and ended with the tragedy of the loss of my father. In between, I suppose there were many good times but I think my early life is best characterized as a serious struggle. I also find it significant that in reviewing this segment of my life, I have said relatively little about my relationships with my siblings. I simply don't have many memories of family relationships. It would seem that I was a loner. I was a middle child, squeezed in between an older brother and sister, and two younger sisters. My focus was on my schooling. I liked to study. And then there were the two tragedies that bracketed the beginning of my life and the end of my adolescence. Despite the difficulties of my early life I survived, and I have learned to struggle on. But my story isn't finished yet.

NOTES

1. From a letter written to the author by Tracey Neustaeter, September 29, 2019, reporting what her uncle, Jacob Heinrichs, had told her about his experiences as a student of my Dad.

2. My growth was also carefully documented in the diary. At 3 months – 11 ½ pounds, 24 ½ inches long. At 4 months – 12 ½ lbs, 25 inches long. At 5 months – 13 ½ lbs., 26 ½ inches long. At 7 months – 13 ½ lbs., 27 inches long. This was after all a "chronological record," though there might also have been a concern about my being properly nourished.

3. Tolstoy is to have said somewhere, "Women do love ugly men."

4. Another difficult passage involves the strange requirements for priests in the Old Testament" (Lev 21:16-23). I remain puzzled about the Leviticus requirement of only "perfect" males being allowed to offer sacrifices. But perhaps one has to live with some hermeneutical puzzles.

5. Paul in Romans 9 is in fact drawing on some Old Testament texts (Isa 29:16; 45:9). We also find the same point made much earlier in the story of the Exodus. God is calling Moses to lead his people out of Egypt, and Moses responds by giving one excuse after another. Just before God gets angry with Moses for trying to escape his call, Moses tries one more excuse, appealing to his speech impediment. God's response: "Who gave man his mouth? Who makes him deaf or dumb? Who gives him sight or makes him blind? Is it not I, the LORD? Now go; I will help you speak and will teach you what to say" (Exod 4:10-12).

6. See, for example, Job 31:2; Prov 16:33; Eccl 5:18; 9:9; 1 Cor 7:17, 20.

7. This quotation is taken from a text I used for my introductory course in philosophy: Loius P. Pojman, ed., *Philosophy: The Quest for Truth*, 4th. ed. (Wadsworth, 1999), p. 526.

8. Thomas R. Yoder Neufeld, *Recovering Jesus: The Witness of the New Testament* (Grand Rapids, MI: Brazos Press, 2007), pp. 174-6.

9. I have recently come across an excellent treatment of the sin of envy – see Rebecca Konyndyk DeYoung, *Glittering Vices* (Brazos Press, 2009). Chapter 2 is appropriately

titled: "Envy: Feeling Bitter When Others Have It Better." Konyndyk sees envy as a spiritual problem requiring a spiritual solution (p. 53). I now realize that I also would have benefited from some spiritual counselling as an adolescent. The key to overcoming the sin of envy is to have a sense of self whose worth and value are "unconditional and noncomparative" (p. 53). Wise advice, given that I was always comparing myself to others as an adolescent. Konyndyk goes on to site Isaiah 43:1-4 as a key to working "from a new, unconditionally loved vision of who we are" (p. 53). "But now thus says the Lord, he who created you, O Jacob, he who formed you, O Israel: Do not fear, for I have redeemed you; I have called you by name; you are mine. . . . You are precious in my sight, and honored, and I love you." Konyndyk adds, "We are loved already and unconditionally – not because of our moral worthiness, our attractiveness, our worldly achievements – but simply because we are God's own children" (p. 53). I needed to hear these words as a teen-ager.

10. I found this idea expressed in John Irvin's, *Prayer for Owen Meany*. Elie Wiesel, in his Memoirs, makes a similar statement: "To strive to seem like what one is not, is to insult the Creator Himself, telling Him He made a mistake" (New York, Schocken Books, 2010), p. 312.

11. Here are some additional biblical passages and stories that I have found helpful in understanding my being born with some defects. Samuel, when he is trying to determine which of Jesse's sons God had chosen to be the next king, gets it wrong at first, and the LORD says this to Samuel: "Do not consider his appearance or his height, for I have rejected him. The LORD does not look at the things man looks at. Man looks at the outward appearance, but the LORD looks at the heart" (1 Sam 16:7). Isaiah, in a passage that is often interpreted as prophetic, describes Jesus as having "no beauty or majesty to attract us to him, nothing in his appearance that we should desire him" (Isa 53:2). "Why was this man born blind?" Jesus' disciples asked on one occasion. Jesus gave an answer that is perhaps not entirely complete, but in some ways profoundly satisfying. "Neither this man nor his parents sinned, but this happened so that the work of God might be displayed in his life" (John 9:1-3). Then there is Paul struggling with "a thorn in my flesh." He repeatedly asks for this thorn to be removed, but God responds, "My grace is sufficient for you, for my power is made perfect in weakness" (2 Cor 12:7-10).

12. As Ernest Hemingway wisely said, "The world breaks everyone and afterward many are strong at the broken places" (*A Farewell to Arms*).

13. One house of the Rhineland village has been relocated to the Mennonite Heritage Village in Swift Current.

14. After leaving home, Ted started Teacher's College in Moose Jaw and quit, then took up a trucking job at Eatons, followed by a two year stint in the police department in Moose Jaw. Here he met and fell I in love with Catherine Sarah McCombe. Ted and Cathy were married on September 5, 1955, at the Alliance Tabernacle, in Moose Jaw. They moved to British Columbia where Ted did a short stint with the C.P.R Police, a job which he hated. He then joined the police department at Ladner, where he stayed until his retirement. Alvina also attended Teacher's College in Moose Jaw for one year after she left home. She felt it would be good to start teaching in a country school even though she could have gotten a teaching position in Swift Current. So she took a job at Ernfold for one year (1955-6), where she taught eight students spread over seven grades. After this she attended university for a year and then began teaching in Swift Current until she left for

MBBC a year after Dad died.

15. My Dad's diary records that I was 54 ¾ inches tall and weighed 63 pounds in 1953.

16. For an excellent treatment of the effects of losing a parent when one is still a child, see "I Couldn't Say 'My Mother' Without Crying," by Hope Edelman (https://www.nytimes.com/2019/08/25/opinion/mothers-childhood-grief.html). In this article Edelman reviews a conversation of Anderson Cooper and Stephen Colbert on the same topic. https://www.cnn.com/videos/us/2019/08/16/colbert-ac360-intv-grief-loss-father-brothers-god-religion-bts-vpx.cnn (Aug. 15, 2019). I quote Edelman: "To lose a parent in the 1980s was to do so in the Dark Ages of grief support. Stoicism, silence and suppression were still the ethos of the day. It would take me five years to be able to say 'my mother' without crying." I resonate with this statement because we as children received very little by way of grief support.

17. Cooper, in the Cooper/Colbert video, and quoted in Edelman, "I Couldn't say 'My Mother'."

18. Edelman, "I Couldn't Say 'My Mother'."

19. Cooper/Colbert video.

20. Ibid.

21. Stephen Colbert closes the exchange with these words (Cooper/Colbert video).

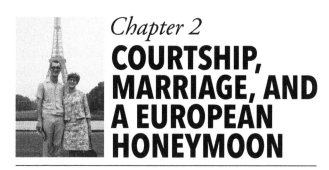

Chapter 2
COURTSHIP, MARRIAGE, AND A EUROPEAN HONEYMOON

In the fall of 1966, Maggie and I both found ourselves at McMaster University – it wasn't exactly an accident. Before the semester got into full swing, I decided to schedule a day of prayer and fasting. As had been my practice for quite a few years, I used this special day to focus on some issues that I was facing at the time. This year, one of my concerns was my relationship with Maggie. In seeking God's guidance on this matter I read the story of Abraham finding a wife for his son, Isaac, as found in Genesis 24. Abraham's servant asks God for some specific signs of His guidance and my study revealed eight such signs. After a long journey by camel to the city in which Nahor, a kinsman of Abraham, lived, Abraham's servant meets Rebekah at a spring of water. Rebekah gives the servant some water from her jar and offers to draw water for his camels, while the servant watches in silence, wondering "whether or not the LORD had made his journey successful" (vs. 21). And then comes the exclamation, "As for me, the Lord has led me on the journey" (vs. 27). I couldn't help but see this story as a model for our developing relationship. I quote from my diary: "We could silently wait and wonder thankfully at God's guidance. I chuckled to myself when I read the next verse where the servant gave Rebekah a ring! Could this be symbolic? I was reassured that I was acting in God's will and could move forward in confidence." That evening I shared my findings with Maggie and we prayed together.

Some explanation might be in order regarding the assortment of topics found in this chapter. The primary focus will be on our courtship, marriage, and the first year of our life together. But all this occurred when I was attending college and university. So, this chapter will describe some aspects of my higher education insofar as this was the context of our courtship and marriage. I will have more to say about my higher education in Chapter 8, where the focus will be on the more academic aspects of my college and university experience. Some overlap is inescapable.

After a difficult summer following my graduation from high school, I was off to the University of Saskatchewan (U of S, 1959-60). I was still grieving the death of my father. I recall times when I would be trying to study at a desk in the library, but instead was day-dreaming, thinking how nice it would be if my father could walk by and see his son at university. I was lonely. There were many times when I cried myself to sleep in the dormitory room at Qu'Appelle Hall. Fortunately, my good friend, Arnold Dyck, had agreed to be my roommate that year. He probably faced some unusual challenges putting up with a rather immature person who was struggling with grief and loneliness. I was also afraid. What would the university environment do to my faith? Here I was helped by the staff of Inter-Varsity Christian Fellowship (IVCF) and also the Christian students who were part of this fellowship. Another worry of mine was that I would not do well academically at university. So I studied terribly hard. In part this was probably a coping mechanism, but I still feel that I was too focused on study. Needless to say girls weren't on the radar at all for me during this first year.

I went to university immediately after high school because I was under the impression that the Kinsman Club Scholarship I received upon graduation could only be applied to university. I probably would have been better off attending a bible school to give me a chance to grow up a little and also recover from the grief of losing my father. Indeed, it had always been my intention to get some bible education. So, after one year at

U of S, I decided to go to the Mennonite Brethren Bible College in Winnipeg (MBBC). My initial intention was to stay at MBBC for one year and focus primarily on the study of the bible. But I ended up staying for three years because I was enjoying my studies and this was a congenial environment for me to mature.

EARLY DATING

During my third year at MBBC, a beautiful girl caught my attention – Maggie Friesen from Vineland, Ontario. I interrupt my story here in order to give a little background to this girl who would eventually become my wife. Maggie's parents, Gerhard and Maria (nee Peters) Friesen, were both born in the Ukraine. Two years after their marriage they emigrated to Canada (1926), eventually settling on a farm in Gem, Alberta, where they stayed for twenty-two years. Maggie was the youngest of five children: Bert, born in the Ukraine, and the rest born in Gem – Rudy, George, and Susie. Maggie (Mary Magdalene) was born on March 15, 1939.

The family moved to Ontario in 1950 where Maggie's father took up an administrative position at Bethesda, a home for Mennonites suffering from mental illness. After several years of schooling in Campden, Maggie attended Eden Christian College for four years, completing her final year of high-school at Beamsville School in 1958. She took a year of teacher's training in Hamilton and then taught at Jordon School for two years. Then she came to MBBC which is where we first met. Sadly her father died during this year, and so she returned to Vineland, teaching at Jordon Station School for two years in order to be a support to her mother.

I now return to my story and my encounters with Maggie during her first year and my third year at MBBC. It was love at first sight, at least on my part. During the college year, I was worried about other fellows who seemed to be paying a lot of attention to Maggie. Thankfully I was given some relief when I discovered that one of them was a distant cousin. Maggie and I did have one skate together on a skating rink near the college, though it was rather awkward as both of us weren't very good skaters. We also played a few scrabble games during the college year.

I got the courage to ask Maggie to come for a walk on March 28, 1963. I had never done this sort of thing before, and so I really didn't know what to do or what to say. Truth be told, I was socially challenged, and so on this our first date, I very bluntly declared my interest in her. Maggie very gently reminded me that we hardly knew each other, that though I was good husband material, she didn't have any romantic feelings towards me. During graduation exercises later that year, I got the courage to ask Maggie out for another date, a walk in a Winnipeg park. I expressed my continuing interest in her, but also said that I realized that this interest had to be mutual. She said her feelings hadn't changed, and thus my initial romantic overtures came to an end, though we did agree to correspond with each other.

I returned to U of S in the fall of 1963 to continue my studies in physics, with the aim of becoming a high school science teacher. However I did take a course in philosophy that same year, after which I got hooked. I was also actively involved with IVCF during these years. I engaged in some extra-curricular activities during these years of study, including some casual dating, which I negotiated a bit more successfully than my first "dates" with Maggie. I had actually come to realize that casual dating might be essential to getting to know a girl before one gets "serious." I was learning a few things!

It was in my second year after my return to U of S, that I went out for my "first formal date," actually a double date with an IVCF friend of mine. We took our girls to see a rather serious play, "The Death of a Salesman," and then went to the Dragon Café for a Chinese dinner. My diary records the total cost of this date as $6.32. I came away from this date not feeling quite sure that this girl was "really my type," though I did ask her out another time when she declined with an excuse. I asked another girl out that same year but this date was decidedly unsuccessful. Later that year, I needed a date for the IVCF banquet, and after several failed tries, I asked one of the girls in my bible study group, Pat Smith, a nurse and definitely not a Mennonite, and she happily agreed. This was a double date with Len Pauls, my former roommate. We had a great time and I think she even liked me. I followed this up by calling Pat when I was in Vancouver the following summer during one of my seismic excursions, connected with my job in Ottawa, but unfortunately she was on call. So, this was not meant to be!

The above reference to my summer job in Ottawa and my visit to Vancouver calls for a brief explanation. In my third year at U of S I was offered a summer job with the Department of Mines and Technical Surveys in Ottawa. This job involved being an assistant in field trips in various remote parts of Canada, doing seismic research. I say more about these delightful summers in Chapter 8, where I will expand on the experiences I had during my post-secondary education.

MORE THINKING ABOUT A SPECIAL GIRL

In the meantime, I had not forgotten about Maggie Friesen. After MBBC Maggie and I were corresponding once in a while. I even got a nice letter from her on my twenty-second birthday. Then on August 26, 1964, I got a surprise phone call from Maggie, while I was at work at Bowman Brothers, informing me that she was in Swift Current. She had taken a train and bus trip to British Columbia and Alberta to visit friends and relatives, and was now on her way home. The bus schedule allowed for a few hours layover in Swift Current, and she was hoping to see me. Well, how to interpret that? It would seem that not all was lost! We had what I thought was a good short visit and parted with a warm handshake. Maggie informed me later that she was not at all impressed with the way in which I handled this short visit. Instead of having a coffee and a conversation at the bus station, I took her home so that my mother could help entertain her. My excuses – I have never handled surprises well, I was confused, and I was a geek.

My diary records a day of bible study, prayer, and fasting I had in the summer of 1964 in which I identified four objectives, one of which was to find God's will with respect to a life's partner. My study of the bible that day included the following passages that were relevant to this objective: Proverbs 31, on the characteristics of "a wife of noble character;" Proverbs 3:5-6, a warning not to rely on one's own understanding; and Romans 8:27-28, promising us that the Spirit prays for us when we don't know how to pray. Interestingly, later that year after my fall exams I felt that it was time to end the rather sporadic correspondence with Maggie. I wrote her a letter thanking her for what she had done for me and wishing her happiness in her future life. Equally interesting was the fact that in the spring of next year, when I was in Ontario for my new job at the Dominion Observatories, and during a visit to my sister, Alvina, and her husband, Abe Klassen, who were living in Vineland at the time, I was "rather disappointed" that I was only able to greet Maggie in passing, probably after a church service.

In the summer of 1965, I received word that I was awarded an Honours Scholarship in philosophy at U of S for the following academic year. This led to a time of reflection on God's goodness and the way He was guiding me, which in turn led me to recommit the matter of finding a life's partner to God. All this prompted me to write up a list of qualities I wanted in a future wife, which "under the direction of the Holy Spirit would help me to choose intelligently." Here is my list of ten qualities, arranged "in descending order of importance." I am sharing these especially for the sake of my granddaughters who I know will get a few chuckles about this list.

1. She must be a girl of spiritual strength and vitality. Her ideals should be founded in Christ and His words.
2. She must be morally pure, the kind of person I would want my children to imitate and follow.
3. She must have a pleasing, loving personality, a woman of charm and grace, someone who would be a good hostess to students and young people, and someone who dresses perfectly, meticulously, though not necessarily expensively.
4. She must be a good housekeeper and cook, and reasonably thrifty.
5. She must have a good education, be intelligent, and have a vocation as a nurse, teacher or secretary, though willing to give up her vocation when a family arrives.
6. I would hope that she belongs to a Mennonite Brethren Church, though not necessarily, and if she is from another denomination, I would expect her to join the M.B. church when we are married.
7. She must be about my age, preferably not over or under two years my own age.
8. She must be reasonably beautiful to make up for her not-so-handsome husband.
9. I would expect her to be reasonably talented and appreciative of music and culture.
10. I would want the blessing of God and both sides of the family on our relationship.

The above list of ten qualities is considerably abbreviated from the original list in my diary. It ended with this note: "I would think that it sounds as though I am looking for some parody of perfection (wrong word, I realize, but I must have been enamoured with the alliteration!). There are few such girls, but I think there are some, and I'm sure God has prepared such a one for me." Well, all this sounds rather idealistic and this idealism would of course create some problems for my future wife. Perhaps I should have added another quality – she must be a person who will be able to extend mercy and compassion to her future imperfect husband!

The following academic year I completed my honours degree at U of S, with a double major in physics and philosophy. After receiving four "A" grades in my philosophy courses and a second class standing in the comprehensive exam I felt encouraged to go on to graduate school in philosophy. However, I was expecting to go to Germany in the following year. This expectation was based on circumstances surrounding an earlier application for a Germany Exchange Scholarship (Deutscher Akademischer Austauschdienst, DAAD). The letter notifying me of my successful application for this exchange scholarship had not arrived on time given my travels related to my Ottawa job during the summer. I was told that my successful application could be passed on to the following year, and therefore was most shocked to discover in June of 1966 that this carry-over had not materialized. I appealed this decision and was in fact given the award in the following year, by which time I would be accompanied by a wife! But in the meantime, I was in despair as I had nothing else planned for the coming year. I then began frantically applying to fifteen graduate schools.

RENEWED RELATIONSHIP WITH THIS SPECIAL GIRL

Thankfully, there were some more positive developments evolving for me on the romantic front. I returned to Ottawa again in the summer of 1966 for my summer job, and on the Victoria Day long weekend in May I visited Alvina and Abe in Vineland. After some teasing and prodding, I finally got the courage to phone a certain young lady who was still on my mind rather often, namely, Maggie Friesen. Amazingly, she agreed to go out on a date, and a very successful date it was – a hike to Ball's falls followed with a dinner at a restaurant. As might be expected, the success of this date left me somewhat confused. Some correspondence followed upon my return to Ottawa, with some "ambiguous" responses, leading eventually to my boldly asking if I could see her once again during my visit to my sister and brother-in-law on the July 1st long weekend. We had a wonderful conversation over dinner at Henley's Restaurant in St. Catharines, during which time I expressed my confusion and hesitancy about asking to see her again on the weekend. She then dropped a beautiful hint, "What shall we do tomorrow?" I was elated.

The following day we went hiking along the escarpment at Grimsby, and after finding a convenient fallen log to sit on we had "a conversation." I told Maggie about my confusion and yet my continuing love for her. She told me about her own confusion, expressed by the fact that she was always waiting for a call from me when she heard that I was coming to Vineland. She confessed that she had changed her mind about me and wanted us to try again. We prayed together, committing our relationship to "our heavenly Father" (we had both lost our earthly fathers). We reviewed past developments in our relationship and then agreed to forget the past and start again. Further visits with family and relatives followed the next day. After all this time, I had finally learned how courtships should proceed!

I was back in Vineland at the end of July and for the first time had someone special waiting for me when I arrived by train. It was a whirlwind weekend, what with dinners at restaurants, dinners with family and relatives, meeting uncles and aunts, boat rides with a nephew and niece (Judy and Leon), and long conversations with Maggie on house steps and a park bench in the moonlight. We also shared our life stories. After all the visiting, Maggie told me that I had won over the whole family. Welcome news!

Maggie was taking a summer class at Waterloo Lutheran University, and so early Monday morning we were on our way to Waterloo, stopping by McMaster University in Hamilton where I wanted to visit the philosophy department to explore possibilities for graduate study. We had an intimate conversation in the car where I expressed my desire to kiss Maggie, but then added that I felt that I shouldn't do so. (Indeed, a first kiss had to wait until our engagement.) But, it felt good to hold a girl in my arms – first time ever for both of us. Maggie then drove on to Waterloo, and after I had completed my interviews at McMaster, I made my way to Waterloo on my own, where we had another good conversation over dinner and then said our goodbyes.

On my way back to Ottawa, I stopped in at York University in Toronto to talk to the head of the philosophy department, Dr. Yolton. I had also visited the University of Calgary earlier that summer. In the end I concluded that these three departments were fairly equal in terms of their suitability for an M.A. program. Each place offered me a scholarship. The final decision was made on quite non-academic grounds – Maggie wanted to finish her degree at McMaster University, and I wanted to be near her, so McMaster is where I went to begin my graduate studies.

Shortly after my return to Ottawa I was on my to Uranium City for one month of seismic work. We set up camp in an idyllic location beside a lake where fish were plentiful, and where we even made some friends with the Gabrielsons who had a cottage on the same lake and who kindly lent us a bike and a canoe. This is also where I shot my first and only bear, a feat which I like to brag about because the story seems so unbelievable to those who hear it (see picture in Chapter 8). On my return, I spent some time at home in Swift Current, had my final surgery on my nose and cleft palate, returned to Ottawa for another week of work, and then finally got back to Vineland where Maggie was waiting for me after two months of separation.

MCMASTER UNIVERSITY AND ENGAGEMENT

Fall, 1966, and we were both off to McMaster University, where Maggie was completing her B.A. in English literature and I was starting an M.A. program in philosophy. I was fortunate to have found an apartment with my cousin, Bob Thiessen (48 Homewood Ave), and very conveniently Maggie was rooming with his girlfriend, Mary Elliot, in an apartment not far from us. It was a wonderful arrangement which facilitated many visits, the girls often cooking suppers for us, shared dates, and of course times of study in between.

During the first week of classes, I decided to have a day of prayer and fasting, focussing on three issues. The first had to do with my fears regarding graduate studies in philosophy. Here I was reassured by the promise of God's presence given to Joshua, and Paul's words in Romans 8:31-9 where he maintains that nothing (including philosophy) can separate us from the love of God. I was also concerned about my witness and was inspired by Paul's words in 2 Corinthians 2:14-15 where Christians are described as spreading the fragrance of the knowledge Christ everywhere. Finally, I was concerned about God's guidance regarding Maggie. Here I read the story of Abraham finding a wife for his son, Isaac, as described in the story at the beginning of this chapter.

I had some difficulty adjusting to graduate school. I was only taking three courses, and we only met once a week for a two-hour seminar in each course. This required much more study on my own and self-discipline. I found myself getting discouraged and lacking in motivation. In part this was no doubt due to the fact that I was preoccupied with other things. But, my overall life-style was probably much healthier than it had been during my undergraduate years. There were the walks and visits and dates with Maggie. We met once a week for bible study and prayer. Weekends were often spent in Vineland. I had purchased a 1960 Rambler Classic in October to meet our transportation needs. I was teaching an adult Sunday School class in the Mountview M.B. Church in Stoney Creek. And Maggie was always around to help me overcome times of discouragement.

As might be expected from a philosopher, I went through a phase where I spent time analyzing whether my love for Maggie was genuine. This surely was carrying philosophy too far, but thankfully, reality had a way of curbing my analytical tendencies, and God also reassured me that I really did love her. The end of the fall semester finally came, and with it also an end to our preoccupation with writing term papers and exams. Indeed, I had other things on my mind – purchasing a diamond ring and having a conversation with Maggie's mother, asking permission to marry her daughter. Permission was granted with a caution about Maggie's "fragile" health – she had an enlarged heart and a damaged heart valve due to childhood rheumatic fever. Maggie had already alerted me to her health problems, but love has a way of taking risks, and I am indeed very glad I took that risk.

On December 21, 1966, at the end of our weekly time of bible study and prayer in Maggie's apartment, I initiated this conversation: " I love you Maggie, and I want to marry you. Will you marry me?" Yes! "Will you accept a diamond as an expression of my love to you and as a symbol to others of our love for each other?" Again a yes! And so we were engaged to be married and I did kiss her! I told Maggie she could call the shots for the day. She had wanted to study but wearing a diamond seemed to change things. We talked, made some initial plans for our wedding and our future, went to her roommate's school and surprised Mary with our announcement, had a fine dinner at a restaurant, went to tell Maggie's mother about the good news, saw the pastor about making the announcement in church the following Sunday (Christmas day), visited Abe and Alvina

and let them finally figure out what had happened, phoned my Mother and Lottie and got them excited, and sent telegrams to our older siblings, Ted and Cathy, and Bert and Marie: "Advice for summer. Come for wedding. Diamond sparkling today. Love, Maggie and Elmer."

Life after engagement became more complicated. The new year started with the excitement surrounding the arrival of my first niece, Florianne Fay Klassen, born on January 12, 1967. I was hoping she would be born on my birthday in which case I had promised to give her a dozen roses each year for her entire life. Maggie and I helped pick her name! Motivation for studies seemed to come easier this semester, though there were "down" moments. Two significant encouragements came my way. The first was a conversation with my favorite professor, Dr. Shaloam, who countered my self-doubts about going on in philosophy. I describe this in more detail in Chapter 8. The second encouragement was a letter from Dr. Frank C. Peters, who was then Dean of Waterloo Lutheran University College, offering me a sessional position in philosophy. So there was a future in philosophy after all! I was tempted to consider this offer, but we had been planning to go to Germany after our wedding, given the promise of the secretariat at DAAD that my original scholarship would be activated for the coming year. A phone conversations with Maggie helped reassure me that we should stick with our original plans to go to Germany.

Weekends were very full, what with dates, planning a wedding, visiting family, and meeting relatives. I was again offered a job at the Dominion Observatories in Ottawa. The major seismic expedition that summer would take our team to the interior of British Columbia, and this allowed me to include some stop-overs on our way there and back to visit friends and relatives, including Maggie's brother Bert and family in Red Deer. I also made several visits to Vineland during the summer, and Maggie came to Ottawa twice as well. In May we finally got word from DAAD regarding our time-table while in Germany, and so were able to settle on our wedding date – August 10, 1967. In July I purchased my third car, a Deluxe Volkswagen Beetle which we would pick up in Wolfsburg, when we arrived in Germany – $1,535.70, with no duty or taxes because we would be living in Germany for one full year. During my last week in Ottawa, I prepared my wedding speech and also spent some time reflecting on how God had led me over the past few years. I was happy to leave my hot upstairs room on 7 Woodlawn Ave., for the last time.

WEDDING

On my way back to Vineland on August 5, I met my Mother in Toronto and we travelled together via bus to Hamilton and then on to Vineland to see my beloved. Then followed days of getting ready for the wedding. My best-man, David Derksen, and I went to a hotel in St. Catharines for my last night as a bachelor. The morning of August 10, we decorated Abe Klassen's big Mercury that he lent us for the wedding, and in the afternoon we were off to see my dear bride and her bridesmaid, my sister, Lottie. Maggie was of course stunningly beautiful in a wedding dress that her mother had made – plain but beautiful. The wedding party then drove to St. Catharines to take pictures and relax for a while. Then off to the Experimental Farm near Vineland to take some family pictures, after which we went home to wait for the actual wedding ceremony.

We arrived at the church at 7:30 p.m., to the beautiful sound of the choir in the balcony singing "My God, I Praise Thee," and "Praise my Soul the King of Heaven." Then came the processional –"Praise be to Thee," as first David and the pastor, Mr. Schmidt, walked up to the front, followed by Lottie, and then Maggie and I, walking together as there was no father to give away the bride. The sun was low so were walking through rays of sunlight and shadow – perfectly glorious. Rev. Schmidt prayed, then came a Scripture reading from Colossians 3:12-18, then the vows, the joining of right hands, prayer, "The Lord Bless You and Keep You," and we were man and wife. The choir then sang, "The Lord is my Shepherd." We listened to a rather disappointing sermon based on Genesis 2:18 which I had suggested as a text – a mistake! Rev. Schmidt gave us Matthew 18:19 as a parting verse: "Again I tell you, that if two of you on earth agree about anything you ask for, it will be done for you by my Father in Heaven" – a rather unusual application, and yet fitting. Joyce Schimky then sang "O Lord our God." We went out to sign the register while the choir sang, "Joyful, Joyful We Adore Thee," "Love Divine," "King of Love my Shepherd is," and "So Nimm den Meine Hände." Then the processional where Maggie and I walked out hand in hand. Except for the sermon, it was a marvelous ceremony, with lots of beautiful music. It was good to have the church choir present much of the music as Maggie had sung in the choir for about thirteen years.

A reception line was then formed in the basement. There was a buzz in the room as people walked around, talking and obviously enjoying themselves. We got a cheer when we handed out the cake to a room of college friends. A small program followed with George Friesen serving as the master of ceremonies. Abe Klassen rehearsed part of the story of our romance and I gave a small speech including the appropriate thank-yous. At 10:30 it was all over. After a brief stop at home so Maggie could change into her going-away dress, we went with Mother to lay some flowers at the graveside of Maggie's father. We returned to the church where Maggie threw her bouquet to have it caught by Irma, our best-man's girlfriend. Then we were off for a couple of days alone, including a visit to the Botanical Gardens in Hamilton. We had to get back rather quickly as we were scheduled to leave for Germany in a few days time.

HONEYMOON IN GERMANY

The next stage of our honeymoon was spent in Vineland, opening wedding presents, selecting which presents we wanted to take along to Germany, packing and shipping our luggage, and visiting family and friends. Then we took the train to Expo 1967 in Montreal where the Russian ocean-liner, the Alexander Pushkin, was waiting for us. We were allowed to use the ship as a hotel while we spent a couple of days visiting the pavilions of Expo which were overcrowded and which we quickly found rather boring. On the final evening in Montreal, my former roommate and his wife, Arnold and Betty-Mae Dyck, took us out for French Canadian dinner and a grand tour of Montreal.

On the morning of August 18, the ship left Montreal and we began another segment of our honeymoon – a nine-day trip across the ocean. It was a time of relaxation and resting which both of us needed. The meals were wonderful, after we learned that the abundant appetizers were only the first course of our meal! The ocean-voyage was surprisingly calm and we experienced no sea-sickness. We set aside a day for bible study and prayer, working through the book of Hebrews, noting especially the various descriptions of Jesus. We also couldn't help but note the admonition to "encourage one another daily" in keeping the faith – a good prescription for marriage (Heb 3:13; cf. 10:24). Our ship stopped in Tilbury, England where we took a delightful tour of London, after which we were on our way to our final destination.

Then followed the final stage of our honeymoon – a year spent in Germany. I like to describe what we did as following the biblical model for newly-weds. In the Old Testament, a man was to be given a year free of all duties after he was married, so that he could "bring happiness to the wife he has married" (Deut 24:5). It was good for both of us to be away from home, away from our dear mothers, and entirely on our own as we adjusted to marriage. It was also good to be away from demanding work schedules and rigid deadlines. The only requirement for myself was the completion of my M.A. thesis. Beyond that I could take courses that interested me and we had time to travel.

Upon arriving in Germany, we took a train to Wolfsburg to get the Volkswagen I had ordered earlier. We had not made any hotel arrangements but a kind German lady took us to a hotel which was already closed for the night. Undeterred, she rang the bell, and when the owner of the hotel stuck his head out of a second-storey window, she "ordered" him to come down and give a nice Canadian couple some lodging for the night. An interesting introduction to German customs! After a tour of the Volkswagenwerk factory the next morning, we drove through the beautiful Harz mountains on our way to Brilon where I was slated to study at the Goethe Institute for six weeks in order to improve my command of the German language. Here again, we met a very helpful Frau Hellwig who cajoled one of her neighbors, the Fritsches, to give us some rooms on the second floor of their new house. They joined forces to get the rooms furnished for us. What an introduction to German hospitality.

The program at the Goethe Institute was intense, with all-day classes for most of the week. It was difficult to measure my progress but towards the end of the six weeks I delivered a half-hour "Referat" on Kafka in German. This would have been impossible for me at the beginning of the program. During my free time, we made frequent trips to surrounding towns and villages, enjoying the beautiful scenery. Our shiny blue Volkswagen often drew admiring glances from people on the streets as the car was a new export model which they had never seen before. We realized that in driving this new car we were seen as rich Americans – a label we didn't exactly like, but certainly could understand. We were indeed very privileged. On our one-month anniversary we had a surprise visit from my cousin, Arnold Voth, and my friend, Len Pauls, who had been touring Europe during the summer. They conveniently sold us their camping equipment so we were equipped for camping for the year. Given their arrival on the weekend, we ran out of most of the essentials in food, because in Germany, stores closed at noon on Saturdays for the rest of the weekend.

After six weeks in Brilon and a farewell party sponsored by Frau Hellwig, we had to pack our trunks and suitcases once again and move on to the University of Erlangen where I was studying for the year, as per arrangements with the DAAD exchange scholarship that I had received. After some hunting for appropriate accommodation, we settled on an unfinished suite on the third floor of a new house being built by Herr and Frau Dietzsch, on Dompfaff Str. 49, in Alt Erlangen. We were told that the unfinished state of the suite was "provisorisch" (temporary). The kitchen never did get finished, but we adjusted and appreciated the lower monthly rent of 250 DM. Our only window was in the ceiling and so we had to be content to look at the sky. At least there was some natural light coming into our bedroom.

After passing the language entrance exam I attended some classes and finally settled on three courses – Analytische Sprachphilosophie (with a seminar) and two classes in German. In the following summer semester I took some theology courses, especially enjoying a course taught by Dr. Künneth, "Grundzüge und Hauptprobleme der Theologie der Gegenwart" (Major Themes and Problems of Current Theology). Dr. Künneth was the leader of the "Erkenntnis Bewegung" in Germany, a movement trying to recover orthodox Christianity. I also took a class in hermeneutics. It was good to dabble in some more in theology and also to wrestle with problems of liberal theology. I also enjoyed discussions with John Walker, a disciple of Francis Schaeffer, and Herr Winkler, from the Baptist church which we attended. I also connected with the "Studenten Mission in Deutschland," the equivalent of IVCF in Canada, and here we made some good friends, including Dieter Weber who invited us to his parent's home in Neckarsulm in southern Germany for Christmas.

My other preoccupation was the writing of my M.A. thesis on Kant's notion of God. I even bought a German edition of Kant's *Critique of Pure Reason*, but gave up reading after one page which consisted of just a few very long and complicated German sentences! In April of the following year I sent a draft of my thesis to my supervisor, Miss Hahn, and a month later received word from her that it was acceptable except for a few minor corrections. We had made the mistake of not taking along printing paper from Canada, and thus had to have paper specially cut for my thesis. Maggie was so gracious as to spend many hours typing the thesis using carbon paper to produce six copies. Corrections were of course difficult to make. Little did we know at the time that computers would make this process so much easier in a few years time. In addition to this task, Maggie was of course cooking, sewing, entertaining many students, and after months of looking for work, she managed to find a part-time job teaching English at a Gymnasium, the German equivalent of our high-school.

Of course our year in Germany included much more than study and writing a thesis. We took full advantage of all that Germany had to offer by way of culture. We spent many evenings enjoying concerts and plays and operas. Erlangen had a beautiful Markgrafen Theater which we visited rather often. Sunday afternoons we often drove to Nürnberg to enjoy an opera at the Nürnberg Opernhaus, usually buying the cheapest ticket available ("stehplätze" – standing places), and then moving to empty seats after the performance began. Then there were museums and castles to visit in the surrounding countryside.

We also travelled extensively. After spending some time with Dieter Weber's family in southern Germany at Christmas, we travelled to Switzerland and Austria. In January we spent a week in Berlin under the sponsorship of DAAD. In addition to many informative seminars we spent a day in

East Berlin, experiencing first hand the effects of communism, what with waiting for two hours while a "Zollbeamter" copied our leader's address book, seeing soldiers on nearly every street corner, observing streets nearly empty of cars, and seeing stores with very little merchandise.

At the end of May we took our first major nineteen-day holiday, visiting the Austrian Alps, driving along old Roman roads still in excellent condition, enjoying orchards on the side of the mountains, experiencing the contrast between the catacombs of Rome and St. Peter's basilica, tramping barefoot along a sandy Mediterranean seashore, and enjoying the art of Florence and the leaning tower of Pisa. We also spent some time at L'Abri, listening to Francis Schaeffer, who in the next few years influenced my thinking in a significant way with his subsequent books. In July we made a short trip to Czechoslovakia, together with Karen McCartney, a fellow student. Here we enjoyed a long chat with a Prague resident who felt the current liberalization of his country wouldn't last. In August we made our final camping trip, visiting Paris, Holland, and Denmark.

While we were enjoying our one-year honeymoon, we of course could not ignore the question of what we would do in the following year. I wanted a break from studies and so I spent time applying for jobs. My search quickly came to an end when Dr. Frank C. Peters, who was then Academic Vice President at Waterloo Lutheran University, offered me a sessional position in the philosophy department. I couldn't quite believe my good fortune. This offer also served to confirm my earlier decision to switch from physics to philosophy. Maggie then applied for teaching positions in Kitchener/Waterloo and in April was offered a position at the Smithson School. We also got a letter from the Henry Thiessens who offered us their furnished apartment in Waterloo, since they were taking an MCC position in South America. God was certainly working miracles in our lives!

Early in August we had to bring our blue VW bug to Emden to be shipped to Canada on a Volkswagen export ship for a mere $600. We then made our way back to Erlangen by train combined with a one-day cruise on the Rhine. On August 19, 1968, exactly one year and one day after we arrived in Germany, we spent a long day travelling home to Canada, starting with a taxi ride, a bus to Nürnberg, a flight to Frankfurt, then Köln, then Montreal, and finally Toronto. Maggie's brother George and his wife Nettie were waiting for us at the airport and took us home to Vineland where we spent a week visiting the family.

All good things finally come to an end, and so did our honeymoon year in Germany. Monthly anniversaries during this year are noted in my diary. I wrote the following in April: "Married life truly is wonderful"! At the time of writing these memoirs, we have already celebrated our 50th wedding anniversary, and I still say, "Married life is wonderful."

FIFTY YEARS LATER

It is surely appropriate to conclude this chapter by fast-forwarding and reflecting on another celebration fifty years later. Of course, by now I was retired and we were once again living in Waterloo – a new home and a new church and a very different family situation. Our children were all married and we now had six grandchildren – our maximum. How did we celebrate our 50th wedding anniversary? We began by having our anniversary recognized at our regular Senior Connections gathering in our church, Waterloo North Mennonite Church, in the beginning of August. We provided the cake, put up a few wedding pictures, and shared a few memories of our wedding and honeymoon. Audrey, Rachel, and Madeleine joined us for this event. Then later in August, the entire family got together for a week at Log Escape Cottage on Lake Manitouwabing near Parry Sound. The week was filled with good food, good fellowship, games, swimming, canoeing, and each evening, a slide presentation, reviewing a section of our fifty years as a married couple and as a family. The children presented us with a lovely fiftieth anniversary book of pictures and tributes. Of significance to us also was the fact that the cover and interior layout had been designed by Greg – a superb work of art. It was a good week which we will long remember.

We continued our celebrations in September with an eleven day tour of Ireland with Royal Irish Tours. Although we were rather disappointed with our tour guide, we nevertheless enjoyed the beauty of the emerald isle and saw some very nice manor houses which was the focus of this tour.

Fifty years is a long time. As already noted, there were significant changes in our life as a married couple in the years between 1967 and 2017. Each of us changed during this time. And these changes required ongoing renewal of our commitment to each other. I trust it has not been too hard for my dear wife to renew her commitment to me as I have become a different person over time.

What a privilege it has been to share life with Maggie, who continues love me and who has stuck with me through the ups and downs of life's journey. And what security there has been in the vows we made at our wedding to love each other until death do us part. It is these vows that have sustained us through the ebb and flow of life together. Yes, there were times when we disagreed with each other, though our children will not have seen us quarrel too many times. Both of us don't like scenes of conflict and so we have in the main kept a lid on our emotions during times of tension. We realize there are marriage manuals suggesting that this is not a healthy way to deal with conflict, but it has worked for us. And we are still together and happily married. God has indeed been good to us, and we are deeply grateful for His grace that has sustained our marriage.

Family at Log Escape Cottage, August, 2017

Chapter 3
EARLY CAREER AND BABIES
(1968-1979)

It was the summer after my first year of teaching at Waterloo Lutheran University (1968-9). After a delightful four weeks in Orillia where I was teaching a summer course, we took an extended holiday to the western provinces to visit relatives and friends and also to attend the wedding of my good friend, Len Pauls, in Lethbridge, Alberta. We then took a bus to Swift Current to visit my mother. The bus stopped in Medicine Hat and we had some time to kill as we waited for a connecting bus that would take us to Swift Current. It was very hot and very windy as we took a walk in downtown Medicine Hat. We still have a vivid memory of the heat and the wind and the tumble-weeds tumbling down the streets. We said to ourselves that we would never want to live in Medicine Hat. Little did we know that we would spend thirty-six years in this fair city. God has a sense of humour!

WATERLOO LUTHERAN UNIVERSITY
AND OUR FIRST BABY *(1968-70)*

Our one-year honeymoon in Germany was over. It was time to return to the real world and experience married life in Canada, and face the day-to-day pressures of work and the uncertainties about the future. After a week at Maggie's home in Vineland, Abe and Alvina brought us to our new abode in Waterloo, an apartment on Hazel Street, near Waterloo Lutheran University (WLU) where I would be teaching, though some distance away from Smithson School where Maggie would be teaching. We plunged into getting settled in our apartment and preparing for our teaching assignments, while waiting to pick up our Volkswagen which still hadn't arrived from Germany. Early in September I had a day of prayer and bible study, focussing on the question, "What does it mean to have a relationship to Jesus Christ?" My reflections on this were eventually published in the *Mennonite Brethren Herald* in 1970, an early foray into religious writing for me. I was also preparing for the defence of my M.A. thesis at McMaster University, which occurred on September 17. My defence was successful in spite of what I thought was a poor showing on my part.

Then on September 23, 1968 I gave my first lecture at a university. Facing a class of sixty students, was a terrifying experience. Who was I, just twenty-six years old, teaching students, many of whom were nearly as old and some even older than I? But I survived! It was a tough year for both of us. Maggie had a difficult remedial class of students in Grades 5 & 6. Both of us were working very hard, with nearly every evening devoted to preparations for classes and marking student essays or homework. Sometimes I had to end a lecture early because I had come to the end of my lecture notes! But after one year of teaching I was convinced that teaching was my cup of tea.

A highlight of this year was the summer spent in Orillia, where I was teaching an extension course for the university. We found a nice house to rent near the high-school where I was teaching. I taught from 8-10 a.m., marked papers and prepared for the next class the rest of the morning. Then in the afternoon and evening we were free to go swimming, canoeing, fishing, golfing, reading, or visiting. And we had a lot of visitors that summer! We also got to know our neighbours, the Palmers, very well, and watched the first landing of men on the moon at their home. These four weeks in Orillia were a lovely holiday with pay!

After my course was finished, we took another extended holiday out West to visit friends and relatives. We flew to Edmonton where we met Maggie's brother, Bert and his wife, Marie. Then another flight to Vancouver where we had to make a quick switch to a new set of relatives on my side of the family – Ted and Cathy Thiessen, and Ruth and Maurice Cunin. We then took a bus to Lethbridge to attend the wedding of Len and Martha Pauls, where I was an attendant. Then on to Swift Current via Medicine Hat, again via bus. The story at the beginning of this chapter describes our experience and our first impressions of Medicine Hat. From Swift Current we travelled by car to Prince Albert where Abe and Alvina had started a church ministry and then on to Glenbush to visit Henry and Susan Pauls and their seven children. Then back to Swift Current, a train ride to Winnipeg and from there a flight to Toronto and a drive home to Waterloo and back to the grind.

I was offered an extension to my sessional appointment at WLU. Two things stand out in my second year of teaching. I was invited by the religion department of the university to participate in a debate with Joel Hartt (my office-mate) on the question, "Is God necessary for modern man?" Joel was my colleague in philosophy, an outspoken atheist, and a person with a flair for words. Needless to say, I was terrified and wondered why I had ever agreed to participate given that I was generally averse to debating in public. I was encouraged by the fact that the InterVarsity Christian Fellowship (IVCF) group on campus was praying for me. The debate took place in a large classroom theater. I drew on Francis Schaeffer's writings to argue that modern man does indeed need God. I'm sure Joel "won" the debate rhetorically, though I felt he missed the point by critiquing arguments for the existence of God. Our topic was not on the existence of God but on whether human beings need God. After the debate my IVCF friends told me that it was my calm and dignified approach to arguing that won that day.

My introductory course included a section on the philosophy of religion which led to my first experiment with declaring my faith in the classroom. I concluded this section with a lecture on "Why I believe in God," handing out a bibliography for students who might want to pursue the topic further. One of my students, who had already come to see me in my office several times over the course of the year, came to see me again and told me that she had actually purchased one of the books on my bibliography – John Stott's *Basic Christianity*. She then informed me that she had become a Christian. Her commitment and growth were beautiful to watch. Shortly afterwards, her boyfriend also became a Christian. A little later both came to the Sunday School class that I was teaching in our church.

My load of extra-curricular activities increased considerably in my second year of teaching at WLU. As already mentioned, I started teaching an adult Sunday School class, consisting mainly of new Christians and non-Christians, at the Waterloo M.B. Church which we were attending, and where Alvin Enns, who became a good friend of mine, was pastor. We also led a mid-week bible study group and had the joy of seeing people become followers of Jesus Christ. In these two years at WLU, I also did some preaching in our church and the Kitchener M.B. Church. I was also invited to give lectures to youth groups in these churches, as well as to the IVCF group on campus. We spent the first Christmas at an IVCF International Christmas, and the following summer attended the IVCF grad camp.

My sessional appointment at WLU was made possible because one of the philosophy instructors at WLU was working on his Ph.D. He returned to the department after two years of study, and so my sessional appointment came to an end. Given my newly found love of teaching, I was of course facing the question as to whether I should begin studies towards a Ph.D., and we agonized over this decision. I had a day of prayer and fasting in which I focussed on this decision, even drawing up a list of pros and cons. A primary consideration for me was the job market in Canada – there was a surplus of Ph.Ds in philosophy in the country and this could only get worse in the three years it would take for me to complete my Ph.D. I also reasoned that an M.A. was generally adequate for positions at junior colleges, and since I loved teaching undergraduates, maybe there was no need to get a Ph.D.

I therefore began searching for a job and sent out about thirty applications for teaching positions at colleges and universities. I got a bite from Medicine Hat College in Alberta where they were about to introduce the second year of their university transfer program. In the end, they postponed their decision to hire a philosopher, but gave me the impression that there might still be hope for a job in the future. We took this as a final sign that God wanted me to continue my studies. I was also being encouraged to do so by my colleague, John Redekop, and by Dr. Frank C. Peters, who indicated that there might be a possibility of getting a position at WLU when I completed my studies. I made a visit to the graduate supervisor at the University of Waterloo (U of W), Dr. Suits, and explored their program and the possibility of getting some financial support. Given my teaching experience, they offered me a class of my own, teaching Social and Political Philosophy – not exactly my speciality, but who was I to question my qualifications, given the $3,000 stipend that was attached to this offer.

During this second year at WLU, Maggie was happy to give up teaching and stay at home, given the difficulties she faced at Smithson School. But she was also pregnant and we were excitedly waiting for our first child. Nine months of waiting seemed like a long time. We spent some time thinking about names for our new baby. Our first choice for a girl's name was "Audrey Lynne." And a girl it was to be.

Dr. Mathies, our family doctor, was monitoring Maggie very closely during her pregnancy, given her heart condition. But he didn't seem too worried about the actual delivery. On a Thursday night in mid-May, the first sign of arrival appeared – Maggie's water broke. The next day all was calm. Early Saturday morning contractions began. I brought Maggie to the hospital at 9:30 a.m. It was a long day with Maggie alone in a room and me alone in a waiting room. Those were the days when husbands weren't allowed to be with their wives during a delivery and so after a few hours of waiting, I went home. Finally after 5:00 p.m., Dr. Walls (an associate of Dr. Mathies) called and announced that we had a baby girl. He had told Maggie as the head appeared that she was giving birth to a football player, but after the delivery, he added, "a female football player." Audrey Lynne arrived at 5:01 p.m. on Saturday, May 16, 1970, weighing seven pounds and three ounces. After a quick supper during which I burned my tongue, I hurried to the hospital to see my wife and child. I saw Maggie just coming out of the delivery room, and she excitedly told me, "she's beautiful." Then I went to see my daughter who still hadn't been washed, and I had to admit she looked cute nonetheless, what with dark hair, a chubby face and definitely a Friesen. I then went to talk to Maggie and we rejoiced together, praising God for this miracle and gift of a baby.

Audrey was slightly jaundiced and so they kept her under a light for three days, during which time Maggie was not even allowed to hold her. Of course fathers couldn't hold their babies either in those days. Dr. Mathies kept Maggie in the hospital for an entire week for observation, again because of her heart condition. She was in fact fine. Indeed, her heart seemed to improve with having babies, as well as having a more active lifestyle. In the meantime, I was busy moving to a house we were renting for a couple of months from the IVCF coordinator, Harry Klassen. I was also teaching a summer school class and taking swimming classes, finally getting my Senior Red Cross Swimming Certificate after a third try. At the end of the summer we moved again, this time to a house on 50 Bricker Ave., adjacent to the WLU campus and scheduled for demolition for future campus expansion. This was an ideal rental property for us as it was close to U of W campus. Our close proximity to both campuses also meant that students could drop in any time. We also rented out two bedrooms to students (John Dinnick and Bob Koop). Following our move, we went to IVCF Grad Camp, where we had an enjoyable holiday and time of fellowship, after which a new chapter of our lives was about to begin.

UNIVERSITY OF WATERLOO *(1970-71)*

My year of studies at U of W felt so different from my year at McMaster where I was working on my M.A. I was more confident and I treated my professors more as equals – after all, I had two years of teaching under my belt. I enjoyed my initial studies in two areas of concentration – the philosophy of religion with Dr. Horne and the philosophy of education with Dr. Hendley. The department of philosophy at U of W had a unique approach to their Ph.D. program – you worked on four areas of concentration, each under the supervision of a professor, and then wrote your thesis. My other two concentration areas which I took later were epistemology and existentialism. What was enjoyable about my studies at this level was that I was able to focus on areas in which I was really interested.

Indeed, my studies were causing me to think through issues and to change some long-standing positions I had held. For example, I especially enjoyed the last paper I wrote for Dr. Hendley in which I contrasted the implications for education of a "yes" or "no" answer to the question of God's existence. I was amazed to uncover some significant differences and was forced to reverse my earlier opposition to Christian schools and colleges. A revised version of this paper was eventually published in the *Mennonite Brethren Herald* in 1974. Even further down the road, my reflections on this question led to my second book, *In Defence of Religious Schools and Colleges* (McGill-Queen's University Press, 2001).

My studies in the philosophy of religion also led to a re-evaluation of my belief that we could rationally prove the existence of God. I will have more to say about this in Chapter 8 where I describe my emerging under-standing of the nature of rationality.

Studies this year were also helped by the fact that life was more bal-anced than in previous years. We had a baby to take care of and I recall times when I was studying with Audrey cradled on my knees. We were also leading a fellowship group which we saw as a small "house church," trying to recapture the New Testament pattern of fellowship where we tried to foster honesty, love, and care for each other. Sadly, some members of our group struggled with the freedoms that others felt they had and eventually left our group. We also enjoyed our involvement with the Waterloo M.B. Church which was considering a building program at the time. Here I am embarrassed to be reminded that I argued strongly against "church build-ings" based on the fact that in the New Testament, we find the church meeting in people's homes. Clearly I needed some further lessons in herme-neutics! The circumstances of the early church just might not apply to the contemporary scene.

After Christmas I wrote a few letters of inquiry regarding teaching po-sitions, mainly following up on some prospects from my job search in the previous year. In the middle of these inquiries I received a letter which we at first greeted with laughter and disbelief. The Pulpit Committee of the Fra-serview Mennonite Brethren Church in Vancouver wrote to me informing me that their pastor, J.A. Toews, had resigned. They were therefore inquir-ing as to my "availability and willingness to consider a call to the pastoral ministry at Fraserview" (letter dated February 9, 1971). Maggie and I were at first dumbfounded at the very idea of a large established church pastored by a veteran M.B. minister calling "a young radical student as minister" – a point I made in my response. But our initial reactions turned to serious thinking and prayer as we asked whether God might be calling us to the ministry. I consulted with John Redekop, who had probably forwarded my name to the church, and John gave me a better understanding of the Fraserview church. Alvin Enns, our pastor at the time, also gave me some wise advice and issued some cautions. I wrote a lengthy letter describing some of my "radical" ideas about church, my "heresies and major short-comings," and my misgivings about my suitability for their church. They didn't even bother replying, though I don't exactly blame them! In retro-spect, it would have been a huge mistake for me to accept this invitation. I have long believed I am better suited to serving the church as a lay person and lay-minister. But this did stop us in our tracks and made us wonder whether we really were open to what God might have in store for us.

A few days after my response to the Fraserview inquiry, I got a phone call from Medicine Hat College (MHC) asking whether I was still interested in a philosophy position at the college. This certainly helped to put the Fraserview inquiry into a better perspective as we could now think about a possible alternative. I responded by saying that I was indeed still very interested in the possibility of teaching at MHC. The president of MHC arranged to interview me at the Toronto airport, together with another person applying for a job in their business program. A little later, the president came to our home in Waterloo for another interview. This led to a job offer which I gladly accepted even though this entailed an interruption of my Ph.D. studies. The job market in philosophy in Canada was not good and I had a family to support. The philosophy department at U of W gave me permission to continue the Ph.D. program on a part-time basis.

So now our thinking shifted rather dramatically to the future move and job. In the meantime my sister, Lottie, moved in with us after having lived in Edmonton for a while. She got a job at the KW Hospital. During the summer months I worked on the third area in my Ph.D. program – epistemology, though I found studying a bit difficult because of the analytic nature of the readings, but also because we were rather preoccupied with preparations for our move. We had heard that the housing market was rather tight in Medicine Hat so I flew to Alberta in June to look for a house. After just three days, I bought a house without Maggie having seen it. The house was only one year old, had three bedrooms with an unfinished basement and was nicely landscaped. Price: $20,300. For the down payment, we had to borrow $2,000 from my mother in order to supplement our meagre savings from two years of teaching in addition to monies acquired from some student loans. This all seemed like a lot of money, but I would soon be on a full-time salary.

Atlas Van Lines picked up our worldly goods on the morning of August 5, 1971. After lunch with Lottie, we were off on the long trip to Western Canada with our Volkswagen, which conveniently had a platform under the back window in which Audrey could sleep when she felt like sleeping, which wasn't too often. Instead, she was constantly on the move, switching from the back seat to the front seat. There were no regulations regarding baby car seats at the time! Her mother remembers singing nursery rhymes and Sunday School songs to Audrey, and then trying to keep her hydrated as we were driving through the hot prairies with no air-conditioning in the car. We spent a few days with my mother in Swift Current, during which time I made a trip to Medicine Hat on my own to buy appliances and a bed. A few days later I was able to bring my family to our new home at 1412 – 26th. St. S.E. in Medicine Hat. Little did we know that we would be living in this house for most of the next thirty-six years.

FIRST YEAR AT MEDICINE HAT COLLEGE AND OUR SECOND BABY *(1971-72)*

A new beginning – a new place, new house, new friends, and a new job. We discovered that it takes about a year to settle down and really feel at home in a new environment. But there is also excitement in venturing out into new territory. We were young and there was much to learn.

MHC had just moved to a brand new campus before I arrived in 1971. It offered university-transfer courses (first and second year) and a variety of technical/vocational programs. I was located in the Department of Humanities and Social Sciences and was the only philosopher at the college. There were eight teachers in our department – a rather odd assortment of people, some 1960s hippies who would come to classes in work-boots and overalls. I, on the other hand, arrived in a suit and tie. Since philosophy was a new program at the college, I spent some time developing posters to advertise my courses (see picture in Chapter 9, p. 253).

Even though I had two years of teaching under my belt, I found my first year of teaching very challenging, what with a workload of twelve hours of teaching per week and four different course preparations. It was simply impossible to do justice to my courses with such a heavy workload. But I did have some bright students and my second year class in the history of Western philosophy (Phil 301/305) proved to be quite exciting, what with people like Peter Boyle, an ex-psychiatric nurse, and Karl Nohr, a brilliant young student who was thinking of switching his major from biology to philosophy. In the end, Karl decided to go into medicine. I made the mistake of getting involved in institutional politics during my first year at MHC. I was appointed to the General Academic Council of the college and soon became aware of long-standing tensions between faculty and administration. Unfortunately some of this rubbed off on me and gave me a rather negative attitude towards my new workplace.

I had made some initial contacts at the Crestwood Gospel Chapel (the local Mennonite Brethren church) when I went house-hunting earlier in the year, and so it was assumed that we would make this our church home. Our initial experiences in the church proved to be rather disappointing and so we were somewhat hesitant in committing ourselves, but in the end we decided to join the church. We soon developed some close friendships with Dave and Martha Rempel, and Ernie and Irma Nickel. Dave was a high school teacher, Ernie, a farmer. Both couples were a little older than we were, but this didn't stand in the way of developing growing friendships. The church had a vibrant social life and often gathered on the Nickel farm. Maggie and I were soon approached about getting involved in the church. In fact, on the first Sunday we were there, Maggie was asked to help in the Pioneer Girls Club, and I was soon appointed as church secretary.

Sadly, it quickly became apparent that there were some significant problems with the new pastor who had been hired just before we arrived. Dave Rempel and I came to the conclusion that something needed to be done. Confronting the pastor about his weaknesses became rather messy, and I was far too young and inexperienced to become enmeshed in a difficult church situation. I spent a day in prayer and fasting, asking God for wisdom in dealing with this situation. With the help of the Alberta M.B. Conference executive, the pastor was eventually persuaded to resign. It was a learning experience for me, but it did serve to cement a relationship of trust and mutual support between Dave Rempel and myself.

I had hoped to spend some time working on my Ph.D. program during the following summer, but didn't get too far on this. Instead, we relaxed, enjoyed holidays, took a one-week trip to Swift Current, Prince Albert, and Glenbush to visit various members of our extended family. We tried to take a holiday in Waterton but returned soon after we arrived because of bad weather. Several trips to the Cypress Hills Provincial Park in Elkwater served as a substitute. We received a good number of visitors – friends and relatives from the East and elsewhere. I also built myself an office in the basement of our house.

Meanwhile, we were awaiting an addition to the family, even as we were enjoying seeing Audrey grow and spend hours on end playing in the sandbox with a neighbor girl, Pammy Pudwell. Audrey began speaking in longer sentences that summer. It would seem that we were copying the Pudwells in family planning. They had a boy that summer and named him Paul, a name that we were considering ourselves if we had a boy. Our child was to arrive on September 13, but  came a week late. My mother had come from Swift Current to take care of baby-sitting needs as the college year had already started. Andrew Elmer was born on September 21, 1972, at 6:50 a.m. He weighed in at nine pounds and seven ounces, and was chubby, some dark hair, and of course cute. I was at the hospital with Maggie though not in the delivery room, despite the nurses' encouragement. I didn't trust myself given my proneness to fainting at the sight of blood. I cancelled my 8:00 a.m. class that morning but managed to teach my other two classes. We had tried to convince ourselves beforehand that we would be happy with either a boy or a girl, but after it was all over we confessed that we were actually delighted with a boy. Another new creation, another miracle, and another precious gift from our Lord.

THREE MORE YEARS AT MEDICINE HAT COLLEGE AND OUR THIRD BABY (1972-75)

Meanwhile, life had to move on. The morale at MHC went from bad to worse, what with threats of needing to fire six to eight faculty members due to a 17% error in projected enrolment. Given that I had just recently been hired, I felt quite insecure about my job and actually wrote to the philosophy department at the University of Waterloo inquiring about the possibility of returning in order to finish my Ph.D. A few joint meetings of the faculty and the administration helped to overcome some of the distrust at the college. I wrote a long letter to the president and the board chairman expressing my initial hopes for MHC, my growing disillusionment, and my renewed faith in them to be able to improve morale. The arrival of Roy Wilson in our department in 1974 helped boost my own morale. Roy was a historian and also led the education program. We became good friends and had similar aspirations for the department.

In other developments related to teaching, I taught an ethics course at Hillcrest Christian College in the winter semester of 1973. Teaching within a Christian setting proved to be an interesting experience and made me aware of how different this was from teaching at a secular college. I also spoke at their chapel on the topic, "The Bible and Emotions." The low enrolment at MHC made it necessary for me to fill my workload with a Social Studies course for adult students in the upgrading program. I certainly didn't feel qualified to teach this course and needless to say this was not a pleasant teaching experience. I also experimented with an evening course in the history of philosophy and had a good class which included a local doctor, Don Lewis, and a theologian, Stan Riegel, who both became friends of mine. I had never learned to type, so I also took a typing course at the college, and am deeply grateful that I finally acquired this skill, given the arrival of the computer in just a few years time.

I was able to accomplish more by way of working on my Ph.D. during my second year at MHC. I completed the epistemology area of my program, writing two papers – a critique of objectivity, and an answer to the relativism that seemed to be implied by my critique of objectivity. The college offered me a one-semester sabbatical the following year to help me to finish my Ph.D. They agreed to spread this over the entire year, so that I taught half-time and studied half-time in 1974-5. This allowed me to work on the existentialism area of my program which I completed in the summer of 1976. Then began the search for a dissertation topic (see Chapter 8).

We became increasingly involved in the church. Maggie continued teaching Sunday School and also became the choir conductor in addition to leading the singing in our worship services. Considerable pressure was put on us to start a youth ministry in the church but we felt this would involve too much work for us, given our young family. Instead we tried to add a few social events to the youth Sunday School class which I had started to teach. Certain needs in the church led to the formation of a lay-ministry in the church to supplement the work of our current pastor, Walter Wiens. So on April 20, 1975 the church appointed four lay-ministers (Lorne Dick, David Rempel, Elmer Regehr, and myself). This was a significant event for me in that it was a confirmation that my gifts lay in the area of teaching and preaching. Working with these three men plus the pastor was most rewarding and also a learning experience for me. In later years, the four lay ministers also served the church when it was without a pastor. Another significance development in the church was the adoption of a new constitution in 1975 which made our church a genuinely inter-Mennonite church. I drew up the final draft of this model for church unity. I also took on the position of moderator of the church in 1977, which was interrupted by a sabbatical in 1978, and then renewed several times after that. As I dealt with problems in the church I was increasingly seeing the need for more patience and gentleness. A book by Gene Getz, *The Measure of a Man,* highlighted the importance of "speaking the truth in love" (Eph 4:15). Good advice also for leaders.

We enjoyed a full summer of holidays after our second year in Medicine Hat. In June we flew to Ontario where I attended my first Learned Societies convention in Kingston. It was good to be in a high-powered academic environment for a change, listening to papers given by scholars across Canada. After I returned to join the family in Vineland, we took Mom Friesen's car and visited other relatives in Ontario, including a visit to Stratford with Lottie and her new boyfriend, Carl Goertz. Later in August we took another holiday at a Family Camp at Pioneer Lodge and had a great time hiking, riding, river rafting, and swimming. We did this again the following summer, combining this with a holiday at Wasa Lake in the mountains near the Alberta/B.C. border. This lake was not too far from Medicine Hat and had a lovely beach with a shallow entrance to the water and so was ideal for a family with small children. In the summer of 1975 I again combined attendance at the Learned Societies with visiting family in Edmonton and northern Saskatchewan. Later we took a one-week trip to Ontario after we discovered that Mom Friesen was too ill to come and visit us as had been planned. Upon our return, we again took a camping holiday to Wasa Lake. Family gatherings at Christmas alternated between our place in Medicine Hat and Saskatoon/Glenbush, and then a series of Christmases at Mom Thiessen's home in Swift Current (1974-5-6).

We had been trying to discern whether we should have more children and in the end decided to let nature take its course. This decision "bore fruit" sooner than expected. Our third child was to arrive early in December and we were hoping that this would happen after my classes were over. After the last class, I gave Maggie permission to have her baby, and indeed on December 6, 1975, at 3:30 p.m., Gregory John was born. He was eight pounds, thirteen and one-half ounces in weight. Both of our Mothers were ill at the time, and so Maggie's cousin, Elly Dueck helped me care for the children at home. Audrey and Andrew were very much aware of what was happening this time and enjoyed their visit to the hospital to visit their mother and new brother, Gregory. We spent Christmas at home, though we did take a one-day trip to Swift Current where I seemed to have impressed everyone with my sense of pride and happiness. Indeed, God had blessed us as a family.

A YOUNG FAMILY (1976-78)

Our family was now complete, though we did consider adopting another child a few years later, an idea that was eventually dropped. Our hands were now very full with three young children and I certainly felt the burden and responsibility of providing for my young family. I remember the routine of my coming home from work late afternoon and caring for the children while Maggie made supper. Then followed the routine of giving the kids baths and reading to them while they had their night snacks. Only after this routine was completed and I had given them a good night kiss would I retreat to my office in the basement and return to my own work. Of course, many times I was away at church meetings in the evening and then Maggie would be on her own. It is perhaps significant that in my yearly diary I make special mention of attending an academic conference and finding it relaxing to be away from the family for a week. Taking care of three children was at times wearisome but clearly God had called us to this task. Of course, there were also many joys connected with raising a young family.

Gregory was quite demanding as a baby, waking up for feedings two to three times per night. But he won our hearts with his quick and ready smile. In the summer we would often take Gregory for a stroller ride after supper – he seemed to need this at that time of the day. He was a very healthy baby and didn't have the tonsillitis infections of the other two children. However, he was allergic to the cat we had acquired and so we had to send Calico back to the farm. The other two children made sure Gregory was aware of their disappointment. At three years old, Andrew was the clown of the family, though very sensitive to criticism or scolding. He was already into building things with Lego and there was never any doubt as to what presents we should give him at Christmas and on birthdays. We could have sent Audrey to kindergarten when she turned five but chose not to. Instead we transformed our basement into what one of our friends called a kindergarten room, complete with a rug, an easel, building blocks, pictures on the wall, a ladder-swing, a lego table, and a playhouse in the corner.

Audrey started going to school in the fall of 1976 and loved it. Her teacher was Mrs. Bartlett, a former student of mine and herself a mother of four. Although we had confidence in her teaching the basics, we were a little concerned about her failure to stimulate creativity. We were happier with Audrey's teacher in Grade 2, Miss Ciona. Once Audrey was able to read, she read voraciously. We did not send Andrew to school after he turned five and so he demanded that we provide formal kindergarten activities for him at home. Gregory entered the "terrible twos" with a vengeance, but also with the ability to charm us with his rapidly expanding vocabulary.

Ours was a very busy street, what with about a dozen children, mostly pre-schoolers, living on our block at one point in time. Mothers frequently got together for coffee and also did childcare for each other. Our house tended to be the neighborhood center for children, what with a sandbox and a carport. In June of 1977 a tragedy struck our family. Andrew was hit by a truck while crossing our street. The screech, the crunch, and a crumpled body on the pavement will forever be etched on our minds. Fortunately Andrew was not seriously hurt, although it took several weeks for him to recover from his concussion. It was an anxious time for us.

With a growing family, we had to face the fact that our car was simply too small. We agonized about the decision to get rid of our dear Wolfgang II which had served us so well since our marriage. Was buying a bigger car good Christian stewardship? We took our time in deliberating on this question, but finally in 1974

Okanagan Lake, 1977

we bought a one-year-old Volvo station wagon which was big enough to carry our children and our camping equipment during our summer holidays, including our big canvas tent. We kept this bright orange station wagon for a long time – all of our children learned to drive in it, and it even served as a wedding car for Gregory's friend, Nathan Kowalsky in 2000 after I had resurrected it for this event. By this time Gregory had a yellow Volvo station wagon and they wanted both cars in the procession. Our Volvo weathered a small accident and was damaged in a hailstorm, after which we dubbed it "the Wounded Cheezy." It was a sad day when we had to retire it in 1998, but I did purchase another used Volvo that same year. On another financial note, we paid off our house in 1978, after just seven years in Medicine Hat.

Meanwhile the political atmosphere at Medicine Hat College only seemed to worsen. There was some hope of moving towards academic excellence when Lorne Dick was appointed Acting Vice-President of Instruction. However, in 1976 the College Board, in a surprise move, appointed Bob Sackley as President, even though Lorne had applied for the position. Prior to this appointment Bob was the administrator of college operations. He was certainly not an academic but he was a good Mormon and the Mormon community ran an effective campaign against any other competitors for the job. I was overwhelmed at the injustice of this appointment and eventually wrote a long letter to the College Board, outlining eight procedural problems I saw in their appointment of the new president.

A few years earlier I had been appointed head of a committee to create a faculty handbook for the College. I even got workload relief for this task.

As is rather typical of me, I plunged into this project boldly, organized what needed to be done, and then began requesting various policies from the administrators. These requests were not well received, and so even though the committee had been working on developing a policy manual for several years, Bob Sackley suddenly terminated the project in 1977. I take some comfort in the fact that many years later, when an outside consultant was hired to evaluate the College as whole, as well as the president at the time, his major criticism was the lack of policies at the College.

My disappointments with the college were creating in me a desire to find another job. And indeed, other career opportunities were presenting themselves and these helped me to put this desire into proper perspective. Early in 1977, I received a letter from Dr. Henry Krahn, President of the Mennonite Brethren Bible College, offering me a position at the MBBC. He visited us later in person and was encouraging me to come to MBBC that fall. In the end, we declined the offer as I did not want to jeopardize the upcoming sabbatical which I had already been promised in order to finish up my Ph.D. studies. Henry Krahn told me that the offer remained open and this led to an ongoing internal debate as to whether I should make the move. These possibilities did, however, serve to boost my morale and also showed me that I was on the right track in getting a Ph.D. in philosophy.

Another morale boost for me was the arrival of Lillian Douglass in 1976, as Director of the Nursing Program at MHC. She was a fine Christian who taught me to laugh at problems. She was also very committed to including an ethics course in the nursing program and this helped boost enrolment in my courses. My morale received another boost when I experimented with offering an evening course in the philosophy of religion in the winter semester of 1977. This course attracted over thirty students, half of whom were auditors. Unfortunately, some dropped out, I suspect because I announced my Christian convictions at the outset – I was still experimenting with different approaches to "teaching from and for commitment." One student wrote this in his evaluation of the course: "uncomfortable course for an agnostic." In the fall of that same year, I also offered an off-campus course in the philosophy of education for the University of Lethbridge (Education 3050). I was particularly happy with the timing of these new courses as they helped me prepare for the writing of my dissertation.

BACK TO WATERLOO (1978-79)

It was time to make a final push to finish my Ph.D. studies. I had completed the four concentration areas that were part of the Ph.D. program at U of W. I had been at MHC for seven years and so was eligible for another half-sabbatical at 40% salary – I had already taken a half-sabbatical in 1974-5. I applied again for a Canada Council Doctoral Fellowship and the long-awaited envelope finally arrived during the first week in April of 1978, informing me that my application had been successful and that I would be receiving a $7,000 grant plus an array of additional benefits. We were delighted not only because this would provide a much needed supplement to our 40% salary but also because this was a confirmation that the choice to interrupt my Ph.D. program seven years ago in order to take a position at MHC was the right one. Indeed, when I arrived back at U of W in fall, I discovered that several of the students I had been studying with seven years earlier were still there, in part because they had been unsuccessful in getting teaching positions.

Everything seemed to work out so well for our move to Waterloo. We were able to rent our house to two nursing instructors at MHC. With the help of some friends in Waterloo and lots of phone calls we found a house to rent in Waterloo near the university on Candlewood Crescent, ($360 per month). The summer was devoted to making these arrangements, saying our good-byes, and finally packing for our trip. Our Volvo was fully loaded with a big box on the roof-rack and with Gregory's plastic motorcycle tied on the very top – something which created amusement for people passing us on the road. On our way to Ontario we stopped in Regina and had a delightful visit with Len and Martha Pauls who had just moved to Regina. We also spent an extra day in Winnipeg to check out the city and talk with faculty at MBBC about the possibility of taking a position there. We took our time travelling to Waterloo and tried to stay at good motels with swimming pools or access to beaches.

After seven days of travel, we finally arrived at our new home where the Jim Whitneys were waiting to give us an orientation to their house before they left for their sabbatical in England. We all felt some disorientation for the first few days, but gradually got acclimatized and felt at home in our house and in the neighbourhood though the children did miss their friends who lived on our street in Medicine Hat. I felt the need for some spiritual reorientation and so spent a day in bible study and prayer, studying the life of Abraham, the gospel of Mark, and 1 & 2 Peter. It was a good day and I now felt ready for the challenges of the year.

We made many visits to the near-by pond where the children loved to feed the ducks. They also enjoyed the neighborhood swimming pool. We bought bikes for each of us so that we could go on family bike trips. Audrey and Andrew attended Keatsway Public School, whose Principal was Mrs. Johnston, a superb administrator and a Christian. Audrey was in a combined Grade 3 & 4 class, taught by Mrs. Shaddick for the first while, and then by Mrs. Young. Andrew began his first day of school and thought his teacher, Ms. Schwieger, was the best teacher in the whole school. Audrey also joined the Mennonite Children's Choir for the year. During this year, we noticed that Andrew was becoming more and more absent minded. On one occasion he went to the bathroom during a meal and then went on to

play with his toys, forgetting all about his supper. Gregory (2 ½ years old) began prefacing any tasks he didn't want to do with the expression, "not quite yet." He would also preface many sentences with "also." Another expression of his: "Gregory is big, Daddy is small," to prove who knows what!

We did a fair amount of visiting in the fall. We tried to go to St. Catharines once a month to visit Grandma Friesen who had moved into Tabor Apartments and was not in the best of health, having been diagnosed with a type of anemia. Then of course there were visits to Maggie's siblings, George and Nettie, and Rudy and Mary. We also had a lot of visitors, many of them friends from our previous years in Waterloo. We also befriended two international students, Abdul Latif and Islam, from Bangladesh, who joined us for Christmas day. For entertainment, Maggie and I got seasons tickets for the K-W Symphony and we also visited the Stratford theatre once during that year. Maggie joined the choir at Wilfrid Laurier University and also sang in the church choir.

Of course, the major reason for our stay in Waterloo was the writing of my Ph.D. dissertation. Here I faced initial disappointment because it was felt that my initial thesis proposal which I had been working on for quite some time needed further revisions. My thesis committee felt that I was trying to do too much, with some members feeling that I should limit myself to the concept of indoctrination. I resisted such a narrow focus at first, but eventually agreed to their suggestion.

I met with my supervisor, Dr. Brian Hendley, about once every two weeks and found our meetings stimulating and encouraging. The first few months of writing were invigorating. However, after a few months of writing I became aware of sense of insecurity and loss of identity due to my very different lifestyle since moving to Waterloo. Activities that had given me a feeling of usefulness, such as teaching and church work, were no longer part of my life. Instead, I was working at home, alone, writing, spending hours and days and weeks at a task at which I might fail. Even my children had problems explaining what their father was doing when asked about this by their friends. I found some encouragement in reading through Genesis in the New International Version of the bible which I had just purchased. God was with Jacob and Isaac as they faced new challenges, and God would also see me through my new challenges. A letter from a former student of mine, Tom Treen, asking counsel regarding his Christian faith also was an encouragement. Here I was suddenly useful again, cast into my former role and I liked it.

A few other outside assignments also helped to give me a sense of usefulness. I gave a lecture to the IVCF group at WLU on the Christian mind. I was also invited to speak at a weekend camp for youth executives in churches of the Mennonite Brethren Conference in Ontario. Serving as a resource person for an extended series of weekend lectures was a first for me. My lectures focussed on the mind, its limits, and its place in apologetics. During the Christmas holidays, I also spoke to the youth at Scott Street Church in St. Catharines. We also started a home bible study group with Bob Kuhl and his wife, Margaret, Ken and Margie Hull, and Linda Neufeldt. It was good to study the gospel of John and do some meaningful sharing.

We had a lovely summer at the end of our time in Waterloo, enjoying the neighborhood swimming pool, the park, the pond, and biking in the area. Finally, on Sunday, August 19, after getting rid of all the bikes we had bought (sold at near the original cost price), we started our journey back home. We took our time again, visiting Dan and Elsie Klassen in Thunder Bay, and Len and Martha Pauls in Regina. We spent a few days in Winnipeg where I gave a series of lectures on "The Core Curriculum," at MBBC. This was an exhilarating experience for me, though we left with mixed feelings about joining the college. We stopped in Swift Current and my mother joined us for the rest of the trip to Medicine Hat. Here we were given a royal welcome by the neighborhood, with a sign on the driveway and flowers in our living room. It felt good to be welcomed in this way and I was happy that my mother was also with us to enjoy the welcome.

The completion of this sabbatical seems to be a good place to end this chapter on my early career and our having babies. I now had nearly a decade of teaching under my belt and I had just completed a full year's sabbatical which enabled me to nearly complete my dissertation and get very close to getting my Ph.D. Our family was complete with three children now ages nine, seven, and four. The Psalmist describes children as a gift from the Lord. "Blessed is the man whose quiver is full of them" (Ps 127:3-5). I was indeed blessed by my Lord.

It felt good to be able to return to our home after my sabbatical. We were no longer rootless and unmoored. Yes, our first impressions of Medicine Hat were rather negative as the story at the beginning of this chapter illustrates. But our home had become more than an address; it was part of who we were and had become. And it would continue to shape us as we continued working and raising our children in Medicine Hat. Yes, living in a particular place involves limits and constraints, but we are finite and limited creatures, and constraints form the context in which we can flourish and engage in mission. So my story continues as I move on in the next chapter to the middle of my career and the growth of our children.

Chapter 4
MID-CAREER
AND GROWING
CHILDREN
(1979-1992)

Our daughter turned into a teen-ager a bit earlier than expected, and her father was worried. The year was 1982 and I had gotten involved in the formation of a Christian school in Medicine Hat. We wanted our children to switch from the public school to the new Christian school, but Audrey was resisting the move (for some understandable reasons, we discovered later). We eventually gave in but had some concerns about her being able to navigate the secular influences of the public school. Dad, the philosopher, believed that all problems could be solved by writing policies. So he drew up a statement entitled, "Commitment of Audrey Thiessen for Grade 7 at Alexandra Junior High (1982-83)." The statement begins with a prefatory note: "Some of the items of this commitment arise because Audrey wishes to attend a secular school rather than the new Christian school."

The statement continues with a series of promises which Audrey was making. Then follows the infamous dating policy – "no dating until at least age 16; no group dating until at least age 15; group activities are acceptable before this time, but again are subject to the approval of parents." The final promise: "I promise to discuss with my parents, problems or things that are bothering me at home or at school." The document was actually signed by Audrey with Dad's signature as a witness. Wow! I think this Dad needed some help in relating to a daughter who was becoming a teen-ager.

But I was still not done with the writing of policy statements. In December of 1983 and in anticipation of the rest of our children becoming teen-agers, Dad wrote up another statement entitled, "Guidelines for Dancing and Related Activities (for the Thiessen family)." This one-page statement is prefaced with some bible verses, e.g. "Do not love the world or anything in the world." (1 John 2:15-17). Then follows the application. "We agree to let our children dance provided they promise to exercise Christian discernment and have the courage to leave a dance or not go to a dance when conditions are such that the dance is not in keeping with Christian ideals as are expressed in the bible verses included in this document." The statement goes on to spell out some conditions which we as parents viewed as not conducive to upholding Christian ideals and where we would expect our children to leave or even decide not to go in the first place.

The statement continues with some specific rules to be followed. Then follows a statement expressing our general concerns about dances not being in keeping with Christian ideals. Next is this significant qualifier: "However, we feel our children must assume some responsibility for deciding issues on their own. We hope and pray that they will live up to the confidence we are placing in them. A betrayal of this confidence will lead to a forfeiture of the privileges in making decisions on their own." The statement ends with another bible verse: "Don't let anyone look down on you because you are young, but set an example for the believers in speech, in life, in love, in faith and in purity" (1 Tim 4:11).

Ah yes, the anxiety of parents trying to raise teen-agers. If only parents were given another chance. But you only have one try at this all-important task. You do your best and hope your children will eventually forgive you for your failures. In retrospect Maggie and I console ourselves with the thought that not everything we did in raising our children was misguided because we are rather pleased with the way our children turned out. But our grandchildren have enjoyed hearing about Grandpa's policy statements.

RETURN TO MEDICINE HAT

The specific dates assigned to the chapter heading call for some explanation. How does one define the middle part of one's career or the stage of family life characterized by growing children? In the previous chapter I dealt with my early teaching career and the birth of our children (1968-79). This chapter begins with my return to Medicine Hat College after a year's sabbatical. In the fall of 1979 I was thirty-seven years old and it was just over a decade since I had begun my teaching career. I have chosen the fifty-year-old-mark as defining the end of my mid-career. 1992 also marked our twenty-fifth wedding anniversary. In 1992 our children were teen-agers and our oldest child, our daughter, was already married.

Upon our return from Waterloo in the fall of 1979, we had some trouble adjusting to life back in Medicine Hat. We even felt a little disoriented in our own house. After a stimulating year in Waterloo we didn't like the feel of sliding back into the same old routines we were in a year earlier – back to work at the College and back to our usual involvements in the church. But we were warmly welcomed back home by our neighbors and our church. We particularly enjoyed an evening of elegant dining at the home of our friends, Dave and Martha Rempel, together with Peter and Pat Mueller. When our shipment of luggage finally arrived nearly a month later, we began to settle in and feel re-oriented to life back at home.

Our two oldest children returned to the Crestwood Elementary School near our home. Audrey was in Grade 4 with Miss Reisdorf as her teacher, a young woman who had been a student of mine earlier. Her teacher also led the school choir and so Audrey was able to continue singing as she had done in the previous year when she was part of the Inter-Mennonite Choir in Waterloo. Andrew was in Grade 2 in Miss Ciona's class and was pursuing new knowledge with great enthusiasm. He would come home with his head in the clouds, formulating grandiose ideas of telescopes and periscopes and the like, which Daddy was supposed to help him make immediately, and of course Daddy would generally oblige. Our children were happy with their teachers and so were we as parents. Gregory, soon turning four years old, was still at home, finding it a bit hard to be at home alone without his older siblings. Maggie therefore had to spend a lot of time playing games with Gregory – played his way, of course. We often heard him talking to himself while playing, sometimes arguing himself out of something using his parent's lines of reasoning. He was also busy inventing vocabulary, at one point trying to recall the word for "sponge," coming out with the word "squish," and we all knew what he meant. Mom was given a break from household demands with two evenings per week spent doing pottery and singing in a choir.

I had to adjust to a new President at Medicine Hat College (MHC). Chuck Meagher, had acquired this position in a rather unique way. He was a pharmacist and not at all an academic, but he was a loyal member of the Conservative party, and at the time of his appointment, he was Chair of the Board of Governors of MHC. So he essentially appointed himself President. It created a fair amount of controversy, but all this happened while I was away on sabbatical. I also discovered that my replacement during my sabbatical, Arnd Bohm, had not really advanced the philosophy program at MHC. No students enrolled for my second year course which therefore had to be cancelled. I had asked for a ¾ workload, but with this cancellation, I ended up with only ½ a course load. This left me with lots of time to revise my dissertation and so I was able to complete the first draft by December. The completion and defence of my dissertation is described in more detail in chapter 8. What a relief to be awarded my Ph.D. in the fall of 1980.

MEDICINE HAT COLLEGE (1980-85)

There were a number of significant challenges that I experienced at MHC during the time period under consideration. The first had to do with my bid for the chairmanship of the Department of Humanities and Social Sciences in 1980. Roy Wilson had resigned and I had decided to let my name stand. In fact, when Roy first got the position six years earlier, he and I had deliberated as to who should run for the position and I finally decided to let him take it. Now it was my turn, though I spent some time carefully tabulating the pros and cons of running for this position. I was the only one running and the department gave me a vote of confidence – eight out of ten members supported me, with two abstentions. However, the administration and the Board of Governors turned me down, exercising their power in accordance with the new faculty contract. No reasons were given, but I suspected that part of their rejection of my candidacy was due to an earlier letter I had written to the Minister of Advanced Education, protesting past appointments of presidents at the College. Indeed, Jim Horsman, our local MLA, had forwarded my confidential letter to the President and the Board!

There were no doubt other reasons behind this decision, such as my being considered "inflexible" while I was working on developing a Guidelines Manual for the College a few years earlier – a project that was cancelled mid-point because the Administration really didn't want to develop firm policies. The administration and the Board were also flexing their muscles and simply didn't want to allow a department to elect its own chairman. They went through the charade of having another competition for the job and I was encouraged to let my name stand once again. Only one other person applied for the job and we were both turned down. How foolish of me to let myself be turned down a second time! Finally, Glen Ennis, no doubt one of the persons who had abstained in the original department vote for me, had the courage to submit his name, and of course he got the job.

I found all this very hard to accept. Glen was a former high-school teacher and only had an M.A. degree, and I didn't consider him to be strong academically. The injustice of this entire procedure overwhelmed me. I knew I had to learn to love my enemies and forgive them, but it wasn't easy. It took me a long while to accept the situation, and was helped by a former student of mine, Mike Page, who suggested that I took things too seriously. He didn't expect more from the world, and thus was not as disappointed when things didn't work out as expected. Maggie also made a comment which helped me – this life is so short in relation to eternity that hardships shouldn't matter all that much. These comments and further study of Scripture helped me eventually to accept my situation. In looking back over this experience, I expect it played a significant role in my own growth as a person.

A second challenge grew out of an evaluation of the Department of Humanities and Social Sciences conducted in 1981 by the Academic Vice-President, Lorne Dick. The procedures used to do this evaluation left much to be desired and the entire department was on edge and unhappy. A major recommendation of the final report was that all members of the department should be working on their doctorates – a rather unrealistic ideal and somewhat of a farce given that the person who had just recently been appointed as our chair would never get his Ph.D. Each department member was also given a short evaluation report and my own report was less than stellar: "In some cases he has been considered somewhat inflexible, a perception that has inhibited his effectiveness. While working on his dissertation, he took limited responsibility for institutional concerns. . . . Sometimes lacks courageous optimism." Interesting, especially when a strong majority of the department had given me a vote of confidence in running for the chair, and when the reasons for my lack of optimism were a result of the significant problems with the way in which the college was being run. I also prefer to see myself as principled rather than inflexible. I was not the only one upset over their individual evaluations. A joint meeting of the department was held which led to a request that rebuttals might be submitted as addendums to our evaluation reports. But this proved to be of no avail with a Vice-President who loved power and saw these evaluations as a way of keeping his faculty humble. I finally went to see Lorne about the blatant distortions in my own evaluation and the growing estrangement that was developing between us. No apology was forthcoming, though he did say that he was sorry that I felt hurt by all of this.

In the summer of 1981, I received an unexpected phone call from Harold Coward, Director of The Institute for the Humanities at the University of Calgary, asking me if I would be interested in a one-year research project dealing with the need for humanities in Alberta's thirteen technical/vocational colleges and institutes. It is perhaps rather surprising that I very quickly came to a decision to accept this offer. I needed a change and this provided a means to get away from the disappointments I was experiencing at MHC. I was also hoping that this might open up further job opportunities in the future. Also, my being seconded to the University of Calgary for the year would require finding a replacement for my position at MHC and I thought that this might be a way to get a job for Gary Colwell, a friend of mine at the University of Waterloo who was still looking for a philosophy position. Everything fell into place very quickly and thus in a matter of weeks, my direction for the year, and perhaps for the future, was changed.

I accepted the secondment on condition that I could still teach one course and was allowed to teach a second-year course in political philosophy. I rather enjoyed the balance between teaching and research.[1] My work on the humanities research project proved to be a little frustrating that fall. I had some difficulties preparing a questionnaire that was to be used in the study. Corresponding with thirteen institutions and arranging for visits proved to be very time-consuming. Then I spent a lot of time traveling, visiting six of the northern institutions in December. We also faced some push-back from the Department of Advanced Education when we sent them some tentative conclusions mid-way through the project. They thought there was a bias in our approach, and for a while Harold was uncertain as to whether we should even proceed with writing a final report. In the end, it was decided that we should proceed and that we would co-author the final report. I spent the following summer feverishly writing the report and continued work on this in fall while teaching full-time. After submitting the report to the Department of Advanced Education we made several visits to Edmonton to discuss the report with them. I also presented a paper based on the report at a conference of the Alberta Colleges and Institutes Faculty Association (ACIFA) in the spring of 1984, and at Lethbridge Community College in the fall of the same year. A paper entitled, "The Need for Humanities in Technical/Vocational Programs," was published in the *Canadian Journal of Higher Education* in 1985.

In retrospect, I think this career decision was a mistake. It didn't open up further opportunities for me in the academic world, and the extensive travel involved was hard on the family, especially Maggie. The children did however enjoy the airline treats I brought home each time. In December, in the middle of my trips to northern Alberta, we got a call from Ontario informing us that Maggie's mother was seriously ill and in the hospital. We decided that Maggie should fly to Ontario with her sister, Susan. My mother came to Medicine Hat to help me take care of the children. On January 6, 1982, we received word that Mom Friesen had finally been released from her ten years of suffering and had gone to be with the Lord. We decided to take the entire family to the funeral and were fortunate to be able to make last minute reservations. The children thoroughly enjoyed the plane trips – it was a first for Gregory, although he claimed that it was his second, given that the first occurred when he was in Mommy's tummy. It was good to say our final good-bye to our mother and grandmother, though it left us feeling a little more alone in this world, and a bit more cut off from the past.

My next challenge at MHC occurred in 1984-85 after I made a last minute decision to run for position of President of the Faculty Association, mainly because I was frustrated with the irresponsible way in which the Association was being run. There were two other candidates running for the position, but I won with a clear majority on the first ballot. I was immediately thrust into a controversy in dealing with a grievance filed by one of our members, a sessional appointee who claimed his contract was not being renewed because of his political activism. The grievance was supported by the Faculty Association even though there was no contractual violation – it was mainly a protest against the administration. It proved to be a long and messy affair which didn't exactly endear me to the administration, but I rather enjoyed processing this issue, especially the challenge of running tight meetings. The faculty finally came to their senses and rescinded their support for the grievance.

Then followed a major confrontation with the Academic Vice-President, Lorne Dick. It all began with the Executive Board of the Faculty Association sending a letter to Lorne, protesting some rather unorthodox hiring procedures. Lorne refused to answer our letter, so I as President of the Association went to talk to the President of the College, Chuck Meagher, who then made Lorne formally respond to our letter. I had also given a report at the fall meeting of the Faculty Association, requesting that a special committee be set up to study the erosion of collegiality at MHC. I had several meetings with the President to discuss the issue of collegiality and at one point he asked me to give him some examples of a lack of collegiality. All this finally prompted Lorne to storm into my office, very angry and literally screaming at me and calling me unprofessional and a tattle-tale. Several of my colleagues in neighboring offices couldn't help overhearing the confrontation and came to my office after it was all over trying to console me.

I was terribly upset for the next few days and had trouble sleeping. I waited a week for an apology from Lorne, but in vain. I therefore brought the matter to the Executive Board of the Association who supported me in writing a letter to the President and the Board of Governors, requesting mediation. Chuck arranged for a meeting with Lorne and myself, and started off by suggesting that we simply forget the whole affair. I replied that we needed to deal with the issues involved and that if I had done something wrong, I wanted to apologize. Lorne sat in sullen silence, but we did manage to review the events leading up to the confrontation. I finally broke down in tears and this led Lorne to admit that he was very embarrassed over what he had done. Although this wasn't a clear apology, I accepted it as such, but added that it would take me some time to learn to trust him again. In subsequent days I made it a point to greet Lorne when we met in the hallway, but our relationship remained strained. All this taught me much about how to confront with love. Prayer was most helpful in creating better attitudes.

During the winter semester of 1985 I had to deal with another matter – disciplinary action being considered by the Administration against one of the instructors.[2] Lorne Dick called me into his office and wanted to show me a list of complaints of students against this instructor, who happened to be a member of my own department. I refused to look at this list of complaints, and told Lorne that my role as Faculty Association President would be to monitor the procedures followed in dealing with these complaints and to ensure that they were fair. Lorne seemed to accept the fact that my role as Association President was to be an advocate for the teacher, although he later denied that he had agreed to my advocacy role. Procedures in dealing with this matter were indeed botched up, and our department chair dared to suggest that the issue had been blown out of proportion due to my involvement in the matter. But the complaints against this instructor were at least softened in the final report.

I also persuaded the Faculty Association to form a committee to study collegiality and faculty morale at MHC, and Roy Wilson was appointed chair of that committee. Unfortunately the Committee's final report was poorly written and the Association turned down the Executive Board's recommendation that the report be forwarded to the Administration and the Board of Governors. This prompted me to rewrite the report and I did manage to get the revised report and its recommendations passed by the Association, though just barely. We had meetings with the Administration and the Board to discuss the findings of the report. Someone leaked the report to the Medicine Hat News and one of the editors wrote a series of articles based on the Report. I had originally hoped for a broader circulation and thus was delighted with this leak. I had also hoped that this document would become a reference point for future discussions about the administration and would in the end lead to some improvements at the College. Lorne Dick was clearly very upset with all these developments and I am sure blamed me for the leak to the newspaper.

After classes were over I did a study of David's relation to Saul as described in 1 Samuel, as a way of assessing my actions in the past year with respect to Lorne. David kept insisting that he had no intention of hurting Saul, but Saul kept feeling more and more suspicious about David, despite his disclaimers. Eventually David simply retreated from the problem and escaped to the land of the Philistines. He coped with the psychological problem of feeling unjustly treated by reassuring himself that a final day of reckoning would come, but it would be God-initiated. I worked on two sermon outlines on the problem of injustice, and told our pastor, David Funk, that I would only be able to preach these sermons fifteen years from now.

I was glad when my tenure as President of the Faculty Association was over, though I would be intimately involved in facing another major crisis a few years down the road. In the meantime, through all these years of political turmoil, I was enjoying teaching. And it was most gratifying to have many students visit me in my office, not only for help in the courses they were taking from me, but also for personal counselling. For example, I got to know Roy very well in 1983-84. He was originally from Quebec but had been working in northern Alberta for a few years and ended up in Medicine Hat, trying to recover from a divorce and a subsequent life of alcoholism and drugs. He came to my office asking searching questions about the Christian faith. I gave him John Stott's *Basic Christianity* and encouraged him to read the Bible. After a few weeks he reported that he had become a Christian, and subsequent changes in his life clearly indicated that he had been soundly converted. He fell in love with one of the girls he got to know through Inter-Varsity Christian Fellowship on campus, of which I was a sponsor. They wanted to get married immediately, despite parental opposition. So Maggie and I got involved in marital counselling, eventually persuading them to wait. We acted as surrogate parents in helping arrange their wedding the following spring. I was asked to give the sermon at their wedding.

So, yes, I was generally enjoying teaching and interacting with students. But there was still the ongoing political turmoil at the College, and because of this I was on the lookout for ways to escape MHC during this middle stage of my career. One possibility that was at the back of my mind during this time period was teaching at the Mennonite Brethren Bible College, after having been offered a position there in 1977 and again in 1979. In any case, MBBC did not contact me again, and I eventually felt at peace about not taking that position. I inquired about a philosophy vacancy at Regent College in British Columbia, but they required a Ph.D. which I didn't have as yet. A position opened up in the education department at Red Deer College in 1982, but they wanted someone with some experience teaching at the K-12 level.

I was also exploring overseas assignments with the Mennonite Central Committee (MCC) and was offered a position at the University of

Khartoom in the Sudan for the fall of 1982. We eventually turned this down, though we were still thinking about this as a possibility for the following year. I also applied to the Nigerian Universities Office in Ottawa, and in the summer of 1983 they suddenly called and wanted me to come for an interview regarding a fall teaching position at Calabar. After the interview and some consultations while in Ottawa, we decided this was not what we should do on such short notice, even though it was a bit tempting.[3] A statement in our Christmas letter of 1982 is significant: "We are resigning ourselves to the prospect of settling down in Medicine Hat for good." But I am not sure how complete that feeling of resignation was, given the next sentence: "Any job offers?"[4]

BEYOND MEDICINE HAT COLLEGE (1979-85)

Upon our return from Waterloo in 1979, we both plunged back into various activities in the church. Maggie was a bit reluctant to direct the choir once again, in part because she didn't have a pianist who could handle the kind of music she wanted to sing with the choir. She also taught Sunday School and organized a drama workshop with Esther Wiens from MBBC. She was of course also very much involved in entertaining church people. We started a home bible study group with John and Irene Derksen, Mike and Susan Page, and Linda Thiessen. This met a real need for Christian fellowship and also allowed us to nurture the faith in others.

In 1980 I was back on the church council as Evangelism Elder and in this position tried to encourage friendship evangelism and small fellowship groups in the church as a means of outreach. I also began teaching a "Basic Christianity" class for new Christians. I was of course still part of the lay-ministers group which experienced some tensions with existing pastors. In 1981, I was co-opted into taking on the role of moderator of the church and tried to work at resolving these tensions. When Jake Penner resigned as pastor in 1982 and we could not find another pastor, the lay-ministers did their best to fill the pastoral role. This continued until David and Shirley Funk served us as summer interns and then accepted our invitation to be our pastor in 1984. In my yearly diary for 1985 I wrote the following: "In the church, I was enjoying my weekly meetings with David Funk. He was doing a superb job and thus my job as moderator was made easy."

Our children were of course growing. In the fall of 1980 Audrey started Grade 5 with Mrs. Lovig as teacher. She was reading at such a rapid pace that we couldn't keep her supplied with books, let alone censor everything that she was reading. Audrey was also developing the ability to use humor to pacify her parents when she was in trouble. Andrew was taking Grade 3 with Mrs. Fischer. He became an avid reader and was developing in self-confidence. His other pastimes included building space lego and collecting rocks. We were toying with the idea of sending Gregory to kindergarten, but decided to stick to our usual practice of not sending our children to kindergarten, in part because we felt Gregory wasn't ready for it as yet. Maggie was babysitting Naomi Derksen for three days a week and this helped to keep Gregory entertained. Indeed, they did a lot of giggling together.

One incident with Gregory stands out in my mind. We were at a church retreat in Elkwater and I took Gregory to the outdoor toilet. Seeing some bugs on the floor, Gregory suddenly asked, "Daddy, do you know what suffering is? It is when you step on a bug and squish it. That's what suffering is." Well, what could I say – my four-year-old son was becoming a philosopher!

Children's activities included piano for Audrey and Andrew (these were the years of Rotary Festival competitions), German school on Saturdays with Mom doing some of the teaching, picking rocks at the farm of Mike and Susan Page, T-ball for Andrew in spring, swimming lessons in summer,  building the boy's a go-cart, building a fort at Art Thiessen's farm with Ronnie and Randy, and building our own little fort beside the house.

Shortly after my sabbatical in Waterloo, I got involved with the Christian Education Society of Medicine Hat whose initial objective was to start a Christian alternative school within the public school system. This entailed speaking in various churches to promote the idea. In the end we had to open as a private school. I was also on the Education Committee of the Board, and so was developing policies for the school. The school opened in 1982, and so we switched Andrew (Grade 4) and Gregory (Grade 2) into the Christian school. Audrey was reluctant to make this switch, in part because she had a bad experience when we first visited the school at an open house. So she started at Alexandra Junior High, with accompanying parental guidelines as described in the story at the beginning of this chapter. Andrew continued attending the Christian school until 1984 when he started Grade 7 at Alexandra Junior High. This change was prompted in part because we didn't have confidence in the teachers he would have had at the Christian school.

Highlights for our family were camping trips during the summers. In the summer of 1980 we finally took a holiday all the way to the West coast (2 ½ weeks). We fell in love with the ocean at Pacific Rim Park, despite the breakdown of our Volvo. I managed to fix the brake cable temporarily with a clothes-line wire. Full repairs were done in Nanaimo after a nerve-racking drive through the Island mountains with only thirteen to fifteen uses of the clutch. We visited Pacific Rim again in 1994. Other holidays were spent in Kananaskis (rained out in 1981), Banff, Big Sky Mountain and Yellowstone in 1982, northern Saskatchewan, Jasper (1983), and several holidays in Waterton. In 1984 Audrey, Andrew and I did a bike trip from Medicine Hat to Swift Current – a 140 mile challenge, with a sleep-over in Piapot, and a lunch served on the second day by our back-up crew consisting of Mom, Gregory, Lottie and Gillian. Audrey and Andrew also started attending Camp Evergreen in summers, with Andrew and Randy Thiessen attending an Inter-Varsity camp in Sundry in 1984.

A final comment on this segment of my life. I was busy. I was wearing many hats – a father and husband, a college teacher and political activist, a counsellor, a church worker, a preacher, a guest lecturer, a visionary of new possibilities in schooling, an academic researcher and writer, and a columnist for the Mennonite Brethren Herald (1980-82). After the completion of my Ph.D., my writing venues expanded when I began publishing academic essays growing out of my dissertation. I also began giving papers at the Learned Societies and other academic conferences. I was asked to speak at a Christmas banquet at Hillcrest Christian College. I also gave a lecture at a nursing graduation banquet and entitled my talk, "Liberal Education and the Problem of Pain in the Nursing Profession." An unusual title I'm sure, but the students who had taken an ethics course from me during their program would have expected me to do something like this. In 1983 I gave two lectures on ethical relativism, one at an International Student banquet at the University of Lethbridge, and another at the Alberta Woman's Temperance Union. This is a topic that I am still giving lectures on some 35 years later. My yearly diary for 1984 includes this comment about my many activities: "I found I was able to work at many projects at the same time, over the years . . . and I could do this without feeling frustrated." I now wonder whether I was trying to do too many things at the same time.

SABBATICAL IN ENGLAND (1985-86)

One of my dreams for the family was to have us live in another country for a period of time. There was some resistance to the idea of an MCC term in Africa which we were considering in 1982 and 1983, so when the possibility of spending a one-year sabbatical in England was suggested, the children were more ready to resign themselves to the fate of fulfilling father's dream for the family. Given the poisoned political climate at MHC, I took every chance I had to get away, and so was happy to accept the offer of a full-year's sabbatical in 1985-86. So it happened that in the spring of 1985, we were busy getting ready for one year away from home. I taught spring and summer courses in order to supplement the reduced 80% salary I would get during the sabbatical. We managed to find a suitable house in Oxford, owned by an Oxford don, Edward Martin, for a reasonable price (320 pounds per month), and also found very suitable renters for our house in Medicine Hat, Steve and Judi Cripps – Steve had just been appointed as the Parks Superintendent for the City (rent $500 per month).

To complicate matters, I was offered a summer course at the University of Prince Edward Island (PEI), and I simply couldn't resist this opportunity as I had been trying to get a summer course in Eastern Canada for a few years. So after some sad farewells, we flew to Toronto and rented a car to take us to PEI. We camped on the way, having shipped our camping equipment ahead of us – another mistake. While we enjoyed the PEI beaches in the afternoons and evenings, there were not too many other redeeming features of our summer experience in PEI. Our apartment was dirty and hot. My philosophy of religion class was disappointing with only four students most of whom were rather mediocre. Audrey went to camp and was crushed when she had to leave the new love of her life, the director's son. The weather wasn't the greatest. Then there was the trip back to Toronto – why go all the way back to Toronto when we could have left from Halifax? Perhaps our PEI experience was a bit disappointing because we realized this was only the first installment of an exciting year's sabbatical in another country. In retrospect, accepting this summer job was a mistake and made things unnecessarily complicated.

On to England. After a six-hour stay-awake flight, we had to endure a two and one-half hour wait to get through customs at the Gatwick airport. We then took a train to Oxford – a challenge given that we had ten large blue duffle bags of luggage which we had to load onto the train and transfer to another train at Reading. When we arrived in Oxford we had trouble finding a taxi that would take all of us plus our luggage.  Our landlord was waiting for us at 28 Squitchey Lane, and after a brief tour of the house, the children chose their rooms, Maggie made the beds, and everyone settled in for a good night's sleep. And sleep we did – Maggie got impatient in the morning and went shopping for groceries before anyone else was up.

The first month in Oxford was spent settling in, adjusting to the rain, cleaning our rather "tatty" house, getting used to buying groceries nearly every day in the nearby Summertown shopping area, purchasing bicycles for everyone, and eventually purchasing a used car, a 1975 Volvo for 465 British pounds – we were after all a Volvo family. The car was a bit rusty, had a steering wheel which was on the wrong side and rattled even more than the U-joint. Future problems included a carburetor breakdown, a door handle which broke off, an odometer that stopped working, and a wheel bearing which was grinding and which eventually led to the sheering of the axle and the wheel simply falling off on the return

from one of our trips to Europe. I still feel badly about exposing the family to this danger because I didn't fix the problem sooner, again because money was tight.

But car problems were just the beginning of our trials in England. Maggie wasn't feeling too well in September and at the end of the month was diagnosed as having endocarditis, and thus was hospitalized for a four-week treatment of antibiotics via I.V. She was in the Radcliff Hospital which was a teaching hospital famous for its cardiac clinic, and so she had a lot of interns taking her history and getting familiar with this rather unusual medical condition. Fortunately, my schedule was flexible and so I could take care of household challenges together with Audrey. We even brought a full hot meal to the hospital for Maggie which was met with mixed reception by the nurses. Fortunately, the doctor diagnosed the problem early enough so that after the treatment, life could return to normal for Maggie and the family.

Our children (ages 15, 13, 10) had to adjust to a new school system, including the wearing of uniforms. The boys attended Bishop Kirk School, a church-aided school just two blocks from our home, while Audrey attended Cherwell School, a state high school about a 20-minute walk away. Audrey had trouble making friends in school and after some bad lunches with fried Spam, she started coming home for lunch even though it was a long walk. The boy's were placed in grades based on their ages, and thus were not sufficiently challenged. Their schooling was also hampered by a work-to-rule campaign on the part of the teachers. This had the effect of introducing us to another family, the Erensons whose daughter also attended the school and started coming to our home for lunches. John Erenson was a Wycliffe bible translator working on his Ph.D. in anthropology – another delightful friendship, started by a teacher's strike of all things. All in all the schooling experience wasn't the best for our children, but experiences outside of school more than compensated for this.

We spent the first month visiting various churches and were happy when this time of a "schmorgasboard Christianity" was over. We enjoyed the liturgies and the beautiful pipe organs in most of the churches. We were attracted to St. Aldates where Michael Green was the rector – the services a strange mix of evangelical preaching, genuine fellowship, and a liturgy which was both formal and informal. Our children didn't like the long services – a communion service would last for two full hours. After a visit to

Wesley Memorial Church in downtown Oxford, where the children were immediately welcomed, particularly by the Eddy children, we decided to make this our church home. Audrey and Andrew were quickly incorporated into the youth group and even joined the choir and learned to sing Latin anthems. For Christmas the church put on a major musical which went on tour. This was certainly a stretching experience for Audrey and Andrew, though when Audrey wrote Grandma Thiessen about the dancing, Grandma was a little concerned, and I had to remind my Mother that her responsibility was to love her grandchildren and leave the raising of them to us.

Another memorable experience for our children was a treasure hunt which included clues placed in some of the colleges of Oxford. It might seem rather incredible to have these famous ancient colleges used for the trivial purpose of a youth treasure hunt. But what better way to get our children into these colleges given that they tended to resist visiting them with their parents. We also enjoyed some warm hospitality on the part of a few families who weren't as reserved as most and who were not frightened by North Americans. Maggie and I also joined a small church fellowship group. The church was certainly more liberal than we would have liked, and I had to reflect on how far they had departed from the original vision of John Wesley and his founding of the "methodological" church – I had read a book on John Wesley before our sabbatical, which in fact had influenced our choice of this church. The children certainly didn't get much bible teaching in their "fizzy" Sunday School classes, but they developed some very positive attitudes about church. When we returned to Medicine Hat, they were inspired to replicate the youth program they had experienced in this Methodist Church. So we are thankful for what this church experience did for our children.

Of course, the main reason for being in Oxford was academic and so I enjoyed the transformation of Oxford from a city of tourists in the summer to a real university city in early October when the students, together with their bicycles, came flooding in to enrol in one of the forty colleges that make up Oxford University. What a privilege to walk or cycle through the cobbled streets of the oldest university in the English-speaking world. I sometimes couldn't quite believe I was actually at this famous university. I sampled a good number of lectures during the first week of the Michaelmas (fall) term and found it most interesting to see and listen to authors of articles or books that I had been studying over the years. It was also somewhat reassuring to hear a bad lecture from one of the Oxford greats, for example, John Wilson, a prominent philosopher of education who had in fact arranged for my membership at Mansfield College. I discovered that affiliation with a college was not really that important for my purposes. I had to miss an invitation to high table at Mansfield College because Maggie was in the hospital at the time, but found their dinners at 7:00 p.m. to be inconvenient in any case, what with a family at home, and my needing my supper at 5:30 p.m. sharp. Eating at high table was also too expensive for our budget and besides, I also found the fellows at the college to be rather unfriendly – you can't really blame them, having to put up with foreign visitors each year.

I thoroughly enjoyed the intellectual stimulation of attending a variety of lectures, many of which were very good. I, together with Ken Konyndyk, another sabbatical visitor from Calvin College, attended a series of philosophy of religion lectures by Richard Swinburne. Swinburne wondered why we were attending his lectures and we had to explain that it was simply good to listen to another professor teach the same classes that we had been teaching. Swinburne also took me out for lunch on one occasion. On another occasion I was even mistaken for Swinburne by a student who was waiting in the hallway for his lecture. What an honor!

I also enjoyed a graduate seminar team-taught by Ronald Dworkin and Steven Lukes on "Liberalism and its Critics." Another highlight was a six-week seminar on "Science and Theology" where I heard lectures by scholars like John Polkinghorne, Donald Mackay, and Thomas Torrance. Then there were the philosophy clubs that I could attend, for example, the "Metaphysicals" consisting of philosophers and theologians who met to discuss various topics in the philosophy of religion. The first session was held in a professor's room at Merton College (John Lucas). What a delight to see a room thoroughly cluttered with furniture that looked as if it had been picked up from an ancient garbage dump.

I was also able to attend a number of philosophy conferences. In the fall I attended the annual meeting of the Society of Christian Ethics, which was quite disappointing and made me wonder why the name "Christian" was even in the name of the society. The Society of Christian Philosophers also met in the fall and this conference was more Christian in orientation. A highlight for me was a paper by Richard Swinburne, recently appointed the Nollith Professor of the Philosophy of the Christian Religion at

Oxford University, replacing Basil Mitchell. His paper was entitled, "Guilt, Atonement and Forgiveness." At his earlier inaugural lecture at the university, accompanied with much pomp and circumstance, he spoke on "The Structure of the Soul." He introduced his inaugural lecture by describing the dark days of the 1950s when the philosophy of religion was not very popular and was being attacked both by philosophers and theologians. Basil Mitchell, who was also at the conference I described earlier, commented on the fact that a philosopher treating a theological subject as Swinburne was doing now, would have been looked upon with suspicion some fifteen to twenty years earlier. Philosophy had come a long way and I was enjoying the respectability which the philosophy of religion had in Great Britain. My hope was that this respectability would eventually transfer to North America.

Libraries are an essential part of academic life, and Oxford had a lot to offer in this regard with its Bodleian library which was then the second largest library in Britain and which had been around for some 380 years. To become a reader, I had to undergo a formal initiation ceremony where I recited a library creed in front of a gowned admissions clerk. The Bodleian was in many ways very antiquated. Although efforts were underway to computerize their holdings, their main catalogue consisted of a series of large scrap books with little strips of paper pasted on each page for each of the 4 ½ million books spread along seventy-seven miles of shelving in the library. Only a few of the books were on open shelves and thus for most books one had to hand in a request for a book one wanted to read, wait for ½ to 1 ½ hours until the book appeared in one of the reading rooms scattered in various buildings throughout the city. It really was a nuisance, especially given that no books could be taken outside the Bodleian.

But studying in one of the beautiful rooms of the Bodleian more than made up for the inconveniences. I also enjoyed reading in the lofty galleried upper floor of the domed Radcliffe Camera which one reached by a spiral staircase "that allows readers to approach their work with dignity." My favourite library was Rhodes House, endowed by Cecil Rhodes – a magnificent structure with a winding staircase, high ceilings and French Impressionist paintings on the walls. I also made use of the theological library in Pusey House. Here most of the books were located on a lower floor which really looked like a dark dungeon as one descended via a steep, narrow, spiral staircase. The crowded shelves were some twelve feet high and it was quite an ordeal to climb up a step ladder to get to some journals on the top shelf. When trying to find an article in a journal, I found it easiest to simply sit on the top rung of the step ladder and do my reading up there.

In the winter (Hilary) term I continued to enjoy the richness of academic opportunities in Oxford. I could attend any number of lectures on any day of the week. The problem was how to pick and choose. I enjoyed a special lecture series on the history of the University of Oxford since 1945. It was fascinating to hear J.O. Urmson describe the work of Gilbert Ryle and J.L. Austin who were at the forefront of the analytic movement in philosophy and made Oxford the "world champion in philosophy" after World War II. I enjoyed some lectures on the history of the philosophy of science by Rom Harré. Then there was A.J. Ryan who started his lectures on the history of political thought in a small classroom that only seated about thirty-five students. He had to change to an auditorium which accommodated about 200 students because his lectures were so popular. I also attended a graduate seminar on "Analogy and Metaphor in Religion" led by Richard Swinburne and Rom Harré, as well as a series on virtue ethics, a topic which was very much in vogue at Oxford at that time.

During this term I also visited Professor Basil Mitchell, who had just retired from his position as Nollith Professor of the Philosophy of the Christian Religion. It was a real treat to be able to visit someone whose writings I greatly admired and whose essays I had taught for many years to my own students. I visited him in his home, an antiquated cottage in a romantic little village outside of Oxford. We spent most of the time discussing indoctrination, and although we agreed on most things, Mitchell was a little more optimistic than I about coming to agreement as to what "indoctrination" means.

I did not accomplish as much as I would have liked by way of my own research and writing while at Oxford. The intellectual stimulation of the plethora of lectures available was simply too enjoyable. Brian Hendley, my thesis supervisor, had invited me to contribute an essay on tolerance and education for a book he was editing. Unfortunately, this book project did not come to fruition. However, I was invited to give a paper on the topic at the Morrell Studies in Toleration, a research program sponsored by a wealthy Quaker who left York University a sizable foundation. I'm not sure this Quaker would have appreciated the rather negative reaction I got to the argument of my paper, namely that contrary to the view of the Alberta Committee on Tolerance and Understanding, private religious schools do not foster intolerance in a society. I also presented this same paper at branch meetings of the Philosophy of Education Society of Great Britain at Cambridge in February and in Wales in June. John Hull also invited me to give a lecture to his M.A. students at the University of Birmingham, where I met considerable opposition to my defense of the notion of truth with a capital "T". I also read a book by Oliver Barclay, *Developing a Christian Mind*, and began writing a lengthy response which was eventually published in the *Evangelical Quarterly* in 1992. I began work on a bible study guide on "Faith and Reason; Knowledge and Doubt: A Study Guide on Epistemological Questions." I was quite keen on this project and sent off a proposal and some sample studies to Inter-Varsity Press, but sadly they weren't interested. The academic atmosphere of Oxford was even inspiring me to think of writing a book myself – tentative title, "Indoctrination and Religious Education," growing out of my dissertation. However, this project would have to wait until after my sabbatical. I describe this book project in greater detail in Chapter 10.

Another significant and generally enjoyable part of our sabbatical was travelling which we did whenever the children had school breaks. Our first trip was taken just three weeks after we arrived in England and before school started. We travelled to the south-west part of England, going all the way to what is appropriately called Land's End. On our way back we visited Bath where one can see some very good ruins of ancient Roman baths. We then travelled to Exmoor National Park and fell in love with a little town of Lynton on the coast where we hiked along the coastline, did some horseback riding on the moors, and enjoyed tea and scones one mid-afternoon. Then on to Exeter and a visit to the beautiful cathedral at Salisbury. We still hadn't purchased our camping equipment so we stayed at youth hostels which were increasingly catering to families. The children loved the hostels because here they could interact with other young people.

In February we took a short family trip to Paris which was somewhat of a disaster, starting with a delayed bus ride, another missed connection, a very noisy and rough thirty-five minute ride on a hovercraft which Gregory and I did not really enjoy, trying to find a hostel closer to the centre of Paris, and difficulties in getting a taxi to take us to our hostel. Besides it was cold – February is not the best time to visit Paris. But we did visit some of the typical tourist destinations – Church of Saint Mary Magdalen, the Palais-Royal, the Eiffel tower, and the Notre Dame Cathedral.

During the school break in early April we took a trip to northern England and Scotland, covering some 1,700 miles. Despite the terrible weather, we had some delightful experiences – visiting Yorkminster Cathedral, driving along Hadrian's wall, a stop in Edinburgh, a lovely youth hostel in Pitlochry, a short search for the Loch Ness monster, and an interesting stay at a castle turned into a youth hostel on the shores of Loch Lomand, where we were put up in servant's quarters, on the top of a flight of seventy-seven steps, but it was worth it. We were sorry that we would not be able to visit Scotland during the summer months.

Finally we spent 2 ½ weeks in July doing a camping trip in Europe – Belgium where we got lost, Germany where we spent a delightful weekend with a Lutheran *pfarrer's family* (Dieter Weber) whom we had met nineteen years earlier in Erlangen during our honeymoon, Austria where we were locked out of our hostel room at Salsburg, Italy where we spent two beautiful days on the Adriatic, Switzerland where we again fell in love with the Alps, France which didn't impress us once again, and then back to Oxford half a week earlier than planned as we were getting tired of travelling.

After another 1 ½ weeks in Oxford, selling some possessions, packing the rest, and saying our last farewells, we returned to Gatwick Airport for the long flight home to Calgary. I have described this sabbatical year in detail because it was an important milestone for our family despite some health problems and less than ideal schools. The children had many enriching experiences, and Audrey and Andrew developed some good friendships, some of which have lasted over time. This year also facilitated the breaking up of some unhealthy friendships for Audrey in Medicine Hat. For me it was intellectually very stimulating though at times I was led to reflect on the futility of the academic life and the seeming unimportance of philosophical questioning. It was also a stimulating year for Maggie, and I felt good about keeping my marriage promise to give her a life full of adventure.

BACK TO MEDICINE HAT COLLEGE AND A CRISIS (1986-92)

Upon our return, I struggled with post-sabbatical blues and perhaps also some elements of a mid-life crisis. In my yearly diary I noted that I had never been so unenthusiastic about teaching as I was that fall. "After all, what challenge is left after one has completed one's doctorate, published a few articles, and fulfilled a long-standing dream to spend a year abroad with the family? Even retirement does not seem that far away anymore!" In order to keep my mind off these depressing thoughts I plunged into renovating a room in the basement for Andrew, painting various rooms in the house, and putting a new carpet in the living room. In part this response also reflected what we usually did after a year away – we were more aware of what needed to be done in the house, and so we got a spurt of energy to do some house renovations.

I also began thinking seriously about writing a book based on my dissertation, surmising that a new challenge would help me to forget about retirement for a while at least. In fact I began work on this book project in the following spring. I describe the writing of this book and the Social Sciences and Humanities Research Council grant I received in order to complete this project in Chapter 10.

I took on a new challenge in 1987 when I got myself elected as the Faculty Representative on the Board of Governors at MHC. My objective in accepting this position was to get the President of the College removed from office. I have already described the rather unusual way in which Chuck Meagher had gotten his position eight years earlier despite his lack of qualifications. In subsequent years we faced a growing problem of low morale at the college which culminated in a vote of non-confidence in the President by both faculty and staff. I describe the political dimensions of the long and difficult journey to unseat him in Chapter 9. Here I will focus mainly on what all this meant for me personally.

Although I treaded very cautiously at the beginning, trying to win the confidence of the members of the Board of Governors, it didn't take long for the President and the Board to turn against me as I tried to help them face the truth about Chuck's weak administration. Midway through this ordeal and in response to the faculty/staff votes of non-confidence in the President, the Board fired the Academic Vice-President, Lorne Dick. After this firing, I felt a sense of utter abandonment. I was just reading the Psalms at the time and found them most relevant, particularly Psalms 91 and 94 where my NIV bible has this note written on the margins – "read many times during the MHC crisis in May 1988." We were also studying Isaiah in Sunday School and the repeated calls for righteousness and justice became very meaningful to me as I dealt with this crisis. After it was all over, I made it a point to review some lessons I had learned from this painful ordeal, drawing often from the Psalms and Isaiah. Yes, these lessons were organized in point form in my yearly diary! What follows is a slightly reorganized, abbreviated, and edited version of some of my points.

1. Lessons about politics and power:

(a) I gained a better understanding of the extent of political power and how power can become corrupted. I came to realize that the boldness of the President and Board members was intimately related to their connections with the Conservative party of Alberta, another and higher level of power. "They pour out arrogant words; all the evildoers are full of boasting" (Ps 94:4).

(b) Again and again I faced abuse and reproach as I was trying to help the Board face the truth. Here passages in Isaiah that describe the suffering servant became very meaningful to me (Isa 50). We are told to expect the reproach of men and not to fear it or be terrified by their insults (Isa 51:7). "Though princes (Board members) sit together and slander me, your servant will meditate on your decrees" (Ps 119:23). Indeed, we are called to suffer for Christ's sake (Phil 3:10; 1 Pet 4:12-19).

(c) I was particularly struck by the dishonesty of the Board, constantly twisting truth, refusing to face up to the truth, and trying to get the truth stifled, even to the point of approaching the editors of the *Medicine Hat News* to keep a lid on reporting on the College crisis.

(d) I came to a better understanding of the extent to which the evil of the world is done unconsciously. I was often reminded of Jesus' words on the cross: "Father, forgive them for they do not know what they are doing" (Luke 23:34). I also learned the meaning of Jesus' sad commentary on human nature when early in his ministry he said that he didn't "entrust himself to them, for he knew all men" (John 2:24).

(e) I also learned how vulnerable a person is in the face of power. I discovered later that the Board had actually discussed removing me from the Board and firing the Association President and perhaps also me.

2. Lessons on how to face evil and injustice in the world:

(a) At first I sensed a calling to remove the President from office. The Psalmist asks, "Who will rise up for me against the wicked? Who will take a stand for me against evildoers?" (Ps 94:16). I felt that God was calling me to speak truth and seek justice in this situation (Isa 49:6-7). In retrospect, I'm not sure I got this right. More on this later.

(b) I began to resolve a long-standing tension in my thinking about what is our part and what is God's part in addressing the problems of this world. I concluded that if we as Christians find ourselves in positions of power, then we are called to speak truth and uphold justice within the sphere of our influence. Therefore, I needed to speak truth to the Board and make motions and vote when appropriate. But, ultimately, all this was in God's hands, and therefore I needed to pray that God would intervene in this situation. I could only offer him a few loaves and fishes of human effort, and I had to trust God to multiply my feeble efforts.

(c) Paul's description of the armor of God in Ephesians 6:10-18 became very meaningful to me. I recognized that my chief weapon was truthfulness. My job was to speak truth to power. Just naming evil and wrongdoing was powerful, and I was constantly amazed at how Board members felt embarrassed when I did this. Sometimes they couldn't even look me in the eye.

(d) I was constantly facing choices about when to speak and when to stay silent. Here I was amazed to discover a truth in my reading of the gospel of John during the Association of Canadian Community Colleges (ACCC) conference in St. Johns, New Brunswick, which I attended with the Board in May, 1988. Jesus "purposely stayed away from Judea because the Jews there were waiting to take his life" (John 7:1). Jesus made a pragmatic choice not to speak truth at that particular place and time. Eventually, though, he did speak truth to power and went to the cross for doing so. I too needed to take a stand on major points, which in fact I had done, but then I needed to back off about speaking the truth on more minor issues. You can't fight evil on all fronts. Jesus, though clearly recognizing his call to expose evil, also recognized that sometimes "the time is not right" (John 7:7, 6).

3. Lessons about God:

(a) God is a God of righteousness and justice, a point made repeatedly in the Psalms and Isaiah and indeed throughout the Bible.

(b) God is also described as one who judges and even avenges. "O God who avenges, shine forth" (Ps 94:1). I found this truth to be most therapeutic because it helped me to overcome vindictiveness which is a constant temptation when dealing with personal injustice.

(c) I developed a deep trust in God during these difficult times and was nourished particularly by the Psalms. "I will say of the LORD, 'He is my refuge and my fortress, my God, in whom I trust'" (Ps 91:2). "When anxiety was great within me, your consolation brought joy to my soul" (Ps 94:19). I needed this comfort because from time to time I was afraid of losing my job.

(d) Finally, I realized that God wanted to be glorified in all this, just as Jesus glorified God in the midst of his suffering (John 12:28). I had vowed that if God would resolve this crisis, I would publicly acknowledge His hand in all of this, which in fact I did at a Faculty Association meeting when I gave a report after it was all over.

4. Lessons about myself:

(a) I realized that I feel deeply about justice as well as the injustices that I experienced. I found myself breaking down again and again, even at public meetings. This isn't entirely a negative thing, but it did raise questions as to whether I was too sensitive a person to be involved in political machinations.

(b) I was forced to admit that I can provide leadership in times of crisis. I need time to think things through, but once this is done, I can then "set my face as a flint" (Isa 50:7). I also realized that once I had made up my mind to do something, I felt much better. It was uncertainty about what to do that led to anxiety. Here again, I needed to be patient – God in his own time would bring clarity out of confusion.

(c) My idealism needed to be tempered with realism. In the midst of this crisis, I consulted with Don Posterski, whom I had met years earlier when he was connected with InterVarsity Christian Fellowship. I met with Don over breakfast at the annual meeting of ACCC mentioned earlier. Don stressed that there comes a point where I must accept injustice and pragmatically work within the system. One cannot make an issue of all things. God in his sovereignty is letting evil forces overpower the good for a time, and we need to accept this, all the while realizing that God's light will eventually shine through the "thick darkness" (Isa 60:2). Indeed it is only after the righteous die that they will achieve peaceful rest. (Isa 57:1-2).

5. Lessons about the church:

(a) I came to appreciate the importance of Christian counsel. Early in this crisis, I met with two friends (Dennis Palmquist and Stan Riegel) and asked for their advice on how to deal with the President in a Christian manner. They suggested a direct confrontation, and so I arranged a meeting with Chuck to explain my position and suggest that he resign. He tried to persuade me to join him in resolving the problem of low morale, but when he found out that I felt there was only one solution to the crisis, he promptly ended the meeting.

(b) I also appreciated the fellowship of prayer. Several faculty members joined me each week to spend some time praying for the college.

(c) I also appreciated Christian friends who encouraged me in the dark times of this crisis. Jim Hayward, a friend and student of mine, sent me a card at the height of the crisis and referred me to the picture of the suffering servant in Isaiah 50:4-9. He also prayed with me on several occasions. Alvin Penner, another student of mine and subsequent friend, also wrote me a wonderful letter of encouragement.

(d) I also came to appreciate the power of reconciliation. Lorne Dick and I had experienced some major conflicts years earlier and by God's grace these had been resolved. Now I could defend him and help him to interpret events and face a difficult future.

This concludes a review of some of the lessons I recorded long ago in relation to the crisis at MHC. Have I really learned these lessons? To some extent, yes, but I still find myself having to relearn these lessons from time to time. In the end, I also had to ask whether I did the right thing when I took on the challenge of removing the President of MHC. Was all the time and energy and emotional investment worth it? At the time I certainly felt called to do what I did. But, in retrospect, I'm not sure I got this right. I think I was simply being too idealistic about creating a better world. Paul admonishes us to submit to authorities, even unjust authorities (Rom 13:1-7). Yes, for a time, the politics of MHC improved. But political turmoil and corruption returned. I found it somewhat ironic that the last President during my tenure at MHC was eventually fired some years after I had retired. We as Christians need to be realistic about evil and injustice in the world. Jesus reminded us that we will always have the poor with us (Matt 26:11). In other words, we will never eliminate the problem of economic injustice. And yet, we as Christians are clearly called to pray for and enhance God's kingdom here on earth. But these efforts must always be tempered with realism, patience, and hope. "Your kingdom come; your will be done on earth as it is in heaven" (Matt 6:10). I am still wrestling with the full implications of this prayer.

Some brief comments on teaching during these years. I had some very disappointing students in my classes when I returned to Medicine Hat College after my sabbatical year in England. I faced low enrolment problems in my senior political philosophy course, a problem exacerbated by the fact that the political science instructor discouraged her first year students from taking this course. Thus, I began teaching at the Brooks campus as a way of filling my workload. Problems of low enrolment in my senior classes continued in the ensuing years. For example, in the fall of 1990 my two senior classes were reduced to one or two students by the end of the semester. Some of my students reported that there were faculty who were discouraging students from taking my courses and this finally prompted me to alert the senior administration about this problem, in part to protect myself lest enrolment should become a more serious problem in the future. I also realized that I would now have to teach at Brooks on a regular basis in order to fill my workload. This did not stop me from experimenting with a new course in the philosophy of science at the main campus of MHC in the fall of 1991, and it turned out to be very successful.

CRESTWOOD M.B. CHURCH (1986-92)

We were getting into a pattern with regard to leaving and returning to the Crestwood Church after our sabbaticals. Before a sabbatical we would heave a sigh of relief as we took a break from all positions. Upon our return, we would once again take up our responsibilities. The church too had to adjust to our comings and goings. Elmer and Agnes Regier wrote this in "An Exposé" of our family written for the church *Chronicle* after our return from England: "To the Thiessen Five we say, we are honored to have you as part of our church family. We will allow you your Volvo, your bike, your beard and yes, your sabbatical leaves (with envy, of course) just as long as you keep coming back quickly."

After Oxford, I returned to the church board as Education Elder and Maggie took on the position of Sunday School Superintendent. A major concern for us was the development of a solid youth program, and Audrey and Andrew were only too willing to replicate their experiences at Wesley Memorial in Oxford. We had the good fortune of having some capable young men and women come to our church who were able to provide some leadership in our youth program in the following years.[5] A highlight was our first bike trip from Jasper to Banff, August 3-8, 1987. This was something I had wanted to do with our family some time, but other young people soon expressed interest in joining us. In the end we had twelve bikers (including myself and Greg Johnson whom Andrew had met in Oxford and who was now living in Ottawa) plus three people providing support (Maggie, Art and Nettie Thiessen). The weather was perfect except for one afternoon and evening of rain. The youth were marvelous and Maggie and I enjoyed working with Art and Nettie in planning, organizing, setting up camp, and cooking. There is nothing quite like seeing the beautiful Rocky Mountains on a bicycle. Everyone in the group will long remember the long ride down the Sunwapta Pass by the Columbia Icefields, where one of our terrified bikers wore out her brakes by keeping them locked all the way down the pass.

The success of this event led to two more bike trips in the following years.[6] In subsequent years we kept up the annual bike trip tradition though we made some changes. We set up camp in Kananaskis Park each year for the long weekend in August. We went mountain-biking instead of road biking. Each family was on its own and young people had to be adopted by a family in order to participate. This made it a lot simpler to organize and more enjoyable for those who had been the support crew on our road trips.

Unfortunately there were some tensions emerging in our church. Our pastor, David Funk, had disbanded the lay ministers on his arrival, and after I returned from Oxford, I discovered considerable alienation on the part of the former lay-ministers. I spent much time in discussions with David trying to help him understand the situation, eventually persuading him to reinstate the lay-ministers, though my efforts weren't without mis-interpretations on the part of some members of the church. Then there was an emerging problem in the adult Sunday School class where discussions were being disrupted because of the hyper-skepticism on the part of some members in the class. I tried to address this problem by teaching a class on the parameters of healthy discussion in church, based on 1 Corinthians 12. I discovered that some members of the leadership did not support my efforts to deal with this problem and so I felt it was wise to withdraw from leadership in the church. In retrospect, I believe I could have chosen a better way to deal with this problem.

Dave Funk resigned as pastor in 1989, and then the search was on for another pastor. The lay-ministers were designated as the search committee for a new pastor and we soon made the delightful discovery of a good candidate, Mark Jantzen, who was studying at Regent College at the time. After some interviews by phone, we had Mark and Sylvia come to our annual church campout and they very quickly won the hearts of our church. I quite liked Mark and was church moderator for much of his early tenure. We met weekly for discussions. The church was growing and plans were underway for a building expansion. The church celebrated its 25th. anniversary in July of 1991. Unfortunately, this event exposed some tensions in the church as the older members of the church viewed this celebration as very important while the younger tended to ignore it. Also, Mark came to question the role of the lay-ministers, and so once again I was driven to defend this body as a stabilizing element in the church.

A highlight for our church and our family was the baptism of our children. Audrey and Andrew were both baptized in 1987 with David Funk as their pastor. Audrey was baptized on June 7, and we appreciated her strong testimony which clearly articulated a "growing into" the faith. She boldly declared that she couldn't identify a conversion date. I wrote her a letter the following day commending her for her courage in saying this, since for many people in the church, this would have been seen as somewhat unorthodox. Andrew made a decision to get baptized in the fall of the same year, together with Tim Riegel. It was good to see two tall, handsome young fellows take a clear stand for Jesus Christ on October 4, 1987. Andrew mentioned that he had had a conversion experience after a week at Camp Evergreen in a 1983. Interestingly, we were not aware of this beforehand.

Gregory informed his mother in February of 1989 that he had become a Christian after a film was shown in our church depicting the life of Jesus. He was baptized by Mark Jantzen in the fall of his final year of high-school. He had developed a good group of friends in the church, and together with Nathan Kowalsky, they managed to survive the challenges of Grade 12. So on November 29, 1992, we had the joy of celebrating our third child's baptism. I gave a short devotional during the communion that followed the baptism, and talked about the fear I had that my being an academic and a philosopher would somehow lead my children to turn away from the faith. God had clearly answered our prayers about sustaining the faith of our children despite my being a philosopher. We gave each of our children a chain and a cross as a special memento of this important day in their lives where they gave an adult affirmation of their Christian faith.

FAMILY EXPERIENCES (1986-92)

A year after our return from our sabbatical at Oxford, Audrey was finishing high school, Andrew was put into an enriched SEAL program at Medicine Hat High, and Gregory transferred from the Christian School to Alexandra. All were doing very well in school. Andrew received the Rutherford scholarship as well as the Lion's Club Award for academic excellence and the Benjamin Lesk Memorial Award for Physics. All the children were also taking piano lessons though we were facing some difficulties here. Audrey was developing shoulder problems because of piano playing so we decided to end her lessons in 1987 while she was working on her Grade 10 piano. We had already pulled Gregory from piano because he was finding this too stressful. He followed this up with some guitar lessons. Andrew was doing well in Grade 9 piano though social interests were taking priority.

Another tradition that we started with Audrey was a Mennonite bar-mitzvah when our children turned eighteen years of age. We took them out to a restaurant of their choice, and then over a nice meal reviewed the past with them, asked them to forgive us for errors made in raising them, and officially gave them more freedom to make their own choices. We encouraged our children to attend a bible school or bible college after high school, We also made it a point to fund the first year of their bible education. So in the fall of 1988 we drove Audrey to the Mennonite Brethren Bible College

in Winnipeg, and on our return were very much aware of the fact that our first child had left home. Of course, we knew she would flourish at MBBC, what with many social opportunities and a greater distance from her parents.[7]

Another important milestone in children growing up is of course getting their drivers license. We kept our sturdy Volvo for this purpose and all three of our children learned to drive in the "wounded cheezy." Meanwhile we purchased a second car in 1987.[8] The decision to buy a second car came with some guilt feelings, but with children driving, life seemed to be less complicated with two cars in the family. Among other incidentals, we built a garage attached to our house in the summer of 1988, Andrew started a bicycle business in our new garage that same summer, and we got a new cat, Mischka, in 1989, with several other cats to follow.

Summer holidays were another important family experience for us. I have already described our annual bike trips which were certainly very significant for our family. Then there were our camping trips, probably most remembered for the old heavy but spacious canvas tent that took forever to set up (see picture in Chapter 3, p. 64). In the summer of 1987, after our return from Oxford, we took a ten-day holiday, travelling with John and Irene Derksen and family to the mountains and then on to Kelowna. The children were certainly happier camping with their friends. Later that summer we had our first and very successful bike trip from Jasper to Banff. Later still, we travelled to Glenbush to attend Lorraine Pauls' wedding. Our children loved going to Henry and Susie's farm. In my yearly diary, I describe this as the best summer in many years, certainly more relaxing than travelling in Europe as in the previous summer.

Maggie and I started taking some holidays without our children, joined by our good friends, Len and Martha Pauls. In 1988 the four of us spent some delightful days at Mount Engadine Lodge in Kananaskis Park. The following year we stayed at Num Ti Jah Lodge – a bit disappointing in terms of accommodation, but we made up for this by enjoying a memorable meal at "The Post" in Lake Louise. We also enjoyed some good hikes, including one at Sunshine Village in Banff. In 1991 we took a rather expensive 3-day holiday at Lake O'Hara Lodge, located near Field, B.C.. The lodge can only be accessed by bus which takes you a good way up the mountain. The view was idyllic, the hikes were marvelous, and the gourmet meals fantastic.

Canoe trips with the boys were another kind of memorable summer experience. In the fall of 1983 I took Andrew and Randy Thiessen on a canoe trip as an advance birthday present for Andrew. Our intention was to go from Bow Island to the Hat, but it was a windy day and so we
only made it to the Ralston Pump House. In 1988 I took Andrew, Randy, and Darren, a newcomer in our church, on a three-day trip down the South Saskatchewan River. Canoeing through the wilderness, venturing through the Suffield army base hoping that the shooting would stop as we passed through, hearing the coyotes at night, and seeing other wildlife during the day, made this an exciting trip. The following spring I did another canoe trip with Gregory and his friend Nathan Kowalsky and his father.

I would be amiss if I did not mention our nearly monthly visits to my mother in Swift Current. She enjoyed the children and they enjoyed her. She would also come to visit us in Medicine Hat and on occasion take care of the children while Maggie and I went on a holiday by ourselves. The children still have fond memories of hunting for their Easter bags of goodies, which Grandma always hid, either in her yard or in a Swift Current park. After nearly twenty years of living in her own house, a house that Dad bought as their retirement home, we felt it was time for her to move. So, in 1978 we moved my mother into Heritage Towers. She was not entirely happy here so in the spring of 1983 she purchased a condo near the Bridgeway M.B. Church.[9] During these years she was also coping with an array of health problems.[10]

A memorable family Christmas was held in 1988 when most of the Thiessen clan met in Swift Current and had a celebration in the Bridgeway M.B. Church (Ruth and her new husband, Bob, Ted and Cathy, Abe and Alvina, Lottie and Jillian, Carey and Shirley, and our family). The grandchildren put on a delightful skit, entitled, "A Thiessen, Thiessen, Thiessen, Cunin, Stubbs and Goerz Family Gathering." It was a grand caricaturing of each set of parents, though oft-times very accurate, even painfully so.

WEDDING

A major event of this period of our lives was the marriage of our daughter to Geoff Wichert on August 4, 1990. This love story began at MBBC, a good place to meet given that this is where Audrey's parents had met as well. Audrey returned to MBBC for her second year of studies in the fall of 1989, and we became aware of a rapidly growing relationship with Geoff. They visited us on the Thanksgiving weekend and we had a good time hiking, canoeing, biking, eating, and getting to know each other. A discussion with them revealed that they were already talking about marriage, though thankfully only 2 ½ years down the road. We saw them again at Christmas when we travelled to Winnipeg with my mother to hear the College choir give their Christmas concert. Audrey came home for Christmas and shared her plans about going to the University of Toronto the following year to join Geoff. Then a week before Christmas we received a surprise phone call from Geoff, asking for Audrey's hand in marriage. We were in a state of shock and suggested that we needed some time to think about this.

It took us a while to process all this but soon came to the conclusion that it was not the choice of a mate that was the problem, since we had come to like Geoff, even though we had only met him a few times. Our concerns had to do with Audrey getting married at such an early age. Hence, we gave Geoff a yes to the hand of our daughter, but we wanted them to reconsider the timing of the wedding and suggested that this announcement be put on hold for a month. After some further processing we released them from the waiting period that we had imposed on them. They were of course delighted and promptly got publicly engaged on January 27, 1990, with the wedding planned for that fall. They were planning to come to Medicine Hat in mid-January to announce their engagement in our church, but decided to wait until the MBBC choir tour to Alberta. We went to Coaldale to hear the choir and brought them to the Hat on Sunday, February 18, at which time their engagement was announced in our church.

Upon completion of the winter semester at MBBC, Audrey returned home for the summer. We were still in England on a research/holiday tour when she returned. As soon as we got back, preparations for the wedding began in earnest. In the meantime Audrey was working part time at a day care center, where she had worked the previous summer. She was also appointed joint summer intern in our church, together with Ron Thiessen. She preached her first sermon that summer and Dad was proud of his daughter. Geoff was in Europe for a music tour with Bill Baerg and returned mid-July to spend some time with us, after which he went back to Winnipeg to work.

The wedding day arrived all too soon. Guests started arriving a few days before the wedding. We had rented a floor of rooms at Hillcrest College for Audrey's and Geoff's student friends as well as the Wicherts and our relatives. We hosted a lot of them for the evening meal two days before the wedding. The next day we had the rehearsal, with the Wicherts taking care of the rehearsal supper. We asked everyone to stay away on the day of the wedding so we could maintain our sanity. After hair appointments, dressing, and the arrival of flowers, Geoff and his best men arrived for the taking of pictures. Geoff was so proud of his beautiful bride, and she was beautiful! Family pictures were taken in a Medicine Hat park.

At three o'clock we gathered at the church for the wedding and Dad had to take that difficult walk up the aisle to give his only daughter away in marriage. Mark Jantzen, our pastor, did a superb job – it was his first wedding in our church, so it was a real test for him. The reception was held at the Hillcrest Church gymnasium – Audrey had been part of their youth group a few years earlier. Andrew and Mike Davies served as M.C.'s at the reception and did a good job.

Soon it was all over. Audrey and Geoff stayed at the Medicine Hat Lodge, where we had reserved a room for them. After the morning church service the next day, we had a reception at the church for the families of the

bride and groom, after which Audrey and Geoff came back for the opening of gifts. The Plante family wanted to leave for their holidays, but the children insisted on taking in every part of this wedding, including the gift opening. Thus ended what was dubbed the church social event of the year and so everyone could move on to their own affairs.

TWENTY-FIFTH WEDDING ANNIVERSARY:

The summer of 1992 seemed to be one long celebration of our twenty-fifth wedding anniversary. It began with a trip to eastern Canada early in July, coinciding with the Canadian M.B. conference in St. Therese, Quebec, near Montreal. I took in part of the conference while also attending the Concord College Board meetings. Meanwhile Maggie and Gregory stayed in Toronto with Geoff and Audrey. After I returned from conferencing, we had a delightful time, spending our first extended stay with our married children – Geoff was just completing his M.A. and Audrey was earning money babysitting. We also enjoyed exploring Toronto, going on a camping trip with Geoff and Audrey, and visiting Friesen siblings in southern Ontario. On our return to Medicine Hat, we did our annual bike trip in Kananaskis. Andrew was able to join us because he was doing a summer internship in our church. It was good to see his leadership skills developing. Audrey was back in Medicine Hat for the weekend of our actual anniver-

sary, serving as bridesmaid for Cory and Lorilee's wedding. We celebrated our anniversary by going out for supper as a family – the children gave us a lovely card listing twenty-five things each of them appreciated about us as parents. On Sunday, some friends in the church joined us for a picnic at Echodale park. The final celebration of the summer was attendance at the International Society of Religious Education and

Values (ISREV) conference in Banff. I took Maggie along so we could also enjoy Banff together. It was a wonderful summer, in which we could celebrate God's goodness to us as a married couple and as a family.

Some concluding reflections. This chapter has dealt with the middle stage of my career and the stage of my life where our children are adolescents. I am thirty-seven years old at the beginning of this chapter and fifty at the end. It is perhaps symbolic that I was attending a full day of Concord College board meetings in Winnipeg on my fiftieth birthday.

It is perhaps also significant that on my day of prayer and bible study in the spring of 1992, the last year covered in this chapter, I was studying the book of Jeremiah. Jeremiah was appointed by God "to destroy and overthrow" and "to build and to plant" (Jer 1:10). This would seem to describe the middle part of my career. God called Jeremiah to speak truth to a nation "where truth has perished" (Jer 7:28). This was not an easy task. "I sat alone because your hand was on me and you had filled me with indignation," Jeremiah says (15:17). But through it all, God was with Jeremiah. "[B]lessed is the man who trusts in the LORD, whose confidence is in him" (Jer 17:7). Throughout all the difficult times of this stage of my life, the LORD was truly my refuge and strength.

NOTES

1. My connections with Harold Coward and The Institute for the Humanities at the University of Calgary led to another project in the fall of 1981. I was asked to host a retreat for the religious studies departments of the universities of Calgary, Lethbridge, and Regina, to be held at Medicine Hat College. A stimulating venture which I hoped would gain me some "brownie points."

2. I was involved in another venture during the 1985 winter semester which bears mentioning. With the support of administration, a committee consisting of community members and college faculty began a religious lectureship series which in fact continued for several years. Our first speaker was John W. Montgomery, and we were pleasantly surprised at the community turnout for this event. I can't quite believe that I took on a leadership role in this venture in addition to all the other pressures I was facing at the college.

3. I was offered a job during the first few minutes of the interview and discovered that the real purpose of this visit was negotiating the terms of the appointment. I spent the night in Ottawa at my cousins, Gordon and Annette Thiessen, and they brought me into

contact with a friend of theirs who was the Canadian High Commissioner to Nigeria. He advised against going.

4. I applied for ten outside teaching positions a few years later (1988-89) but was not called for an interview in any of these applications. For an analysis of why I was having problems in finding a university position, see Chapter 9, pp. 271-2. Several people at Trinity Western University were encouraging me to apply there, but somehow I felt God had called me to teach within a secular context.

5. These included a summer youth pastor, Erwin Neufeld (1987), Dwight Block, Beryl Schultz, and Janet Heller.

6. These bike trips included the Golden Triangle (Castle Mountain, Radium, Golden, Takakawa Falls) in the summer of 1988, and the Glacier/Waterton trip in the summer of 1989, where the boys especially enjoyed the breath-taking ride down the Logan Pass, going even faster than the cars on the road.

7. Andrew attended MBBC in 1990, and Gregory followed three years later. Audrey graduated in 1991, Andrew in 1994, and Gregory completed two years at MBBC.

8. We purchased a 1980 Pontiac Parissienne Brougham for $5,500, a rather big car, but it was comfortable!

9. Purchasing this condo at $32,500 involved collecting some loans that Mom had made to her children as well as a $1,000 gift that she had given to each of us. As it turned out, her two-bedroom condo at #4, 1187 Ashley Drive was a more suitable place for her and she was much happier there than she had been in the Heritage Towers (#212 – 325 Sidney East).

10. Mother had a major surgery earlier in 1974 in Saskatoon to correct a pinched nerve in her neck which was solved by a bone graft. Unfortunately, she had to have surgery again two years later to deal with pain in the hip due to infections resulting from the earlier surgery. She was in the hospital for a month after Christmas in 1982. In 1986 she had surgery once again to have some gall stones removed. She became very sick in the winter of 1990, eventually going to Regina where a urologist discovered a large tumor of puss near her kidney. Removing this tumor involved a serious surgery and recovery took a long while. We nearly cancelled our planned 22-day trip to England, and were relieved when we heard that Ted and Cathy were planning to spend some time with mother in Regina. The other siblings living closer to Regina also visited her. I brought Mother back home after our England trip and she recovered in the Swift Current hospital.

Chapter 5
FINAL CAREER STAGE AND EMPTY NEST
(1992-2000)

1993. I was very conscious of the fact that this was the last year at home for our last child, Gregory. Therefore I was happy occasionally to bring Gregory and his friends to Cypress Hills Provincial Park in Elkwater for some skiing. I remember a time early in January when I took a carload to Elkwater (Andrew Wiens, Jeremy Derksen, Amber Holmes, Richard Nickel, and Gregory). It was interesting to hear them talking in the car on the way there and back. They exhibited a wonderful sense of humour, certainly better than mine! But they also enjoyed each other and had a lot of good clean fun. I will miss this next year. I dropped them off at the ski hill, and was most thankful that I didn't have to stay in that yuppy environment. I often went cross-country skiing in Elkwater, and this time I decided to go to the top of the hill near the golf course where some new trails had just been created. The weather was perfect, about ten degrees above, with the sun shining. About three-quarters of the way down the trail there was a group camping site, so I found a picnic table with no snow on it, lay down for a while, had my lunch, and then did some reading - two essays in *Your Daughters Shall Prophesy* – essays by Linda and Gordon Matthies, and Ron Geddert – very good, I thought.[1] I was all by myself and it was perfectly quiet. It was a real treat. I then made my way back to the crowded and noisy ski hill, retreated to the car to do some more reading until the rest were finished with skiing at 4:00 p.m. Then an enjoyable forty-minute ride home listening once again to teen-agers talking.

PREPARATIONS FOR ANOTHER SABBATICAL (1992-93)

Believe it or not, it had been seven years since my last sabbatical and so I dared to think about another sabbatical, and another way to escape from Medicine Hat College. In May of 1992, I read about a new missions venture in Lithuania, the founding of a Christian college, funded by the Art Defehr Foundation. I contacted Dennis Neumann, one of the co-organizers of this new venture, and he responded about a month later with a phone call, quite excited about our interest in serving at the college. When he found out that Maggie was a teacher he was even more excited, and then when he heard that I was going on a sabbatical, he suggested that we use one semester of my sabbatical to teach at the college. When I explored this possibility with our Academic Vice-President, he was most supportive, so I submitted a sabbatical proposal, involving one semester of teaching in Lithuania and one semester of research and writing. This was approved by the administration in the fall of 1992, so we could begin planning this rather exciting venture. We felt it would be a good way to adjust to the empty nest syndrome that we would be facing the following year. In fact, we hesitated a little in committing ourselves, because we thought it might be better for us to stay in the country for Gregory's first year away from home, but in the end, the children all assured us that it would be alright.

Gregory had a good final semester in Grade 12. He was growing physically – three inches in five months, and this was increasing his confidence. He surprised himself and us on how well he was doing in school – he liked the sciences and did very well in English. We also became aware of his interest in a certain pretty girl, the first of a number of girls we got to know because of Gregory's ability to charm members of the opposite sex. In June we went through high-school graduation exercises for the last time and they were a drag, both for us and for Gregory. We had purchased a casual black jacket for him in Toronto, with Audrey's help. Audrey had phoned him ahead of time and told him that he would really like it, just to prepare him for this new experience of dressing up. The rest of the outfit – tie, dress shoes, casual pants, white shirt – were purchased in the Hat right at the last minute with Andrew assisting. The graduation banquet was long and boring, with Orville Kope trying to amuse us with humour in decidedly bad taste. It was a fit-ting conclusion to our feeling guilty about sending our children to public schools. But that was now over. We need Christian schools – after all that was what I was writing about!

At the college, I was teaching four sections of ethics – a bit tiresome, except for the occasional bright spot. One week I had a wonderful series of discussions in class and in my office. One student had been expressing very anti-religious feelings several times during class discussions. One time after he had raised yet another objection to Christianity, I replied, "I think you are being a little hard on God, John," which brought quite a few chuckles from the class. Then a few lectures later, while I was finishing my introduction to ethics, he asked me very seriously, how one could be moral when it was so difficult. How is that for a teachable moment? I was able to explain that we needed forgiveness for failure and help to try again, and the only adequate foundation I knew of on both of these counts was God. John's attitude seemed to have mellowed from previous times when he had raised similar issues.

Another student came to my office for a second time. After raising some questions about the next essay, he asked if he could deal with a more personal issue. He then proceeded to grill me for an hour about various questions regarding Christianity. Did we need religion to be moral? Did I believe in the end of the world and Armageddon? Did I believe in evolution? Were the Scriptures reliable? Which translation should one read? Which church was authentic? He shared that he was finding himself at the end of his rope and was searching for something more. It was these kinds of experiences that made teaching worthwhile for me.

In February/March I had to complete the final stage in preparing my first "real" book, *Teaching for Commitment*, for publication. Proofreading and indexing – what a chore! All else had to be put aside for this intense task. It was good to complete this process and realize that very soon I would be able to see my book in print. I then discovered that a decision had been made to publish it only in hardcover. I wrote a letter of protest and Mc-Gill-Queen's University Press reversed their decision. Later that spring I received word that the book would be co-published in Great Britain by Fowler-Wright. I was of course delighted with this development.

1993 was also the year for conferences. I made a total of four visits to Ontario, one being in February in connection with board meetings for Concord College. In April I attended an Evangelical Fellowship of Canada consultation on education in Orillia. In May/June, I attended two conferences back to back, one at the University of Waterloo, a 30th. anniversary celebration of the graduate program of the department of philosophy. I presented a paper on "Liberal Education and Commitment," and felt good about the response. Audrey and Geoff picked us up and took us to their apartment in Toronto. The next day, we all went to Ottawa, where I had booked two rooms at Carleton University, where the Learned Societies meetings were being held. We had a wonderful time, despite the rain – eating out, visiting parliament hill, attending the CBC youth music competitions, and visiting with the Johnsons, our friends from England who also took Geoff and Audrey kayaking. Later that summer I got a call from Dennis Neumann asking whether I would come to Ottawa as part of a group of six people from Lithuania Christian College, in an effort to get some funds from the Canadian government. Although I didn't really need another trip, I went out of a sense of duty to the college.

As for family affairs, Andrew was back home for the summer and very quickly got a job at the Lawn Shop. However, he hated the work and this led eventually to the termination of his employment. After a while he got a job delivering parts at Zelmor Automotive, a job which he liked much better, although the pay wasn't that good. At the end of June, we had an interesting visitor, a girl who Andrew had been helping all winter at MBBC. We had been concerned about Andrew's involvement with this girl who had some deep needs, and had warned him about the dangers of a male/female relationship in such a situation. He assured us that he was not getting romantically involved with her. However, during this visit, they informed us that they had decided to begin having a special relationship. What could we say? Later we had a formal talk with them, using prepared notes! We felt we had to express some of our concerns about this relationship, but at the same time we wanted to assure them of our support if this relationship should develop. We were thankful when this romantic relationship was terminated a few months later.

During the summer, Andrew and I had fun becoming a father-son speaking team. On one Sunday he spoke at Crestwood, while I spoke at Seven Persons. Then later, we switched places. I was thankful that my work as moderator of our church was coming to an end given my upcoming sabbatical. I was becoming increasingly concerned about the direction our church was taking under our pastor's leadership. I was saddened to see the difficulties that were emerging in working together as a team. But I also realized that he needed support, and so it was just as well that we were leaving. I did tell the incoming moderator, Dave Rempel, who only wanted to serve for one year, that there was a real question as to whether I would step into this role again when I returned. Here was another tension that I needed to work through theologically – a pastor cannot survive without support from some of the key lay-leadership, but what does one do when there are significant differences about the direction the church should take?

In the meantime, plans were well underway for our sabbatical. Early in the winter semester I spent a lot of time choosing texts and preparing a library order for Lithuania Christian College. Then during the summer I was busy preparing lectures. I had chosen a new text in ethics and this required some added preparation, and then I had to prepare for a brand new course for me, "Faith and Learning." We also made the somewhat difficult decision to stay at Stapleford in England for the winter semester, even though I was promised a 500 pound grant at St. David's University College in Wales. However, Trevor Cooling and John Shortt really wanted me at Stapleford, and kept writing to me about additional speaking assignments. I concluded that working within an evangelical context would be a better fit for me, and Trevor and John obviously had a lot of connections that might open some doors for me in the future.

LITHUANIA CHRISTIAN COLLEGE (FALL, 1993)

My semester of teaching at a newly formed Christian college in Lithuania Lithuania Christian College (LCC) in the fall of 1993 was probably the most invigorating teaching experience of my entire career. We left Medicine Hat on August 24, not exactly looking forward to a gruelling seven segment, 24

½ hour trip to Lithuania. The Kowalskys drove us to Great Falls in their big van. Their son Nathan was coming to Lithuania with us for the first three weeks, on his way to a Capernwray Bible school in Germany. After a night in Great Falls we flew to Minneapolis/St. Paul, where we met the rest of our volunteer group coming mainly from Winnipeg. Then followed a stop at O'Hare airport in Chicago, a four-hour stopover in Warsaw, on to Vilnius where we discovered that three out of our four pieces of luggage were missing, and finally a three-hour bus trip to Klaipeda. The next morning started with a welcoming breakfast, some information for orientation, and the giving of our allowance – $60 for the two of us per month. In the afternoon we got a tour of the building and surrounding area, and we also went to an exchange depot to get some Lithuanian currency. The exchange rate had been getting worse – now at 3.40 lita for one U.S. dollar – the coming of the pope seemed to have had something to do with this.

Our orientation included some lessons on Lithuanian history. Lithuania had just achieved its independence from Russia a few years earlier. What we didn't realize was that we would have the privilege of witnessing an important milestone in Lithuanian history during our first week in Klaipeda. We were still immersed in orientation sessions when our language instructor, Professor Jane, from the University of Klaipeda, excitedly told us that after fifty years, Lithuania would finally be completely free – in the morning of August 31, there would be a final withdrawal of the last Russian troops.

So, after a hard day of work in orientation sessions, most of the staff walked down to the nearby Russian base that used to house about 20,000 troops, to see if anything was happening. We saw history in the making. We arrived at the entrance of the base just as one army van was pulling out of the gate, so we quickly snapped some pictures as one Russian officer angrily pointed thumbs down at us. We crossed the street to get closer and an elderly Lithuanian woman was at the gate, ecstatically trying to communicate with us. With prompting, we got the message, "Heraus," "Aufwedersehen," accompanied repeatedly by appropriate gestures to the departing troops. Sure enough, inside the compound was a long convoy of trucks, ready to depart. Somewhat hesitantly, we poked our cameras through the heavy steal barred fence and took some more pictures.

We then noticed some civilians walking into the compound. So we cautiously proceeded through what used to be a very heavily guarded entrance. There seemed to be no signs of resistance from the soldiers that we saw in the distance. Then we were met by a soldier who spoke a somewhat incoherent German, partly because he had been drinking "schnaps" for the last three days, he told us. He informed us that we should feel free to wander around, except for one area of the compound, which was still off limits. We should also feel free to take pictures, except with a movie camera. We were told that they were waiting for 5:00 p.m., the official time of departure. It was now about 4:30 p.m.

Most of the soldiers, including a commandant, were very friendly, especially with the one single girl in our group, Theresa. We made some efforts at communication, through our friendly but rather drunken soldier. They even offered us cigarettes. One soldier invited a member of our group into his car, offering him some champagne, as he proudly showed off his collection of Western rock music, some of which was blaring from his cassette player.

Most of the soldiers were simply standing around and waiting, looking at us and other Lithuanians strolling through the base with some amusement. In one corner of the compound, there was a bonfire, into which soldiers were throwing various documents, a new approach to shredding secret materials. We took many pictures. The Lithuanians were already looting the buildings, so some of the younger members of our group stayed behind and brought home many artifacts including two soldier's hats, two truncheons, an employee of the month plaque in Russian, of course, and some photos. On their return, our looters were appropriately chastised by the ethics professor of the college (me), but to little effect as they proudly displayed their wares.

Lithuania Christian College (LCC) was a joint venture of the Christian Charity Fund of Lithuania, headed by Otonas Balciunas, Logos, a mission agency in Germany, and the DeFehr Foundation of Canada. It had been started a few years before our arrival as an English language institute, and was now offering two years of what would eventually be a four-year liberal arts program, in addition to the language institute. We were twenty-one teachers and staff, serving about fifty-five students in the language institute, forty students in the first year of the college program, and another twenty-seven in the second year college program. Ernie Reimer, a former school superintendent, was the President of the college, and Len Loeppky, a retired high school teacher, was the Dean. We were housed in the second floor of a newly renovated dorm of the University of Klaipeda, with classes being held on the first floor of the same building. Our rooms were rather sparse with large and very drafty windows, and we shared a common kitchen. Hot water was centrally controlled by the city and only came on once a week until cold weather set in later in fall when it was supplied continuously. The students were housed in two dilapidated apartment blocks at the outskirts of the city.

Our teaching loads were heavy. I taught three classes, two sections of ethics at a first and second year level, and a new course for me, "Philosophy of Faith and Learning," involving an exploration of different worldviews and a treatment of what is meant by integrating the Christian faith into academic disciplines and professions. Maggie went to the Klaipeda State Oil Terminal twice a week to teach English to about eight executive and office personnel. This was her favourite assignment with the two-hour sessions passing very quickly because the atmosphere was very relaxed and included a lengthy coffee break. She also taught ESL two evenings a week to classes of students from the community – doctors, businessmen, seamen, bartenders, and anyone willing to pay the 40 lita to take the course. At that time there was a long waiting list of people wanting to get into the program. Another assignment was added to her workload well into the semester – teaching two classes at the Pedagogical Institute, helping budding teachers of English improve their oral English. On her first lecture, one of the teachers grabbed the resource book she was using and photocopied the entire book – teaching resources were that scarce in Lithuania. Sadly, many of these teachers would never get to teach English in the school system as the pay for teachers was very low and they could make much more money in the business world where there was a need for English language skills.

The first challenge was reading the student lists in each of my classes. Here are some first names: Beata, Dovile, Birute, Jovita, Raimonda, and

Enricka – all girls names. Boys names included Darius, Dallius, Roman, Vaidas, Mindaugas, and Jonas. The last names were even more problematic – Skukauskaite, Vaitkeviciute, Jonusas, Plestyte, Butkus, Seibutyte, Marcincute, and Jakaitytė. My first class was with the second year students taking ethics. Then after lunch, I met with the first year ethics students. I began each class with a short word of prayer – the first time that I had been able to do this at the college/university level and I wasn't going to miss it. The administration had advised against this practice, giving as a reason that we had chapel each morning. I felt the administration was a little too cautious about exposing the students to Christian values – they needed to read my book!

I was somewhat nervous, as I'm sure the students were as well. However, they warmed up very quickly, laughed at my cartoons on philosophy, and engaged in some good discussion on the usual three questions I give at the beginning of my philosophy classes. Several students gave good definitions of philosophy. A few expressed the view that there was no truth in philosophy or that truth was relative. One gave a very clear social science perspective on philosophy, saying that our opinions are shaped by the background from which we come. Another asked how I could grade papers, given that they would be expressing their own opinions and surely each opinion was as valid as any other. What were their expectations? Some students wanted to learn to think, to express themselves, to discover the meaning of life, or to learn to think about things from several points of view. What were they afraid of? Some were afraid of not finding any answers, of being lost, of the course being dry and impractical, One student was afraid the course would be like psychology! One was afraid of exams. I was delighted with the first classes. I didn't even finish reviewing the course syllabus, but that didn't worry me – the main objective of the first class was to establish rapport with the students.

After the second class I gave them an assignment – reading some pages on the nature of philosophy in the library. One student approached me and said she couldn't find the appropriate book in the library, so I went over with her, only to discover that many of my students were already in the library trying to access these reference books. Unfortunately, there were not enough books for them – the $1,000 budget I had been given to purchase library books for each course didn't go very far. Clearly these students were keen, and it would be joy to teach them.

My classes were soon going very well. Indeed, by the end of the week I was having trouble controlling discussions in classes. I asked students to raise their hands when they wanted to speak, but even that didn't seem to help. I was getting the impression that they were welcoming the opportunity to participate in discussions and the chance to wrestle with deeper issues. Some private discussions with two of my students, Ausra and Vaidile proved to me that these students were very capable of deep thinking.

My earlier visit to the student dorms gave me the idea of going there on a regular basis and having office hours out there. I explored this with the students and they were most supportive of the idea. So at the end of the first week, Maggie and I visited the student dorm. We were a little late but by the end thirteen girls sat with us in a T.V. lounge for 1 ½ hours, enjoying Maggie's cookies and hot tea. One girl, early in the evening, said she would write to her parents that here the teachers came and brought you cookies – they wouldn't believe it, she said. After a while, I asked if any of them had some questions, and a few were raised about an assignment I had given them.

Then Rasa showed us a painting by a famous Lithuanian artist who just had an exhibition in Vilnius during the pope's visit. It was a painting of despair, showing naked men in the darkness, beside a ladder, on top of which was a platform covered with blood. At the bottom, was a girl, brightly dressed, and we discussed whether the painter had intended to have this girl symbolize hope. We discussed conditions in Lithuania and possible causes of the crisis in the country. Some spoke of the loss of faith during the Communist regime. Their grandparents had faith, but their parents didn't because of atheistic indoctrination. One student told of a painful incident in which a child had brought a Christmas present to a teacher, a symbol which had some Christian connotations. The teacher had openly ridiculed the child. Our visit was most gratifying. The students thanked us profusely for coming to visit them. Vaidile approached me and expressed her delight at my coming here to teach. She said she wanted to see me very often during the semester, to make sure she learned as much as possible from me during our short time in Lithuania.

I was soon having many conversations with my students outside of class. Here is a sample of one day of conversations and classes. It was a Thursday and I had had two classes in the afternoon and was just working on grading the first set of term-paper assignments. I had an appointment with Vaidile who had already seen me several times in the preceding weeks. She was very worried about the last quiz which I had already marked and had brought with me. She had reason to be worried, as she had done poorly. But what was significant was that with further studying, she had already realized that she had done poorly. I corrected her English and we discussed some conceptual problems in her paper. She was very concerned about understanding every detail of her readings. She was worried about doing well and I assured her that she would indeed do well in my classes as I could tell that she was very bright. I suggested that she was being a little too meticulous about details and that this might be rooted in a perfectionist streak in her, which I could understand, being a perfectionist myself. She agreed and we had a good discussion on techniques she could use to handle her perfectionism.

At noon Maggie came back from her second class at the oil terminal, all excited about conversations there. She had been given a rose from their rose garden. They had a wonderful time discussing how to conduct telephone conversations. Midway through the class they proudly led Maggie away for a coffee break, following up a suggestion she had made at their first session. We invited Vaidile to join us for lunch at the Klaipeda University cafeteria – a first for her even though this was her second year at LCC. We had a nice soup and something we thought was fish, but it turned out to be a fried potato patty with spices – a very Lithuanian dish, plus an apple crisp. It cost us about 2.85 litas for the three of us (71 cents, U.S.).

I then taught my first year ethics course, returning the quizzes they had handed in. The first year class was still struggling with their English, and I realized that I would have to lower my expectations with them and be more careful in explaining concepts. We completed our discussion on the moral crisis in Lithuania and began discussing the question of the meaning of life as one prerequisite for morality – a good lively discussion.

Continuing with my day of teaching and counselling, Rasa approached me after class and said she had found my assignment very difficult. She had worked on it until midnight and finally was so angry that she had thrown her work on the floor and tried to go to sleep, She was upset that I had asked them how a religious person might respond to an atheist's position that life is meaningless. She herself was not religious, so how could she answer that question. She also said her problem was that she knew so little about the religious point of view, though the bible classes last year had helped her. Unfortunately, she had not been able to sleep after her little temper tantrum, so she got up and worked on the assignment a little more. She got an "A-" on the quiz, and did very well on the religious response to an atheist's treatment of life as meaningless. I realized that she was really very bright.

I then met with the second year students for the course on faith and learning. The course was going very well, even though this was the first time I was teaching such a course. It felt good to be teaching on a subject that I cared about so deeply. We were discussing the nature of worldviews when one Christian student suggested that Christian presuppositions would not have any effect on our thinking about law or government – well, you can imagine how that got me going. I even drew on John Howard Yoder and noticed later that one of the students had signed out Yoder in the library.

After class, Jonas approached me and wanted to continue a discussion he had begun after the sermon I preached the previous evening, "Now we know only in part," based on I Corinthians 13:9, 12. He disagreed with my claim that doubt was a normal part of Christian experience, an implication I drew from Paul's claim that we only know in part. He equated doubt with unbelief. Then he asked me a trick question: Did I know for sure that he was wrong about doubt? Well, I didn't fall for his little trap!! I was a little concerned about Jonas as he was a new Christian (converted from communism), and tended to see everything in black and white.

Then Vaidile wanted to continue the discussion on her questions. We went at it for another three-quarters of an hour. One interesting question: What did I mean that God was a personal God? After a while I suggested that I was getting rather tired – could we meet some other day to continue. I deposited my books in our room and then went down one floor to the lounge area to relax and read the *Baltic News*, an English language paper. However, I was soon interrupted by Ausra. First she had a question on my sermon – did I say that we should worship God because we are ignorant of his nature? No, but I had said that recognizing the limitations of our knowledge in the face of God's infinite knowledge can lead to worship – I had ended the sermon by reading from Romans 11:33-6. She raised some questions about her own deistic worldview which we had discussed earlier. Then she announced that after my sermon she had decided not to argue with me anymore regarding her worldview. I simply knew too much and she wouldn't be able to defend her worldview. I asked whether she was afraid that maybe her worldview was mistaken, and whether this decision was perhaps a defence mechanism. She smiled, though I noticed her eyes were watering. She also asked how I was able to present arguments so well for positions that disagreed with my own worldview. I was pleased that she was seeing this level of objectivity in my teaching.

Well, I was getting very tired after counselling and teaching for nearly five hours straight. It was soon time for supper which Maggie prepared in our common kitchen. Sometimes we would go out for a walk after supper, if we had not been out in the afternoon, but I needed to do some more preparation in the evening, what with all the time spent with students. Later that same evening Ernie Reimer, the president, stopped in and asked how we were doing. He informed us that last year when they had considered us for this work, he had done a survey of the students to see if they would rather have a course in psychology or philosophy in the following year. Nearly all of them had said they would prefer psychology! We were glad that philosophy was chosen in the end. Ernie also asked if we could come to a meeting in ten minutes, in which they were doing some planning regarding worship services. So we were at a meeting for another hour. We were thankful when it was finally time for bed.

There were other activities that were keeping us busy at LCC. Ernie asked me to do a devotional for the staff for the first Sunday evening that we were there. Then he asked me to preach at one of the International English church services that he had begun early in the semester. He said he was so delighted to have a larger staff at LCC this year and with a variety of gifts. Ernie and Len would also consult with me on occasion, Ernie being very aware of the fact that I was the only staff member at LCC who had a Ph.D., with teaching experience at the post-secondary level. Indeed, at one point he told me that he had thanked God many times that I was at LCC this semester. I also initiated conversations with the philosophy department at the University of Klaipeda early in the semester and over time was able to break down some of their seeming defensiveness. They even invited me to give a lecture to the department but unfortunately this only occurred at the very end of the semester. We had a faculty retreat at a Palanga resort in October where I was asked to do a series of in-service workshops for the staff on teaching from a Christian perspective. I was also writing the occasional article describing our experiences for the *M.B. Herald* and *The Amber Link*. Maggie and I also led an eight-week bible study on basic Christianity for students.

In October, Otonas Balciunas, one of the Lithuanian founders of the college and an evangelist, asked me if I would be willing to do a series of lectures on topics in the philosophy of religion as a preliminary to a series of evangelistic meetings he wanted to hold in Silute. So began a new venture, with Inga Kalvinyte serving as my translator. The series seemed to be well received and so Otonas asked me to give some lectures in other cities, for example in Gargzdia, where a teacher who had recently become a Christian had expressed interest in the topics I was dealing with – Moral Standards: Relative or Absolute; The Problem of Suffering and Pain; Commitment without Fanaticism. Otonas then asked whether I would be willing to do another series in Kaunas. So this kept us rather busy on weekends.

Otonas finally invited me to speak in his own church in Siauliai at the end of November. After the service Otonas and his wife Raimonda took us to a private room of a friend who catered for them when they had special guests. The table was decked out beautifully and was loaded with good Lithuanian food. We sat at the table for about 3 ½ hours talking about the church in Lithuania, LCC, and the shallowness of North American Christianity. Otonas was very aware of some of the tensions I was facing at LCC and I discovered that he was quite sympathetic with my approach to teaching from and for commitment. He even suggested that I should be an advisor for LCC in the future – something that never happened. Otonas also asked if my pre-evangelism lecture series could be translated into Lithuanian as he was working on producing Christian literature for the church in Lithuania. This Sunday was certainly another highpoint of our stay in Lithuania. And what a thrill to have Otonas see the potential of philosophy in doing evangelism. What an affirmation of my own calling to be a philosopher.

Although we were very busy, we did take some time for outings and concerts. We enjoyed frequent walks in the forest nearby. We enjoyed many a meal at restaurants, our favourite being the Green and White. We enjoyed visiting the market, a huge area, partly in open stalls with a roof overhead and partly in a building. You could buy anything at the market – clothes, fruit and vegetables from local gardens, all kinds of meat – we actually saw someone chopping a pig's head on a very well used chopping block, i.e. a tree stump. Maggie purchased many a bundle of home-spun yarn at the market. Shopping for groceries in the store near our apartment building was also always an adventure. Produce in the store was behind the counter or in wire cage shelves so that you couldn't pick up anything in order to read the label. And trying to get the price of produce from the vendors outside the store was always a real challenge. Early in the semester the LCC staff went to Kaunas, one of the most Lithuanian cities in the country, very prosperous, and quite a contrast to Klaipeda. We bought some linen at a factory there. It was here that Maggie had her wallet stolen by a pick-pocket – very professionally executed so we hardly noticed, except that Maggie did recall that she got bumped at one point in the crowded store. Losing $30 did make us more careful from then on.

Philosopher's Pose

On another Saturday we took a four-hour drive to Panevezys, on a state-run bus, which only drove 70 km. per hour as per state regulations. The main purpose was to visit a cottage factory making candle houses. On our way back we stopped at the Hill of Crosses at Schilute, which the pope had just visited. Unfortunately it was raining, but the large number of crosses was quite a testimony to the living faith of the people of Lithuania, despite opposition from communism. In fact, we liked to attend the Catholic church in Klaipeda on some Sundays, in part for the music, but also to get a feel for Lithuanian piety on open display after years of persecution by the communists. On another occasion a group of us took a ferry and went to Nida, where we enjoyed the sand dunes, the Witches Hill with its many carved figures, and the Tomas Mann museum, where we were guided by a student from the Language Institute. In November the staff went to Riga, Latvia, and we all had a wonderful time being in a very modern city once again. Here we enjoyed shopping, a view from the tower of St. Peters church, lunch with John and Kay Unger, and Ernie and Elfrieda Reimer, a wedding with some organ music at another church, and a bathroom stop at the very plush Roma Hotel.

There were also unexpected events. In November we had an unusual visitor from Kiev – a contact one of the staff had made in the previous year.

Paul Kostiuk was a young merchant marine engineer interested in philosophy and he wanted to meet me. We took him out for lunch and he then joined some of my classes and loved them. After one class he handed me a letter he had written, and asked if we could meet to discuss it. So I invited him down for some tea in the evening even though I was rather busy. His letter was well written, self-effacing, and told of his interest in philosophy. I agreed to help him explore the possibility of taking some correspondence courses at the University of Waterloo. He was obviously a very bright chap, and really should go on to further studies. Two weeks before the end of the semester, Paul Kostiuk suddenly showed up again. He had returned from Kiev in order to attend my final two weeks of lectures. I was flattered! He stayed after each class, and would always have a few comments to make in response to the lecture. Sadly, this relationship had to end, though we kept up correspondence for a while and he would surprise me with an occasional phone call when his ship happened to be in Canadian waters.

I faced some interesting challenges during this semester of teaching. My first year students had more difficulty understanding philosophical ideas because their grasp of English was still weak. So I had to explain concepts more carefully. I also let them hand in their essays in two stages which allowed me to check their first drafts focussing only on English grammar and spelling.

About mid-semester I realized that not all was well in my second year classes and so I decided to have the students do a class evaluation. This confirmed that there was some dissatisfaction with the Faith and Learning class. About half a dozen students expressed concern about the fact that the course was being taught from a Christian point of view, that I wasn't spending more time teaching non-Christian worldviews, that the course was compulsory, and that there should be more freedom to express their own thoughts. After informing Len about the problem he encouraged me to follow this up with a further discussion in class. I reminded the class that this was a Christian college and reviewed the mission statement of the college. The students protested, arguing that originally this wasn't supposed to be a Christian college. This took me by surprise but I suggested that the original mission had always been the same. I also explained that although this was a Christian college it was also a liberal arts college and so they were free to challenge what was being taught. I said I was mainly concerned about attitudes and expressed the hope that we together could make this a good class.

Dennis and Renee Neumann arrived that very week, and interestingly, informed me that during their last year's visit to the college, they had faced a similar protest about the college's identity. They invited me to a meeting with the administration to discuss the problem. It was a fascinating discussion, so very relevant to the book that I had just written and that would be coming out soon. I realized there were several problems at issue here. I suspected there must have been some ambiguity regarding the original founding of LCC. My hunch was that some of the original founders of LCC were not entirely honest about the Christian identity of the college with the first students who enrolled at the school. Otonas clearly had a very different vision for LCC than did these Canadian administrators and businessmen. I also suspected there were a few staff in the first year who might have been too aggressive in pushing their Christian convictions in the classroom and this suspicion was being arbitrarily carried over to my class this year. There were also differing views about the nature of Christian education and liberal education. I disagreed with their suggestion that the problem might be my approach to teaching or that I was arguing too persuasively in the classroom. After all philosophy is all about arguing and what better way for students to learn to argue than to argue with a philosopher. Besides, some students had expressed their surprise about my arguing for positions which were contrary to my own convictions and that I was even raising objections to the Christian faith. I reminded everyone at the meeting that I taught in exactly the same way in a purely secular context. Neutrality is impossible. All teaching is from and for commitment, but it is possible to combine this with genuine freedom of thought in the classroom.

I also realized that the students had trouble distinguishing between their earlier communist education which clearly involved indoctrination and the kind of education I was giving them. They felt they had simply exchanged communist indoctrination for Christian indoctrination. Of course here I couldn't resist doing some clarification of the notion of indoctrination. Yes I was teaching from a Christian point of view but they were perfectly free to disagree with me. I tried to be fair in my treatment of various viewpoints in the classroom and would present arguments and objections to all viewpoints. Students began to appreciate this when essay assignments were returned and they discovered that some Christian students got low grades and those who were very sceptical of the Christian faith got high grades. In further discussions, some of the students informed me that they were having some difficulty in expressing objections because of language difficulties. I resolved to try to help them state their objections. One new student, Tomas, suggested that these students wanted their own views to be respected, but weren't willing to extend that respect to others. I also concluded that there were a few students who were very hostile towards Christianity and thus were objecting to any Christian content in any college classes.

I discussed the matter further with Ausra on our way back from Panevezys. She gave me two helpful insights. She suggested that this was the first time someone had clearly articulated the philosophy of LCC and this had taken the students by surprise. Ausra also pointed out that Lithuanian students tend to be very attached to their beliefs, and hence when I objected to their beliefs, they took this as a personal assault. This is why she didn't like small group discussions, since these tended to become too personal. I reminded myself that I needed to teach my students to distance themselves from their beliefs and to be more open-minded. Fortunately, the atmosphere in the class improved over time. I was also reassured when twelve years later during our return visit to LCC, Jim Mininger, the new President, told me that he had faced another "crisis" in his early tenure regarding the identity of LCC and that my book had given him a new vocabulary to articulate his position.

The last two weeks at LCC were very busy, what with marking exams, a lecture at the philosophy department at the University of Klaipeda, last conversations with students, meetings, packing for the move to England, and saying our good-byes. We turned our last classes into a bit of a party, supplying refreshments and saying our good-byes. The staff at the state oil-terminal put on a big celebration for Maggie and presented her with all kinds of gifts. Indeed, we were rather overwhelmed with the expressions of thankfulness we were receiving when we had only been in Lithuania for such a short time. I would have more time for conversations if any of them wanted to see me during this last week, and several did take me up on this offer.

Ausra was probably one of the students I had had most conversations with during the semester. Towards the end of the semester and in anticipation of our leaving, she seemed even more intent on meeting with me. On one occasion she came to see me after a class in which I had highlighted the need for open-mindedness. She recalled a conversation we had had early in the semester, when after some discussions about her own worldview, she had told me that she didn't want to talk to me about her deistic worldview anymore. She was finding my criticisms a little too unnerving. I respected her request, but now at the end of the semester she wanted to open up the topic again, and of course, I was only too willing to do so. She asked me why I hadn't been pushing her and I told her I didn't have to – the Hound of Heaven (as C.S. Lewis put it) was quite able to get to her without my help. She appreciated the freedom to make up her own mind. She confessed that something had happened to her this year and she couldn't quite explain it. She felt more open about Christianity and said she needed to talk to me about what was involved in becoming a Christian. She didn't think she was one yet, but what did it mean? I explained the essentials of the faith and she even took notes on what I was saying. She was afraid of becoming closed-minded like another Christian student in class. Ausra joined us for our last concert in Klaipeda. After a beautiful Schubert mass, I told her that one reason I believed in God was because of music like this. She agreed with me. On our final visit with her, Ausra said that she couldn't imagine next semester without me at LCC teaching philosophy.

Thus ended what I still view as the most stimulating and rewarding semester of my teaching career. Never had I taught students who were so eager to learn. Yes, there were some challenges in teaching, but my research and writing on Christian nurture prepared me to face these challenges. We worked terribly hard. Living conditions were not ideal. And yet our immersion in the lives of students was most enriching. I trust that some of them were helped. At our farewell, Ausra and Mindaugus said this about me: "I think many of us were pleased to have a teacher who loves teaching philosophy. His courses helped us to understand that morality is not only an abstract concept but also is a guide in making decisions. I think a lot of my colleagues would agree that without studying philosophy one feels lost in the sea of various ideas, concepts and worldviews. I think, for many of us, Elmer's courses clarified our beliefs and taught us how to defend our opinions." I kept corresponding with several of these students for quite some time after we left LCC. Some of them actually told me that they missed my demanding philosophy essays. Audra wrote, "Never before have I thought that philosophy could be such an interesting and practical subject." Ausra wrote to me after our son Andrew arrived at the college in the following year: "I think it is good for him that you came to Lithuania first. The reason for this is that you have a very good reputation among our students, so all think that the son is very much like the father."

We had the privilege of having several of my students visit us in Medicine Hat in 1995 when they were on an exchange program with Concord College. What a delight! Then, when we returned to LCC some twelve years later, I was again able to connect with some of my former students, several of whom were now on staff at LCC. More on this in the next chapter.

ENGLAND (WINTER, 1994)

Our transition from Klaipeda to Nottingham, England was fraught with every conceivable problem . On the way to the airport in Vilnius our van, packed with nine people plus all our luggage, hit an ice patch, spun around the highway twice until we finally hit the guard-rail and came to a stop. Rather scary! When we arrived at the airport our Lithuanian Airlines plane was delayed because they had encountered some technical difficulties – not exactly a good way to encourage faith in the airline. Half an hour later we climbed onto a plane that was dirty with crumpled rugs, seats that were floppy, and had water dripping from the ceiling. Russian workmanship at its best! Then in Amsterdam, as we were loading our eight pieces of luggage onto the train and after the departure bell had rung we realized that my briefcase had been left behind on a bench. I ran out, yelled for them to wait, found it on the bench and ran back, just in time. After our ferry ride across the channel, we missed a good connection to Nottingham and so had to go all the way down to London and then back up again to our destination. Then began the second leg of our sabbatical, and what a contrast to our experiences in Lithuania.

Our good friends, Trevor and Margaret Cooling, had arranged for a flat at The Grange, a residence of St. John's College, an evangelical seminary founded by Michael Green. The fridge and cupboard were already stocked with food, and on the table was a surprise – a copy of

my first "real" book, *Teaching For Commitment,* just published and which I still hadn't seen. On the second day Trevor took me to a Christian mechanic he knew who had a good deal on a car, a Lada which I purchased for 595 British pounds. Our boys and Nathan Kowalsky, who had been on a skiing holiday in the French Alps, arrived a short while later and so we were able to celebrate Christmas and News Years with them We had some good times together, hiking in the Pennines and visiting Oxford where we had lived during our last sabbatical.

Once the boys had left we plunged into our new activities at the Stapleford House Education Centre, a research and resource centre for Christian teachers. Maggie did some volunteer work for the Centre. I started by putting the finishing touches on a paper I was to give at the annual Christian theory of education conference held at Stapleford. The weekend was superb – wonderful fellowship and vigorous intellectual exchanges. Brian Hill from Australia was there and the two of us were repeatedly referred to as international heavyweights – clearly more appropriate for Brian. In fact, Brian was concerned about my defence of religious schooling and parental rights in educating children, even suggesting that British evangelical educationalists were in danger of marginalizing themselves – a veiled reference to my arguments.

Then followed a consultation where four of us (Trevor, Brian, John Shortt, and I) spent four days planning for a new book, "An Agenda for Educational Change: An Evangelical Perspective." I was again impressed with the deep devotion of British evangelical academics – we spent the first half hour of each day singing around a piano, praying, and being led in a devotional. We managed to arrive at a consensus as to what should go into such a book and who the contributors should be. We were trying to be forward-looking, addressing educational questions that might be on the agenda in the next two decades.

The following week was spent getting ready for two lectures I was to give at a Bridgehead for Education workshop in Bristol, again sponsored by the Stapleford Centre for Education. I was amazed at the dedication of Christian teachers in England – about twenty teachers coming together for ten weekends in a row to hear papers on a Christian approach to education. I repeated the paper I had already given on parental rights and gave a lecture in which I attempted to review my book – very interesting to quote from my own book and then autograph copies of my book that many of them purchased. Trevor and I had some good long discussions on our way to and from Bristol and managed to sort out some of the areas where we disagreed. We also discussed my next book project about which I was feeling somewhat ambivalent. Trevor encouraged me to write for the popular market using IVP as a publisher.

Much of my four months at Stapleford were spent writing chapters for my next book, *In Defense of Religious Schools and Colleges*. I also gave a paper at the University of Durham, "The Embarrassment of Teaching for Commitment." I attended the annual meetings of the Philosophy of Education Society of Great Britain held at New College in Oxford. We visited Cambridge where I consulted with Terry McLaughlin and heard a lecture by Richard Pring. In March Maggie visited her friend, Penny Adamsen, our neighbor in Oxford

New College, Oxford

many years ago and now living in Ireland, while I went to Exeter to give a paper and consult with Mark Halstead. I then went on to London and spent some time at the Mennonite Centre, headed by Nelson Kraybill who took me on a walk to visit Karl Marx's grave. I also spent a delightful time with Luke Bretherton, of CARE – Christian Action, Research and Education, who was very interested in hearing about our experiences in Lithuania.

Of course we also spent time exploring the countryside, hiking, visiting new churches and magnificent cathedrals, and enjoying wonderful choirs. Our four months in England came to an end all too soon. What an intellectually stimulating time it was. Just before we left we spent a lovely evening with Debbie from Stapleford, and her fiancée, who told us some British Lada jokes: How do you double the price of a Lada? Fill up the tank with petrol. How do you triple the price of a Lada? Put the petrol tank cap back on. What is the difference between a common cold and a Lada? You can get rid of a cold. Thankfully we did get rid of our Lada and for a fairly good price at that (400 pounds). We attended St. Helens Anglican Church on our final Sunday after which Trevor drove us to Hull to catch the ferry to Rotterdam where we boarded a plane to take us to Minneapolis and then on to Great Falls. Ernie and Irma Nickel were waiting for us at Great Falls, where we stayed for night and then it was on home after eight months away.

BETWEEN SABBATICALS (1994-2000): A GRADUATION AND SOME BIRTHS

Yes, there is some significance to the heading of this section. My teaching career was in some ways defined by the sabbaticals I had when I was at Medicine Hat College (MHC). Sabbaticals were the highpoints of my career. They allowed us to escape the rather narrow confines of life in Medicine Hat. They were invariably very stimulating intellectually. Sabbaticals also allowed me to escape from the messy politics of MHC. Our sabbatical years enriched our lives significantly and I am deeply grateful for my four sabbaticals.

Upon returning home in April, we had to face some of the usual headaches that accompany having renters in one's house – our strawberries had been dug up (who knows why); and the utility and phone bills had not been paid for the last few months, though after a reminder, our renters were quick to pay up. We had to hustle and get ready for a trip to Winnipeg to celebrate Andrew's graduation from Concord College. On our way, we stopped at Swift Current to visit my mother who was overjoyed at seeing us again, and even got up the courage to come with us to Andrew's graduation. It was good to see Andrew and Gregory again, and interesting to sit down at Andrew's guest table at the graduation banquet, with all his friends, mainly girls, whom Grandma was eying very carefully. There were only eight people graduating so it was a rather small affair. The baccalaureate service was held on Sunday, after which we took Andrew out

for brunch (after he got a ticket for making an illegal U-turn on Henderson Highway). I had been asked to give an address at the graduation ceremonies, where I made another plea for teaching for commitment.

After our return from Winnipeg it was time to settle into our home and into a routine. I had given myself two weeks to get reoriented, but instead needed about four weeks. Part of this time was used to get ready for teaching in fall. It was most discouraging to return to the department at MHC. The morale was worse than when I had left and the behaviour of some of my colleagues was much worse – literally yelling at each other and alcohol consumption in offices, to name just two problems. Eventually I decided to write a letter to the Vice-President Academic, and this did get some things straightened out, though I had to face some criticisms in the department for lodging a complaint with the administration. Ralph Weeks didn't keep his promise to interview several other members of the department, before he took action, but then what could one expect from Ralph. He was preoccupied with applying for the Presidency, and eventually got it, despite my writing a letter to the Board, urging them to hire an outsider. At least it wasn't a crowning – Ralph was given a 3 ½ year contract, with a full year's probation.

The second big event after our return from England was the birth of our first grandchild. Indeed, in this period between sabbaticals we had the joy of welcoming three grandchildren. Madeleine Justina Wichert was born on May 14, 1994. The birth occurred in the middle of the night, with Audrey phoning us from the delivery room, happily announcing that a girl had been born, seven pounds, one ounce. In typical Audrey style, she asked to be released from the hospital on the second day, and they showed off their baby to a church college and career group on their way home. Then they went on a camping trip the second week they were home. We had decided not to go to Toronto since Geoff and Audrey were planning to come home for a visit in a few months

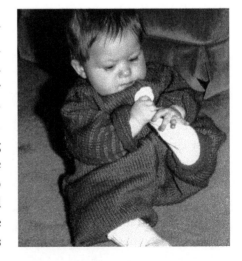

time. In the meantime we waited anxiously for pictures, so we could see our granddaughter. Audrey and Geoff and Madeleine visited us for two weeks in July, and we had a wonderful time. Our granddaughter was a delight – beautiful, good-natured, and quiet – we never did wake up at night because of her crying. She developed in the short time she was at our place – focussing on people's faces, giving us charming smiles, controlling her hands enough to look at them, and lifting her feet. We very much fell in love with her and enjoyed the adjustment to grandparenthood.

Three years later, we welcomed our second grandchild. Sylvie Berthe Wichert was born on January 28, 1997. Sadly, her Grandmother Wichert had taken very ill earlier in the year. Audrey and Geoff were hoping that she would still be able to hold this new grandchild in her arms and she did, as Audrey was up and around just a few days after Sylvie's birth. Bertha Wichert died a few days later. We finally got to see Sylvie in November when Audrey came down to visit us with her two girls. We had wonderful time – Sylvie was eight months old and just at that delightful stage of childhood. Madeleine was showing all the characteristics of a 3 ½ year old – we had a couple of difficult sessions while Audrey was visiting Grandma Thiessen and we were left alone with the children. But still, our grandchildren were a lot of fun, though we found the time rather intense. Audrey spent a lot of time with her Grandma, which she appreciated. I had great fun getting to know Sylvie better during their visit with us during the Christmas of 1998. Things were going well the first week, but during the second week, she kept saying, "No Grandpa" when I looked her way.

Ariane Maria Wichert was born on Oct. 15, 1999. We had decided to have Maggie attend this birth, but had difficulty

Three grandchildren at Red Rock Park, Alberta, 2000

determining when to fly to Toronto. We booked a plane a week after the due date, hoping that the timing would be about right, but as it turned out, Grandma arrived just after her grandchild was born. I got to see Ariane for the first time when our entire family got together for my mother's funeral in Swift Current in December of the same year. Indeed, I carried Ariane in my arms in the processional, and drew attention to this fact when I told my mother's story during the funeral service, pointing out the appropriateness of celebrating a birth and a death at the same time.

BETWEEN SABBATICALS (1994-2000): SOME DEATHS

Births and deaths – they come together in real life and certainly did so during this time period in our lives. We were rather preoccupied with taking care of my mother during the time between my sabbaticals. She was still living in her own condo in Swift Current and we were increasingly concerned about issues surrounding her aging. Mother celebrated her 90th birthday in May of 1996. She said she didn't want a family celebration, so we arranged to have all her children come and visit her around the time of her birthday. She enjoyed this arrangement, though she did regret that we couldn't take a family picture. We were worried about reports of her fainting and falling down occasionally. She complained a lot about being ill and was gradually accepting help in keeping her apartment. She surprised us in the fall of 1996 when she informed us that she was moving into a senior's home in Herbert where her brother Henry was now living. However, we got a call a few hours later telling us that she had changed her mind because she realized that she would have to share a bathroom with another resident.

A year later we showed her the new assisted living apartments at Chinook Village in Medicine Hat and when we mentioned the possibility of her moving to Medicine Hat she expressed interest. One apartment soon opened up and it did not take long for her to make up her mind. It was obviously time for her to make a change. Lottie and Joseph, and Ted and Carey helped us to move her in June of that same year. We realized this would change our lives considerably and it did. Mother was very disoriented at first and we had some issues that had to be worked through. She overcame her disorientation in a few weeks and generally loved her new home including the meals. We had to tell the occasional white lie in order to overcome some hurdles, e.g. promising not to use the bank machine in order to withdraw money for her.

We had from the start told Mother and the rest of the family that we might be leaving Medicine Hat after a couple of years when we were planning to retire. We were also becoming increasingly concerned about Mother being in an apartment by herself, and her neighbours were urging us to find a place with more care. Eventually Ted found a good nursing home in Abbotsford and was indeed urging Mom to make a move so that he could do his part in taking care of her. We moved her in June of 1999 and then realized how much of our lives had been preoccupied in caring of her. Ted and Cathy worked very hard at making her happy. We visited her in the summer and felt terrible when she suggested that we had come to take her back home.

I was working at home on December 8, 1999 because classes had already ended, when I got a call from our sister-in-law, Cathy, saying that Mom had been taken to the hospital, after she was found sitting in her chair before breakfast, completely unresponsive. A few hours later Cathy phoned again, reporting that Mom had had a massive stroke and the doctor felt it would just be a matter of hours or days before she died. She died at 4:55 p.m. on Thursday, December 9, shortly after one of her former pastors, Peter Klassen, had visited her. We decided to have a memorial service in Abbotsford as well as a funeral in Swift Current. I decided to go to Abbotsford to help Ted and Ruth with funeral plans. Both Peter Klassen and Peter Nickel, two pastors of Mom in Swift Current, officiated at the memorial service held in B.C. on December 11. I then flew home and was immediately involved in planning for the funeral in Swift Current to be held a few days later. Our entire family drove up together in a van that Andrew had rented for his trip from Calgary to Medicine Hat. The funeral was somewhat disappointing, perhaps because of the stress I was under, but also because I had already experienced a beautiful memorial service. It was bitterly cold and we made it a point to also visit Dad's graveside, which was just a short distance away. We were unable to bury Mom beside Dad's gravesite, as we had planned (see pictures of the gravesites at the end of Chapter 1). The church at Swift Current went out of its way to make a meal for the family at noon, and then serve a lunch after the funeral. The family stayed around and we ordered some Chinese food for supper, after which we all went our separate ways.

Mom had spent only six months in Abbotsford. Was it the right decision to move her? Was her stroke a result of her unhappiness there? These were the questions that I had to process, as I faced some more guilt about the decision to move Mom. There were no clear answers to these questions. We did the best we could. Her move allowed Ted to care for her for a while. She was able to make contact with her siblings in B.C. Ruth and Bob were able to be with her during her last hours. So, perhaps it was the right decision after all.

Unfortunately, this was not the end of deaths during this period of time. Maggie had three brothers die in just over a year. Her older brother Rudy (age 73) died of a heart attack on January 13, 2000. With the death of a sibling – a first for us – we now faced a new question. What to do about attending the funerals of siblings? I encouraged Maggie to attend this funeral – I couldn't as classes had already begun. So here we were again making last minute plans for another trip to Ontario for Maggie. We attended one of our concerts in Calgary on Friday and I brought Maggie to the airport early Saturday morning. Audrey joined Mom for the funeral in St. Catharines.

Sadly, this was not the end of deaths in the family. Maggie's oldest brother Bert, living in B.C., was struggling with cancer and in March of 2000 we heard that he had been given only a few more months to live. Maggie postponed paying a final visit with him to make room for visits from the immediate family. But, in the end, we waited too long. We had booked flights for the end of April, but when the time came, Marie advised against coming. Bert (age 75) died shortly afterward on May 2. We both flew down for the funeral and had a good visit with the family. All this was a strong reminder to us of the brevity of life. "Teach us to number our days aright, that we may gain a heart of wisdom" (Ps 90:12).

George was also struggling with cancer. We were hoping that we would be able to spend some time with him during our sabbatical stay in Toronto in the fall of 2000. This was another reason why we chose Toronto as the venue for part of our upcoming sabbatical. When we arrived, we had to postpone visiting George and Nettie – George was not strong enough to continue chemo treatments. We managed to have one good visit with him later in the year. He died on February 7, 2001, just before he turned seventy. We were in Victoria during this time, enjoying the second half of our sabbatical. Maggie flew to Ontario for the funeral. Nettie, George's wife, died less than two years later, on December 3, 2003.

BETWEEN SABBATICALS (1994-2000):
OUR CHILDREN AND ANOTHER WEDDING

Gregory returned to Concord College in 1994 together with his good friend, Nathan Kowalsky. Gregory was not too keen on returning in the following year and decided instead to begin a three-year program in Visual Communications at Medicine Hat College. He was the only child that benefitted from the free tuition my children could get at MHC given my status as a faculty member. After graduation he moved to Calgary where he experimented with some jobs, finally ending up working for FedEx. So in 1999 we finally faced the proverbial empty nest. It was during our Christmas holidays in Ontario, while we were at Camp Crossroads with the family that Gregory informed us about his discovery that his long-standing struggle with needing to check things was called an Obsessive Compulsive Disorder (OCD). Of course as parents we asked ourselves what we could have done earlier to help Greg with this problem. We had always known that he was anxious as a child, but weren't aware of the more serious nature of this problem as he was growing up. We were thankful that he had opened up about his condition and resolved to do all we could to help him cope with his problem.

Audrey and Geoff were on their way to Paris early in 1995 where Geoff was doing research for his Ph.D. dissertation in history. Unfortunately, he could find little material related to his research topic and so had to change his dissertation topic midstream. Upon their return Geoff continued work on his Ph.D., while also applying for teaching positions. There was much excitement when he was shortlisted for a position at Atlantic Baptist University in Moncton and was even given the impression that he was the top candidate. I had the privilege of giving Geoff some advice as to what he might expect when he, together with Audrey, flew down for a final interview in March. In the end, all this came to nothing and Geoff made the painful discovery that his interview was really just a front to make the process seem like a genuine competition, given that there was another favored candidate all along. My role then switched to trying to help Geoff and Audrey cope with the pain of this disappointment and also to caution Geoff against doing anything rash by way of protesting procedures that were obviously flawed and unjust. Further conversations with people at ABU revealed that it would not have been an ideal teaching environment in any case. This incident no doubt contributed to Geoff eventually giving up his pursuit of a Ph.D.

Andrew attended LCC as an exchange student in the fall of 1994, and then graduated from Concord College in the spring of 1995. Andrew spent another year getting a B.A. from the University of Winnipeg. Summers were spent working at Redi Enterprizes and Camp Evergreen. He was looking for a youth pastor position in the summer of 1995 and when no openings came up he spent some time fixing up an old Volvo he had purchased after which he moved to Toronto. Here he took up a succession of jobs – a security firm, then social services, and finally a youth pastor position in Vineland, the home church of his mother and grandmother.

The more significant event for Andrew and for us was his marriage to Rachel Giesbrecht on July 17, 1998. We were hearing rumors of a budding romance in the fall of 1997. Andrew had met Rachel at Camp Crossroads the previous summer. She drove a Honda Civic and had driven Andrew home from camp at 160 kms per hour – this sounded like a possible negative. We heard she was a lively, vivacious girl, beautiful, with blonde hair, and very active in the church, playing piano and singing in a trio. Greg was impressed with the fact that she had a tape of the rock band – Stryper. Well, events unfolded rather quickly. Andrew was home for Christmas and loved talking about his Rachel who had sent along presents for each of us, with two presents for Gregory – a cap-gun and fleece socks. She knew how important it was to win over a brother.

Soon Andrew and Rachel were talking about suitable dates for a wedding and this date kept being advanced until it was set for the summer of 1998. But we still hadn't met this girl. They promised to visit us in February but wanted to get engaged before that. So on a Sunday when Rachel and the entire Giesbrecht family were in the Vineland church, Andrew announced from the pulpit that he had met this wonderful girl, after which he came down and knelt before Rachel, proposed, and gave her the ring, all this causing many of the women in the church to weep with joy. The following week they came to Medicine Hat and we finally were able to meet Rachel and were quickly impressed with this forthcoming addition to our family. We got another chance to get to know Rachel a little better in the summer during our annual trip to Ontario, alongside my visit to the Learned Societies (now Congress). We had a lovely family dinner at the Prince of Wales Hotel in Niagara-on-the-Lake and then enjoyed a performance at the Shaw Festival – Major Barbara. The following weekend we made a repeat visit to the Burgetz's cottage and had a good family time with everyone there except Gregory. We, of course, also enjoyed getting to know Sylvie better (now sixteen months old) and Madeleine who had just turned four.

This trip had been planned before we knew about the upcoming wedding, so one month later, we again were back in Ontario, this time with Gregory. Our family stayed at Ernie and Mary Reimer's basement with Audrey and Geoff – it was an ideal arrangement – air-conditioning during some very hot days, with lots of room to spread out. Audrey had arranged a Medicine Hat gathering for the first night we were there. The following day we had the rehearsal and after that, a rehearsal supper at the Tallman's funeral home.

Pictures were taken at Niagara Falls in the afternoon of the wedding day. I had the privilege of giving the wedding sermon on the topic, "The Problem of Particularity and Universality, and Marriage." Fortunately, the title was not included in the bulletin, but I did have one pastor taking notes.

Unfortunately Rachel had been struggling with a migraine headache all day and this took full effect during the reception line which went on forever, what with 300 guests. Her headache continued into the program after the meal, much of which she missed.

Gift opening was the following day and by then Rachel was fine. It was a tough start for a marriage, but we encouraged her to simply forgive herself and accept a wedding day that was less than perfect. Our side of the family had given Andrew and Rachel some camping equipment as a wedding gift. They flew to B.C. the following day for their honeymoon – a camping holiday on Vancouver Island and the Rockies, ending up in Medicine Hat for an after-wedding on August 4. We had Mark and Debbie Penner cater for us, and so we had a fairly relaxing time as we entertained nearly 100 guests. I had encouraged Andrew and Rachel to include a more formal program as part of the celebration and this turned out to be a good idea, as many individuals paid some wonderful tributes to Andrew.

There were many memorable holidays that we had with our children during this period of time. Given the arrival of grandchildren, we made it a point to connect with our children in Ontario at least twice per year. Christmases were often spent in Toronto. There were also summer visits which we tried to combine with my attendance at academic conferences. Our annual bike trips to Kananaskis continued for some of these years. Among the memorable times together were the following: a sixteen kilometer Crypt Lake hike in Waterton with the whole family, including baby Madeleine in the summer of 1994 when Geoff and Audrey paid us a two-week visit in Medicine Hat; a backpacking trip with the boys on the Carthew Trail in Waterton in the summer of 1995; family gatherings at the lovely Burgetz's cottage on Lake Huron in the summers of 1997, 1998, and 1999; and a canoe trip with Greg and Nathan, Keith Kowalsky and myself, in the summer of 1996. Maggie and I also traveled to B.C. in 1996 for a Peters' cousins gathering. We also enjoyed a delightful stay at Mount Engedine Lodge in Waterton with our friends, Len and Martha Pauls, and Rob and Marriane Twigg.

BETWEEN SABBATICALS (1994-2000): ACADEMIC WORK, CHURCH, AND BEYOND

Perhaps it should not be surprising that my return to MHC after my last sabbatical was once again fraught with some political turmoil. I had originally been scheduled to introduce a new second-year course on political ideologies in the winter semester of 1995. However, I discovered that Terry Chapman, our history and political science instructor in the department, had put pressure on the administration to eliminate this option for me. Interestingly, my "Political Science" plate on my door also mysteriously disappeared, even though I had been teaching a second-year history of political philosophy course for many years. It seemed that I might have a battle on my hands to retain even partial responsibility for political science courses. I ended up writing to the senior administration about this and other problems in the department (e.g. alcohol consumption in faculty offices in our department), but as usual, not too much was done to address these problems.

I had my usual mix of good and bad classes during this time period though there were a number of very good classes. A highlight of the 1995 winter semester was a course in the philosophy of religion with twenty-three students in the class, the highest number registered in this course in at least fifteen years, and a healthy mixture of atheists, agnostics and believers. Students were quite willing to engage in discussions and so I did less lecturing. Indeed, discussions were so lively that I had to move into a refereeing mode from time to time. At the end of the semester I asked the students if they would like to have a philosophical party and they were enthusiastic about the idea. So after the exams I scheduled a Sunday evening get-together in our home. I had told the students beforehand that they could ask me any questions they liked and this led to a lively discussion in a very relaxed atmosphere which lasted until after midnight.

I also had a good winter semester in 1997 with one very interesting new student, Bob Stevens, a retired geologist, who was taking every philosophy class he could from me. He was desperately searching for meaning in life and was often in tears as we spoke on serious topics relating to his quest. He married a much younger woman, Anne Marie, and they subsequently had five children which Bob amazingly helped to take care of despite his senior years. We got to know the family well over the years and we continued to have religious discussions, invariably at Bob's instigation.

I received some interesting comments on my classes during the 1999 academic year. Lee, a Vietnamese student, informed me early in my Philosophy 201 class, that a philosophy class was a better place to learn about God than in church. A student in my introductory Religious Studies class described the course as a therapy session. Angelina, a single mother with a very interesting background, told me that when she was in my ethics classes, she felt that she was back in church. Should I worry about my philosophy classes feeling like church? Not if you believe in teaching for commitment.

The publication of my second book led to a lot of academic activity during the time period under discussion. The summer after I returned from England I gave four papers at the annual Learned Society meetings in Calgary.[2] I was also invited to speak at a number of faculty retreats at Christian colleges and universities.[3] I was pleased that my academic work also led to invitations to speak in churches on topics related to my research.[4] I also received some inquiries or invitations to apply for administrative or research positions at other Christian educational institutions.[5] Another preoccupation of mine during this period was the writing of my third book, *In Defence of Religious Schools and Colleges*. A revised draft was completed in the winter semester of 2000, with me having to lengthen my work days to 12-14 hours, six days a week, in order to complete this project. The book was finally published in 2001. I describe this book project in more detail in Chapter 10.

I was asked to serve as moderator of our church once again upon our return from our sabbatical in 1994 but was reluctant to agree to this given the many complaints we heard about what was happening in our morning church services. I eventually agreed to return to leadership after a long conversation with our pastor, Mark Jantzen, who promised to return to a more traditional style of worship. At this point the church was in the middle of a building expansion program and cost overruns were giving me sleepless hours at night.[6] A dedication service was held on September 10, 1995. Differences of opinion regarding worship style and my feeling that I didn't have full support for my leadership on the part of some of the other leaders in the church led to my withdrawal from the moderator role in the church in 1996. In so doing I was very consciously trying to follow Jesus' example of accepting powerlessness in the face of conflict. Interestingly, during this time I was also getting push-back from some members in the church about a sermon I preached on doubt and a Sunday School lesson where I refused to take a teetotaler position on alcohol. You can't win them all! Donna Jantz took over as moderator of the church but she was soon consulting with me about growing dissatisfaction in the church, with some people even leaving the church. This was resolved when Mark resigned in 1998.

Meanwhile I focussed on preaching and teaching Sunday school, tackling some longer books of the bible like Romans and Jeremiah. I was appointed chair of the search committee for a new pastor and this led to the appointment of Murray and Dianna Schmidt who were just completing their seminary studies. The church again faced tensions regarding worship style. Thankfully I was not moderator, though I was asked to serve on a pastoral review committee which did reveal some dissatisfaction in the church though these were understated by our moderator at a church business meeting. In the end I realized that significantly different visions for the church (including the issue of child baptism) suggested that I needed to resign from the lay ministry. Thankfully, my upcoming sabbatical provided a convenient excuse for withdrawing from leadership entirely.

Maggie continued to teach Sunday School and was also involved in a ladies coffee hour on Tuesday mornings. In addition she was volunteering at Global Gifts and was able to make a trip to Ontario to visit the self-help headquarters in April of 1995. She began helping with ESL instruction at Saamis Immigration after Global Gifts shut down and this new work turned into a part-time job beginning in 1998. We were both enjoying singing in the College choir for a number of years. I was also appointed to the Ethics Committee of the Palliser Health Authority and served on that committee for several years. I also joined a book club that was organized by Dan Reinhardt, pastor of Hillcrest Church, who had just returned from a sabbatical, and Dallas Miller, one of my former students and now a lawyer.[7] In order to supplement the rather meagre cultural diet offered in Medicine Hat, we got seasons tickets to the Calgary Symphony in the year, 2000.

This chapter has focused on the final stage of my career and our facing the proverbial empty nest on the home front. Much of this chapter has been devoted to describing our 1993/94 sabbatical experiences in Lithuania and England. The reader will have noticed that all subsequent sections included the phrase "between sabbaticals." This is just one indication of how important sabbaticals were in my life. The next sabbatical will be described in the following chapter even though it really belongs to my final career stage. Placing this event in the following chapter where the focus is on my semi-retirement can be justified in part by the fact that my final sabbatical had all the characteristics of being semi-retired. Truth be told, part of my reason for doing so is to even out the length of these chapters.

NOTES

1. John E. Toews, Valerie Rempel and Katie Funk Wiebe, eds., *Your Daughters Shall Prophesy: Women in Ministry in the Church* (Kindred Press, 1992).

2. Other academic papers were given at the Philosophy of Education Society Meetings in San Francisco in 1995, the Learneds at Brock University in 1996, three "With Heart and Mind" conferences – Regina in 1995, Toronto in 1997, and Trinity Western University in 1999, and another Learneds in Ottawa in 1998.

3. Faculty retreats included the following: North American Baptist College in Edmonton in the winter of 1995, Canadian Bible College in Regina in the fall of 1995, Concordia University College held on Rudy Wiebe's retreat centre outside of Edmonton in 1996, and Providence College near Winnipeg in 1998.

4. Church invitations included the Lendrum M.B. Church in Edmonton in 1994 and the Bridgeway Church in Swift Current in 1995. Our experience at LCC also led to some invitations to give a report in our own church in 1994, and to speak at missions conferences in Swift Current in 1994 and Lethbridge in 1995.

5. I received phone call from the President of Providence in January of 1999 inviting me to apply for the position of Academic Vice-President at Providence – this was in fact a second inquiry from them. Other queries relating to academic or research positions were received from ICS in Toronto, Concord College, and Prairie Bible Institute.

6. In the end we had a cost overrun of about $200,000 with the total project costing about $650,000.

7. Other members of this book club were Keith Kowalsky and Elwin Kershaw, both dentists, Henk Hak, a doctor, and Jeff Scott, a mechanic. One of the first books we studied was Tolstoy's *The Resurrection*. This book club continued for a good number of years and provided a delightful opportunity for intellectual engagement.

Chapter 6
SEMI-RETIREMENT AND A FINAL WEDDING (2000-2007)

Although thoughts about retirement from Medicine Hat College (MHC) were never far from my mind, I applied for another half-year sabbatical for the 2000-2001 academic year. This time I was asked to appear before a committee of administration and faculty to defend my proposal for a sabbatical. I really didn't think I had a chance to get another sabbatical and so didn't take the interview too seriously. First they asked me why I wasn't applying for an entire year as I was eligible for a full-year's sabbatical. I replied that I wasn't good at arithmetic and so hadn't counted the years that had elapsed since my last sabbatical. I think my real reason for only applying for a half-year sabbatical was that I felt I would have a better chance at getting this. Then they asked me what my career goals were – they were obviously going through a standard set of prepared questions. What does one say about career goals when one is thinking of retirement in a few years. So, I rather flippantly replied that my career goal was getting ready to die! As we proceeded, I realized that they were taking my application quite seriously and that I might even get another full year's sabbatical, so I began to respond to questions more carefully. In the end, I was awarded my fourth and final sabbatical at MHC.

MY FINAL SABBATICAL (2000-2001):
UNIVERSITIES OF TORONTO AND VICTORIA

My proposal for this sabbatical involved work on a new research program on the ethics of proselytizing or evangelism, as well as preparation for a new course in bio-ethics for the Nursing Program at MHC. We considered going back to England for part of our sabbatical, but in the end we did not do so and decided instead to go to Toronto for the fall semester so we could be closer to our children and grandchildren. I managed to get an appointment as a Research Reader at the Centre for the Study of Religion at the University of Toronto. Then in January we moved to Victoria where I was granted a Visiting Research Fellowship with the Centre for Studies in Religion and Society, headed by Harold Coward, an old colleague and friend of mine.

We postponed our departure to Toronto because I had been asked to speak at the wedding of Nathan Kowalsky and Stephanie Toonstra in Edmonton and we also wanted to attend the wedding of Randy Thiessen and Lana Engel, to which Andrew and Rachel were coming. After these weddings were over, and after giving a brief tour of the house for our renter, Julia Morch, a new faculty member at MHC, we were finally able to depart in mid-September. We had decided to take our time, with two stop-overs at friends, Len and Martha Pauls in Regina, and Dan and Elsie Klassen in Thunder Bay.

We arrived in Toronto five days later on a Sunday afternoon, being welcomed, of course, by Audrey and Geoff and their girls who took us to our new home on 990 Woodbine Ave., only a short distance from their own house. Audrey had gotten the key for us earlier. It felt strange to walk into a house that we had never seen before, knowing that this would be our home for a few months – a repeat of our Oxford experience. It also felt odd to walk into a stranger's house – like a massive invasion of someone else's private domain. The two-story house was located near the busy intersection of Woodbine and Danforth, with a subway station just across from the house – a wonderful convenience, we discovered. After a short while, we got used to the place and I especially enjoyed my upstairs office and a T.V. room. However, there were also some later challenges with this location – lots of noise, a bank robbery next door, drug needles left in the alley, and a homeless person who sometimes spent the night on the lawn next to the bank.

I went to the university a few days later and got my library card from the Centre for the Study of Religion and my carrell assignment at the

Robarts library. I also picked up any information I could on concerts and special lectures. One occurred the following day, a lecture on a new statement on Jewish-Christian relations by a prominent Jewish scholar, David Novak. So the fourth day we were in Toronto, I was attending an excellent lecture that was relevant to my research – something I just happened to come upon. Thursday of the first week we attended the first of the Graduate Christian Fellowship (GCF) film series that Geoff was organizing. On Saturday we spent time swimming with our granddaughters and on Sunday we had Audrey and the girls down for lunch. The following Monday we attended a wonderful matinee concert at the Roy Thomson Hall, which included Dvorak's violin concerto. I was warmly welcomed at the Institute for Christian Studies (ICS) a few days later and had a very fruitful discussion with Jim Olthius on Emmanuel Levinas who he thought would be helpful in my research. I attended several lectures the second week, and couldn't quite get over the wealth of opportunities I would have at the university. The first two weeks were a good initiation into life in Toronto.

We had a wonderful time with our family. We thoroughly enjoyed our three grandchildren – Madeleine was now six and in Grade 1, Sylvie was now 3 ¾ (and the ¾ was very important), Ariane had just turned one and we enjoyed watching her learn to walk – this was the first time we were able to experience this with a grandchild. She was a delight and she knew it, especially with two doting grandparents around. Geoff was extra busy in the fall because he had accepted a job with Elections Canada, doing the computer work involved in preparing the voters list. Thus we gave Audrey some help with baby-sitting so she got some relief time during the rather busy fall. We also enjoyed several trips to St. Catharines where Andrew and Rachel had recently purchased a house. Andrew was youth pastor in Vineland at the time, and Rachel was continuing her work as a nurse at the Tabor Nursing Home in St. Catharines. Of course we visited them several times over the semester.

Maggie and I also thoroughly enjoyed the cultural life of Toronto. By the end of our stay, we had attended nineteen concerts, two operas, one play and three movies. It felt so good to have a choice as to what we wanted to do on a Friday night – often we had to choose between several excellent options. We also enjoyed several hikes with our children, a visit to Casa Loma, and a stroll through the St. Lawrence Market, crowded with yuppies buying "natural foods." We attended a number of churches, but finally settled on the Toronto United Mennonite Church (TUMC) which Audrey and Geoff attended and where we very much enjoyed the preaching and the music. Sadly, we also had to go down to Vineland for the funeral of a good friend of Maggie's, Annetta Toews. We also went to Kitchener a couple of times to visit Maggie's brother, George, who was in and out of the hospital being treated for cancer.

I accomplished a fair amount with regard to researching materials for my next book on the ethics of proselytizing. I focused mainly on gathering materials and reading though I did write the occasional article. In addition, I consulted with a number of scholars and attended a variety of special lectures at the University of Toronto. In November I had a series of speaking engagements – a lecture on "The Ethics of Proselytizing," at the university, a sermon at the Fairview M.B. church at St. Catharines, and a couple of chapel services and a philosophy lecture at Eden (Christian) High School. In December I checked the proofs and prepared indexes for my third book, the official title of which had been changed to *In Defence of Religious Schools and Colleges,* to be published by McGill-Queen's University Press.

We had a good Christmas with the entire family – Gregory joined us a few days before Christmas. We spent time at all three homes. While in St. Catharines, I did something very uncharacteristic of me – I changed our plans for getting to Victoria by car, at the urging of Maggie and the children. Via Rail had a two-for-one special for seniors, and so we decided to travel by train and ship the car separately by train which turned out not to be too expensive. There were further family celebrations in Toronto, a gift exchange, a good time of sharing with Gregory informing us of the results of his counselling sessions – they had come to agreement that he was suffering from an Obsessive Compulsive Disorder (OCD), together with depression often associated with OCD. He had prepared a handout for us, on the advice of his counsellor. He asked for patience as he tried to work through this problem. I preached in the Vineland M.B. Church on the final Sunday of December. Given our change of plans we had to vacate our house so the owners could again take occupancy, and so we stayed at Audrey and Geoff's for our final days.

We boarded our train on January 6, 2001 for our three-day trip across Canada. This was certainly better than spending eight hours a day in a car, driving. We were both busily reading the proofs of my book and this took up a good deal of our time (see picture in Chapter 10, p. 294). With the days being so short, it was dark much of the time and so there was little opportunity to enjoy scenery in any case. We especially enjoyed the meals in the dining car, visiting with different people nearly each meal. Our car had already arrived in Vancouver when we got there, so after a long taxi ride, we picked up the car and were on the way to the ferry and then on to Victoria. Craig McQuigan and Martha McCalister, owners of the house we were renting, were waiting for us, and were in fact ready to start on their expedition to Mexico and South America. After a one-hour visit with them, we were left on our own and we could once again move into what we would call our home for the next five months (2620 Dean Ave).

The next day, the Centre for Studies of Religion and Society at the University of Victoria had an orientation session for new fellows, so I had to shift gears rather quickly. I was still finishing up revisions on the index of my book, and so my mind was rather preoccupied, so much so, that I even forgot where I had parked the car after one afternoon session at the university. The police had to be called to help me find it. The proofs were sent off by FedEx by the end of the week, and then work began on organizing my very nice office at the University and also setting up my office in the basement of our home.

I soon felt at home at the Centre and enjoyed engaging in the many dialogues during our coffee-breaks, attendance at which was a requirement. The secretaries called us to coffee each morning by ringing a sheep-bell – a fine tradition. I had a large office with a big window overlooking the beautiful campus. There were tables on three sides of the room to spread out my research materials – the nicest office in my entire career. In talking with Harold Coward, the Director of the Centre, the first week, I suggested that I would find it very helpful if I could have some of the fellows review a preliminary table of contents for my book before I began serious writing. He immediately suggested that we arrange a meeting with the scholars at the Centre who gave me some good feedback, raising questions about the Christian orientation of the book, the ethical foundations from which I was evaluating proselytizing, one even suggesting that this was a very big project and would take years to finish. I had lunch with Harold later that week and we sorted out some of issues that I needed to resolve in writing my book. Again, I found the discussion very helpful and felt that all these suggestions saved me a lot of time by making me face some questions of orientation of the book early on in my writing. I was deeply appreciative of the kind of help that I was receiving – a true community of scholars. I even suggested to Harold that I felt that I had arrived in academic heaven.

Another requirement of each of the fellows was to give a public lecture at the university. Mine came at the end of the semester and I felt quite good about the response – about thirty in attendance, with none of the antagonism that I felt at the University of Toronto lecture in the previous year. Several members of the Saanich Community Church attended, and Adele Wickett wrote a piece on my lecture for a Christian newspaper that she edited. Dr. Don Lewis and his wife also surprised us by showing up for the lecture – I had forgotten that they had retired in Victoria. We went to their home later. Don had attended some of my evening classes many years ago when I began teaching at MHC.

I met with Harold again at the end of my stay, and expressed my surprise at how easy the writing seemed to be going – I had nearly completed two long chapters of my book. He suggested this was due to my growing maturity as a writer and also because I had a clear idea of where I was going. Indeed, I was becoming more convinced that I should be more modest in what I was trying to do in this book – limit myself to a consideration of objections to proselytizing, a defense of proselytizing, and then a development of some criteria to distinguish between moral and immoral proselytizing. Harold concurred and encouraged me to get on with the project. He alerted me to a dialogue on the ethics of proselytizing occurring on a Hindu-Christian listserve prompted by the Dalai-Lama's condemnation of proselytizing earlier in the year. He also suggested that I submit my manuscript to SUNY press, where he edited a series – this was very encouraging, because SUNY is one of the best publishers in the area of religious studies.

On the first Sunday in Victoria we attended the Saanich Community Church (MB) and were most unimpressed – a church without a pastor and in search of a new identity, using outside consultants to find themselves! So we spent the first month or so church-shopping, but didn't find any church that seemed suitable or even hospitable. In the end we decided to give Saanich another try – this time, Marvin Schmidt was speaking, He had been appointed interim part-time pastor. It was good to connect with Marvin again, and he and Eunice were very hospitable, both seeming to appreciate our friendship. We got together several times and even visited their home on Pender Island, just before they went on an extended holiday to Europe. Marvin did not wait long to ask me to preach – in fact, I preached a second sermon in May, "Coping with Chaos and Confusion." We also enjoyed getting to know Ben and Linda Stobbe. Ben had recently retired from his administrative position in the British Columbia Corrections Branch, was the moderator of the church, and seemed very much like me in orientation and approach to life and faith.

We again enjoyed the expanded cultural opportunities of the city – especially the Belfry theatre, the Victoria Symphony, and the La Fayette string quartet. All told, we attended twenty-five concerts (seven choral and twelve string), three plays, and one opera, plus six noon-hour student recitals for me. Again we were making up for the cultural dearth that we had to live with in Medicine Hat. We also enjoyed exploring the city, especially the beaches. At times I would cycle by the beach on Oak Bay near our home after a day at the university. Or we would go for a walk along the beach after supper. On weekends we would do more extended hikes or drives into the beautiful countryside. I especially enjoyed a day of kayaking around Salt Spring Island with one of my former students, Morley Myers.

We also had a lot of company. On Friday of the first week, during supper, we were surprised by a knock on the door, and our first visitors – nephew and niece, Merv and Judy Hempel, who had just moved to Victoria, together with Marie and Val. It was especially good to have Greg and Laura down about five times during our stay. Again, how providential that Greg had transferred to FedEx in Vancouver at the beginning of our stay in Victoria. This move was also prompted by the fact that his now official "girl-friend," Laura Earle, was studying in Vancouver. We had some good times together, a highlight being our visit to Port Renfrew where we had rented a cottage for the weekend. Nathan and Stephanie also joined us and we had a wonderful time exploring the Botanical Beach, as well as other beaches on the way to Port Renfrew. I also had a good dialogue with Nathan regarding his future. Rachel surprised us early in the semester by coming to Victoria for a weekend with Ariane. Then later in the semester Audrey and Geoff came on their own, as part of a 10th anniversary celebration which had been postponed. My brother Ted, and his wife Cathy, came down a couple of times. We also made a couple of trips to Vancouver and Abbotsford during this time – one time for a funeral of my Uncle Abe, which gave me an opportunity to see some Thiessen relatives whom I had not seen for a long time.

Our time in Victoria ended on a rather sad note. The week before we left we got word that Marvin Schmidt had had a fatal heart attack while on a holiday in Europe. The church was in shock at the loss of their pastor. We were glad that we could attend the church that final Sunday when they had a brief memorial for Marvin as part of the morning worship service. Again, a powerful reminder of the brevity of life. On our final evening in Victoria, we were invited to the home of some new friends in the church and had such a good visit that we had a hard time leaving, even though we needed to get ready for our move the next day. All this made it more difficult to leave Victoria – we had come to love the people and made a few good friends who were encouraging us to retire in Victoria.

We took our time going home, spending a couple of nights in Abbotsford visiting Ted and Cathy, then a couple of nights at Vern and Marj Borne in Kelowna where we met with two sets of cousins, and then two more days to travel home to Medicine Hat. Coming back after such a wonderful sabbatical was difficult. I actually lay awake one of the first nights, getting panicky about settling into routine in this prison-like atmosphere. Two more years here – but that should be bearable, surely! This sabbatical had convinced us that we could adjust to new cities and that we needed to move to a bigger city for retirement. Of course a move would be unsettling but God would be with us. Upon our return to Medicine Hat we started reading *Daily Light,* for our morning devotions and the first few readings were especially meaningful. "Forgetting what is behind, I press on toward the goal to win the prize for which God has called me heavenward in Christ Jesus." "The Lord himself goes before you and will be with you; he will never leave you nor forsake you." "I am always with you; you hold me by my right hand. You guide me with your counsel, and afterward you will take me into glory."

RETIREMENTS (1999, 2003, 2007)

Why the plural in the heading? Because my retirement was complicated. Even as I am writing this autobiography I still prefer to talk about myself as semi-retired because I am still doing some teaching and writing. So I like to see my retirement as taking place in stages. The first date represents a near-retirement. In the spring of 1996, the administration at MHC offered a special early retirement package to a number of senior faculty members – nearly a full year's salary upon retirement three years down the road. I agonized over the decision to take early retirement in the intervening three years and was exploring various options to get support for a five-year teaching stint at Lithuania Christian College (LCC) as part of our retirement plans. But in the end I decided against retiring at this time – it was simply inadvisable financially. I couldn't quite understand what I was experiencing at the time – the mixed messages I seemed to be getting, the disquieting feelings, even panic, at times. But it all fell into place in the fall of 1999, when much to my surprise, I was offered a full-year's sabbatical which I have already described in the introduction to this chapter.

I was contractually required to continue teaching for two more years after my sabbatical, but interestingly, I was again exploring the possibility of taking a "later" early retirement package in 2002. Why? I was increasingly feeling trapped at MHC. I was not enjoying teaching as much as I used to. For someone who has always taken pride in teaching and doing it well, it was difficult to admit that the long-standing thrill of teaching was no longer there. There were a number of factors behind this gradual erosion of my interest and excitement in teaching. Medicine Hat College was undergoing a major shift in identity in the 1990s, becoming more and more a technical/vocational school, with the humanities and social sciences department increasingly becoming a service department, providing courses for various programs. For example, in my final year, I taught informal logic to a class of police and security students, an ethics course for massage therapists, and a biomedical ethics course for nursing students. And these students were often not that interested in humanities courses, seeing them as peripheral to their programs. In addition, many of these students were not high academic achievers – the entrance requirements for some of these programs was lower than for the university transfer program, and besides, the college had an open door policy with regard to admissions. It also seemed to me that students were increasingly less serious about their studies. Most of them had jobs and so studying was something they did only if they had some extra time.

More broadly, I came to realize that I was not proud of the place where I worked. Another reason for my early retirement was burnout. In a typical semester, I was teaching five courses, which involved four different course preparations. Given my commitment to having students do a lot of writing in my classes, I was repeatedly marking over 100 papers and other assignments throughout the semester. I was working ten to twelve hours per day and was feeling more and more like a teaching machine. And I had very little time for research and writing which I needed to do for my own sanity. I was also hoping to do some overseas teaching at the end of my career and so I needed to make room for these dreams. There was a final non-academic reason for retiring. We had, for quite a few years, been very unhappy in our church. We needed to move from Medicine Hat so that we could get into a healthier church environment.

All this should explain why I felt so much at peace about submitting a letter of application for early retirement on December 16, 2002. I had been negotiating with my Dean, Len Vandervaart, beforehand regarding the possibility of continuing to teach part-time at MHC after my retirement until I turned sixty-five. This was eventually agreed on, in addition to the 40% retiring allowance as specified in the contract. So my full-time status at MHC ended in the summer of 2003 when I was sixty-one years old and after I had been at the College for thirty-two years. I felt as though I had been released from a prison. Despite the fact that I would be returning to part-time teaching at the same institution, I nonetheless felt free. I was no longer bound to the hectic schedule that made me feel like a teaching robot. I was no longer bound to MHC, or to Medicine Hat. We were free to leave at any time. It was indeed time to retire.

But there was still one more stage of retirement ahead. The understanding with the administration was that the arrangement of part-time teaching at Medicine Hat College interspersed with occasional overseas teaching stints would continue for four more years and that all ties with MHC would come to an end when I turned sixty-five. So the year 2007 marks the end of living in Medicine Hat for thirty-six years and also the beginning of another stage of semi-retirement which will be described in the following chapter.

Saying good-bye to a thirty-six year teaching career at MHC was difficult. At my earlier "official" retirement in 2003, there were constant reminders of an ending – letters giving instructions for exit, the last lecture, the grading of the last final examination, a college retirement banquet, and a departmental dinner to honor the retirees. Then a few years later when I "really" retired in 2007, I had the unusual experience of seeing my position being advertised in the newspaper. And colleagues were clamoring for my office long before there was any indication that I would vacate it. Ah yes, but eventually I did have to give up my office to which I had returned, day after day, for thirty-six years (less sabbaticals and occasional leaves). And now I would be a person with no fixed professional address and with no more professional development perks. Indeed, at first I seemed to be in a state of denial with regard to my retirement. I didn't want to admit that I had come to that point in my life. This would require a change of identity. It would require faith in myself and faith in God. Indeed, the morning of the day that I began an earlier draft of these reflections, we read some words of reassurance from our devotional book, *Daily Light*. "Even to your old age, I shall be the same; and even to your graying years I shall bear you. . . . Jesus Christ is the same yesterday and today, yes and forever" (Isa 46:4; Heb 13:8).

PRE- AND POST-RETIREMENT TEACHING AT MEDICINE HAT COLLEGE

I have been getting ahead of myself so it is necessary to back-track a little. After my sabbatical in 2000-2001, I had to face a few more years of teaching full-time at MHC. The winter semester of 2002 proved to be a challenge in a number of ways. I faced a large increase in the number of students I was teaching, totaling about 100. I had also chosen new texts or new editions of texts in all my courses which entailed more work in preparing lectures. Then there was a new course in biomedical ethics for the nursing program. Given that this was a new course, I felt a bit insecure and this probably led to my being a bit too advanced in my lectures and giving too many C's on student papers, which in turn led to a group of students complaining to Deans Joyce Engel and Len Vandervaart who seriously mishandled the complaints. Fortunately, students came around to better attitudes – I even had some students who loved the course, and the final student evaluation of the course was quite positive.

That same winter I also had an accident walking home from the college – I slipped on a piece of ice and broke my ankle, both the tibia and fibia, the latter with multiple breaks. This of course required surgery but I only missed three days of lectures. I video-taped my classes for a week and a half and then was back at the college lecturing from a wheel-chair – a humbling but insightful experience. That same winter I also experienced increasing problems with my mental health, a recurrence of problems I had begun to experience earlier, what with the stresses of teaching and planning for retirement in the past few years. I will have more to say about this health problem later in this chapter.

In the fall semester of 2002, I was pleasantly surprised to have some excellent classes particularly my two sections in introductory philosophy – good discussions and some bright students who had a lively interest in philosophy. Ray came to see me every three to four weeks, to discuss ideas he was scribbling into his notebook. He was literally writing a book. He was taking a few electives at the college in order to finish his degree in bio-chemistry from the University of Calgary. We had some wonderful discussions and he was getting increasingly nervous about his materialistic, deterministic position, given my defenses of the spiritual dimension in life.

I had one new class, a logic class for the police and security program. After all the terrible things I had heard from my colleagues about these students, I was not at all looking forward to teaching this class and so I started by being as harsh and threatening as I could possibly be. This seemed to work, as they seemed to be quite orderly and serious. There were a few weak students and I had some problems with attitudes in one corner of the room, but one angry outburst on my part put them in place. In the end I really didn't mind teaching the class. Unfortunately, my ethics course for massage therapists in the following semester was very weak, but it was the last time I would be teaching this course and so it was bearable.

In the meantime I was applying for some sessional positions for my post-retirement – one at the University of Victoria, and a couple in New Brunswick. A position also came up at the McMaster Divinity School. I had initiated a brief correspondence with Alven Nieman from the University of Notre Dame regarding a review of my book that he had written, and he encouraged me to apply for a fellowship at the Centre for the Study of Religion at Notre Dame. Perry Glanzer had also encouraged me to apply for an annual visiting fellows program at Baylor University. Eventually I got word that I was not successful in either of these applications. My job applications also were negative (except for a late offer from the University of New Brunswick, St. John's Campus, which I turned down). So, in the end, I had to adjust to the idea of staying at Medicine Hat College after my official retirement, teaching two courses each semester, and working on my next book. This is why I had been so insistent in my negotiations with the college. I needed this as a fall-back position. And basically, I was content with this. Only, I kept reminding Maggie that we definitely had to do something different the following year. Maggie was just as happy about staying in Medicine Hat for a few more years, as she was enjoying teaching at Saamis Immigration.

My official retirement date was the end of June, 2003. The department had a farewell for me at which time I gave a review of my years at MHC. The Faculty Association also honored retirees at their annual fall banquet in October of 2003 at which time I gave another lengthy speech reviewing the high and the low points of my career at MHC. They had consulted with me about a retirement gift and I suggested a sculpture from one of my former students, Morley Myers, who now had a studio in Salt Spring Island. He appropriately chose a recent sculpture he had made, "Inspiration" or spirit, a figure floating in tranquility with the face of God sweeping past. I am sure the sculpture was worth much more than the Faculty Association paid for it, so it was as much a gift from Morley himself, and one that I have cherished through the years.

The summer of our retirement we took a one-week holiday to the mountains, retracing some of the stops that we made on our bicycle tour from Jasper to Banff many years ago when our children were teenagers. We also spent some time in Edmonton where I attended a bio-ethics conference and where we also did some exploration of the city and housing, with a view to making this our retirement home. Then in October we returned to Banff to attend a seniors retreat put on by our church conference. Yes, now that we were retired, we were beginning to stop pretending that we were not getting older. It was a wonderful retreat where we met many old friends and made some new ones.

In the fall after my retirement I was quite enjoying the reduced teaching load of two courses per semester. Indeed, in our Christmas letter of 2003 I noted that the joy of teaching had returned. The following year I made note of the fact that the morale in the department was terrible, but interestingly, my colleagues often commented about my always having a smile on my face. I guess semi-retirement was good for me.

BELGIUM (WINTER, 2005)

In March of 2004 I had a long and delightful conversation with Dr. Heinrich Loewen, the upcoming president of the Evangelische Theologische Faculteit (ETF), in Leuven, Belgium. He had heard about me from some Mennonite Brethren leaders in B.C., and was interested in having me come to his school in Belgium to teach, perhaps on a long-term basis after our full retirement from MHC. After some further conversations it was mutually agreed that I come for a one-semester exploratory visit and so our plans for the winter semester of 2005 included an overseas teaching stint. Sadly, Heinrich's vision for ETF and for our involvement in the school was unrealistic and his term as President only lasted a couple of years.

But we still had a delightful semester at ETF, though our apartment in the musty building was rather small. Fortunately I could retreat to a spacious office in another part of the building and another couple gave us access to their large apartment for a couple of weeks while they returned to the U.S. for some deputation work. My central assignment was teaching a graduate course, "Worldviews and the Christian Mind." It was a challenge to adjust to a graduate course, a European style of education (only two separate weeks of classes, two hours each day), and a small class of seven students (three from the Ukraine, three from the Netherlands, and one American/German). Several of the students commented on the fact that it was refreshing to take a course that wasn't a theology course – this despite the fact that I did a lot of theology in the course. But I think they enjoyed thinking through the practical implications of the Christian faith with final essays covering some interesting topics – art, rock music, economics, artificial intelligence, South American machismo, and genetic engineering. But I had a difficult time convincing them that work can be a form of worship.

One of my functions was to help the school make connections with the broader academic community so they were happy to support my giving a paper at a conference in the University of Nijmegen in the Netherlands. Later I was invited by Siebren Miedema to give a paper at the Free University of Amsterdam. I also audited a course taught by Gie Vluegels at ETF on early church history, "The Apostles and the Creed." Gie was doing some fascinating research refuting claims that there was not one version of orthodox Christianity in the post-apostolic church and that an official orthodox version only emerged with Constantine.

We also took Flemish lessons twice a week. The state offered these courses for all newcomers and it was free, so why not! This was part of the Flemish attempt to retain their identity – a bit like Quebec trying to retain the French language in their province. Maggie spent some time each week helping Marjorie Weber in the library and also did some essay-editing for students whose first language was not English. Maggie also baby-sat for Nathan and Stephanie Kowalsky once a week. Nathan was doing his Ph.D. at the Catholic University of Leuven, while Stephanie was working. He needed time to work on his dissertation and so they asked Maggie to help take care of their little Anya. We visited various churches, but finally settled on the International Church of Evangelicals in Leuven, where I even preached a sermon on Palm Sunday.

We enjoyed living in the beautiful city of Leuven, home to the Catholic University of Leuven, founded in 1425, having about 30,000 students, including over 3,500 foreign students. Seeing downtown Leuven late in the evening was quite an experience, especially on a weekend – hundreds of students on the streets, some quite inebriated. Visiting the magnificent Gothic structures of Leuven, brightly lit up in the dark night was quite awe-inspiring. We enjoyed many good concerts and lectures. Mid-way through the semester our social life picked up considerably with the arrival of Bjorn and Reidun Fjeld from Norway. Bjorn was President of the Ansgar Bible College/Seminary in Norway and was on a three-month sabbatical. They had a car and so were able to take us along on various trips exploring Belgium, including visits to Ghent (a city with a fortress where many

Mennonites were tortured and killed) and Ottignies Lovain - la - Neuve, (which was built up from scratch in the 1970s to provide a location for the French portion of the Catholic University in Leuven, and which has no cars in the heart of the city). Our friendship with the Fjelds has continued through the years and we have exchanged visits in each others homes.

Greg and Laura also joined us for a week towards the end of our semester. After we had sent them to Paris for a few days on their own, we made a trip to Switzerland in a rented Mercedes, no less, (of course, a compact model as befits humble Mennonites), and we again fell in love with the country. Highlights included a hike and supper in a quaint village high up in the Alps and on our return, a stop at a Lambourgini museum which Greg quite enjoyed.

On one of the last Sundays in Belgium, Nathan and Stephanie persuaded us to come to Mechelen for a parade, an elaborate affair with segments telling the story of the city of Mechelen, then the Christian story, and then a special story about an icon of Mary that was floated down the river each year, when at one point, it stopped at Mechelen – hence a yearly parade to celebrate Mary. It was a 1 ½ hour procession with 2,000 participants, 100 horses, 20 floats, 160 musicians, choirs and dancing groups. We were very impressed. The Catholics do some things right – what a way to evangelize and teach children.

LITHUANIA (WINTER, 2006)

We returned to Lithuania Christian College (LCC) in the winter of 2006, in part to explore this as a possibility for a five-year teaching commitment after my forthcoming "real" retirement. So much had changed from when we were in Lithuania in 1993. When we arrived in Klaipeda this time around we stopped at a grocery store before we went to our apartment and we simply couldn't believe the contrast with our shopping experiences 12 ½ years earlier. We entered a fully modern, brightly lit grocery store, iKi, with automated cash registers using bar-codes for tallying our bills. I rather facetiously mentioned that it would be good to have some barbequed chicken for supper, given two days of irregular meals on planes and in airports. Our host said, no problem, and brought us to a counter with hot barbequed chicken – amazing! A short drive later and we were grateful to finally get to our own apartment.

The next day revealed that we were living in a Soviet cluster of eight apartment blocks, grey and dingy, with balconies that looked like they might crumble at any time. But our "orange apartment" was up-to-date and fully furnished with heated towel racks and a real shower with hot water each day. The next week we were taken to the newest mall, the "Acropolis" which announced its presence with a glaring ten foot neon sign. Inside was the Maxima store, something like a giant Superstore with groceries and many other goods. This seemed to be the only useful store in the mall, as the other stores had luxury items – we counted seventeen shoe stores. There were luxury vehicles displayed in the corridors of the mall which also included a skating rink and many restaurants. Yes, things had changed.

The new LCC campus was about a fifteen-minute walk from our apartment, fully modern, with beautiful classrooms and computer labs. Of course, the college was much bigger – about 550 students with forty faculty. I soon ran into three of my former students who were now on faculty or staff at LCC. The feel of the college was very different – an established institution, more professional, a new President, Jim Mininger, and a new Academic Vice-president, Marlene Wall. The college had in the meantime been actively recruiting students from various countries in Eastern Europe and central Asia. So the names took some getting used to – Altynai Kudaibergenova (a girl from Kyrgyzstan), Kseniea Tjapkina (a Latvian girl), Taras Mikhailiuk (a boy from Belarus) and Simona Stopinaite (a girl from Lithuania), Lyubov Mattykhina (a girl from the Ukraine), Olesia Gurina (girl from Russia), and Dorarta Hyseni (a girl from Albania). I tried to learn at least the first names of my students.

I was scheduled to teach three classes – introductory philosophy, introductory logic to mostly third and fourth year business students, and a philosophy of a religion class. Maggie had a heavy teaching load, with morning classes at Limarco, a shipping company, twice a week, and then ESL classes four evenings per week. So we were very busy. Sadly the students were very different from what we experienced in 1993. Yes, there were still some very fine students who were conscientious and eager to learn, but there were others who now displayed many of the same attitudes of so many North American students who are spoiled and take their wealth for granted. We had to remind ourselves that the current LCC students had not lived through the deprivation and suffering of the Soviet occupation. They took freedom and their much higher standard of living for granted. Many of them were well-off and there were quite a few cars in the college parking lot – some even quite expensive. There were, of course, exceptions – many of the students who came from Eastern bloc countries were poor and were able to attend LCC only because they were on scholarships and these students tended to be very keen to learn.

The one thing that hadn't changed from our previous time at LCC was the privilege of having delightful conversations with students. For example, Victoria, a Lithuanian, but of Russian background, took me by surprise one day when she appeared in my office. She was rather quiet in class, but when she came to see me, she was very talkative and came prepared with a list of philosophical questions that she wanted to discuss. After a discussion in which she revealed some very good insights, she asked me what I thought about students who didn't ask questions in class. Did I think they were stupid? I assured her that I didn't think that at all, and that there were many reasons why some students didn't feel free to discuss in class. She also shared a problem she was encountering at home when she tried to discuss philosophy with her parents. They were not very keen on philosophical discussions at the dinner table. So, I had to do some family counseling as well! One can never tell what will come up in discussions with students!

One of my students, Taras, from Belarus, was in my office two to three times per week, wanting to discuss philosophy and questions of faith. He had become a Christian as a young adult and had worked for Campus Crusade for quite a few years in Minsk. He was rather conservative theologically, and early in the semester he told me that I was "beating the arrogance out of him," given my emphasis on the fallibility of human knowledge. After a semester of thinking through various problems in philosophy he was realizing that maybe some issues weren't quite as black and white as he had originally assumed. Later in the semester he described the overall effect of my course as making him more unsettled in his Christian convictions and this worried him. We had a good discussion of the relationship between objective theoretical uncertainty and practical passionate Christian commitment. At the end of the semester he came to my office once again to ask a favor – could I write a letter of recommendation for him. He wanted to leave LCC and was applying to Union University, a Baptist University in Tennessee, where his girl-friend was studying. I was a bit worried about how the department chair would take this news as Taras was one of the very few theology students at LCC.

One Friday afternoon I met with two of my students, Ruta from Lithuania, and Dorarta from Albania, both of whom had attended my special lecture at the faculty forum several weeks earlier. They wanted to discuss what I said about "Teaching for Committed Openness." I was looking forward to this conversation because they were good students with positive attitudes. Well, they peppered me with questions. How does one decide what to commit oneself to? Dori expressed fear about exploring options for commitment. What if she became a Buddhist and got it wrong? Is there such a thing as truth in the area of religion? How does one choose a career? It was wonderful to hear the two of them exchange ideas. They were obviously close friends and so felt free to criticize one another. So Ruta told Dori that she was too concerned about success and also too materialistic. Dori admitted that she was too idealistic – I was certainly qualified to speak to that issue! It was a wonderful, relaxing conversation. I wished I had more time for this sort of thing. But teaching three different courses kept me very busy.

We did have some times of relaxation, though weather made it very difficult to go on outdoor excursions. It was very cold for most of the semester and even our walks to the college were trying. We attended some concerts and often went to restaurants with some of the faculty. During the spring break we did get to Kretinga, a smaller town near Klaipeda and visited a botanical garden there. We made a couple of visits  to the spit, which involved taking a short ferry ride to a long strip of land just off the mainland. This spit makes Klaipeda such an ideal harbor for ships. There is a Maritime museum on the spit as well as a little resort town named Nida where we climbed some sand dunes and then enjoyed a good long meal in a warm restaurant – our usual response to cold weather.

We took a couple of tours towards the end of our stay. The President's wife wanted to go to a nearby town of Plunge, to pick up a carved angel that she had ordered, and she offered to take some of the faculty along. We also visited a linen factory there. On a beautiful spring day, we took a bus to Palanga in the morning (½ hour ride), had a leisurely stroll to the Amber Museum, walked along the beach, had a leisurely lunch at a fish restaurant, walked for a bit, had our dessert of waffles dipped in chocolate, and then came home. If we had been able to do this sort of thing during the spring break, this semester would have been a lot more tolerable

Overall, our experience at LCC this time around was not a very positive one and this was not only because of the bad weather. The college had changed. It was much bigger and more impersonal with the business program much more dominant than in 1993. The students had changed, with quite a few taking on North American attitudes towards their studies. While before the administration and staff were mostly Canadian, the atmosphere was now decidedly American with quite a divide between older and younger faculty. Although we had a nice apartment, we felt more isolated than in 1993 when we all lived on the same dormitory floor.

Although I had some good classes, particularly my logic class, my philosophy of religion class was one of the worst classes that I have taught in my entire career. The class was small and most of the students were in the class because other elective classes had been full when they registered and so I faced bad attitudes from the start. They weren't handing in their assignments on time and I had some discipline problems. I am sure I could have done a better job of handling the problems I was facing, but I simply was not up to this challenge at the time. In the end both the students and I were happy when this terrible class was finally over. I resolved never to put myself into a position where I had to teach a class like this again. I was after all retired and had no need to teach students who don't want to learn. It was this class that I blame for the recurrence of some health issues towards the end of our stay in Lithuania. I was experiencing increasing digestive problems and also the occasional panic attack. This was the beginning of a more serious three-year bout of anxiety and depression.

During the final week, the President and Dean, both arranged for official exit interviews. But these turned out to be rather perfunctory. We answered their questions and left it at that. After all, with only four months here, we really didn't have a right to be too critical. I had already intimated that we would not be returning to LCC in the future, so this may have set the tone for these formalities. I realized that I didn't want to devote five years of my retirement, teaching at a college that was in the main a business school trying to export capitalism to Baltic and East European countries.

On the final Sunday, there was a class reunion of the 1996 graduation class. These were the students that I had taught in the fall of 1993, so it was a real privilege for us to join them. Several of them reflected on my teaching 12 ½ years earlier. Beata said she would be a different person if she hadn't taken my courses. Several commented on my frequent demand to summarize things in one sentence. Several also mentioned the cookies and muffins that Maggie brought to the dorm on several occasions. We recalled that they ate voraciously as though they were still hungry. Asta and Rasa both mentioned the problems they had faced in their careers, trying to live according to the values taught at LCC. All these were good memories, and sadly our stay at LCC in 2006 would not provide us with as many pleasant memories.

On our final day we were driven to Vilnius where I had reserved a B&B in the heart of the city, on a quaint narrow street, run by a charming old couple. We spent two wonderful days in Vilnius, hiking, eating, visiting the old castle at Trakai, and the weather was perfect. We then left for Norway where we had arranged to spend some time with Bjorn and Reidun Fjeld whom we had met the previous year in Belgium. We spent one night in Oslo, enjoying an evening walking along the grand street to the kings palace. We then had a wonderful train ride to Bergen, where we took a boat ride up a fjord, and enjoyed eating in outdoor restaurants because the weather stayed perfect the whole time. We then took a bus to Kristiansand, to visit Bjorn and Reidun. In my letter to them later I wrote this: "We will cherish all the memories that we have of our time together – the good conversations, the exploration of Kristiansand, the evening meal of shrimp, the walk around your fjord, the excursion to Lillisand, the surprise birthday party, meeting your lovely family, and the care you gave for our every need. Thanks for your love and listening ear. It was an encouragement to us. We trust you were able to catch up with your work after we left. We also hope that we will be able to entertain you sometime in Canada."

MORE GRANDCHILDREN (2001-2006)

I now want to back track again and review some of the other events of our lives in this semi-retirement stage of my life. First, the completion of our roster of grandchildren. We had enjoyed our three grandchildren during our sabbatical in Toronto in 2000. But more were on the way. In 2002 we were looking forward to two more grandchildren. Andrew and Rachel were expecting their first child on Christmas day. Audrey and Geoff were expecting their fourth child a month later. So we found an excuse to go to Ontario in November – to see our two pregnant girls.

Christmas excitement began earlier than usual in 2002 with the arrival of Andrew and Rachel's baby on December 16, 2002. Josiah Andrew arrived a week early. Andrew was very excited and Rachel was delighted that they were now going to be able to attend a Goossen gathering at Camp Crossroads. As was the custom with each grandchild, I wrote a prayer for Josiah on the day of his birth.

Beatrice Lilith Wichert was born on January 31 of 2003, to Geoff and Audrey, a fourth daughter and our fifth grandchild. Of course, this required the writing of another prayer. The year 2003 was very preoccupied with seeing grandchildren. We made four trips to Ontario that year. Having two grandchildren arrive at nearly the same time motivated us to do a bit more travelling. We even squeezed in a visit between two of my exams just before Christmas.

The following year we welcomed the birth of our sixth and final grandchild – Lauren Rachel, born to Andrew and Rachel Thiessen on November 10, 2004. Modern technology allowed us to get a picture of Lauren on the day of her birth. So Grandpa had to write out another prayer and send the parents another baby-bonus. We promised each of our children a baby bonus of $500 as a way of encouraging them to have babies.

ANOTHER FAMILY WEDDING (2004)

Another excitement for us in 2004 was the marriage of our third child. It was a long wait. Mother and father had already been "courting" Greg's girlfriend, Laura Earle, for a long time. There were also long parental conversations with Greg about marriage. We had some good holidays with both Greg and Laura while they were living in Vancouver and we were on sabbatical in Victoria in 2001. But our patience was being taxed and father was nearly ready to propose on his son's behalf. Finally on March 15,

2004 we received a phone call from Greg, informing us that he and Laura were engaged and were planning for a wedding in July. We were elated. Finally our third child was getting married and to a wonderful young woman. So the spring was very busy planning for this wedding and, of course, plans for family visits were now focused on getting together for the wedding.

Greg and Laura cut their ties to Vancouver in June and visited us early in July and then left for Cremona to get ready for the wedding. Andrew and Rachel arrived in Calgary a few days before the wedding and stayed at the home of Ed and Dorothy Reimer. They also made some visits to Cremona to help with wedding preparations. Audrey and Geoff and family arrived on Friday before the wedding. We picked them up with two vehicles (borrowing Ralph Erb's van once again) and went on to a camp-ground near Cremona where I had reserved some cabins which were more primitive than we had expected. But with the grandchildren this was probably still the best arrangement for accommodation in the immediate area. Marie, and Susan and Henry joined us later in the campground. The wedding rehearsal on Saturday was held on the farm and we provided the rehearsal dinner complete with sausage from Ralph's famous Premium Sausage outlet in Seven Persons.

The wedding, held on July 11, 2004, went quite well except for the weather – there was a brief let-up in the rain during which time we rushed through the ceremony. Andrew officiated and I felt honored to be asked to give a brief homily. So it was a father-son team marrying off a son and a brother – quite special. Greg and Laura's vows were a creative mix of original and traditional – very meaningful. Laura was, of course stunningly beautiful and the two of them made for a very handsome couple. The reception was notable for the involvement of a very supportive group of their friends.

Greg and Laura spent the first night at a near-by cabin, and returned to the farm the next day to open gifts. They stayed around the area for the next day or so while the rest of the family went on to Kananaskis. Greg and Laura, much to the astonishment of their friends, joined us for one and a half days of camping and hiking in Kananaskis. They then went to B.C. for the rest of their honeymoon. On their return they were most anxious to get to their recently rented house in Lethbridge. Laura's parents moved their belongings from the farm to Lethbridge and we joined them in order to help with moving and house preparations.

CHURCH (2001-2006)

Sabbaticals provided convenient escapes from the problems we were facing at the Crestwood M.B. Church in Medicine Hat. As might be expected, returning to a less than ideal church situation after our rather exciting 2000-2001 sabbatical in Toronto and Victoria was not easy. I was no longer in leadership, found myself marginalized. and was not being invited to teach or preach. Thankfully other opportunities for church-related ministries arose. A highlight for me was a year of pulpit-supply in the Seven Persons Community Church in 2001-2002, together with Jake Penner. I was approached about serving as the Moderator of the Alberta M.B. Conference, but I wisely agreed to only serve as Assistant Moderator provided that they find a Moderator, which in fact they were unable to do. Then in 2002 I was asked to make a presentation at the M.B. National Youth Convention in Calgary and ended up with fifty young people crowded into a room to hear my lecture, "Philosopher's Stone: A Christian Philosopher's Journey." At the local level I joined one of our Christian doctors, Henk Haak, in starting an evangelistic bible study in 2003, attended by fellow doctors, professionals, and students.

Perhaps it was somewhat symbolic; on the day that I got my final cheque as a full-time employee at MHC, I received an invitation from Lexington Christian Academy to serve at a faculty forum in April of 2004. The invitation from this rather elite private school near Boston came with an offer of an honorarium of $1,000, the biggest that I have ever received. What was most encouraging was the note in the letter of invitation explaining why I was being invited – the academic director was an avid reader of my books. Another highlight in the spring of 2003 was the paper that I gave at a conference in Saskatoon focusing on "The Future of Catholic Higher Education in Canada." The chair of the conference was very pleased with my paper and informed me that some of the bishops present were ready to induct me into the Catholic church. I discovered that Canadian Catholics were resisting the pope's "*Ex Corde Ecclesia.*" The chair of the International Catholic Universities Association was also there and complimented me on my paper, and invited me to visit him in Paris sometime. Gladly!

Closer to home, I was asked to speak at the wedding of Dan Barbour and Renae Kowalsky in 2003. Then in the fall of 2006 I gave three series of lectures/studies on a Christian worldview – a college and career group in our church, a home fellowship group in Seven Persons at the home of Ralph and Elaine Erb, and another series at MHC initiated by Adam Brown.

Meanwhile, given escalating problems in the Crestwood church, people not willing to take on board positions, tensions regarding worship, and people leaving the church, I was facing increasing pressure to return to leadership. The tensions in the church included a generational divide and I couldn't help but note that the requests for me to return to leadership came from both the young and the old. A series of meetings was scheduled in 2003 which included the current board and lay-ministers as well as past leaders like Dave Rempel, Ernie Nickel, and myself. We made some good progress in identifying the problems in the church, but unfortunately, these were glossed over at a congregational meeting at which Dave Rempel and I both agreed to return to the lay-ministry. I had requested an opportunity to give a little speech before the vote, and here I explained why I had finally agreed to return to leadership and why it was important to name the problems we were facing. But all this was rather awkward given that the leadership had refused to give a clear summary of the problems that had been identified in the series of meetings we had with the extended leadership.

Subsequent attempts to address these problems were met with strong opposition on the part of a few in the church. People were making personal attacks against me by phone, behind my back, and at meetings. There were repeated attempts at reconciliation between myself and some leaders in the church who opposed me but these were invariably incomplete and didn't lead to subsequent changes in behavior on the part of those advocating for change and new directions in the church. My yearly journal records that 2004 was "the most difficult year of my life in the church," and indeed seemed at times "like a taste of hell." In the end, I felt I had no choice but to resign from leadership once again. I simply couldn't help the church. Even my preaching and teaching and writing were constantly being challenged by a few leaders in the church.

My hurts were deep and no doubt contributed significantly to my experience of a season of anxiety and depression. How did I survive all this? I received some wise counsel from Christian brothers outside the church. And of course, Maggie was always by my side. I found nourishment in the Scriptures, particularly the Psalms where David is repeatedly wrestling with the problem of enemies who are maligning him and where even his friends abandoned him (Pss 7 & 17). In the end David rests his case with a righteous God who tests minds and hearts and will ultimately judge his enemies and so I was reassured that I could leave the vindication of my cause to God (Ps 7:9-11). But this God is also a refuge, a shield, a rock, and a fortress (Pss 7:1,10; 18:1-2). These were some of the reflections I recorded on my day of prayer and fasting on June 22, 2005.

What is further significant is that I was meditating on 2 Corinthians 11-12 on three of my yearly days of prayer and fasting during this difficult time period. Here Paul is very upfront about rumors, gossip, and false charges that he has faced, but he goes on to say that he has learned to accept all this because it keeps him cut down to size, weak, and dependent on God. In the end he rests his case on the fact that he loves Jesus Christ and has tried his best to love the church. Again I found this so applicable to my own situation. I also received this wise advice from Jake Doerksen, a seasoned Alberta pastor and friend who during a visit in our home shared the "Doerksen law" that he had formulated over time: The more insecure people are, the more pious they will sound, and the more they will use piety to manipulate others.

After our return from our second teaching stint at Lithuania Christian College, I made some attempts to heal relationships, but these efforts proved rather futile. It was time to leave Crestwood, and fortunately we were planning a move away from Medicine Hat after my retirement and so we simply tried to make the best of a bad situation. My yearly diary in 2006 includes a careful analysis of mistakes I and others made in trying to resolve the crisis at Crestwood. But such an analysis is probably a reflection of my being too introspective, too prone to analyzing situations, and too sensitive to criticisms. My analysis included one item of self-affirmation: "Following Jesus' example by not retaliating, by putting myself into a position of powerlessness as a leader, was the right thing to do. And I think by this I averted what could have become a major church split. So here is a positive thing I did."

It has taken years to put this difficult chapter of my life behind me. In preparing to write this section, I reviewed my extensive journal accounts of these difficult years and some of the pain returned. But doing so helped me to see that my heart was generally in the right place even though I made some mistakes. I was just dealing with a no-win situation, and I was unable to bring the church back to health. I have to admit all this and then focus on that which is ahead. God has graciously helped me to do so. It is no coincidence that the day that I was writing this section, I was reading Isaiah 49 where you have the first hints of a description of a somewhat enigmatic servant of the Lord who says this: "I have labored in vain, I have spent my strength for nothing and vanity; yet surely my cause is with the Lord and my reward with my God" (Isa 49:4). I tried hard to be God's servant in the Crestwood Church and so I will rest my case in "my God who has become my strength" (Isa 49:5). I also must be careful not to forget the many earlier years of successful service and leadership that I gave to the Crestwood Church.

FINAL YEAR IN MEDICINE HAT AND MOVE TO WATERLOO (2006-7)

Deciding where to move after retirement was not easy. Edmonton, Calgary, and Vancouver Island were all possibilities we were considering until the final year of our stay in Medicine Hat. During our visit to Ontario at Christmas in 2006, our children were begging us to move closer to the grandchildren – actually gently chastising us for not taking them into account enough in our planning for the future. Gradually, this option seemed more right to us. We couldn't give a time when we made a decision. Rather, we found ourselves having made the decision over a period of time.

Upon our return from a teaching stint in Lithuania and a holiday in Norway I was approached by the administration of MHC and asked if I would be willing to take on an increased workload for the 2006-7 college year. The person they had hired to replace me while I was gone wasn't to their liking and so they wanted me to take over the philosophy program for the entire year, teaching three courses rather than the usual two. I was also reminded that this would be my last year of part-time teaching at MHC as they wanted to hire a full-time philosopher to replace me. So for my final year at MHC I was teaching three courses per semester but was only being paid on a part-time basis – what a bargain for them! But it kept me rather busy.

Health: I was facing increasing mental health problems during my final years in Medicine Hat. Early in 2002 my yearly journal records that I was experiencing a return of anxiety attacks at night and I even had a panic attack in my office. I made an appointment with our new doctor, Tom Mohanraj, and he quickly assessed me as having a mild depression and was ready to prescribe anti-depressants. I resisted the same and we agreed to do some further tests. I also experimented with some light treatment with the Lightbook we had purchased. I seemed to be coping for a few years, but experienced serious digestive problems and panic attacks while we were in Lithuania in the winter of 2006. Upon our return to Medicine Hat I was experiencing significant depression, repeated panic attacks, and intense mood swings, often within the same day.

What was the cause of these mental health problems. In retrospect I have come to realize that there were a number of circumstantial factors that were contributing to my condition. My final years at MHC were difficult and I was experiencing burnout because of the heavy workload. Decisions regarding retirement were also more stressful than I realized at the time. I was also facing some very difficult problems in our church. Then there was the stress of a difficult winter semester at LCC where, in fact, I began experiencing renewed panic attacks and anxiety. I was also facing uncertainty with regard to the future. Our original plan to spend the first five years of our retirement teaching at LCC was no longer viable, given the difficulties we had faced in 2006 when we were at LCC. Then there was the problem of where we would retire. I also had to face the fact of my getting older, given that I was turning sixty-five in 2007, and so had to fill out applications for the Canada Pension Plan (CPP) and Old Age Security (OAS). I also had feelings of being trapped – trapped within an unpleasant church situation and trapped in terms of future choices.

I finally saw our doctor in June of 2006 and he prescribed some Rivotril, a short term drug that could be used as needed when I faced anxiety. He reassured me that I was normal though my being a very sensitive person made me more vulnerable to the intensity of feelings that I was having. I needed to embrace this condition, because it was this which also made me a writer. So my weakness was also my strength. Over time, I discovered that I was also having more trouble with my hypoglycemia and that there was a close correspondence between low blood sugar and feelings of anxiety or depression. Eventually my doctor put me on an anti-depressant (Celexa), and later referred me to a psychiatrist, Dr. Boodhoo who helped me to understand my failure to balance work, rest, and play. Amazingly I continued teaching throughout the year, though I recall times where I had to hold on to the lectern because of dizzy spells caused by my medication. During this difficult time I also prepared and reviewed lists of bible verses which I posted in our spare bedroom where I would spend some time in meditation and prayer each day after supper. Over time the anti-depressants restored me to near normality and I was able to cope with life more optimistically. Thankfully, I was able to wean myself from anti-depressants under the direction of Dr. Lisa McFarlane in Waterloo in 2009.

Manuscript: My final years of semi-retirement at MHC were of course preoccupied with completing my book on the ethics of proselytizing which I had submitted to McGill-Queen's University Press. Finally, in December of 2006, I received an email from Roger Martin, my editor, informing me that the Aid to Scholarly Publishing Program (ASPP) had rejected my application for a subvention, and as a result, McGill-Queen's could not publish my manuscript. His email included these words: "Elmer, I have to tell you that I am absolutely shocked. Between the merits of the application and the track record of your scholarship, I had every expectation of receiving an approval of the application for a publication subsidy." His earlier comments on my project included the following: "I believe – no I am convinced – that this is an important and timely book. . . . I am thoroughly convinced this book needs to be out there (i.e. in the public domain)." In an email written as I was working on a reply to the referee reports, which Roger himself helped me with, he wrote: "Each time I go through the reply I'm reminded anew of the importance of the book." Roger was clearly very distressed with the ASPP rejection and I felt so badly for him that I wrote him an email trying to console him. I was surprised how well I took the bad news. I certainly would not have been in any shape to get this news a few months earlier at the height of my depression, or if this had happened with one of my earlier books.

So I had to start from scratch once again in my search for a publisher. I immediately sent out about forty proposal inquiries to publishers via email or regular mail. I had an expression of interest from Columbia University Press in New York but they eventually decided against publishing the manuscript because I was advocating a position! For a more detailed description of this rejection, see Chapter 10. Catholic University of America Press expressed interest but in the end turned it down because it was not Catholic enough. Thankfully there were other expressions of interest, but in the end I settled on Paternoster Press in England who eventually sold North American distributing rights to InterVarsity Press. The book was published in 2011.

Milestones: There were a number of milestones in 2007. I celebrated my 65th birthday on January 18. The previous day I had an encouraging word from my psychiatrist and in the evening I had a massage at the College, as well as a call from Lottie, who wished me birthday greetings. My birthday began with a meditation from Peterson's *Leap over a Wall*, Chapter

13, on "Growth." It was the story of David finally taking the throne. Petersen translates II Samuel 5:10, as David proceeding from that moment with "a longer stride and wider embrace." The preface to the chapter quotes Jesus in Matthew 5:48: "In a word, what I'm saying is, Grow up. You're kingdom subjects. Now live like it. Live out your God-created identity. Live generously and graciously towards others, the way God lives toward you." How fitting a challenge for my birthday. The children also sent me a package of birthday cards listing 65+ "reasons why we love you." Reading these was very affirming – I hadn't changed really, despite my depression and the difficulties of the past year. We also celebrated our fortieth wedding anniversary later in fall, but this celebration took place after our arrival in Waterloo and so will be described in the next chapter.

Church farewell: The church held a farewell for us on July 15, 2007. I was asked to preach in the morning service, though even this request came about via quite unusual circumstances. I spoke on "Stations-in-life as Callings," using I Corinthians 7:17, 21, 24 and Ephesians 5:21-6:9 as my main texts. I had preached this sermon once before in Lithuania, but this time added a section focusing on old age as a station in life and as a calling. I wanted to help the elderly in the church (and myself) to think about this period of life as a calling. After the sermon, we were called to the front and the lay-ministers prayed for us.

There were quite a few visitors at the service and also later at the pot-luck, including several people from the Seven Person's church and a couple of members of my book club, Jeff Scott and Dr. Henk Haak. Quite a few of our own people were away on holidays, but given the number of guests the church was really not that empty. The basement was well-decorated for the pot-luck, with white table cloths and flowers, thanks to Jane Roth and Martha Rempel. A display had been set up with some old photos, including weddings of our children. Janet Heller had baked a large cake for us. Maggie, in her speech mentioned that this was also the year of our fortieth wedding anniversary and the atmosphere felt a bit like a wedding, with glasses tinkling at one point, to which we responded appropriately.

Arnie Nickel chaired the program after the meal and there were a good number of sincere tributes paid to us. Martha Rempel began by describing our coming to Medicine Hat in 1972 with our charming baby and their efforts at making us feel welcome. She remembered my sermons and Sunday school lessons, and Maggie's contributions in the choir and her singing in duets with Pat Mueller or in trios with Irma Nickel and Mary Klassen. Sadly David Rempel did not feel well enough to come to the mike and say something. He did talk to me afterward, but said only one sentence, "You have done a lot for this church." Other tributes came from Ernie Nickel, Ralph Erb, and Donna Janz. Linda Fenrick came up and gave just a short tribute. "Her son thought that we were cool, they as parents thought we were cool, and her parents also thought we were cool. We really appealed to all generations."

Richard Nickel then came up and thanked us for always making him feel welcome at our home. He also thanked Maggie for her baking and me for the bible studies I had led. Greg and Laura were also there and Greg gave a fine speech, thanking us for his upbringing, and saying how hard it was for him to see us leaving. He pointed out that this really began a new chapter in his life as well. He took many pictures during the pot-luck and was very much a part of the celebration.

Donna then presented us with a gift from the church – a Jim Marshall etching of a tree at Police Point. This would go well with the etching of the United Church that Maggie got from Saamis Immigration and the one of the railway station that we already had. There was also a card and some sheets of paper with tributes – mainly from those who didn't say anything during the open mike. Maggie then gave a speech, reviewing the past and reminding the church of its past strengths. My emphasis was also on the better times. All in all it was a good farewell celebration. The church went out of its way to honor us. We tried to be as positive as possible and thanked the church for what it had done for us and for the family. But, in the end, we were very glad to be leaving the church.

Finding a house in Waterloo: We spent quite a bit of time on the internet in 2007 studying the housing market in Kitchener/Waterloo. Audrey made a couple of visits to Waterloo, looking at areas in the city and possible houses we might like. Kelly Kroeker, a friend of Audrey's living in Waterloo, also looked at houses that we were interested in from our internet search. We also drew up a list of requirements for a house. Through the advice of Grace Neeb we chose her sister-in-law, Ruth Leeson, as our real estate agent. We had to wait until the end of my spring course to fly to Ontario to do some house searching for ourselves. We flew to Ontario the first week of June, dedicating a week to do our search for a house. We arrived in Waterloo at noon, and fell in love with the second house that Ruth showed us. After looking at about ten houses during the rest of the day we realized that we were always comparing these houses to the second house we had seen earlier in the day. After a long and tiring afternoon, Ruth asked us if we wanted to keep looking or take a second look at the house at 305 Bushview Crescent. We chose the latter option and after another careful look at this house we decided to buy it, making an offer at the listed price ($262,000). We were afraid of multiple offers on the house because the housing market was rather hot in Kitchener/Waterloo at the time. I usually don't make important decisions like this in one day, but we did it, and after hearing Ruth's report of the owners of the house, we felt even better about our decision. The next day we were still quite comfortable with our decision.

Upon returning to Medicine Hat, we realized that having a home to move to made a huge difference in our thinking. We knew where we were going and it made the preparations easier. We then dived into preparing to sell our Medicine Hat house – there were many things to fix up or paint (e.g. deck and garage). We had decided to sell the house on our own and over three weeks had about fifty inquiries and forty visits, but no offers. We finally decided to sell the house through a real-estate agent, and chose Ed Benning whom I knew, and who had in fact already brought several clients to the house. He set the price at $269,500 and felt that it would sell in a short time. Unfortunately Ed had to undergo heart surgery and so we were left with his assistant, Patrice Morrison, who eventually recommended that we drop the list price. About a month after our move to Ontario we finally sold the house for $257,000 with Patrice agreeing to lower her fee because of some less then professional dealings on her part.

The move: Of course there were a good number of farewell visits/suppers with our friends before we left. We spent many days packing things for the move. My office and the garage were left to the last, and I didn't get to do the sorting and culling that was needed so in the end we just moved everything in my office and the garage. We thought we were progressing so well that we took a little holiday visiting Rod and Susan Reynar in Olds, spending a night at our favorite B & B at Kananaskis, enjoying a final beautiful drive through the foothills, visiting Henry and Susan at their new home in Coaldale, and then back to Medicine Hat for a final week of packing.

Andrew had found a mover for us – a fellow church member who ran a bee business and had a driver and truck with a fifty-three foot trailer. He had a delivery to make near Winnipeg about the time of our move and his driver, Dan, wanted to spend some time in the mountains. So arrangements were made to leave the truck in Medicine Hat for a week, which gave us the flexibility to load it at our convenience. The cost of this move was amazingly under $5,000. Loading day was Saturday, July 28, 2007. Greg and Laura came the day before and helped us with last minute packing and loading. Peter Reimer was very pleased to drive the truck/trailer from the church parking lot to our house. We had a good crew out from the church, as well as a few people from Seven Persons, and then a few others like Mike Page and Vern Lawrence, who happened to drop by a few days earlier and offered to help us. It was all done in about four hours, including the loading of our new appliances which we picked up from Sears. We fed most of them pizza for lunch. There was a good spirit in the group and it was a really good day.

Adding to the stress of the move, our Volvo broke down a few days before, just when I was going to pick up blankets from a U-Haul in Redcliff. Doug Dirk who had been servicing our Volvos confirmed that I had blown a head gasket, and maybe also warped the head, depending on how long the engine had been overheated. There was also an oil problem, probably due to a faulty turbo. We decided to say good-bye to the Volvo and

Good-bye, Medicine Hat

Doug agreed to take the car, repair it, and share any profit when he sold it. So after loading the trailer we went car shopping with Greg and Laura, Greg very excited, and trying to sell us on the idea of a Jetta. In the end we purchased a new Toyota Corolla for $22,000. So, on July 31, 2007, we took possession of a new car as well as a new house in Waterloo.

A few days later our household goods left with Dan and the truck and trailer. A little later we left Medicine Hat with our new car.. We really didn't shed too many tears about leaving. We were no longer attached to the house. In fact, we were glad to leave the house and Medicine Hat. This ease of departure was no doubt a result of a long process of adjusting to the need to move on in our lives.

We took our time travelling to Ontario, staying at Len and Martha Pauls in Regina one night, and at Al and Sue Enns' beautiful cabin north of Winnipeg the next night. The next day we phoned the children after supper to see how the unloading of the trailer had gone. They begged us to hurry on so we could meet everyone in our new house. So we drove a few more hours and stayed in a terrible cabin in small town in northern Ontario. The next day (Sunday, August 5) we drove sixteen hours and arrived in Waterloo about 11:00 p.m. Amazingly, all of our possessions were already at the house, most of our belongings were unpacked, and much of the furniture was already in place. We had a good time of celebration and then went to sleep in our own bed in our spacious bedroom.

We were woken up by the grandchildren in our bed the next morning – how suitable – this was in part why we had moved. During our breakfast we enjoyed looking at our backyard which was suitably cluttered with a variety of cardboard creations of turtles and airplanes and houses which the grandchildren had made out of the boxes containing our belongings and new appliances. Thus began the settling in to our new home.

Chapter 7
RETIREMENT AND AGING

Soon after our arrival in Waterloo in 2007, Maggie began volunteering as an assistant in an ESL program at the Sunnydale Center for low-income housing, home to many recent immigrants. She was asked to work one-on-one with Alex Rhatushnyak, a young Russian computer engineer, whose English was better than most and so could benefit more from individual conversation. Alex wanted to meet me as he was interested in philosophy and over time we developed a relationship with him. He was already engaged to a girl in Russia and soon brought his new bride, Anastasia, to be with him in Canada. The relationship with this young couple has continued for many years and we had the joy of being an integral part of the birth of their first son, Yegorka (the diminutive for Georgiy, in Russian) on August 10, 2009 (our anniversary date). Maggie even accompanied Anastasia in the birth of their second son, Timothey, on September 1, 2014.

In July of 2014, Alex and Anastasia stayed in our home for a week during a transition to a new job. Whenever they were in our home, we made it a practice to pray before meals. Of course, we didn't insist on this when we were in their home, although on one occasion Anastasia did ask me to pray before a meal because she "sort of liked this practice." During the week that they were in our home Yegorka suddenly expressed an interest in learning to pray. We explained why we prayed to God before a meal and then Anastasia gave Yegorka the Russian name for God. Maggie then guided Yegorka in his first table prayer. The next time, he was on his own, and he went on and on thanking God for various things he had experienced during the day. Sometime later we had a conversation about God. Yegorka wanted to know why people killed other people. Then he asked why God let other people kill others. The conversation then moved on to ethical questions. Could good be bad, and bad be good? I suggested to Yegorka that this was relativism, and then tried to explain why relativism didn't work – if I hurt him really badly, would he call this good? An amazing philosophical discussion with a child not yet five years old.

ADJUSTING TO RETIREMENT

As already mentioned in the previous chapter, retirement came in stages for me. This chapter focusses on the stage of my retirement beginning in August of 2007 when we left Medicine Hat and moved to Waterloo, Ontario. But even after our move, I still didn't think of myself as fully retired. Indeed, when asked to introduce myself at various events I often described myself as semi-retired, because I was still doing some teaching, writing, and presenting of papers at conferences. So this chapter will describe my semi-retirement and my gradual transition to full retirement.

Our first year in Waterloo was of course focused on adjusting to a new house, a new neighborhood, a new city, new friends, a new church, and new experiences. The first few weeks after our arrival were spent on settling into our house, finding where our children had placed things, rearranging furniture, unpacking my books, and organizing my office "in my own space" on the second floor of our house. Not surprising perhaps, both of us were suffering from back problems from all the packing and unpacking of the previous weeks and so needed some visits to chiropractors and physio-therapists, though Maggie's problem was exacerbated by a serious fall. Greg and Laura arrived towards the end of our first week and we appreciated their giving us advice as to how to arrange some of our furniture, especially in our huge master bedroom. We had a wonderful time with them, visiting St. Jacob's market and traveling in the countryside, including Elora Gorge.

Both of us quickly fell in love with our new house and the neighborhood in which we lived. Just a few blocks from our house is the Laurel Creek Conservation Area, a large natural park with a lake and many trails. We immediately bought a season's pass and have over the years enjoyed many walks in the park throughout the year, and cross-country skiing in the winters. We also discovered the famous St. Jacob's Market a short drive from our house which we have frequented nearly once every week as we stock up on fresh produce and sometimes apple fritters. We have come to appreciate the fact that we live in the north-west corner of Waterloo and are just two blocks from the country-side, and so we have often enjoyed a walk along the perimeter of the city on Benjamin Road where we can take in the scenery of Mennonite farms and occasionally a Mennonite horse and buggy on the road.

Of course we especially enjoyed getting to see our children and grandchildren more often. Initially it was only about a 1 ½ hour drive to each of our children living in Toronto and St. Catharines, and so we made spontaneous visits from time to time, even doing some baby-sitting occasionally. Here is just a  sample of family visits we made that first fall season in our new home. On the last Thursday of August, Audrey and the girls came down and we had a great day, walking to St. Jacob's market via Benjamin Park and giving everyone a horse and buggy ride to a Mennonite farm. Andrew and Rachel came down the following Sunday after church. We again took a walk through Benjamin Park and Josiah enjoyed an hour at the Lego store in the Outlet Mall near us. Andrew and Rachel came to see us again one Sunday afternoon early in September. Later we went to St. Catharines to baby-sit for Rachel. We also were in Vineland for their church's 75th anniversary. The last Saturday of September we went to Audrey and Geoff's to help with building a fence. Then everyone came over for Thanksgiving Saturday, and we had a delightful time at the Nauman's pumpkin farm. We went to Toronto again for Thanksgiving Sunday, in part to see Geoff's parents.

Later in the year it felt good to have everyone in our home for Christmas – Audrey and Geoff mentioned several times that this was the first time in twelve years that they were in a parent's home for Christmas. We were glad that we had decided to host them in our home rather than go to a cottage or camp. This would be the test as to whether our home was big enough to accommodate everyone. We put Andrew and Rachel and their children into our bedroom. Geoff and Audrey and family were in the basement, complete with a new bathroom. It all worked very well, with the children playing in the basement much of the time. We opened presents in the evening of the first day. The following day we all went cross-country skiing and tobogganing in the Laurel Creek Conservation Area and had a great time.

What were our children doing at this point in time? Geoff was working in the Engineering Department at the University of Toronto as data-analyst, as well as serving half-time in the campus ministry program of the Christian Reformed Church on the U of T campus, more specifically with the Graduate Christian Fellowship (GCF). Audrey was of course busy with her family of four growing girls. Andrew had quit his job as youth-pastor at the Vineland M.B. Church in 2005 and was now working at a surveying company in Niagara-on-the-Lake. I even joined Andrew on a surveying assignment in Northern Ontario in the French River area in the fall of 2007. Rachel was a nurse at the Vineland Mennonite Seniors Home. Of course we missed Greg and Laura still in Lethbridge, where Greg would soon be working in the marketing department at Lethbridge College and Laura was counselling at Family and Community Support Services, in addition to working on her Master's degree in social work at Dalhousie University. Then there were our delightful grandchildren: Madeleine (age 13), Sylvie (age 10 ½), Ariane (age 7 ½), Bea (age 4 ½), Josiah (age 4 ½), and Lauren (age 2 ½).

We attended our first concert in Waterloo on August 27. We saw a poster in St. Jacobs while shopping – Kitchener/Waterloo Chamber Music Society, clarinet, violin and piano trio, in The Music Room at 57 Young St. W. in Waterloo, at 8:00 p.m. It sounded good and so we decided to go. We had trouble finding the place because there was no church or concert hall at this address. After asking a stranger where this concert might be, she pointed to a house with a messy front yard. We hesitated going into this house but people were entering without knocking and so we followed, climbed some stairs, and came into a crowded room with an odd array of chairs and benches and couches and non-matching blinds. There was a bit of a library and lots of music cluttered in a corner beside a gleaming Steinway grand piano. I had to go downstairs for some tickets and there met Jan Narveson, an ethics professor whom I knew from my University of Waterloo days. This was his house, and then I remembered that in my student days I had heard that Professor Narveson had concerts in his house, though we never attended because we were too poor and too busy. Now, thirty-seven years later, he was still sponsoring concerts.

The concert started late because they had trouble seating the seventy-five people who had come. We were treated to a wonderful two hours of music – Stravinsky, Brahms, Beethoven and Bartok. During the intermission, we discovered that this music society sponsored about sixty concerts per year. A season's ticket cost $240 for seniors. We attended the next concert the following Saturday then bought season's tickets.

We had not realized that the cultural scene was so strong in Kitchener/Waterloo (K/W). During that first year we probably averaged about two concerts per week. We thought we had arrived in cultural heaven. Since then we have regularly bought season's tickets for the K/W Symphony and the K/W Philharmonic Choir. In the summers we usually take in several plays at the Stratford Festival. We also discovered the Elora Festival and have regularly attended some of their concerts in the summer, setting a record of nine concerts in July of 2019.

In our first year in Waterloo we also joined the University of Waterloo choir that performed Mozart's *Requiem* and some Schubert pieces in December. After a few years in this choir, the conductor, Gordon Burnett, went on to further studies but conducted occasional benefit concerts and we continued to sing under his baton for a few years. In 2019 we also sang in the Mennonite Mass Choir. I have also enjoyed attending the occasional lecture at one of the universities or colleges. Having access to first rate libraries has also been a huge bonus. Maggie began taking courses offered by the Life-long Learning program at Wilfrid Laurier University, her first course being offered by Len Friesen on Dostoyevsky (2008). Other courses included an art appreciation course taught by Elsa Friesen (2009); a study of Jane Austin (2010); and Bach Cantatas taught by Jan Overduin (2011).

Another challenge for us in our first year at Waterloo was choosing a church and we decided to give ourselves a few months to make this decision. On our first Sunday in our new home we visited two churches – Waterloo North Mennonite, at 9:30 a.m., and at 10:45 a.m., the Waterloo M.B. Church where we had once attended many years earlier. We thoroughly enjoyed the service in the first church – a good sermon and good congregational singing of hymns in four-part harmony. We thought we would be complete strangers at this church and were very surprised when during the welcoming session towards the end of the service, someone got up and introduced us. We did not recognize this person, but after the service we met and discovered that I had in fact taught John Thiessen in Sunday School some thirty-nine years earlier. I had also taught his wife Betty at Waterloo Lutheran University at the same time. In fact, we discovered that we were living on the same street. There were two other couples there that we knew – disaffected M.B.'s from our former church. It was a grand welcoming party. The second service at Waterloo M.B., our former church, was less to our liking. That church had evolved in directions that we couldn't appreciate, so it was rather easy to rule out WMB as our future church home.

In October we began our second round of visits to churches that we considered to be serious possibilities for us. Grace M.B. Church went out of its way to welcome us but in the end we decided against this church – it was small and seemed to be struggling with its identity. We also considered the Kitchener M.B. Church, but the congregation seemed small and old, and besides, the church was rather far away from our home. We rather brazenly joined an outing of the seniors group (50+/-) at Waterloo North Mennonite Church (WNMC) for a Wednesday when they visited the Mennonite Centre in St. Jacobs. A little later we attended the Matins service and Sunday school at WNMC. It was a good Sunday and we were feeling more and more comfortable with the idea of joining WNMC. In fact by Christmas we had pretty well decided to join this church. We liked the location of the church – within walking distance, the hymns, the richness of the language used in the church, the open appreciation of their Mennonite heritage, more lay-involvement, and the inter-generational character of the church. It was also a church where I wouldn't be put into a position where I was being envied because I had too much influence. There were obviously many very capable leaders in the church. The church had a policy of having new at-tendees wait a year before they became members so we only became official members a year later.

Another part of our adjustment to this new phase of my retirement was looking for some kind of work. It didn't take me long to begin exploring pos-sible teaching opportunities and to follow up on some letters of inquiry I had already written while still in Medicine Hat. Early in September I had an ap-pointment with Steve Roy, the academic Dean at Emmanuel Bible College. He was thinking of having me teach a course for them in the winter semester – the philosophy of religion. However, I soon received a letter informing me that enrolment was down and so they could not justify adding an elective to their curriculum. I also visited the philosophy departments at several of the universities and colleges in the city but none of them had any job openings. In October I visited Heritage College and Seminary and was given a warm reception by Stan Fowler but no offers of a course. I also visited Conestoga College (it felt so much like Medicine Hat College), and was told that there might be a course available next fall.

I had been encouraged by Ron Richmond in Regina to contact Carla Nelson at Tyndale University College in Toronto, who was heading up a new education program at Tyndale. She asked for my resume and this immedi-ately prompted her to arrange a meeting with her Dean, Dan Scott. I visited Tyndale mid-November, not entirely sure whether this was a formal inter-view or not. We had a very good discussion and they gave several hints that they really wanted me in the program. But, they were still waiting for gov-ernment approval of their program and so no commitments could be made.

I was relatively relaxed about my search for teaching opportunities. I needed the fall semester off in any case in order to settle into our new house. I would have liked a course for the winter semester, but that didn't happen. Opportunities would come. And we could also consider overseas appoint-ments, once we had settled into our new house.

Another option for both of us was volunteer work. Indeed, I had not ap-preciated this as a possibility prior to this stage of my retirement. In Septem-ber I joined our neighbor and friend, John Thiessen, on a food distribution program that he was involved with at the Sunnydale Centre for low-income housing. It was an interesting experience and I offered to help John with this on an occasional basis, but I was not convinced that I wanted to do this on a regular basis. However, while at Sunnydale, I checked about ESL instruction and found a contact person for Maggie. She followed this up and was soon helping them once a week. The volunteer position at Sunnydale changed over the years and became a conversation program in which Maggie continued volunteering on a regular basis until 2019.

In 2009 I began volunteering at Generations, a Mennonite Central Committee thrift shop, and enjoyed working in the receiving department for a good number of years, together with John Cornies – the two of us were labelled "the dream team" by management. I also enjoyed having  our grandchildren join me occasionally for an afternoon of work when they visited us. When MCC consolidated their stores in 2013 and opened a bigger store, Thrift on Kent, I transferred to the book department. Unfortunately, morale at the store deteriorated with the hiring of a new manager in 2018 and I began considering other options for volunteer work. We got involved with the friendship program for new immigrants at Reception House in 2018. Here we were assigned to a Syrian family who had already been in Canada for three years. We enjoyed getting to know Mohammed Al-Rachid and his wife, Noufa Al-Ibrahim, and their five beautiful children, Hanan, Ahmad, Rayan, Alaa and Mahmoud. In 2020, I began volunteering as a driver and grocery shopper for Waterloo Home Support Services. These volunteer assignments certainly helped to enrich and give meaning to our lives.

Another aspect of our adjustment to retirement and our new environment was making our house really our own. Shortly after our move to Waterloo I began building a bathroom in the basement for any guests we might have. I had to get some help with the plumbing, but did most of the work myself. We were not entirely happy with our kitchen so in early 2008 we had new custom cupboards installed by a Mennonite craftsman, Marvin Weber. I then had the fun of installing the old cupboards into the garage and the basement. I felt a lot happier after I had my garage organized so that I could find my tools. We then discovered Rick Moore, living in our neighborhood, who does landscaping and takes on projects on the side. So we hired him and his boys to put in a curved stone sidewalk in the front of our house. We then developed a flower bed with trees and shrubs to accent the new stonework. Our back yard had an upward slope against the back fence and Rick also helped us design a rock garden in the back, complete with a dry river-bed and little stone bridge.

ANNIVERSARIES

It is perhaps appropriate, after describing our adjustment to retirement and our new home, to focus briefly on anniversaries. One seems to be more conscious of anniversaries after retirement. And there seem to be so many anniversaries once one has retired. Perhaps time goes more quickly when we age.

Our first anniversary was in fact celebrated just a few weeks after we moved to Waterloo. We were married in Vineland, Ontario, on August 10, 1967, and mathematics dictates that we had been married for forty years in 2007. We had just been in our new house for five days on the actual anniversary date so it is perhaps no surprise that we didn't do much by way of celebration on the exact day of our anniversary. But we still intended to do

some celebrating a bit later. So two Sundays after our arrival in Waterloo, we drove to Toronto after church to have a 40th anniversary celebration with all of our children. We found a Thai restaurant in the city-center and had a great meal and visit – adults only.

The next anniversary was my 70th birthday in 2012. We had planned a one-week family winter holiday at a resort in Mexico early in the year to celebrate this birthday. Unfortunately Maggie experienced some significant heart problems just before we were about to

Princess Resort, Mexico holiday

leave and so we had to make the painful decision to stay at home. We encouraged the rest of the family to go without us and they had a good time, giving us a full report soon after their return. Not being able to join our children during this Mexico holiday was a huge disappointment, though Maggie and I returned to this same resort the following year and tried to imagine the fun our children had had in the previous year. We did compensate for this disappointment by celebrating my 70th birthday at a family Christmas gathering at Kimbercote Farm that same year, and I even gave a formal speech describing what it meant for me to turn seventy years old.

By the time we celebrated our 50th wedding anniversary, we were of course very much settled into our new home and environment. So we spent the entire month of August in 2017 celebrating fifty years of marriage. I have described these celebrations in the concluding section of Chapter 2, and so will not say more here.

The next anniversary was Maggie's 80th birthday in 2019. I took her out to a restaurant on the day of her birthday. The following day Audrey had the Ontario family members all down for a grand celebration with a seven-course meal, where Maggie was asked to recount a decade of her life after each course.

Of course my 80th birthday comes three years after Maggie's and so will happen in 2022. Since the writing of this autobiography is being done before my eightieth birthday, I cannot predict how we will celebrate. But one part of the celebration will include the giving of these memoirs to our children and grandchildren.

TEACHING IN ONTARIO AND OTHER COMMUNITY ACTIVITIES

One of my hopes for retirement was that I would be able to do some part-time teaching. My first teaching assignment was in a newly established education program at Tyndale University College in Toronto. I was asked to teach a course entitled "Democratic Values, Christian Perspectives, and Education." I was also appointed Professor of Research in Education for a three-year term. It was great to get paid for what I was doing in any case. The course was to be taught in two segments, two weeks in July of 2008 and then a third week in May of the following year. The course was a challenge in many ways – a rather broad course title which I found difficult to cover in just three weeks and which led me to overprepare, a large class (nearly seventy at the beginning), an intense program, students who had outside jobs despite the intensity of the program, students with weak English language skills, and concerns about the course being too demanding and too difficult. I discovered that the expectations in an education department are simply different from that of an arts and science department.

While there were some student complaints, I was generally pleased with the student evaluations at the end of the course. I was even given a long, standing ovation at the end of the final class. I had many good discussions with students individually and in class. Surprisingly, many of the students were not Christians and so the Christian perspectives dimension of the course led to some serious inquiries on the part of some of the students. One Christian student appreciated my emphasis on the practical implications of the Christian faith and considered the class "a divine intervention" in her life. In the end, I was left wondering whether I would teach the course again in the following year and only after I finally inquired was I told that they had other plans, which was probably just as well. However, my position as Research Professor continued for the full three years.[1]

I was made aware of the Laurier Association for Life-long Learning (LALL) at Wilfrid Laurier University which offers courses for seniors as part of their Continuing Education program. I applied and was invited to teach an ethics course for them in the fall of 2009 – "Ethics for a Pluralistic-Postmodern World." I couldn't help but think that it was rather appropriate for me to start and end my career teaching at the same university. I had a class of twenty-two students, many of them retired professionals who really wanted to learn. One class per week. No exams. No marking.

No discipline problems. It was wonderful. Indeed, I continued teaching LALL courses for the next ten years, courses in logic, applied ethics, philosophy of religion, Plato's Republic, and the ethics of persuasion. I was especially pleased with a course I offered in 2018 on intellectual virtues and vices which led to a full class of thirty students, with another twenty on the waiting list. The course seemed to be addressing some concerns regarding contemporary culture and it prompted a lot of participation in class discussions.

I made another attempt to connect with Emmanuel Bible College (EBC) in the fall of 2011, and this time Steve Roy met with me and explained that they were having trouble with a required course they were offering – a Worldview Studies Seminar. Would I be willing to teach this course? Of course! It was good to be back in the classroom again in the winter of 2012 for an entire semester, though there were some challenges teaching twenty-eight students, mainly young, and most of them rather conservative and not familiar with the demands of a philosophy course. One student even came to me during the break and said he felt sorry for me having to teach at a bible college, what with the narrowness of some of the students.

Another challenge I faced was adjusting to only meeting once a week for a three-hour lecture. I tried to break up the class into different segments and included more discussion but all this took extra preparation. Indeed, as with all my teaching after retirement, I put a lot of extra work into the lectures and courses I taught because I had the time to do it. I believe I did some of my best teaching after retirement. In the end I was very pleased with the student evaluations of my first course at EBC.[2] I had hoped to continue teaching at EBC until I turned eighty. However, the school was facing declining overall enrolment coupled with financial problems. I continued teaching for EBC until 2018 when I had only five students which prompted me to reduce the teaching stipend so the course could still run.

So, for a good number of years I had a wonderfully balanced cycle of teaching a six-week course in the LALL program at WLU in the fall semester, and teaching a twelve-week worldview course at EBC in the winter semester. I thoroughly enjoyed teaching a wide array of courses in the LALL program each fall, and discovered that my background at Medicine Hat College – being a generalist and teaching at an undergraduate level

– had prepared me well for teaching courses to seniors who wanted introductions to various divisions of philosophy. Teaching at a bible college was also a stretching experience, given my many years of teaching within a secular context. I had to remember to pray before each class and I now saw my task as trying to broaden the horizons of these Christian students, many of whom came from a very conservative background. I had some good students who appreciated my approach of trying to prepare them for living in the "real world." I am very thankful for having been able to continue teaching in my retirement all these years.

Another interesting avenue of teaching opened up for me – teaching in retirement residences. In 2008 I was asked to do a five-week lecture series on "Ethics for a Pluralistic Society," at the Waterpark condos, arranged for by a member of our church, Erica Jantzen. I gave a single lecture at Luther Village a year later. Then in 2019, Bev Suderman-Gladwell, chaplain at Parkwood senior homes, asked me to do a four-lecture series on philosophy as part of their wellness program at Parkwood. Again, these were enjoyable experiences that allowed me to indulge in my love of teaching. I was scheduled to give a 3-lecture series on philosophy at the Chartwell Clair Hills Retirement Residence in the spring of 2020, but these had to be cancelled due to the pandemic outbreak.

I was also involved in several community related activities. Soon after we arrived in Waterloo I wrote an op-ed piece for the *K-W Record* on the election controversy regarding the funding of faith-based schools. While they didn't publish this op-ed piece, they did print a letter to the editor on the topic. Later that fall I noticed an announcement in the *Record,* inviting applications to their Community Editorial Board, so I applied, submitting a revised version of the article I had written earlier on faith-based schools and how this played into the election results for Dalton Mc-Guinty. My application was successful and I was delighted with this new opportunity to work in the area of my calling – writing that attempts to bridge the religious and secular worlds. I was pleased when they extended my term for another year. In addition to several smaller reflections, I wrote twelve op-ed pieces during these two years, most of them focusing on ethical topics (2008 & 2009).

I also served briefly on the Ethics Committee of the Grand River Hospital in 2008-9, and then on the Board of the Waterloo Public Library for four years starting in 2011.

TEACHING OVERSEAS

Another hope I had for retirement was to be in a position to offer my services for overseas teaching assignments at Christian colleges, universities, and seminaries, and to be self-supporting in taking on these assignments. I am thankful for several opportunities given to me over the years of my semi-retirement. Though each of these appointments were challenging in different ways, the experiences were nevertheless meaningful and fulfilling.

Evangelische Theologische Faculteit (ETF): My first opportunity came as a result of my renewing contact with Martin Weber at ETF in Belgium in 2008. In the end we agreed that I would teach a course in the philosophy of religion in the following year. So we returned to Leuven towards the end of March, 2009, for two weeks of teaching and one week of holidays together with our good friends from Norway, Bjorn and Reidun Fjeld. When we arrived there was much that looked very familiar. Even the smells of the dormitory were familiar. We were warmly welcomed by the faculty and the new president of ETF who was very frank about some of the difficulties they had faced since I was there in 2005.

I had twelve students in my class, some very good, some average, and some not so good. I worked very hard during the two weeks of actual classes, but it was worth it. Contrary to European professorial practice, I had open office hours, including in the evenings, and I had a number of very good discussions with individual students in my office. The chapel talk that I gave early in my time there ("On being a Christian Academic and Philosopher") led to some further interesting discussions. One student described my class as very practical – the highest compliment that anyone can pay me for my approach to teaching philosophy. The students were very intrigued with my having taught in a secular setting for most of my career. Some were also asking me how I could survive within an evangelical setting as a thinking philosopher.

Meserete Kristos College (MKC): I took on another overseas teaching assignment in the summer of 2011. John Peters from our church had already taught at MKC in Ethiopia several times and I was keen

on joining him on his next assignment. After some inquiries I was invited to teach a three-week course with a rather multi-layered title, "Introduction to Philosophy, Theology, and Logic," which required quite a bit of advance preparation. This was my first trip to the continent of Africa and also the longest time that I had been separated from Maggie. So already at the start, I was feeling anxious. The trip itself only exacerbated the problem, what with a nine-hour stop-over at the Heathrow airport. The final leg of the trip was most interesting as I followed our progress on the map and saw that we were flying over Egypt, the Sudan and the Red Sea. I had never been in this part of the world before.

Then came my initiation to Ethiopia, starting with touching down at the airport in Addis Ababa with dilapidated planes strewn haphazardly beside the runways. One of the administrators, Wondwossen, was at the airport to pick me up and took me to a bank where I was met by a policeman guarding the entrance. Then on to a grocery store, a market where I could buy some fruit, and finally to the home of Negash Kebede, the President of the College, who drove me to the college later – a one hour drive, with the air literally black with smoke from old cars and trucks, and of course again, we were dodging vehicles, people, and even horses, cattle, and donkeys on the road. Upon arrival on campus, I was taken to the guest house which was quite modern, except for an open shower in a smelly bathroom and a rather messy kitchen. The stress of the trip and the heat, together with all the other adjustments to a radically new environment, all contributed to a recurrence of my anxiety coupled with digestive problems. Fortunately, as adjustments were made, routines put in place, and some sleeping pills which the President of the College acquired, I was able to get back to normal mental health. But it was a rough start and I learned one important lesson – take along some medication for anxiety when travelling.

It was exciting to begin teaching my twenty-five students, most of them mature adults with quite a few years of pastoral experience under their belt. The initial classes went very well and I was pleased to discover that most students were very keen to learn. I told the students at the beginning of the course that they should simply address me as Elmer, but most of them simply couldn't adjust to this level of informality. In the end I questioned the wisdom of doing this, but one of the students did tell me after the course was over that my insistence on them calling me by my first name had made an impression on him. So perhaps I did convey an important lesson to people for whom the label "pastor" was very important and in fact meant release from manual labor.

I scheduled small group discussions in the third hour of each class. In one of my early lectures on the relation between philosophy and the Christian faith, I drew on the first chapter of 1 Corinthians and Colossians 2:8. I decided that the discussion question for this class would be to prepare a sermon outline of five to six points based on these texts and dealing with the relation between philosophy and the foolishness of the gospel. This surely would relate to their lives as pastors! This prompted lively discussions but after fifteen minutes I realized they were far from finished. So I made a quick decision to make this their next quiz – a group assignment they could work on during the rest of the day. They all did a fairly good job with this assignment, except for one group who obviously copied from a commentary. What was particularly rewarding was a group of students who came to see me the following day after class, asking me a bit more about sermon outlines. Should they do this even with exegetical sermons? They found my few tips very helpful. I was delighted that I could also teach them some homiletics.

I was thoroughly enjoying many conversations with my students outside of class. After one of my evening walks I met one of my students, Gebrie Alem, and stopped to talk to him. I listened to his amazing story. He was an evangelist in southern Ethiopia. His attendance at MKC was not being supported by his church as was the case with most of the other students who were pastors – the church didn't have the money to send him. So his family was supporting him and he was also earning a bit of extra money working in the library. He was still single and when I asked why, he said he was afraid of divorce – it was so common among young people today. He spoke of persecution in his area, especially because of his active evangelism. One time he had been tortured, made to eat thorns and thistles, beaten without any clothes on, dragged through the streets naked, and put in prison for a week. It reminded me of Paul in the New Testament – these people were so much closer to New Testament times than we who live in North America. But my student recalled that Jesus had saved him and he continued to find great joy in evangelism, and people were being saved. I had to wonder how my course would be relevant to his life and so I asked him about this. He was very appreciative of the course – it was broadening his horizons.

As the course progressed, I became more aware of some of the challenges I was facing in the class – the usual cultural barriers, very weak English language skills, a deep suspicion about philosophy, and their failure to do the readings, probably because they simply couldn't understand them. They also had a lot of trouble with the logic section of the course. They were very afraid of the final exam which I had already revised to make it easier. I provided them with a lot of help with the take-home essay which was part of the final exam. In the end I was able to pass them all, though I'm sure the marks weren't as high as they had come to expect in other courses which they had been taking at MKC. I left with some questions about the approach being taken to educate the church leaders at MKC. Surely giving them an education in Amharic and closer to their own homes would be more helpful and convenient.

But all in all it was a memorable experience, though I am not sure I want to go back to Africa again. The heat was at times unbearable. Then there was the graduation ceremony which John and I were expected to attend, cloaked in heavy hot gowns – I eventually escaped, as I was afraid of fainting from the heat. Yes, I did enjoy a meal at a fancy restaurant on a lake built by the Hailie Salasie family. I also enjoyed my early morning hikes to a hill behind the college that overlooks a beautiful volcanic lake. Then there was the international restaurant (Tomi) on the edge of Debra Zeit which I went to nearly every two days for a good meal with meat, getting there and back by hiring a "bajaji," an Indian three-wheel motorized cart, for 10 birr (about 60 cents). On Sundays we went to a Dutch church in Debra Zeit – a small congregation made up mainly of young people working on various projects to help the poor in Ethiopia – accessing good water supplies, huge gardens, a cattle farm, and also a chicken farm. Also memorable were the many power outages which limited our use of the internet in connecting with the family back home. I never did get used to the engira or the rice with a bit of meat and tomato salad when I tried the meals prepared by the kitchen on campus. Oh the challenges of living in Africa!

Caribbean Graduate School of Theology (CGST): In the fall of 2013 I had the privilege of teaching a four-week course at CGST in Kingston, Jamaica. This invitation came via contacts made by Joyce and Graham Gladwell who knew the President, Las Newman. I was happy that Maggie was able to join me for this trip.

We faced an array of practical problems soon after we arrived. We were accommodated in a townhouse on campus which was dirty, some of the cooking utensils were rusty and unusable, many light bulbs were missing, and when we went to bed we couldn't help but feel the springs in the mattress. A few days after we arrived we were woken up in the morning with someone banging on our door and window. When I went down, I noticed much of our floor was covered in water. A tap in the kitchen had sprung a leak. Fortunately, we didn't have too much of our stuff on the floor. A custodian and maid came to repair the leak and mop up the floor. Sadly, the flooding problem wasn't over, and after a third flood we insisted on getting this fixed properly and the President hired a plumber. The President's secretary also went out with Maggie to get us a proper frying pan. We finally bought lightbulbs ourselves only to discover that some of the sockets were so rusted that the new bulbs didn't work in any case. But the bedroom did have air-conditioning and they had stocked the fridge with some food before our arrival. Be thankful for small mercies.

I also ran into some immediate problems with my teaching. We visited the library the day after we arrived and discovered that the library holdings were rather sparse, with old books, very much used, and looking rather musty due to the humidity. And then there was the problem of bookworms – yes, there really are bookworms! The Dean, Ives Bergeron, didn't have any firm idea of the number of students I would have in class – five had paid up so far, but I was told that students often pay up on the day that classes start. Students kept trickling in so that by the end I had twelve students with one dropping out later. Then there was the problem of textbooks. The Dean had told me beforehand: "Students won't buy the textbooks, or read them, and they won't have time to study." The Registrar told me later that past foreign instructors had brought along a supply of textbooks to sell to the students. I would gladly have done this, if only I had been told to do so.

I also had quite a battle getting some essential materials for my course photocopied – they preferred to have course materials put on their on-line Moodle platform. A few days into my course I got a stern lecture from the secretary to the Dean, not to duplicate any more materials for students, e.g. my two-page outline of each lecture. "You are spoiling them." So I started getting all my materials duplicated at my own expense.

I had some excellent students, many of them already in professions – teachers, engineers, pastors, counselors, and businessmen. Most of them were making huge sacrifices to get a theological education. I discovered that one of them was a medical doctor who had practiced for about twenty years. And she was studying theology. Wonderful! Another older student, was a counselor at a school, ran a farm, and pastored two churches near Mandeville where he lived. He drove about 1 ½ hours each evening to be in my class – talk about dedication. During the second week of classes he excitedly told me how much he was learning in my class and how this class was transformative for him. He appreciated my starting on time and teaching the students discipline. He liked the precision of my thinking, due he thought to my physics background. He was also coming to see the importance of presuppositions in all disciplines. He had clearly prepared his speech as he was rather quiet in class.

Another of my students, Everton, was an engineer working at the shipyards. He was also a deacon in a church, and taking theology to help him in his church work. The Dean informed me that Everton was also an advisor to one of the ministers in the Jamaican government, so by teaching him, I was affecting the future of Jamaica. When I mentioned that Everton had not told me this, the Dean told me that Everton was too humble to tell me this. I was in fact very much enjoying having Everton in class. He told me later that he found the class very helpful. When he said this, I mentioned that at first he had seemed a bit skeptical about what I was doing in class. He agreed, but he had changed his mind as the class proceeded. Interestingly, Everton chose as his essay topic, a Christian perspective on politics.

I did however have to counter some rather conservative and fundamentalist thinking on the part of my students. In week three I brought up the topic of creation/evolution in my class, outlining my position of theistic evolution and this resulted in a near rebellion. Most of the students were die-hard creationists, so I had to work hard at trying to unglue them from their dogmatism. Some weeks later during a class break the medical doctor asked me what I thought about the prosperity gospel. I mentioned that I saw some dangers in this approach, but didn't really want to get into this issue as it was not directly related to the course. But a lively discussion followed among the students during the break, with the doctor valiantly defending the practice of giving God seed money so He will bless us.

During our four weeks in Kingston we did some exploring in the neighborhood, despite the fact that we were warned not to do so. At the end of the second week the Dean took us to his home town of Mandeville and had us stay at the Golf Hotel. Mandeville is higher up in the mountains and hence was a bit cooler. The Golf Hotel had a swimming pool but overall it was a two-star hotel – definitely not a resort! But it was good to be out of hot and noisy Kingston. In the evening, Yves and his wife Vinette, picked us up and took us to a nice restaurant on a hill overlooking Mandeville. Vinette was a French teacher in a high school. They had four children and had named two of their boys Martin Luther King and Billy Graham. Yves took us to their church on Sunday – a very charismatic Church of God. This experience helped me to understand my students better, as I was sensing that many of them were charismatic and were reacting to my rather rational approach to the Christian faith.

At the end of our third week we treated ourselves to a holiday, staying at Strawberry Hill Lodge, in the Blue Mountains just above Kingston. It was rather expensive, but we felt we deserved some luxury. We were welcomed to the Lodge in grand style, told to have our free breakfast until our room was prepared by our maid. Then on to our quaint plantation style suite – old but of high quality, with a wall of shuttered windows, a canopy bed with mosquito netting, and a lovely big old desk. On one side of our deck was a wall of broad leafed palm trees, giving us privacy, at the end of the deck we could see a large mountain valley, and on the other side we could see the city of Kingston far below. Quite lovely really and a welcome contrast to our townhouse in Kingston.

We had a delightful weekend, walking around the grounds which were very hilly with a variety of plants and flowers that Maggie quite enjoyed. We enjoyed many hours swimming and reading beside a lovely pool overlooking the city of Kingston below. We enjoyed some fairly good meals on the deck of the grand house. The President of our school picked us up after our weekend retreat and gave us a running commentary on our way down. We discovered that Prince Charles and Camilla had stayed at the Lodge. The roads up the mountain used to be in much better repair, Las informed us. The government was bankrupt and simply couldn't afford maintaining the infrastructure. The mountains were also being eroded by poor farmers building huts and planting small coffee groves on the steep hillsides.

The night before we left we attended the school's Christmas party, sponsored by the graduate students. This was an experience! The party was held outside, complete with a decorated Christmas tree and lights. The temperature was twenty-six degrees above zero and it was dark, with a full moon in the sky. We arrived on time, at 6:00 p.m., and there were only two other people there. Slowly, very slowly, people arrived, and the program finally began at 7:00 p.m. This was normal for Jamaica. My poor students who had to adjust to me starting nearly on time each evening! I talked to one of the board members and he commented on the lack of discipline among Jamaicans and the many manpower hours lost because meetings started late. Then we listened to a band playing Jingle Bells, but there was no snow! A program followed with lots of hallelujahs, singing, admonitions to worship God more enthusiastically, and a little play which we couldn't understand because the two actors spoke Jamaican English.

I proctored my final exam the following day. The next day the President took us to the airport – no debriefing, and we had decided that it would be best not to initiate any evaluation ourselves. All in all, it was in interesting experience even though there were some challenges.

OTHER ACADEMIC INVOLVEMENTS

My research, writing, publishing, and speaking engagements at conferences will be described in greater detail in Chapter 10. Here I will only highlight the fact that I continued these other academic involvements after my retirement. This is one of the advantages of an academic career – one can simply carry on doing what one has always been doing, even after retirement. I had already completed several drafts of my manuscript, *The Ethics of Evangelism: A Philosophical Defense of Proselytizing and Persuasion* before we moved to Waterloo. Further revisions were made after Paternoster Press agreed to publish the manuscript. After some hassles with the copy-editor, the book was finally published in 2011. It took me a while to get motivated to keep my promise to publish a sequel to this book, but eventually *The Scandal of Evangelism: A Biblical Study of the Ethics of Evangelism* was published in 2018. Work on these memoirs began shortly afterwards. Although I had promised that my second book on the ethics of evangelism would be my last book, the reception of my lectures on intellectual virtues and vices in the LALL program at WLU and in Sunday School classes in our church has put some fire in my belly for another book on this topic. We shall see!

I also started blogging in January of 2010. My self-description for the blog was uncreative and rather bold: "Elmerjohnthiessen's Blog: a Commentary on philosophy, theology, education, church, evangelism, persuasion, and social trends."[3] My motivation for starting this blog was in part to locate some of my previous writings on the internet. But I have added some original articles and book reviews over the years.

Another aspect of my academic activities after retirement has been the giving of lectures at conferences and retreats. Some of these were related to my previous work in the philosophy of education.[4] One was related to my teaching on bio-medical ethics.[5] The publication of my first book on the ethics of evangelism led to a number of conference papers.[6] Here I will focus on three international conferences that were highlights for me.

The first was **a Global Triennial Consultation of the Micah Network**, held in Thun, Switzerland, September 10-14, 2012. The Micah Network is a loose global alliance of over 330 evangelical Christian relief, development, and justice organizations trying to overcome the dualism between evangelism and social action that has historically characterized evangelicalism. At its first global consultation, held in Oxford, UK, in 2001 the network members crafted a "Declaration on Integral Mission" based on Micah 6:8. I was invited to be a plenary speaker at this conference by Sheryl Haw, the executive director of the Micah Network who was excited about my 2011 book on the ethics of evangelism which she had just read. She was hoping I would provide a needed balance to the agenda of the Micah Network which tended to focus mainly on social action.

I went to this conference with mixed feelings. After the initial invitation the executive director changed my assignment to a "semi-plenary lecture" – now scheduled as one of several concurrent sessions. This of course left me wondering why this change had been made and why they were paying for all my expenses. I was assured there would still be about 200 people attending my session and that the change had been made to give me more time. I suspect the real reason was that Sheryl was getting some pushback from some of the leadership who didn't agree with the inclusion of the topic of evangelism on the program. She also added another workshop to discuss a statement of guidelines I had prepared on the relation between evangelism and relief/development. I decided that I would make the best of it and simply enjoy the conference. In fact I heard some inspiring sermons as well as a hard hitting lecture by Johannes Reimer from Germany who expressed some concerns about the secularization of Christian relief and development organizations as well as a lack of emphasis on evangelism. It felt good to hear someone affirming what I believe was the reason I was invited – to reconnect relief/development with evangelism.

A number of logistical problems surrounded my presentations. Changes in scheduling and location of my sessions resulted in only about fifty people attending my semi-plenary address and about thirty-five attending my workshop. Despite these problems, I felt quite good about my main presentation. Several leaders of Christian relief and development organizations asked to meet with me for lunch after my presentation and we had a good discussion. I certainly learned a lot at the consultation and developed a clearer idea as to how to organize my next book on a biblical study of the ethics of evangelism.[7] I was also pleased to get an email from Sheryl Haw in the fall of 2019 informing me that the Micah Board was planning to review the definition of "integral mission" as they realized the concept had led to misunderstandings. I interpreted this as an affirmation of a suggestion I made that there be a moratorium on the concept of integral mission.

I quite enjoyed the location of the conference and the accommodation I was given. Thun is a beautiful city beside a lake high in the mountains. They had put me up at the Adler Hotel in Sigriswell, a village beyond Thun and higher up in the Alps. From my hotel, you could see the Igor and the  Jungfrau mountains (about 4000 feet) in the distance. I enjoyed several good hikes in the mountains, past farms with cowbells ringing and sheep grazing, up steep paths, through forests, and along mountain streams. I had a wonderful time quite apart from the conference.

The second international conference I attended grew out of an unexpected email I received in April of 2014 from Mark Oxbrow, head of Faith2Share in England. Mark invited me to give a plenary address at an **Evangelical-Orthodox Consultation** in Albania in September of the same year. He had heard me at the Micah Convention in Switzerland a few years earlier. This consultation had its roots in the 2010 Lausanne Congress in Capetown and was aiming to bridge the differences between evangelical and Orthodox Christians. Each time they met they tried to address some "hard issues," with this consultation focusing on the issue of evangelism.

There were some excellent papers presented at the consultation, after each of which we were divided into small group discussions.[8] I had been asked to provide a brief review of my book on the ethics of evangelism, and then deal with the specific problem of proselytizing, sometimes referred to as "sheep-stealing." Orthodox leaders have long been concerned about evangelicals doing evangelism in countries where the Orthodox church is dominant. I was disappointed with the two official responses to my paper.[9] But it was good to work on this project and I got some further ideas for my forthcoming book. Given a second invitation to deal with what was really an application of my forthcoming book on the ethics of evangelism, I decided that it would be good to combine my biblical study of the ethics of evangelism with a section on some applications – the ethics of evangelism in health care, education, relief efforts, and then also add the issue of the ethics of proselytizing as sheep-stealing. This adjustment served to renew my motivation to start working on this book.

The highlight of the week for me was the visit to the Orthodox Cathedral in Tirana and hearing the head of the Orthodox Church in Albania, Archbishop Anastasios, describe the work of rebuilding the church in Albania after the fall of communism in the early  1990's. Part of his vision for such rebuilding was the construction of the magnificent cathedral in the heart of the capital, Tirana. The old cathedral was destroyed by the communist regime in 1967. The new cathedral is appropriately named "The Resurrection of Christ." I was deeply impressed with Archbishop Anastasios who in fact faced considerable criticism for his openness to evangelicals and for hosting this consultation. This was just another example of the man's courage in the face of opposition.

So, after a very stimulating week at the beautiful Orthodox monastery of St. Vlash, one hour away from Tirana, it was back to the airport and on to Istanbul. Maggie and I had decided to combine my engagement (which was self-funded) with a two-week tour of Turkey with Insight Vacations. It was rather strange meeting Maggie in the Marriot Hotel in Istanbul with both of us having coming from different parts of the globe.

In January of 2017, I received another invitation to attend an international consultation sponsored by the **Global Christian Forum** in cooperation with the Catholic Church (Pontifical Council for Promoting Christian Unity), the Pentecostal World Fellowship, the World Council of Churches, and the World Evangelical Alliance (WEA). The purpose of this consultation was to develop a statement entitled, "The Call to Mission and Perceptions of Proselytism: A Global Conversation."[10]

The consultation was held June 8-11, 2017, in Accra, the capital of Ghana, at the Pentecostal Convention Centre, a huge complex with lots of green space, dormitories, auditoriums, and a seminary. About thirty people were present, with representatives from Orthodox, Catholic, Pentecostal, Evangelical, and mainline churches, as well as representatives from the World Council of Churches. Thomas Schirrmacher introduced me as an expert in the field and also told me to introduce myself as his advisor. In the end we discussed a draft statement on proselytism that a committee had prepared. This statement never saw the light of day. Nor did we move the discussion forward on this topic. There are simply too many deep differences in theology between the Orthodox or Catholics, and evangelicals or Pentecostals. Evangelicals and Pentecostals believe that they should be able to evangelize wherever there are unbelievers or nominal or lapsed Christians, not only in Orthodox and Catholic domains but also in other Western countries. Schirrmacher and I eventually published an article outlining the evangelical position on this topic.[11]

One interesting highlight of this week was another "Royal Conference" going on at the same time and at the same Pentecostal Centre. This was an evangelistic conference sponsored by the Pentecostal Church of Ghana in which they invited all the tribal kings and queens and chiefs of Ghana. We made a brief appearance at this conference and it was a sight to behold – about 600 kings and queens and chiefs dressed in all their finery. This was the second such conference sponsored by the Pentecostals. Amazing, really – Christians in Ghana reaching out to the upper strata of their society.

There is one other academic involvement that I will mention briefly. In 2019 I joined the Society of Christian Scholars, "a global community of, by, and for missional Christian scholars." I was delighted that one of the services provided by the society is a mentorship programme, because all too often graduate programs offer little by way of helping new instructors with the all-important task of teaching. I volunteered for this programme and was assigned to a young philosophy instructor, who was now teaching part-time at Indiana University – Purdue University Indianapolis. We connected via email and Zoom, sometimes on a weekly basis. I enjoyed our conversations about a variety of issues relating to course design and teaching. It helped me to feel useful, even in old age!

CHURCH AND CHURCH-RELATED MINISTRIES
I have already described how we chose Waterloo North Mennonite Church (WNMC) as our church home during our first year after moving to Ontario. We officially became members of the church on November 16, 2008 and were relatively at peace with this decision. We were soon co-opted into serving as table parents for children in an excellent Logos program held every Thursday evening and were involved in this ministry for two years. I organized a book club in our church in the fall of 2008 and this continued with changing membership until the present time. We also joined a church care group in the fall of 2008, but in 2012 we were asked to lead another care group which we have continued to be involved with until the present time. In 2009, Maggie was appointed to the Congregational Care Team of our church, with the responsibility of caring for parents with new babies. She also attended many of the meetings of a Parents and Tots program in the church on Monday mornings.

One of the things that attracted us to this church was the senior's group in our church, somewhat misleadingly labeled the 50+/- group, which met every second and fourth Wednesday morning. We were asked to take over the leadership of this group in 2010 for a two-year term together with Henry and Elsie Flaming as our advisors. Maggie was in charge of coordinating the snacks, while I coordinated the "cognitive" dimension of our get-togethers. We rotated between four types of events – members telling their life-stories, guest speakers, presentations on "Aging and Dying," and times of fellowship. The group grew in size during our tenure and reached an average attendance of 50 people. We continue to appreciate this life-line of fellowship with the seniors in our church. I have also joined a group of senior men who go cycling once a week during the summer months on the many trails made out of abandoned railway lines in the Waterloo region.

We attended the main worship service at WNMC for a number of years, but some concerns about this service made us switch to the earlier more liturgical matins service in 2016. I have had the privilege of preaching fairly often in both services, though eventually I was mainly giving homilies in the matins services.[12] I had my name entered in the guest speakers list of Mennonite Church Eastern Canada and this led to invitations to preach in a number of churches in the Waterloo area and beyond.[13] A highlight was a weekend series at the Leamington United Mennonite Church where I did a series on biblical ethics in the fall of 2018. I also taught a number of Sunday School series in our own church.[14] A highlight here was a two-part series I did on intellectual virtues and vices in the fall of 2019.

I was hoping to somehow get connected with the university environment after we got to Waterloo. I soon joined a book club on the WLU campus which gets together every two weeks during the fall and winter semesters. The group consists mainly of Reformed and Mennonite professors and is led by Brian Bork, the Reformed chaplain on both campuses. Although discussions have at times been dominated by a few individuals, the meetings are nonetheless stimulating and I have continued attending throughout my years of retirement. I was also hoping to get involved in campus ministries in some way and so I initiated contact with the local branches of InterVarsity Christian Fellowship and Campus Crusade for Christ, soon after we arrived in Waterloo. Little came of this.

In 2017 I connected with Ryan Kreuzer, the staff leader of Power2Change, the new name for Campus Crusade. We met to discuss my interest in doing a four to six week course on one or both of the university campuses on "Worldviews and the Christian Mind." This led to an invitation to speak to both groups at their regular meetings in 2019. I was a bit taken aback by the hyper-evangelistic overtones of both groups, but tried to steer them to a more balanced perspective in my lectures. I was asked a little later to do a four-week study series on worldviews on the U of W campus and was pleased to see that it was mainly upper year students who were attending, with attendance increasing to over a dozen by the end.

We have faced some interesting challenges at WNMC. When we officially joined the church I made a statement to the effect we appreciated the clear Mennonite theological identity of this church, and that in some ways, we felt as though we had come to our theological home. Sadly, we can no longer say this. Over time we discovered considerable diversity of theological opinion in the church. I had studied the Mennonite confession of faith before we joined and liked it, but what we didn't realize was that the confession of faith was seen as optional by some (many) members of the church, including people in leadership, with some (many) leaning towards a rather liberal theology. Learning to navigate these waters has been an interesting learning experience about which I will say more in Chapter 11.

We have taken a number of steps to address the feeling of theological isolation that we have been experiencing at WNMC. For one, I have had to clarify for myself the boundaries between orthodoxy and non-orthodoxy. Reading has also played an important role in nurturing my orthodox faith. As already mentioned, we made a gradual switch to attending mainly the matins services where the liturgy involves more reading of Scripture, the singing of the Lord's Prayer, and the reciting of one of the church creeds. There is less room for error in a liturgical service! I have also on occasion attended other churches in person or on-line.

Since 2012 we have also been part of a Care Group which I lead and which usually includes bible study and prayer. I have also been part of two book clubs, one at WLU and a church book club. Although there is some diversity of theological opinion in these groups, the general orientation is more orthodox. Since 2016 I have also been meeting monthly with two other Christian academics, Len Friesen and Markus Poetzsch, for fellowship and theological discussion. Though we attend different churches and represent different age groups, we agree on orthodox faith and our discussions have been most invigorating and encouraging. Spiritual nourishment has also come via music – the annual concerts of the Grand Philharmonic Choir, singing Handel's Messiah or Bach's Christmas Oratorio, and Bach's St. John's or St. Matthew's Passion at Easter. I have also been spiritually fed by the Bach Vespers Services of the Spiritus Ensemble led by Ken Hull. Bach certainly gives expression to an orthodox faith and he clearly loved his Savior and Lord. Thank you Johann Sebastian Bach.

HOLIDAYS

Since retirement, holidays have been a much bigger part of our lives than in the past. Yes, during my career we had family gatherings at Christmas and we always did some major holidaying during the summer months, but after retirement we had more time for holidays. Besides, our children were now married and had families of their own and so we enjoyed different kinds of holidays. In August of 2008 we went on a camping holiday at Awenda Park with our Ontario children and six grand-children. In the following year, after our return from Belgium, we had to make a quick adjustment to an Easter weekend holiday with our family, at a large cottage in the Crieff Hills retreat center, near Guelph. Greg and Laura were down for a week, so it was good to have the entire family together once again. That same summer we went camping at the Pinery with our Ontario children and grandchildren. We also got together as a family at Christmas a few times.[15]

Of special significance for us were two one-week holidays in summer with the entire family. In August of 2014, we had a delightful family holiday at Loghaven Cabin, on Lake Manitouwabing, near Parry Sound.[16] We had several days of rain, but this didn't really dampen our spirits as there was enough space in the cabin to spread out. Our entire family was there, with Greg and Laura stopping by on their way back from a holiday in Iceland. Audrey was our main chef and served us many gourmet meals. We had lots of fun swimming, sailing, kayaking, canoeing, cliff-jumping, playing tennis, doing puzzles, going on hikes, and enjoying some good conversations. Maggie and I also spent some time with our children and spouses talking about our health, finances, and arrangements for care as we get older. We had such a good time that we resolved that we should do this again. So in 2017, the year of our 50th wedding anniversary, we had another celebration at Log Escape Cabin, which was in fact located just beside Loghaven Cabin which we had rented earlier. I have already described this celebration in the concluding section of Chapter 2.

New for us after retirement were winter holidays spent in the Caribbean. We took our first winter holiday in January of 2010 – a one-week stay at the "Playa Pesquero" resort, in Cuba, a sixty-minute drive from the Holguin airport. It was good to relax and enjoy the sunshine and I certainly enjoyed the swimming. But we found the atmosphere of such a resort quite decadent. What we probably enjoyed most was a tour through the country-side, including a visit to a typical farm, complete with a display of a 1948 Plymouth, still in working condition, obviously the owner's pride and joy. I probably took note of this car because my Dad bought a brand new 1948 Plymouth when we lived in Saskatchewan many years earlier.

After a number of further Caribbean holidays, we made a decision to try something different for our winter holidays.[17] Rather than arranging for another holiday with the entire family, we decided to take each family separately for the next few years. Their job was to entertain us! We started with Greg and Laura in February of 2015. Laura had always wanted to go to St. Martin and so we found a lovely small hotel, Le Petit, on the French side of St. Martin and right on the

St. Martin, 2015

beach. The rooms were charming, and the hosts were most gracious, welcoming us with some brandy on the beach. Breakfast was included and it was so good to enjoy leisurely breakfasts on our balconies, overlooking the

ocean. St. Martin is known for good restaurants, and we thoroughly enjoyed many a gourmet meal. The following year we took Andrew and Rachel, and Josiah and Lauren, to Costa Rica. Highlights here were trips to the rain forest and a chocolate factory. In 2017

Costa Rica, 2016

it was the Wichert's turn, though collecting everyone was a bit more complicated as Madeleine was at Canadian Mennonite University in Winnipeg and Arianne was at Rosthern Junior College. We tried something different

this year, renting a villa at the Silversands Resort in Jamaica. The Villa came complete with two cooks and they were delighted when we encouraged them to feed us real Jamaican food – jerk chicken, jerk pork, lobster, shrimp, and some fine soups. The meals were a highlight for the

Jamaica, 2017

entire family. Another highlight was a visit with our friends, Faith and Ivan Linton and their Cranbrook Nature Resort, complete with a long hike in a rain forest.

Following these holidays with our family, Maggie and I returned to taking our winter holidays on our own.[18] Since our retirement, we have also taken some major holidays involving tours and cruises.

Turkey: In the fall of 2014 we did a two-week Insight Vacation Tour of Turkey, after my participation in the Evangelical-Orthodox Consultation in Albania. It was rather romantic to meet Maggie in the plush Marriot Hotel in Istanbul after the Consultation. This was the first time that we had gone on a tour like this, where everything was pre-planned, and we rather liked it. We had an excel-

Aspendos, southern Turkey; one of the best preserved Roman theatres in the world

lent tour-guide and bus driver, and a good group of fellow-tourists, mainly from Australia. The tour was divided into two parts. The first week covered inland Turkey and included Bursa, once the capital city of the Ottoman Empire, and a charming Cumalikizik Village. We also enjoyed our time in Cappadocia, the unique region of volcanic landscapes and Goreme's rock-carved churches. We found the stories of early Christians hiding in these mushroom shaped "fairy-chimneys" to be quite moving. After the first week we got to the southern coastline and I enjoyed a swim in the Mediterranean in Antalya. Then over the Taurus mountains and on to various ancient ruins, including Ephesus, where I knelt and kissed the ground to pay homage to the apostle Paul. Visiting the sites that were important in early church history was a moving experience for us.

Russia/Ukraine: In the fall of 2016 we did a two-week tour of Russia and the Ukraine with TourMagination. We enjoyed the splendors of St. Petersburg even though it was raining for much of the time. After Petersburg, we boarded a high-speed train to take us to Moscow. It was cold in Moscow, so we were thankful that we could spend a good chunk of the time in the many magnificent cathedrals, museums, and art galleries in that city.

We then spent an entire day getting from Moscow to the Ukraine via Munich, Kiev, Dnepropetrovsk, and Zaporoszhye. A direct flight would have taken us only four hours. The weather in the Ukraine was finally sunny and warm, and we enjoyed our tours of the former

Halbstadt Zentralschule

Mennonite colonies of Chortiza and Molotscha. What were the highlights of our one-day trip to the Molotschna? Seeing the prairie landscape, much like our Canadian prairies. Driving through the Mennonite villages, trying to imagine what life was like during the time of our Mennonite forebearers. Seeing grape arbors in front of many of the houses. Standing in front of the Halbstadt Zentralschule – this is the school that my Dad attended, and where 200 students were trained and armed to form a formidable little army – a Mennonite Selbschutz. In Halbstadt, we also visited the Mennonite Centre, supported by a group of Mennonites in Canada who are involved in providing aid and sponsoring various projects in the area.

After lunch, we travelled through Tiege where Maggie's father, Gerhard, was born in 1901. We also drove by Kurushan, where Maggie's parents met while working at an old folks home. Towards the end of the day we came to the village of Lichtfelde. It was here where Maggie's mother was baptized in the Lichtfelde Allianz Church and where Maggie's parents moved after they were married. Gerhard then got a job as a secretary/treasurer in his uncle's store in Lichtfelde. It was here that their first son, Edelbert was born in October of 1925. It was from here that they emigrated to Canada in October 1926. The Thiessen family also lived in Lichtfelde, moving there shortly after my father John and his brother Jacob began attending high school, an all boy's school, which was really a trade school, in Alexanderkrone.

We then passed through the village of Kleefeld, which was the last home of the Thiessen family – my Dad was teaching in Friedensruh at the time. Next we visited a farm in the village of Alexanderkrone where both of our families had connections. From the site of an old Dutch-type windmill,

I could see some fields where the village of Friedensruh used to exist, and where my Dad had his first teaching position (age twenty-five). He enjoyed his work so much that he nearly decided not to join the rest of the family when they emigrated in 1923.

Unfortunately, it was getting dark when we got to the villages that were of special importance to me and so we were a bit rushed. We did get off the bus at Rueckenau for a few minutes while a few of us walked part of the main village street where my Dad spent the first fourteen or fifteen years of his life. At the end of the village we saw the M.B. Church where my grandfather was pastor. We got out briefly and I made a point of kissing the ground where my father had probably walked many years ago. Then on to Fuerstenwerder, where my grandmother Thiessen was born, where my grandfather got his first teaching appointment, and where my Uncle Jake also taught later. Visiting my father's birthplace and the villages where he lived and first started teaching felt very much like a pilgrimage for me.

Ireland: I have already alluded to our eleven-day tour of Ireland in the fall of 2017 with Royal Irish Tours as part of our fiftieth wedding anniversary celebrations (see concluding section of Chapter 2).

River Cruise: In May and early June of 2019 we took a nine-day river cruise from Budapest to Bucharest. This was the first time we did a river cruise and we quite enjoyed visiting various cities along the Danube in Eastern Europe. All told we visited six countries, starting in Austria, then Hungary, Croatia, Serbia, Bulgaria, and finally Romania.

Canadian holidays:  Closer to home, we have enjoyed many shorter holidays. We started with a bang in 2008. Andrew took me on a canoe trip in the French River district of northern Ontario in May. (I enjoyed two other canoe trips with Andrew in the following years). After a family camping experience in Awenda in the fall of 2008, we tacked on a short more luxurious holiday in Tobermorey, staying at a B&B. Given our new status as retirees, who could take holidays at unusual times, we took another week's holiday to the Gaspe Peninsula in Quebec later in September. A beautiful trip, though the weather was a bit cold and windy. Later still, we flew to Alberta for a weekend visiting our children in Lethbridge before Christmas. We have enjoyed taking many other planned and spontaneous holidays in Ontario over the years. Another highlight was a two-week holiday to Newfoundland in June of 2010.

We have also tried to visit Greg and Laura in Alberta on a regular basis over the years. This has also allowed us to get our mountain fix from time to time, as we miss the Rocky Mountains after our move to Ontario. In this regard, several trips out west stand out for us.[19] In the fall of 2013 we met Greg and Laura at their new condo at the Fernie ski resort. We celebrated Laura's birthday with a gourmet dinner at the Island Lake Lodge high up in the mountains. We had a delightful time exploring Fernie and hiking up to a beautiful lake in the mountains. Greg and Laura left on Sunday but we stayed on for a few more days and enjoyed their condo. Before returning home, we flew to Saskatoon to visit Alvina and Abe, my sister and brother-in-law. This was the first time we had seen Abe after he began suffering from Alzheimers, so it was a bit difficult seeing him in this condition. A few weeks after we returned, Abe was moved to Luther Care Home, after which I spent many hours on the phone helping Alvina adjust to this new reality.[20]

In August of 2019 we flew out west for a thirteen-day holiday. We first went to Lethbridge to see Greg and Laura who were in the middle of adding an addition to their house to accommodate Laura's counselling office. The following day we all went to Island Lake Resort high up in the mountains near Fernie. We enjoyed many good conversations over gourmet meals during our three-days at the resort. We even did a hike in the mountains, with Greg helping his mother over some of the rough spots. The weather was perfect. Maggie and I then did a major road trip (thirty-five hours of driving), visiting friends and relatives in Alberta and

Saskatchewan – a total of sixteen visits with individuals or families. We also stopped in Swift Current to visit the gravesites of my Mom and Dad (see pictures in the final section of Chapter 1). Then it was on to Medicine Hat where we visited our former church and renewed acquaintances from our 36-year stay in the Hat.

HEALTH ISSUES

We are very thankful that we have both experienced fairly good health during our retirement. But we are getting older and this brings with it increasing health concerns. Soon after our arrival in Ontario we were able to find a family doctor, Lisa McFarlane, who has been a superb doctor, caring and conscientious, who follows up issues personally on the phone, and is even willing to admit when she makes mistakes. I was still on anti-depressants when we arrived in Ontario, but Dr. McFarlane soon came to the conclusion that I had regained mental stability and so no longer needed them. I am now much more sensitive to stress levels and so can monitor my mental health which has been surprisingly good since retirement. I encountered significant back problems soon after our move to Ontario but finally found a physiotherapist who has prescribed core-muscle exercises that have in the main helped me to avoid further problems. Dr. McFarlane has also prescribed treatments for my osteoporosis. I have worked hard at keeping myself healthy, doing exercises, walking each day, swimming once a week, and cycling during the summers.

In the summer of 2010, Maggie experienced several weeks of increasing racing of the heart and irregular heart beat or atrial fibrillation. This resulted in two visits to the emergency department at St. Mary's Hospital where she was treated for congestive heart failure (July 28, 2010 and January 26, 2012). I found the first of these visits rather frightening, because I didn't know what congestive heart failure was and assumed the worst. Maggie was also put under the care of cardiologist Dr. Rinne who recommended an ablation which was attempted at the London Health Sciences Centre in January of 2014, but with no success. We therefore had to settle for continuing treatment of her fibrillation and flutter by medication.

We had for many years been aware of the possibility that Maggie might need heart surgery at some point in time. In 2017, decreasing energy levels, increasing coughing, and increasing doses of Lasix to drain fluids in her lungs led Dr. Rinne to suggest that surgery would be needed soon.[21] So in the fall of 2018, Maggie underwent heart surgery to replace the mitral heart valve and repair the tricuspid valve. I was happy to have Audrey with me to navigate this day. After a 4 ½ hour wait our surgeon finally came to the waiting area to inform us that the surgery was done and everything was fine. She was released after six days and made an amazingly rapid recovery. After participating in a seventeen-week cardiac rehab program, her energy level was clearly much better than before surgery We were and are thankful to God and to the advances of modern medicine for her new lease on life.

But our troubles weren't over yet. In mid-October of 2019, Maggie noticed a lump in her left breast. She visited her doctor a short while later who quickly arranged for some tests at the Freeport Cancer Centre. A later visit with the surgeon, Dr. Maurice, confirmed that this was cancer and he recommended a lumpectomy. The surgery was scheduled for December 5, and amazingly after just eleven hours in the hospital, we were both back at home. Unfortunately the pathology report given by the surgeon in a follow-up appointment suggested that not all the cancerous tissue had been removed. So another surgery (a mastectomy) was scheduled for January 9, 2020. Recovery this time around was even better than with the first surgery. Thankfully no radiation was thought to be necessary by the oncologist but Maggie was put on some medications to lessen the risk of further cancer.

DEATHS

It is perhaps to be expected that the last section of a chapter on retirement and aging might end with the subject of deaths in the family. Deaths of some of Maggie's siblings came earlier (see Chapter 5). In October of 2009, I made a trip to Quesnel, B.C. to visit my sister Ruth who had been diagnosed with pancreatic cancer in the summer of that year. I had some difficulty making the decision to visit Ruth as our relationship was not that close. But it was good to spend time with Bob and Ruth, and also with Lottie, who was in Quesnel taking care of Ruth. Etched in my memory is hearing my younger sister crying out that she really didn't want to die. Ruth died on May 4, 2010, a few hours after she had made the decision to go to a hospice.

I was somewhat ambivalent about going to the funeral as we were getting mixed messages from the family and we didn't know what the funeral would be like. In the end Alvina and I decided we would both fly to Abbotsford, and Ted and Cathy would take us all to Quesnel for the memorial service held on May 11, 2010. At the beginning of the memorial celebration, we were informed that the family had requested that there be nothing religious said at the service. I paid a tribute to Ruth, commenting on her early life and ending with a Latin benediction from Verdi's *Requiem* which was indeed religious in nature but wouldn't be understood by the family. I couldn't help but feel rather numb over the hollowness of an "ir-religious" memorial service. Ruth deserved better than that. It was hard to believe that my younger sister was no longer with us.

Abe Klassen, Alvina's husband, had retired in 2007, but was soon de-clining because of Alzheimers. Alvina tried to take care of him at home for a few years, but eventually he had to be put in a specialized nursing home. The family wasn't entirely happy with the care he was receiving and Alvina tried to make up for this by visiting him nearly every day. He had a bad fall one night in the spring of 2015 while he was walking about, and his death a few weeks later might have been related to this, though the cause was un-known. He died on June 11, 2015, at the age of eighty-two. In some ways it was a relief for everyone – his debilitating condition with Alzheimers was finally over.

My only brother, Ted, died of a heart attack on January 22, 2018, while at work in his own company that he had formed since his retirement, Kerith Creek Auto Transfer. News of his death came as a shock because he was in good health even though he was already eighty-six years old. Alvina and I both flew to Abbotsford for the funeral. I was asked to give a tribute at the service, and it was sobering to reflect on Ted's early life which in some ways was more difficult than mine, given that he was ten years older than me. It was good to meet with the family in a restaurant after the fu-neral. So now two of my siblings were gone – a sobering reminder for the three remaining siblings.

How does one conclude a chapter that describes one's retirement and aging? Perhaps a brief update on the lives of our grandchildren would be in place. They are after all an important gauge of our own aging. (See the latest fam-ily picture at the end of Chapter 2.) When we moved to Waterloo in 2007 they were all still children, though the oldest had already entered her teens. Madeleine graduated from the Canadian Mennonite University in 2017, and has worked in social services in Winnipeg for a few years. She returned to Ontario in the fall of 2020 to take a Masters of Teaching program in environmental education at the Ontario Institute for Studies in Education. Sylvie graduated (virtually) from the University of Toronto, Scarborough campus, in the spring of 2020, with a degree in Environmental Science and is currently working for the Impact Assessment Agency of Canada, tracking the progress of government environmental initiatives. Sylvie is also a prolific writer of fantasy novels which are being published on Wattpad.

Ariane is majoring in equity studies with minors in psychology and human geography at the University of Toronto and will be getting her degree in the summer of 2021. She has a passion for helping the marginalized. Beatrice will graduate from a high school that specializes in mathematics, science and technology in the spring of 2021, and is very much involved in dance and ballet. Josiah graduated from high school in the spring of 2020, but was unable to attend a formal graduation ceremony due to Covid-19. He is most proficient in computer programming and is hoping eventually to get a job programming computer games. He is currently taking a gap year, working in a grocery store. Lauren, our youngest grandchild will be taking her Grade 11 virtually in 2020-21, due to the pandemic which is creating havoc for schools. She has a passion for learning about other cultures and is hoping to get training in ESL instruction and then go to Korea to teach English. We are proud of all of our grandchildren and have enjoyed seeing them grow up and become young adults.

Of course, we too are growing older. But it is not over yet. As I am reviewing this chapter for the second time in April of 2020, we are in the midst of the corona virus (Covid-19) pandemic. Indeed, on Maggie's 81st birthday earlier in March, Canada was essentially put on lock-down, with the warning that the elderly were particularly susceptible to the virus. Thus began a long wait and a long lesson in dependence on God. I was studying Philippians during this time, and couldn't help but notice what Paul said about living and dying. "For me to live is Christ ... (and to die) is to "be with Christ," so it really is a toss-up as to which is to be preferred (Phil 1:21, 23). Christ is central in all this. So this philosopher's journey will also end with Christ. That is a consolation.

NOTES

1. Following my year of teaching at Tyndale University College I was asked to give a lecture on "The Call of the Teacher" at their annual Faculty Retreat in August of 2010.

2. 91% of the students gave the course a 4 or 5 rating (out of 5) on the question, "An excellent course?" Most of the written comments were very positive, with several students saying the course was the best course they had ever taken and one that they would recommend to others. Even those who described the course as very challenging, most often added that they had learned a lot, that the course had made them think, or that the course was "hugely worldview altering."

3. The blog can be accessed at https://elmerjohnthiessen.wordpress.com/

4. In the fall of 2010 I gave a lecture on "Teaching for Committed Openness" at the Ontario Christian Teachers Association Educators Convention, held at Redeemer University College. I was also invited to participate in a workshop on "Religious Education in a Democratic Society" at McGill University in Montreal in January of 2016.

5. In October of 2015 I was asked to give two plenary addresses on "The Ethics of Assisted Suicide," and "Dignity and Dying," at the Canadian Mennonite Health Assembly, held in Waterloo. Available at https://www.commonword.ca/ResourceView/48/18495

6. I gave a lecture on "The Ethics of Proselytizing within the Context of Pluralism" at the 40th Anniversary Conference of The Toronto School of Theology, which had as its theme, "Ecumenism and the Challenges of Pluralism" (May 7-8, 2010). I also presented a paper, "The Ethics of Evangelism," at the International Cultic Studies Association (ICSA), held in Montreal, July 5-7, 2012. I was very pleased to be invited to give a plenary address on "The Ethics of Witness in the Health Care Context" at an annual conference of the Centre of Spiritual Life and Wholeness held at the Loma Linda University School of Health Sciences, California, January 17-18, 2014.

7. The Swiss/French contingent of the assembly put together an anthology based on the presentations made at the consultation and asked me to contribute a chapter. So I wrote "The Ethics of Evangelism and Integral Mission," which was translated into French.

8. My group was chaired by Richard Harvey, working with Jews for Jesus in the UK. Other members of my group included Grace Mathews, co-chair of the consultation, Sergyey Koryakin, a convert to Orthodoxy, but still teaching at the Moscow Evangelical Christian Seminary, Katerina Pekridou, a Ph.D. student from Greece, with whom I had several conversations, Alfred Golloshi, an Albanian evangelical preacher, and Metropolitan Mar Diascoros, from India. This group was really a good representation of the diversity present at this consultation.

9. Responses to my paper were given by an evangelical, Dr. Danut Manastireanu, head of World Vision in Romania, and by Metropolitan Dr. Youhanon Mar Demetrios, head of the Syrian Orthodox Church in North India. I (and others) felt that both responses really didn't wrestle with the key focus of my paper, which was on ethical norms. Instead, they both highlighted past ethical failures in evangelism. And both responses said little about the last section of my paper dealing with the tensions between evangelicals and Orthodox on the issue of sheep-stealing. In any case I responded to these papers later in "Reply to Responses (by Danut Manastireanu and Metropolitan Yuhanon Mar Demetrios)" in *The Mission of God: Studies in Orthodox and Evangelical Mission,* edited by Mark Oxbrow and Tim Grass (Oxford: Regnum/Brookline, MA: Holy Cross Orthodox Press, 2015), pp.148-154.

10. This invitation came from Larry Miller who had heard me at the Evangelical-Orthodox Consultation in Albania. They were hoping that I would come at my own expense or raise the necessary funds. I had tried getting some money for my Albania trip, but was unsuccessful, so I simply declined the offer. A few months later I got another letter from Larry Miller, informing me that the WEA had agreed to pay for all of my expenses. Thomas Schirrmacher, President of the WEA, who had written a favorable review of my earlier book on the ethics of evangelism wanted me there as a consultant. I really didn't have any other good reason to decline, so I accepted the invitation.

11. "An Evangelical View of Proselytism," in *Evangelical Review of Theology*. Vol 42, #4, (2018), pp. 308-318.

12. As of September 1, 2020, I have given a total of 35 sermons or homilies at WNMC.

13. As of September 1, 2020, I have given ten sermons at Grace M.B. Church, plus another seventeen sermons in churches in the Waterloo region and beyond.

14. Early in our stay at WNMC I did a series on biblical ethics – rather daring, I realize now. I taught several series of bible studies as a second adult Sunday School class – studies of Amos, Daniel, and 1 Peter. I also did a three-part series on a Christian Worldview in March 2015.

15. In 2012, we all spent Christmas together at Kimbercote Farm, near Collingwood, Ontario, with Greg and Laura joining us for the four days of celebration. We did this again as an entire family in 2018, this time at a cottage near the Blue Mountain Resort.

16. I had spent a lot of time researching cabins big enough for our entire family and finally settled on a beautiful and spacious log cabin right on the lake, owned by Morley Spiderman and his wife who rent out their family cabin when they aren't there themselves. The cost was a bit steep ($7,000 for the week), but it was worth it.

17. Other winter holidays included a week at a B&B in Jamaica in 2011 with our long-time friends, Al and Sue Enns. Earlier in this chapter I described our planned one-week family winter holiday at a resort in Mexico early in 2012 as part of my seventieth birthday celebrations (see "Anniversaries" section earlier in the chapter). Unfortunately we could not join our children for this holiday because Maggie experienced some significant heart problems just before we were about to leave. We did however book our winter holiday in the following year at the same resort, and had fun imagining our children enjoying this resort in the previous year. In February of 2014 we went to Bermuda together with Maggie's cousin, Irene Klassen and her husband John.

18. In February of 2018 we travelled to St. Petersburg, Florida for a one week holiday. The weather was beautiful, though our time here was marred with Maggie getting the flu, but we did get to see the efficiency of a first-class U.S. hospital. In 2019 we were back in Florida once again, this time spending a week at a B&B in St. Augustine, the oldest city of the USA, first settled by the Spanish.

19. In March of 2011 we spent some time with Greg and Laura at a condo in Canmore. We returned to Lethbridge for a few days and while there visited Henry and Susan Pauls, as we usually do on our visits out west, and also Marj and Dallas Miller, former students of mine.

20. In the summer of 2015, we were delighted to have my sister Alvina join us for our week of holidays out west. The weather was perfect and we had a wonderful time driving

through the mountains in our rented Jeep Cherokee, visiting Jasper, Lake Louise, and Banff. After a week of touring, we went on to Lethbridge so we could spend a few days with Greg and Laura.

21. This led to a catheterization in April of 2018 resulting in a verdict that surgery was indeed needed.

Chapter 8
HIGHER EDUCATION, SCIENCE, REASON, AND FAITH

It was my final year at the University of Saskatchewan (1966). The local chapter of Inter-Varsity Christian Fellowship held a Christian mission on campus that same year and the main speaker was John W. Montgomery, an historian, Lutheran theologian, and Christian apologist. He was also invited to give a lecture in one of my philosophy classes and I was deeply impressed with his clear reasoning. I asked if I could meet with him to discuss my doubts and also a paper I had prepared, "A.J. Ayer and Religious Knowledge," which I was going to present to the philosophy club. He readily agreed to meet with me and so I gave him a copy of my paper. We met later and his first comment was, "This is a great paper. You should definitely go on in philosophy or theology."[1] Just two sentences! Dr. Montgomery didn't realize that I needed this kind of encouragement at the time. Indeed, as I reflect back on this incident I realize that it was this little word of encouragement that played a significant role in having me continue my education in philosophy. I hope that in my teaching career I will have offered similar words of encouragement to my students needing the same.

I spent much of my life getting educated. Hence the need for a chapter describing my experiences during the various stages of my undergraduate and graduate education. Interwoven in these descriptions there will also be reflections on developments in my own thinking with regard to my studies in science and philosophy, and their relation to the Christian faith.

This chapter marks a shift of approach in my memoirs. The first seven chapters have been more chronological and autobiographical in nature. The chapters that follow are topical in nature and will in fact be more memoir-like. In these chapters I want to reflect on certain aspects of my life, on how my faith intersected with my studies, on my experiences as a teacher, on my research and writing, and on my church experiences. Obviously there will be some overlap between these chapters and the earlier more autobiographical chapters. I have tried to avoid unnecessary repetition. Most often, when there is some overlap, I will have given an abbreviated version of events in the earlier chapters and an expanded version in these later chapters.

In this chapter I am reflecting on my experiences as an undergraduate and graduate student. I did well in the sciences in high school. After graduating from the Swift Current Collegiate Institute in 1959, I received a scholarship to attend university and so proceeded to the University of Saskatchewan to study science with the aim of becoming a high school teacher. It was a very difficult year, in part because I was grieving my father's death in the previous summer; in part because of loneliness; in part because I simply wasn't mature enough for university; and in part because I was scared about what a university education would do to my faith. Indeed, my dear grandfather, a well-known Mennonite Brethren preacher, was opposed to my going directly to university from high school. I survived the year, thanks in a large measure to the support of a Christian community on campus – InterVarsity Christian Fellowship (IVCF). I will have more to say about my initial and later experiences at the University of Saskatchewan shortly. But first a "religious" interlude in my education.

MENNONITE BRETHREN BIBLE COLLEGE (MBBC)

It had always been my intention to get some bible training at some point in my education. Given the many difficulties I faced during my first year at university, I decided to interrupt my university education in order to study at MBBC in Winnipeg – my intent was to stay only one year with a focus on getting a better understanding of the bible. During my first year, I took every available bible course and thoroughly enjoyed getting a deeper understanding of the Scriptures. David Ewert's courses in particular showed me how careful scholarship and a love of Scripture can go hand in hand. In the end, I stayed at MBBC for three years, graduating in 1963.

I benefited enormously from my three years at MBBC, not least in terms of simply growing up. I was immature for my age, self-absorbed, and struggling with an inferiority complex.[2] I was probably the youngest student at MBBC, as many students at that time already had a degree or profession. I am thankful for the roommates who put up with me, for example, Walter Penner during my first year, who was an example of mature stability and who encouraged me to "be myself." I was often an instigator of water fights in the boys dorm during the first year, probably to the annoyance of the rest of the fellows in the dorm. But they put up with my feeble attempts to be myself. I am also thankful for the close friendships I developed over those three years. Of particular significance here were Nick Wiens, David Derksen, and John Regehr, who was my roommate in my final year, together with Vic Neufeldt.

My sister Alvina was also attending MBBC during this time, and I owe her special thanks for supporting me and giving me the encouragement that I needed every once in a while. During my second year, I had the pleasure of observing Abe Klassen courting Alvina. They were married July 28, 1962. My own foray into romance began rather clumsily during my third year and is described in more detail in Chapter 2.

Two incidents stand out for me in terms of hampering the development of my self-confidence while at MBBC. I was taking piano lessons and doing quite well, even completing the Grade 8 Royal Conservatory exams. I remember a conducting class with Victor Martens where I had to play the piano for a certain hymn and where he then proceeded to critique my playing of the hymn in front of the whole class. Then there was J.J. Toews, who liked pulpit-thumping despite a missing finger, and who was teaching a class on "Christian Education," or something to that effect. I hated the class and went to his office to discuss dropping it, whereupon he suggested that I should continue because I would never become a pastor or preacher given my physical handicaps. Of course I knew what he meant. Ah yes, even teachers at bible colleges have their weaknesses. May God be merciful to these men of God!

During the graduation banquet I was introduced as having questions, questions, and more frustrating questions. This would suggest that during my three years at MBBC I was raising a lot of theological questions in my classes as well as in conversations with students. Elsewhere I have described MBBC as doing little by way of encouraging critical thinking.[3] Answers were at times too pat and there was a bit of a fortress mentality at the College. But perhaps this is somewhat unfair. I was clearly allowed to ask questions. But beyond giving me a good grounding in the Scriptures, the College did little by way of preparing me for the challenges I would face when I entered the field of philosophy. However, my studies in theology and the history of the church did help me to develop some competence in the humanities – I nearly failed an introductory English course in my first year of university.

Of course, there was another dimension to my college and university experience – summer months. I came to appreciate the cycle of studying during the fall and winter semesters and then working in the summer months. By the end of a college or university year I was ready to do something very different, and by the end of the summer I was quite ready to get back to studies. I was fortunate to find a summer job at Bowman Brothers, an auto parts distributing centre in Swift Current, after my first year at the University of Saskatchewan. I kept this job for a good number of years, even getting raises – my salary was increased to $250 per month in 1964. I also did a lot of work at home during the summers, maintaining our large garden and even doing some house renovations. Our home situation was of course difficult with no father around. My two younger sisters missed their Dad a lot, and my Mother feared the worst for them. I am not sure that I as an older brother was enough of a support to my sisters during these early years without a father.

UNIVERSITY OF SASKATCHEWAN (U OF S)

I returned to U of S in 1963 to finish my science degree. During that first year of my return I took a course in philosophy and got a 90% in my final grade, and after that I was hooked. In the end, I went on to complete an honours year (i.e. a four-year B.A.), ending up with a double major in physics and philosophy. My first philosophy teacher was an ex-Baptist, turned agnostic or atheist. Professor T.Y. Henderson loved to spend the first fifteen minutes of many a philosophy class heaping ridicule on the Billy Graham column of the local paper, the *Saskatoon Star Phoenix*. I still remember one of the essays that I wrote for him in a later course in the philosophy of religion in which I made a valiant effort to provide a rational defence of religion – my first feeble attempt to integrate the faith of Athens with the faith of Jerusalem. When I got the paper back, Professor Henderson had written the equivalent of another whole essay of comments in glaring red ink. But he still gave me an "A" on the paper. I also remember a philosophy professor who often came to class drunk. Somehow we as students managed to cope with this.

Why did I switch from science to philosophy? It wasn't easy to make this change. Indeed, in my diary, I recorded times of confusion and doubt about making this transition. Some members of my family were strongly opposed to my entering the field of philosophy which they viewed with some suspicion. But I was facing increasing disenchantment with physics. Yes, there was something satisfying about precise formulas on a blackboard, but how did these formulas relate to existential questions about life and its meaning? Learning about the laws of science seemed to me to be increasingly unimportant and superficial. After all, science itself rests on philosophical assumptions, and it was these assumptions that I was finding increasingly intriguing.

My final course in the sciences was Physics 351 – an Introduction to Modern Physics. I had told my professor that I was considering switching from physics to philosophy and thankfully he empathized with my divided loyalties. He loved to tease the class by pushing the boundaries of science into discussions of philosophical assumptions underlying nuclear physics. I loved these integrative excursions, and it made my transition to philosophy easier. But Professor Montalbetti was a bit ahead of his time in recognizing that ultimately science is shaped by worldviews and perhaps even theology!

In part, my enchantment with philosophy was also due to the tensions it created with regard to my Christian faith. I wanted to test my faith. I wanted to see if it could withstand the challenges of rigorous thinking, and philosophy seemed to be the area where the challenge might be the hottest. I still remember my hesitation in reading Bertrand Russell's *Why I am not a Christian*.[4] It remained on my shelves for quite some time before I mustered the courage to read it. I was rather delighted to discover that the book wasn't as threatening to my faith as I thought it would be. The margins of my copy of this book are scribbled full of my rebuttals to Russell's objections to Christianity.

SCIENCE, EMPIRICISM, AND THE CHRISTIAN FAITH

Here let me reflect a little on my background in science and my resulting struggles with the Christian faith. There were parts of science that I loved. It was precise, it dealt with the observable, and it produced clear-cut answers. I absorbed the typical twentieth century attitudes towards science, attitudes that were shaped by the Enlightenment. Science is objective, and it gives us certainty and knowledge. My studies in science also shaped my philosophical outlook. It gave me a very healthy respect for empiricism, which claims that knowledge must be based on the five senses. I still believe this, at least in part. Although reasoning is important, and no good scientist would deny this, our rationality is ultimately rooted in the data we get via the five senses. All of us are fundamentally reliant on our five senses in acquiring the beliefs we hold. Think of a child – fascinated with seeing, touching, feeling. We as adults are no different. When we demand of someone, "prove it to me," we generally mean, "show me." That is the best way to clinch an argument.

Of course, empiricism seems to create a significant challenge to the Christian faith. God is beyond sense experience. Small wonder that the so-called "Enlightenment," with its devotion to reason and science, led to an increasing scepticism about religious faith. David Hume, eighteenth century British empiricist, argued that any claims that could not be empirically proven should be banished to the flames. German philosopher, Immanuel Kant, proposed that we deny the possibility of knowledge (i.e. scientific knowledge) in the religious sphere, in order to make room for faith. My M.A. thesis explored Kant's resulting notion of God.

The issue of empirical verification was at the heart of the logical positivist movement that began in the 1920s and had its greatest influence from the thirties to the mid-fifties. But the influence of logical positivism extended well beyond this period, and I believe it is still very influential, contrary to many philosophers who say that logical positivism is dead and buried. I wrestled with the challenge of logical positivism to religious faith in my early studies in philosophy. During my fourth year at university, we studied A.J. Ayer's *Language Truth and Logic* (1936), and I couldn't help but be impressed with Ayer's verification principle: a genuinely factual statement must be empirically verifiable. During my early years of teaching a second year course in the philosophy of religion I even used a major 552-page anthology on the topic of verification and religion.[5] And this was only one of four texts for this course! I am still embarrassed about this colossal failure in adjusting the course to the appropriate level of philosophical development of my students.

But, where does the principle of verification leave God? Are not most religious claims immune to empirical verification? These questions were raising significant doubts about my Christian faith during my undergraduate studies in philosophy. Indeed, it was during my fourth year at U of S that I experienced a crisis of faith and was beginning to wonder whether intellectual integrity didn't demand a rejection of the Christian faith with which I had grown up.

It was during this same year (1966) that Inter-Varsity Christian Fellowship (IVCF) held a Christian mission on campus with John W. Montgomery as the main speaker. The story at the beginning of this chapter describes my interactions with Dr. Montgomery. Montgomery also addressed my doubts concerning the verifiability of the Christian faith, highlighting the significance of the Word becoming flesh (John 1:1-11). God entered space and time in the person of Jesus Christ. The birth, life, death, and resurrection of Jesus provide empirical proof of God's existence. I also purchased Montgomery's little book, *History & Christianity,* published by Inter-Varsity Press in 1964, which provides an outline of an historical argument for the existence of God. A later edition includes an appendix, "Faith, History and the Resurrection," where a number of scholars debate the place of faith and presuppositions in understanding the historical evidence for the resurrection. This booklet has played an important role in shaping my thinking and my faith.[6]

Over the years I have come to appreciate the significance of the incarnation as the foundation of the Christian faith. For many people, including philosophers and theologians, this foundation might seem rather flimsy, based as it is on contingent historical fact. Indeed, this is in part what lies behind Paul's claim that the preaching of Christ crucified is "a stumbling block to Jews and foolishness to Gentiles" (1 Cor. 1:23). But Paul dares to suggest that if Christ has not been raised from the dead, then "our preaching is useless and so is your faith" (1 Cor. 15:14).

It is this historical event that continues to be the bedrock of my Christian faith – God became flesh in the person of Jesus Christ. Of course there are complicating issues that need to be addressed. For one, are miracles like the virgin birth or the resurrection even possible? I have taught David Hume's classic "refutation" of the possibility of miracles many times in my introductory philosophy courses, and each time I am amazed, and a little embarrassed, to find a brilliant philosopher like Hume, so obviously arguing in a circle. I often refer to C.S. Lewis's little book entitled *Miracles* (1947), for an illuminating and trenchant critique of Hume's argument. The admission of the possibility of miracles finally hinges on a question of one's worldview and the presuppositions that underlie one's worldview. If the empirical world is all that there is to reality, then yes, the miracles of Jesus' birth and resurrection are impossible. But the claim that reality is confined to the empirical world is itself a presupposition that stands in need of justification. I will come back to presuppositions and their justification later in this chapter.

There is one further insight in the philosophy of science that I have found most helpful in articulating and defending my Christian faith. Harvard philosopher, Willard Van Orman Quine, in his analysis of "Two Dogmas of Empiricism," makes an interesting observation about the status of physical objects in science, as well as atomic particles and forces.[7] He suggests that the epistemological status of these entities in science is the same as that of the gods of religion. I think Quine has got this right. Scientists posit entities such as atoms, electrons, and quarks in order to explain what we do observe, but these posits are not directly observable. I believe it is helpful to think of the God of Christianity as a useful posit that helps believers to explain the world that we live in. The sharp distinctions often made between science and religion are unwarranted, as I have argued elsewhere.[8]

A concluding comment on what I have retained from my scientific background and my philosophical study of the verification principle in logical positivism. I still have a very healthy respect for science and the scientific method. We as human beings are deeply indebted to our five senses for most of what we believe and claim to know. God gave us these five senses to help us navigate the complexities of living in the world He created. I also have a deep appreciation for the way in which science is correctible. Any claims made in science must be verifiable and open to being critiqued. Of course this ideal is not always actualized, because scientists are after all still fallible and sinful people whose egos want protection. But the scientific ideal is still a good one. This ideal is also captured in the principles of verification and falsification of logical positivism. While I have problems with a underlying metaphysics of logical positivism, I believe there is still something right about the principles of verification and falsification. Not only scientists, but all of us, need to ensure that the claims we make can be supported by evidence and argument, and we should also always be open to having any claims we make challenged. Meaningful dialogue and debate in all areas, including religion, end when this is not the case. Failure to pursue truth and closed-mindedness are intellectual vices. Over the years I have come to a greater appreciation of the importance of intellectual virtues and hope to do some further research and writing in this area in my retirement years.

LIFE DURING MY YEARS AT THE
UNIVERSITY OF SASKATCHEWAN

I have already alluded to my first year at U of S (1959-60). It was a very difficult year for me. This was also a lonely year. I would sometimes cry myself to sleep. I recall sitting in the library wishing that my father could come and see his son studying and be a little proud of him. I also remember a visit to Uncle John (Voth) and Aunt Alice (my Dad's sister) on a Sunday, I believe. When I saw the entire family sitting at the table with a father at the head of the table,

I burst out crying. Aunt Alice kindly took me aside and comforted me until I could regain my composure and return to the table. Fortunately, I had Arnold Dyck, a close friend from Swift Current, as my roommate at Qu'Appelle Hall on campus for that first year.

Upon my return to U of S in 1963, after three years at MBBC, I was boarding at the home of George Balzers, where I was often given white buns with jam for my lunch. Given my hypoglycaemia (discovered much later), it is small wonder that I was having trouble with energy and mental health that year. The following year I stayed at the home of Mrs. Martynes, a widow, and was rooming with Len Pauls in a basement room (his brother and another boarder were upstairs). The next year I was going to room with Alvin Pauls, Len's brother, but discovered that he had been killed in an accident that summer, so I was put up in a room on the main floor by myself, and as a result was quite unhappy. I therefore made a switch after a few months, and joined Jake Hamm who was batching on his own in a basement room of a house near the university. I still feel badly about making this switch as it must have left Mrs. Martynes short of much needed earning power.

In my early years at U of S I studied terribly hard, six days and six evenings a week, though I did make a resolve not to study on Sundays. As I recall, I only took one coffee break during my first year. From my yearly diary I have discovered that my studies in the sciences and maths weren't as easy as I have tended to assume. I was worried about my grades and sometimes did poorly in science exams. Calculus was very difficult for me. On top of that I was always wondering whether I should switch from the sciences to philosophy. A 96% in a philosophy course in my third year at U of S "confused" me, I wrote in my diary. As the years progressed, I recall worrying less about my grades, and as a result, my marks kept going up. In looking back on my undergraduate years, I feel I was too conscientious and too studious. I should have relaxed more and simply enjoyed being a student.

Throughout these years I was also struggling with the meaning of life and the meaning of my studies. I found myself overwhelmed at times about the dull routine of life. During my honours year (1965-66) I went through a particularly difficult time. In the fall I was having serious doubts about my faith and was "rapidly becoming a nervous wreck." In November, I wrote this in my diary: "This was the darkest month in my life. Everything turned black. I was completely discouraged. I only saw problems. I lacked ambition and motivation. I was ready to quit school. I questioned my faith. Somehow the promises of God didn't seem to come true in my own life. I wasn't experiencing the joy and the peace of God. My work seemed hopeless. I flunked a physics exam." I was helped by an IVCF sponsor who shared that his honours year had been similarly difficult. I also recall some helpful advice from the head of the philosophy department, Professor Miller, who asked me what I would do if I quit university. If I had no plausible alternative, then surely it was best to hang in there. I am thankful that I did in fact soldier on.

Another component of my university years was of course what I did in the summers. I have already mentioned that during my early undergraduate years I was working at Bowman Brothers in Swift Current. In my third year at U of S I got a "lucky" break with an offer of a summer job with the Department of Mines and Technical Surveys. This government sponsored job was offered to students majoring in the sciences. I would be stationed at the Dominion Observatories in Ottawa, but would be assisting in field trips in various remote parts of Canada, doing seismic research. The first year we did tests in the middle of the Hudson Bay, on Gilmour Island, off Povungnituk, as well as the interior of British Columbia. The following year I spent a month on a lake near Uranium City, where I shot my first (and only) bear.

It is these summer work camps where I got my first taste of outdoor camping and also developed some coping skills in camping. Life in Ottawa was also very rewarding – I found a lovely home in the Glebe district of Ottawa, within walking distance to work, run by two caring spinsters who served three of us boarders breakfast only – suppers were at a restaurant. I enjoyed many good times at at the home of Uncle Dave and Aunt Ella, as well as at Uncle George and Aunt Isabelle's cottage. I also started attending the Alliance Church in Ottawa during the first year and connected with a fine group of young men in the church. This job continued for three summers until my boss informed me that I would not be able to continue in the following year, given that I was switching to philosophy and this job was meant to launch prospective scientists on their careers. But this summer job was a wonderful gift for me, freeing me from my obligations at home and expanding my horizons considerably.

One final comment on the academic side of these undergraduate years. I was blessed with a number of scholarships that helped me cover the costs of my education and even allowed me to purchase my first car during my fourth year at U of S. One of the reasons I  chose to go to university immediately after high school was that I was given a Kinsmen Scholarship of $200. I felt I needed to go to university in order to cash in on this scholarship. On returning to U of S after MBBC, I received a Leonard Foundation Scholarship of $400, which in fact I continued to receive for a number of years. I was awarded a $200 undergraduate scholarship from U of S in 1964/5 and also received an Honours Scholarship from the philosophy department in my final year at U of S. During that final year I also applied for a Germany exchange scholarship (Deutscher Akademischer Austauschdienst, DAAD) and must have been very sure of getting it as I didn't make any alternate plans. So when I received the news that I didn't get the scholarship, I hurriedly began applying to graduate schools. I appealed the DAAD decision and then got word that I had been given the award, but the news came too late for me to accept it for that year. In the end I got the DAAD scholarship the following year, after we were married, and even got an extra 100 Deutschmark for having a wife, and so we enjoyed a one-year honeymoon in Germany.

GRADUATE STUDIES: MCMASTER UNIVERSITY AND UNIVERSITY OF WATERLOO

My rather frantic last-minute search for a university where I could continue my studies towards an M.A. degree resulted in three offers – Calgary, York, and McMaster. In the end I chose McMaster University to begin my graduate studies. My very "rational" choice to go there was dictated in a large part by the fact that a very special young woman named Maggie would be attending McMaster that year to complete her B.A. in English literature. The year at McMaster (1966-7) was a challenge because my background in philosophy was not that strong given my double major in physics and philosophy in my undergraduate studies. Often during our seminars, I found myself struggling just to keep up with the discussion, and I very seldom participated in class discussions. Indeed, I was seriously questioning my decision to continue studies in philosophy.

I remember one incident that helped me to overcome my skepticism about my philosophical abilities, at least to some degree. I had presented a seminar on Wittgenstein's mysticism and later talked to my professor who asked me what I would be doing after completing my M.A. I told Dr. Shalom that I was thinking of quitting philosophy. He was surprised and interrogated me further on this, and so I shared with him my ongoing doubts about my ability to do graduate work in philosophy. He encouraged me to go on because he felt that I was doing well. I had presented two good papers in his class. I needn't worry about not contributing to class discussions because this wasn't that important, and besides, the students who were actively involved in these discussions were probably talking about stuff they didn't really understand. Dr. Shalom felt that I was a clear thinker. He confessed to being a slow thinker himself. He reminded me that lack of confidence was common among philosophers.[9] Wittgenstein is said to have asked Bertrand Russell whether he should go on in philosophy or whether he was simply a dunce. It was this short conversation with my favorite professor that played a significant role in encouraging me to continue my studies in philosophy.

My McMaster year was of course colored by love and courtship. I was rooming with my cousin, Bob Thiessen, and Maggie was rooming with his girlfriend, Mary Elliot, a very convenient arrangement. I'm not sure how focused I was in my studies, but I certainly lived a more balanced life, and Maggie provided the encouragement I needed when motivation was low.

That year I also bought my second car, a 1960 Rambler ($720.00), which facilitated my weekend visits to Vineland. We were engaged shortly before Christmas, and after a summer back in Ottawa, we were married on August 10, 1967. I abbreviate here as all this has been described in more detail in Chapter 2.

Soon after the wedding we were on our way to Germany, This year included six weeks of language study at a Goethe Institute in Brilon, near Kassel, after which we moved to Erlangen where I initially enrolled in some more German courses and a seminar in analytic philosophy. In later semesters I took some courses in theology and hermeneutics. Of course, the bulk of my time was spent completing my M.A. thesis on the concept of God in Immanuel Kant. Maggie was so kind as to type my entire thesis – six copies using carbon paper to make the duplicates. A first draft was completed in April of 1968, and a final draft was sent to the McMaster philosophy department in early July.

During this year I was also applying for jobs as I wanted a break from studies. Surprisingly, despite an incomplete M.A., I got a sessional appointment at what was then Waterloo Lutheran University (WLU), thanks to the intervention of the Academic Vice-President, Dr. Frank C. Peters, a former instructor of mine at MBBC. I defended my thesis on September 17, before my classes began. My experiences during these first two years of teaching at WLU are described in more detail in the following chapter. Despite the challenges of teaching, I found teaching invigorating and sensed a calling to teach philosophy, and so after two years at WLU, I began my Ph.D. studies at the University of Waterloo (U of W). The choice to continue my studies was not made lightly – I still have a list of pros and cons that I drew up at the time to help me make the decision.

In the meantime, we had our first child – studying philosophy with a baby cradled on one's knees is not easy! But family responsibilities had a way of keeping my life balanced. I started applying for jobs once again, in part because I was very conscious of my responsibility to support a growing family, but also because philosophy positions in Canada were scarce at the time. Thus I did not hesitate to accept an offer from Medicine Hat College (MHC) when it came, even though I had only completed one year of Ph.D. studies (1970-71). As a result, work on my Ph.D. was stretched out over the next ten years.

The Ph.D. program in the philosophy department at U of W consisted of four concentration areas. I chose philosophy of education, epistemology, philosophy of religion, and existentialism. Two of these were completed during my initial year at U of W. Two were completed during my first years of teaching at MHC, during which time I also took a half-sabbatical in 1974-75 so I could spend more time on my studies.

A few years later I took another half-sabbatical so we could return to Waterloo and work on writing my dissertation on a full time basis (1978-79). Fortunately, I was also awarded a Canada Council Doctoral Fellowship of over $7,000, plus an array of additional benefits. This eased our financial worries as I was only getting 40% of my salary from MHC during this half-sabbatical. I decided to write my dissertation under the supervision of Dr. Brian Hendley who had just returned from a sabbatical at the London Institute of Education, where he had connected with R.S. Peters and Paul Hirst, who were some of the key scholars in the philosophy of education at that time.

I had some trouble deciding on a dissertation topic, considering quite a variety of possible topics.[10] I even developed a page of principles that should govern the choice of a dissertation topic. It became clear that I wanted a topic which combined my interests in ethics, epistemology, and the philosophy of religion. I eventually narrowed it down to the problem of indoctrination. I was very fortunate to have several faculty in the department who were sympathetic to Christianity and to my wanting to deal with a topic from a Christian perspective.

Soon I was into a routine, meeting with Brian about once every two weeks. I especially appreciated his sharing of struggles he himself had gone through in graduate studies. My confidence was shaken a bit after getting to know one of the graduate students whose external examiner hadn't given his stamp of approval to his dissertation even though the department members were happy with it. As a result this student had to spend an extra six months revising his dissertation. I also attended several dissertation defences and realized that I would probably be at my weakest when it came to my oral defense. Brian tried to reassure me by suggesting that it was the written work that really counted.

The winter months were spent writing chapters on the four criteria often used to define indoctrination. I had some difficulty sorting out my own thinking about the best way to define the concept of indoctrination. At first

I was inclined to adopt a methods criterion, focusing on rationality. But a presentation I gave at the Institute for Christian Studies (ICS) in Toronto gave me pause.[11] Hendrick Hart convinced me that all teaching is in part non-irrational and thus irrationality couldn't be the defining characteristic of indoctrination. After my presentation I received a nice letter from Robert VanderVennen, Executive Director of ICS, expressing his excitement about the work I was doing. What he found interesting was that I was formulating my ideas in ways that would make sense and be acceptable to secular thinkers, adding that this was a challenge that many of the faculty at ICS had not faced given that they had their doctorates from a Christian university. Over the years, I have become very aware of the fact I have had to face unique challenges because most of my academic work has been done within a secular context.

My yearly diary describes how my feelings about the work on my dissertation underwent rather drastic changes throughout that year. Initially I faced discouragement as I ran into difficulties narrowing the topic of my dissertation. When I began the actual writing of chapter one, I found the work invigorating. Then, followed a period of despondency about my having exchanged the usefulness of being a teacher and church worker to the seeming futility of sitting at home and writing a dissertation. In February, my spirits began to lift somewhat. I gradually came to see that my thesis wouldn't be the last word on indoctrination, and that I couldn't exhaust the topic. Other philosophers would disagree with me. In fact, it really was all a rather futile exercise, a puny mind trying to understand a problem but barely able to scratch the surface of an immense topic. I lost my respect for the Ph.D. degree, realizing that claims to have done a lot of research and to have acquired great knowledge were really pretense and sham. I gained a new appreciation for Socrates' insight: "He is wise, who knows how little he really knows." I began to see that getting a Ph.D. was really a game, and if I played it right I would probably get the degree even though I didn't deserve it. What an amazing "con job" all academics, including myself, were able to play on each other and the population at large!

We returned to MHC in the fall of 1979 where I worked on final revisions to my dissertation while teaching full-time. I sent in a near final draft of my dissertation in January of the following year, and was pleased to hear that Brian Hendley and the committee were generally happy with my work, though they suggested a few revisions. I completed these in spring and the final draft was sent off mid-July. My defense was set for September 4, 1980, a day after classes began at MHC. Maggie and I both flew to Ontario so we could also visit Mom Friesen. The flight was terrible and I didn't get a good night's sleep, but managed to get through the 2 ½ hour defense the following day. Dr. Penelhum, my external examiner was not happy with the constructive part of my last chapter, including the "logical howler" in my treatment of a combination of criteria of indoctrination, which he later told me my committee should have caught.

So I had to make some further revisions, though Dr. Penelhum reassured me that these revisions were really quite minor – drop one section and revise one section of the last chapter. In the end Penelhum downplayed the importance of analyzing concepts, even suggesting that philosophers didn't know what they were doing.[12] What a way to conclude the work on my dissertation! I completed my revisions that fall and even managed to convocate that same year. Finally, after ten years, I was awarded my Ph.D. in the fall of 1980. Two celebrations were held that fall in honor of my accomplishments, one sponsored by the department at MHC with Rod Harvey reading an epic poem he had written. Dave and Martha Rempel also hosted a church party for me.

REFORMED EPISTEMOLOGY AND
A CHRISTIAN WORLDVIEW

I conclude this chapter with some further reflections on my attempts to integrate my thinking in philosophy with my Christian faith, and here I will move beyond my years in graduate studies . My philosophical outlook has been shaped to a significant degree by what has come to be known as "Reformed epistemology." Indeed, I often say that I owe my philosophical salvation to the Reformed philosophers who have built on the writings of John Calvin.[13] I was first introduced to this philosophical tradition by the writings of Francis Schaeffer in the late 1960s.[14] I found Schaeffer's overview of the history of ideas most instructive. He introduced me to the notion of presuppositions, underscoring the importance of penetrating to the underlying assumptions of a belief system in order to really understand someone's ideas. Maggie and I even paid a visit to Schaeffer's L'Abri retreat centre in Switzerland in 1968, during our one-year stay in Europe after our wedding.

Reformed epistemology challenges the notion of the autonomy of human reason. Ultimately a person's reason is shaped by a pre-theoretical faith commitment. It is the heart that determines the direction of human reason. Thus faith is a necessary ingredient in all knowing. Or as Anselm put it, it is always "faith seeking understanding." I have often told my students that all knowledge begins and ends with faith. Our thinking is further very much influenced by our history, our environment, and even our psychology, and so we need to give up the Enlightenment idea that rationality is all of one piece, that we all reason in the same way, and that all rational people will come to the same conclusion. Hence the appropriateness of the title of Alistair MacIntyre's book: *Whose Justice? Which Rationality?*[15] Indeed, these insights of Reformed epistemology have been reinforced by any number of post-modern critiques of the Enlightenment.

These insights have profound implications for trying to prove the existence of God. They also call for nuances to the historical argument for the existence of God mentioned earlier in this chapter. Because objectivity is impossible and because faith is a necessary ingredient in all knowing it is impossible for a non-Christian to look at the data concerning Jesus Christ in an objective way. To appreciate the significance of the Word becoming flesh, we must start with the presupposition that God exists, and this is grasped by faith prompted by the Holy Spirit. As we work out the implications of this presupposition, we will find (if we are open-minded) that it agrees with reality and experience, including the historical data concerning Jesus Christ. This approach has also helped me to better understand 1 Corinthians 1 & 2, a passage that had baffled me for a long time. Paul's description of the foolishness of the gospel is addressed to people who don't respond to the Holy Spirit's prompting.

This emphasis on presuppositions and the subjectivity of reason seems to lead to epistemological relativism and ultimately social constructivism. It is these problems that I have been wrestling with in the last few decades of my career and I have gradually come to adopt a position of critical realism. While we can never access reality as it really is, there is still an objectively "given" reality that we are trying to comprehend, however incompletely, and against which our interpretations rub. We must therefore always be open to critically examining our present understanding of reality, in hopes of moving towards a better and more complete understanding. While our thinking is shaped by our pre-theoretical faith commitments, we still live in a common world and there is still a baseline of commonness in the reasoning of ordinary people in ordinary life. I have found John Rawls notion of overlapping circles helpful in trying to do justice to both the uniqueness and the commonness of human rationality.[16]

Regarding relativism and truth claims, I have found that confusion abounds when we fail to differentiate between the search for truth and Truth itself. The human search for truth is relative – we are often forced to admit that we have got it wrong. But Truth is objective and absolute in some sense – eternal and unchanging. To pretend that we can arrive at absolute Truth is to be conceited. But without absolute Truth as a goal, our search for truth becomes empty. The Scriptures are, I believe, very clear in making the distinction between the human search for truth and truth as an objective ideal. Paul in his famous chapter on love stresses that we know only in part, that we only see the truth dimly. It is only when we escape the limitations of human rationality here on earth, that we will know fully and that perfect Truth will be known (1 Corinthians 13:10, 12). I will develop these ideas further in the final chapter.

The limitations that surround our search for truth highlight the need to be open-minded, another theme that has been the focus of my attention in the last few decades.[17] Indeed, I believe open-mindedness is a key intellectual virtue. But like all good things, this intellectual virtue can be distorted. We can be so open-minded that we forget about the goal of coming closer to the truth. We can be so preoccupied with the search that we forget the desperate human need of arriving at some settled convictions. This danger is well illustrated in G. K. Chesterton's description of H.G. Wells as a man who "reacted too swiftly to everything," who was "a permanent reactionary" and who never seemed able to reach firm or settled conclusions of his own. Chesterton goes on: "I think he thought that the object of opening the mind is simply opening the mind. Whereas I am incurably convinced that the object of opening the mind, as of opening the mouth, is to shut it again on something solid."[18] Paul describes people like this as "always learning but never able to acknowledge the truth" (2 Tim 3:7). Somehow we need to find a healthy balance between commitment and open-mindedness.

Over the years, I have also become increasingly concerned about an overemphasis on questioning and critical thinking that is so prevalent today in education, philosophy, and theology (e.g. the hermeneutics of suspicion). French philosopher, René Descartes, is generally seen as the father of modern philosophy. Descartes should also be seen as the father of our current preoccupation with questioning and critical thinking. Descartes begins his famous *Meditations* (1641), by acknowledging that from his earliest years, he has accepted many false opinions as true. This prompts him to systematically subject all of his former opinions to doubt in hopes of finding at least one belief that is absolutely certain. Unfortunately for Descartes, his one certain truth, "I think, therefore I am," is not quite as certain as he thought it was. Indeed, there are problems with the very goal of absolute certainty that drove Descartes' methodological doubt. It is also impossible to question or doubt everything. You simply can't start from scratch. There are a number of assumptions Descartes makes that remain unquestioned. The individualism that pervades Descartes' approach can also be called into question.

What is the alternative? We need to recognize the importance of the community in coming to know, including the community of past generations. We need to acknowledge that we can only question if we have first been given something to question. As Ludwig Wittgenstein taught us, "The child learns by believing the adult. Doubt comes after belief."[19] Questioning and critical thinking are dependent on our first being initiated into a particular tradition of thought. A conservative posture is therefore the appropriate response to tradition. We should cherish the beliefs that we have inherited from previous generations. This does not preclude critical thinking and questioning. (After all, this is what attracted me to philosophy in the first place.) As fallible and sinful creatures, we always need to be open to reevaluating what we believe. But this should be done carefully, assessing beliefs and assumptions one by one, not by a wholesale rejection of everything we have been taught. Our epistemological stance should again be one of committed openness. We should be honest and admit the "answers" that we tentatively hold at the present time. At the same time, we should be open to critically evaluating these answers, always with a view to discovering more complete answers and coming closer to the truth. We also need to be patient, realizing that we will only know fully and completely in the *eschaton*, when we will see Jesus face to face.

In the last few decades I have also explored the notion of "worldview," and more specifically a Christian worldview, and have been teaching courses on this subject since my retirement.[20] I have already dealt with the notion of presuppositions which Reformed writers like to describe as pre-theoretical faith commitments at the heart of one's belief system. One of the difficulties I have been trying to sort out is to describe precisely how these pre-theoretical commitments relate to theoretical belief systems. In any case, these presuppositions shape our worldview, which in turn shapes our thinking in all areas. A Christian worldview maintains that God is sovereign over all aspects of reality, life, thought and culture. I have been inspired by a statement made by Abraham Kuyper, a Dutch journalist, politician, educator and theologian, who in the climax of his inaugural address at the dedication of the Free University of Amsterdam in 1880 stated, "there is not a square inch in the whole domain of our human existence over which Christ, who is Sovereign over all, does not cry: 'Mine!'"[21]

This summarizes a long-held passion of mine for developing a uniquely Christian mind in all areas of human thought and endeavour. Like Paul, I want to "take captive every thought to make it obedient to Christ" (2 Cor 10:5). Here I am indebted to a book I read while I was still an undergraduate student, *The Christian Mind*, by Harry Blamires.[22] Another essay I discovered later in my career and which I found deeply inspiring was written by Alvin Plantinga, entitled "Advice to Christian Philosophers."[23] I have also found the notions of presuppositions and worldviews immensely useful in teaching, and in explaining why and how individuals come to disagree so profoundly about many things. Sadly, the idea of a Christian worldview has been running out of favour among Christian scholars, and so I have published a number of articles defending this notion.[24] Even more sadly, there are many Christian scholars who deny outright the very idea of a uniquely Christian perspective on their disciplines. Hence my continued urging of Christian scholars to be faithful in following Jesus Christ in their academic careers.[25]

NOTES

1. I recall this paper drawing extensively from an article in *Christianity Today*. So, I'm not sure it was deserving of the praise it was given.

2. For some comments about what struggling with an inferiority complex meant for me while attending MBBC, see Chapter 1, pp. 6-11.

3. See my autobiographical essay, "Love of Wisdom and Truth," in a special issue of *Direction: A Mennonite Brethren Forum*, on "Scholarship and Faith," Vol. 46, #2, (Fall 2017), pp. 218-231.

4. Bertrand Russell, *Why I am not a Christian* (Allen & Unwin, 1957).

5. Malcom L. Diamond and Thomas V. Litzenburg, eds., *The Logic of God: Theology and Verification* (Bobbs-Merrill Press, 1975).

6. My copy of this booklet also has an interesting history. I have lent it out to students, one of whom did not return it, and so her father, who was in fact our dentist, replaced it by ordering a used copy for me. For a more recent book that has helped me to think through some of the skeptical questions that have arisen surrounding the history of Jesus, see James D.G. Dunn, *A New Perspective on Jesus: What the Quest for the Historical Jesus Missed* (Baker Academic, 2005). See also Richard Bauckham, *Jesus and the Eyewitnesses: The Gospels as Eyewitness Testimony*, 2nd. ed. (Eerdmans, 2017).

7. W. V. Quine "Two Dogmas of Empiricism," found in his book, *From a Logical Point of View* (Harvard University Press, 1953), pp. 20-46.

8. See my *Teaching for Commitment* (McGill-Queen's University Press, 1993), chap. 4.

9. I have indeed found that feelings of inadequacy are common among philosophers. This theme comes up repeatedly in a biography of Dallas Willard. See Gary W. Moon, *Becoming Dallas Willard: The Formation of a Philosopher, Teacher and Christ Follower* (IVP Books, 2018), pp. 98, 102, 127, 138, 140. Rebecca Konyndyk DeYoung, whose family we got to know while at Oxford, and who eventually followed her father in becoming a philosopher, describes her own insecurity in philosophy in her superb treatment of *Glittering Vices: A New Look at the Seven Deadly Sins and their Remedies*, (Grand Rapids, MI: BrazosPress, 2009). She describes herself as feeling "like an impostor" during her first year of graduate school. Years later she read Thomas Aquinas on the virtue of courage and the vice of pusillanimity which means "smallness of soul." "Those who are afflicted by this vice, wrote Aquinas, shrink back from all that God has called them to be" (p. 9). I found this analysis illuminating when I read this book during my retirement. I suffered from "smallness of soul" as a student. My life has been a long journey in acquiring the virtue of courage in doing philosophy, thanks to the grace of my loving Lord.

10. Some topics I was considering for my dissertation: religion and the public school, the nature of presuppositions, reason and emotion, epistemological dilemmas, ethics without God, and the uniqueness of a religious view of reality and truth.

11. I was also invited to give a summary of my work at Conrad Grebel College in May of that sabbatical year and was encouraged here by Conrad Brunk, the resident philosopher, who quite liked the work I was doing.

12 Dallas Willard has similarly said that "nothing is gained by talking about words instead of ideas" (quoted in Moore, *Becoming Dallas Willard*, p. 99).

13. A reformed epistemology is often traced to Dutch philosopher and statesman, Abraham Kuyper (1837-1920), and Dutch philosopher, Hermann Dooyeweerd

(1894-1977). I am probably the only Mennonite scholar in North America who owns all four volumes of Dooyeweerd's dense, *A New Critique of Theoretical Thought*, first published in Dutch in 1935-6, and translated into English in 1969. This does not mean that I have read all four volumes, though I have appreciated a summary of Dooyeweerd's thought as found in L. Kalsbeek, *Contours of Christian Philosophy: An Introduction to Herman Dooyeweerd's Thought* (Wedge, 1975). Today's foremost representative of Reformed epistemology is Alvin Plantinga, whom I have encountered at several conferences. Other writings within this tradition that have influenced me include George Mavrodes, *Belief in God: A Study in the Epistemology of Religion* (Random House, 1970), Nicholas Wolterstorff, *Reason Within the Bounds of Religion* (Eerdmans, 1976), and William P. Alston's essay "Religious Experience and Religious Belief" (1982), later expanded into a book, *Perceiving God* (Cornell University Press, 1991).

14. See Francis Schaeffer, *Escape from Reason* (IVP, 1968), and *The God Who is There* (IVP, 1968). See my review of these books in the *Mennonite Brethren Herald*, May 30, (1969), p. 24.

15. Alistair MacIntyre, *Whose Justice? Which Rationality?* (University of Notre Dame Press, 1988).

16. John Rawls, "The Idea of an Overlapping Consensus," *Oxford Journal of Legal Studies*, Vol.7, #1 (1987), pp. 1-25. See a diagram to illustrate this overlapping consensus in my *In Defence of Religious Schools and Colleges* (McGill Queen's University Press, 2001), p. 176.

17. See my essay, "Religious Education and Committed Openness," in *Inspiring Faith: Studies in Religious Education*, edited by Marius Felderhof, Penny Thompson, and David Torevell (Hampshire, England: Ashgate Publishing, 2007), pp. 35-46. "Teaching for Committed Openness," in *Cultivating Inquiry Across the Curriculum*, edited by Kim A. Winsor (Lexington, MA: Lexington Christian Academy, 2008), pp. 159-185. An abbreviated version of this essay appeared in *Christian Educator's Journal*, Vol.51, #1 (2011), pp. 23-6.

18. Quoted in my *Teaching for Commitment*, p. 152.

19. Ludwig Wittgenstein, *On Certainty*, edited by G.E.M. Anscombe and G.H. von Wright; trans. G.E.M Anscombe (New York: Harper & Row. 1969/1972), para #160.

20. Here I am indebted to David Naugle's book, *Worldview: The History of a Concept* (Eerdmans, 2002), and two books which I like to use as texts in my courses on a Christian worldview: *The Transforming Vision: Shaping a Christian Worldview*, by Brian Walsh and J. Richard Middleton (IVP 1984/2009), and *Creation Regained: Biblical Basics for a Reformational Worldview*, by Albert Wolters (Eerdmans, 1984/2005). I have also used James W. Sire's *Naming the Elephant: Worldview as a Concept* (InterVarsity Press, 2004) as a text. More recently Michael W. Goheen and Craig G. Bartholemew have published, *Living at the Crossroads: An Introduction to Christian Worldview* (Baker Academic, 2008).

21. Quoted in Richard J. Mouw's, *Abraham Kuyper: A Short and Personal Introduction* (Eerdmans, 2011), p. 4.

22. Harry Blamires, *The Christian Mind* (SPCK, 1963).

23. Alvin Plantinga, "Advice to Christian Philosophers," *Faith and Philosophy*, 1.3 (1984), pp. 253-71.

24. For some of my articles defending a Christian worldview see: "In Defence of Developing a Theoretical Christian Mind: A Response to Oliver R. Barclay," *The Evangelical*

Quarterly: An International Review of Bible and Theology, Vol. 64, #1, (January, 1992), pp. 37-54; "Refining the Conversation: Some Concerns about Contemporary Trends in Thinking about Worldviews, Christian Scholarship and Higher Education," *The Evangelical Quarterly: An International Review of Bible And Theology*, Vol. 79, #2, (2007), pp. 133-152; "Educating our Desires for God's Kingdom," a review article on *Desiring the Kingdom: Worship, Worldview, and Cultural Formation*, by James K.A. Smith (Grand Rapids, MI: Baker Academic, 2009), in *Journal of Education and Christian Belief*, Vol. 14, #1, (2010), pp. 47-53.

25. See the articles referred to in the previous endnote as well as my chapter entitled, "Curriculum After Babel," in *Agenda for Educational Change*, edited by John Shortt & Trevor Cooling (Leicester: Apollos, 1997), pp. 165-80. See also my article, "Temptations Facing the Christian Academic," in *Direction: A Mennonite Brethren Forum*, Vol. 37, No. 1, (Spring, 2008), pp. 60-70.

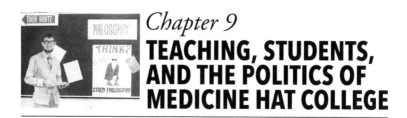

Chapter 9
TEACHING, STUDENTS, AND THE POLITICS OF MEDICINE HAT COLLEGE

In the fall of 1994 I was teaching an introductory philosophy class in Brooks, a satellite campus of Medicine Hat College. The class included several mature men and women, who were all very keen on exploring ideas. One of these students, I will call him Luke, was a seasoned contractor and was very open in class about his confusion about and disillusionment with religion. During a break in one of the early classes, he told me he was experiencing a lot of insecurity and that he felt this was due to his not getting connected to a divine power. He had also been badly hurt in church sometime in the past. This conversation helped me to understand why he was constantly attacking Christianity in class discussions. He and I had a lot of fun discussing religion and I think he had a lot of trouble trying to figure me out. I had students write a philosophy journal that year and in his journal he wrote the following early in the semester: "Roots of Insecurity: lack of firm beliefs; insecurity of existence (being connected); I becoming God; deep suspicion the economy is going to collapse; my inability to deal with and live with uncertainty."

After the final exam, I had a one-hour talk with him and asked him about his spiritual pilgrimage. He was born a Roman Catholic but became disenchanted with the church. He was mentored by a Mennonite for a while, joined an Evangelical church, and then a Baptist church. In these churchly expeditions he became increasingly upset about the doctrinal wars going on between pastors. He went on to explore New Age thinking for a few years and then dabbled with Indian spirituality. He described some sessions in an Indian sweat hut – a group of naked men crowded into a sauna – the closest he would like to come to being in hell. More recently he was is in a men's support group which brought in various speakers from the United States. What an example of modern man's insecurity and confusion. Interestingly, he was repeatedly objecting to the exclusive truth claims made in Christianity, when in fact he himself was so desperately searching for truth. I described him as an eclectic and he didn't know what that meant. He complimented me on my open-mindedness, and was surprised that I actually took the Bible seriously and thought some parts of it to be literally true. He invited me to an Indian sweat lodge session, but I refused with a smile, saying I didn't need to explore that kind of a thing. He told me he had most recently spent five Sundays in a Lutheran church – clearly he sensed that truth was to be found in Christianity, but commitment was a problem for him.

The above story is just one of many stories I will tell in this chapter about my interactions with students while teaching. The primary focus of this chapter is on my life as a teacher at Medicine Hat College (MHC), the institution where I spent the bulk of my teaching career – thirty-six years total, including my years of contract teaching at the end of my career, minus a few sabbaticals. I will also have something to say about the politics of MHC, which were mainly messy. I start by giving a brief overview of my teaching career, saying a bit more about my early years, about which I said little in Chapter 3. In giving this overview, there will of necessity be some overlap with what was said in previous chapters, but I will try to avoid repeating myself as much as possible. My purpose is to provide a summary of my teaching career for those who might not have read the details found in the earlier chapters.

My search for a college or university teaching position began in Germany in 1967-68, when I was on an exchange scholarship, enjoying a one year honeymoon, and finishing my M.A. dissertation on Immanuel Kant. After nine years of post-secondary education I was getting tired of studying and so started applying for teaching positions. Among my many letters of inquiry, one was written to Dr. Frank C. Peters, who had been my teacher at the Mennonite Brethren Bible College (MBBC) and who was now Vice-President Academic at Waterloo Lutheran University (WLU). He forwarded my letter to Fred Little, chair of the philosophy department at WLU, and I suspect this was coupled with a recommendation and even some pressure to consider me for a sessional appointment. Fred asked about my plans for the future and more specifically whether my plans included doctoral studies after a year or two of teaching. I responded by saying I was unsure about doctoral studies, but felt that a short teaching stint might help me to decide whether a career in philosophy was what I really wanted. In any case, I received a letter from Dr. Peters in January of 1968, offering me a one-year position as Lecturer in Philosophy which I gladly accepted at a salary of $7,600.

My workload for the first year consisted of two sections of introductory philosophy and a second year course in philosophical classics. This involved a rather heavy teaching load for a university – thirteen hours of teaching. The department had restructured the introductory philosophy classes that year, introducing larger classes (about seventy-five students in each section) with two hours of lectures and three tutorials per class. In my yearly diary I wrote that my first university lecture given on September 23, was "a terrifying experience," with sixty people staring at me. I recall working many long hours preparing for lectures that first year. While I became more comfortable with my introductory class, I never did feel secure about my second year class, in part because my background in the history of philosophy was weak, but also because the class consisted of a rather strange mixture of some radical students and some who didn't say a word. But I survived the year, and in the end concluded that "teaching was my cup of tea." My contract was extended for one year, and during this year I began to seriously consider doctoral studies with the encouragement of John Redekop and Frank C. Peters.

It seemed only natural to consider the University of Waterloo for my doctoral program and so I made initial inquires there. Given my teaching experience I asked for and was given a class to teach, "Social and Political Philosophy," for engineering students. This course was a stretch for me, as I had next to no background in political philosophy, so I relied heavily on a text/manuscript written by Jan Narveson, an eminent political philosopher in the department.

As I look back on these first experiments in teaching, I find myself rather embarrassed. What was a twenty-six-year-old with a rather weak background in philosophy (due to my earlier major in physics) doing teaching students, some of whom were nearly as old as I was and some even older? In my lecturing I was very dependent on my notes and didn't allow for much discussion. I recall ending lectures before the hour was up because I had come to the end of my notes. I smile at all this now. A leading question or two can always fill in a few spare minutes if one does not want to begin another topic. Insecurity has been replaced with confidence. And though I seldom, if ever, did this, I really could give a lecture with little or no preparation, on topics that I have covered many times before.

But I survived my early experiments in teaching and can only hope that my students benefited at least a little from my teaching. Perhaps surprisingly, I have cards and letters of appreciation from those years, with students expressing thanks for my teaching.[1] One student came to me after the year was over, expressing frustration about my critiquing the philosophers we were studying. His real concern, however, was my challenging his faith in man's reason and man's ability to solve the problems of this world, thus leaving him in despair. When I suggested that his faith in man might be problematic, and that there was hope in Jesus Christ, he responded by saying that he couldn't accept "a humble Christ." Yes indeed, human pride is man's basic problem.

Early in my second year at WLU (1970) I began looking for another teaching position, sending out thirty letters of inquiry. This was prompted in part by my feeling the need to support my growing family (Audrey was born May 16, 1970), and my concerns about the job market in Canada – there were very few job openings in philosophy, in part due to a great influx of American professors in the preceding years. I got a letter from Medicine Hat College expressing some interest in my application as they were in the process of expanding their offerings to include a second-year program in the sciences and humanities. In the end, they postponed their decision to hire a philosopher, but I was given the impression that my application would be kept on file. This helped me to decide to begin my studies towards a Ph.D. Sure enough, during the following year, I received a call from MHC asking me if I was still interested in the job I had applied for earlier. I was offered the position after some interviews and so began a long career at Medicine Hat College.

Medicine Hat College and my office for 36 years

The College had just moved to a brand new campus when I arrived in 1971. It offered first and second year university-transfer courses and a variety of technical/vocational programs. I was a member of the department of humanities and social sciences, an interesting mix of instructors in English, Psychology, Sociology, Geography, Anthropology, History, Political Science, and Philosophy. I was the only philosopher in the department. In retrospect I have come to appreciate this for two reasons. Being the only philosopher meant that I was in control of the philosophy program at MHC. I also had to become a generalist. I taught a wide variety of introductory and second year courses in philosophy and also had to teach a number of courses for the different vocational programs at the College. This combination of teaching challenges forced me to clarify and simplify ideas so students with no previous background in philosophy could understand. I am still grateful for the philosophical and pedagogical discipline provided by this experience.

One problem I faced at MHC was a result of the College being too small to sustain a full-time position in philosophy. So I was constantly having to fill part of my workload with other duties. In my early years I was asked to take on the job of placing education students in schools in the city for their practicum. I also taught a Social Studies course for the upgrading program. Later I taught courses in Brooks for many years. Eventually, my course load was filled with service courses to other departments – bio-medical ethics for nursing students, logic for the police and security program, and ethics for the massage therapy program. Further details about my long teaching career at MHC are found in earlier chapters.

My teaching experiences beyond MHC have also been described in detail in previous chapters. A highlight was teaching at Lithuania Christian College in the fall of 1993 during one of my sabbaticals (see Chapter 5). Other overseas teaching experiences after my semi-retirement included a return to LCC in 2006 (see Chapter 6), and two short courses at the Evangelische Theologische Faculteit (ETF) in Leuven, Belgium in 2005 (Chapter 6) and in 2009 (Chapter 7). Further overseas teaching experiences after our move to Ontario included a course at Meserete Kristos College (MKC) in Ethiopia in the summer of 2011, and a four-week course at the Caribbean Graduate School of Theology (CGST) in Jamaica in the fall of 2013 (Chapter 7).

Closer to home, I have had three significant teaching opportunities since we moved to Waterloo in 2007. My first teaching assignment in Ontario was a three-week course in the education program at Tyndale University College (2008-9). I was also appointed Professor of Research in Education for a three-year term at Tyndale. In subsequent years I was able to arrange for a delightful rotation of teaching courses for the Lifelong Learning Program at WLU (now Wilfrid Laurier University) in the fall semesters (ten years), and teaching a Worldview Seminar at Emmanuel Bible College (EBC) in the winter semesters (seven years). Unfortunately, low enrolment at EBC ended my tenure there as an Adjunct Professor after 2018, and the worldwide coronavirus pandemic forced WLU to cancel a spring course I was scheduled to teach for them in the spring of 2020. These teaching experiences are described in detail in Chapter 7. My focus for the rest of this chapter will be on my experiences at MHC. But first some comments about my approach to teaching philosophy.

TEACHING PHILOSOPHY

As I look back on my career I am very thankful for having had the privilege of teaching philosophy all these years. I happen to believe that all students should study philosophy at some point in time, that is, if it is taught properly, which sadly is often not the case. It is after all the foundation of all disciplines. There was a time when philosophy was understood to include all wisdom and knowledge. The word "philosophy" has its origins in two Greek words, *philein* and *sophia*, meaning the love of wisdom and knowledge. As

human knowledge expand-
ed, various specific disciplines broke off from philosophy. But these disciplines
are still grounded in philosophy. Each discipline is necessarily rooted in basic philosophical presuppositions
that provide the foundation
for the discipline. Or to put
it another way, all thinking

Promoting my courses at Medicine Hat College in 1971

is undergirded by a specific worldview. Philosophy can therefore be seen
as the most general science that brings unity to all disciplines. So studying
philosophy is important for all students.

At the beginning of each course that I teach I tell my students that
there are three essential elements in the study of philosophy. (a) As stated by
William James, philosophy is simply an unusually obstinate effort to think
clearly and deeply about fundamental questions. Philosophy involves "big
picture" thinking. I love helping students wrestle with the big questions
and to understand and critically evaluate their own and other worldviews.
(b) Teaching philosophy also involves helping students to clarify their ideas
and the language they use to express these ideas. My hope is that students
will also learn to organize their thoughts, give coherent expression to their
ideas, and write good essays. (c) Of course, studying philosophy also involves learning to argue and to evaluate the arguments of others.

To accomplish these goals my approach has always been to encourage
students to read original philosophical works, have lots of discussion in
class, and also have students write essays. In my introductory courses, students were generally required to write three to six short essays (300 words)
during the semester, and then another essay as part of the final exam. Of
course this entailed that I spent a lot of time reading and grading essays.
But I believe writing essays is key to helping students grow in their philosophical understanding and abilities. And it has been very gratifying to
see students progress in their ability to write essays that are readable, well
argued, and coherent.

Another challenge I have faced in teaching philosophy has to do
with being transparent about my own Christian commitment. I believe

in teaching from and for commitment. I have after all written a book entitled *Teaching for Commitment*.[2] Over time I have become increasingly comfortable about being open about my own Christian commitment in the classroom. I have experimented with different ways to declare my commitment. Sometimes I have told my students that I was a Christian in the very first lecture of a new course. One problem with this approach is that it puts some students who are very hostile to religion on guard and it takes some time to win their trust. At other times I have waited until well into the course to become more open about my Christian commitment. Whatever approach I use, sooner or later I make it a point to openly declare my Christian commitment and to warn my students (with a smile) that they are stuck with a Christian philosopher and that my commitment will color everything that I say in the classroom.

I don't think it is possible to be neutral within the classroom. Nor is it desirable. Having a professor who teaches from and for commitment is much more interesting for students. Indeed, I believe integrity demands openness about our ideological commitments, especially in a subject area like philosophy. Obviously there are some professional and ethical constraints to being open about one's faith in the context of philosophy lectures in a secular classroom.[3] Within this pluralistic context, the Christian faith has to be presented as one option among others. I have also always tried to create an atmosphere in the classroom where students feel free to offer differing points of view and where all points of view can be openly discussed and criticized. And I have tried to be fair in presenting the differing points of view on any topic. I have also tried to be very sensitive to the power-imbalance inherent in a professor-student relationship. There is always the danger of abusing one's authority in the classroom. I therefore keep telling my students that they can disagree with me and still get an "A" grade. Towards the end of my career I even encouraged students to call me by my first name. After all, I am still a learner like they are, so why not level the playing field?

I find it significant that despite my approach to teaching for commitment, I was very seldom accused of being overbearing and indoctrinatory in my teaching. Instead I would sometimes get comments such as the following from a student in a course evaluation at the end of a first year ethics course: "I appreciated Elmer's honesty about his beliefs and the fact that I did not have to share them to enjoy this course. I felt comfortable disagreeing, and never felt my grade would suffer because I had a different opinion. I had a real love-hate relationship with Phil. 249. I loved it in class and hated the degree of difficulty of the essays (but I do think they sharpened my skills greatly, if only because of fear!). I think Brooks campus and the main campus are very fortunate to have the calibre of professor that I found in Elmer. Thanks Elmer." And I too am grateful for this honest and generous evaluation.

One of the less pleasant aspects of teaching is dealing with students who plagiarize. Two cases stand out for me. In a Religious Studies course that I taught for a number of years, I used an anthology of religious autobiographies as one of my texts. I then had students write their own religious (or irreligious) autobiographies as one of the major essay assignments in the course. One year as I was reading these student autobiographies at the end of a semester, I had a vague feeling that I had read one of them before. I had been collecting the essays that I liked over the years and so I recovered this file of earlier essays and sure enough I found an essay that was identical to one I had just read, with only the name changed. So I had to phone the student who had handed in someone else's religious autobiography and confront her about the problem. At first she denied that she had plagiarized, but when I told her that I collected student essays and had found an essay from a previous year that was identical to her essay she acquiesced. I then had to inform her that she would be failing the course. Sadly, she was a school teacher and I had to wonder what kind of a role model she was to her students.

In my last year at MHC I had two students in a nursing program who were taking an ethics course from me. They were good friends, and perhaps more than friends. I discovered considerable overlap in one of the essay assignments they handed in during the semester. I was then faced with the problem of trying to find out who had copied from whom. I met with them a number of times, both individually and together. At first they denied any wrongdoing, so I called them both in and showed them their papers, highlighting a number of sentences which were identical in both papers. Still denial. After some time, they returned to my office, one at a time, tearfully admitting what they had done. And finally, I could apply some grace. One of the students was on probation and was in danger of being kicked out of the program. I met with the program director and encouraged her to be merciful to this student. I think she had learned a valuable lesson.

A final dimension of my approach to teaching deserves mention. I enjoyed my contacts with students beyond the classroom. I never limited myself to the contractually required four or five office hours per week. And it was most gratifying to have many students visit me in my office, not only for help in the courses they were taking from me, but also for personal conversations. Some of them even became my friends. For example, in the 1980s one of my students, John Lerner, introduced me to the adventures of two to three-day hikes in the mountains in Waterton Park.

Tamarack Trail, Waterton, 1983

SOME STORIES ABOUT TEACHING AND STUDENTS

A significant part of my love of teaching has been the conversations with students that were prompted by my lectures and class discussions. In this section I want to share some of my interactions and conversations with my students. These stories are based on notes I have taken over the years about my significant encounters with students. Student names have been changed and in some cases some factual details have been altered to hide the identities of students involved.

An introductory ethics course always was my favorite while teaching at MHC. My ethics courses were also the most popular philosophy courses I taught. I would often have to teach two to three sections of introductory ethics. For most of the students this course was an elective. I am sure the students were well aware of what they were getting into when they registered for this course. Word gets around at a smaller college of 2,000 students. But, they kept coming. Oh, yes, sometimes they were furious with me. I recall one student who was enrolled in the business program and who came to see me after having taken my ethics course. He told me that at first he had thought that I was crazy, but by the end he had come to realize that I might just be right after all.

In this introductory ethics course I challenged the rampant relativism in student attitudes and thinking about ethics, and I also explored various foundations for objective universal ethical norms. I always included an exploration of a Christian foundation for ethics in the course and would identify some of the unique aspects and advantages of such a foundation. Of course, in good philosophical tradition, I also made it a point to identify the problems inherent in a Christian approach to ethics. In later years I concluded the course with a lecture in which I issued a very personal challenge to students to live the moral life. I also explored the difficulties inherent in accepting this challenge, including the problem of moral failure. And then, very briefly, I mentioned the need for forgiveness when we experience guilt as a result of moral failure. Here I suggested two options – either forgive yourself or find forgiveness in a super-cosmic Forgiver. You could usually hear a pin drop during this final lecture in my ethics courses.

On the final exam of my ethics courses I often added a Postscript at the end of the examination instructions: "It is one thing to know what is right and wrong. It is quite another thing to do the right and avoid the wrong. Thus it might be better to see the final examination of what you have learned in Philosophy 249 as taking place throughout the rest of your life. Unfortunately (or fortunately), our testing procedures are not able to evaluate this aspect of what you may have learned in Philosophy 249. The instructor suggests an annual self-examination!" One student, a Muslim girl, told me after the exam that she appreciated the added note. Another student, in an evaluation of one of my ethics courses wrote, "This was a great class, Dr. Thiessen. Unfortunately you opened my conscience up; is there another class I could take so I can shut it off!" Of course, I didn't offer such a class, because I believe in teaching for commitment.

The following exchange occurred in 1985, after a lecture in my introductory ethics course in which I introduced the idea of objective and universal moral absolutes, even suggesting that this might ultimately require a transcendent law-giver. After class, one of my favorite students came to see me – yes, I did have my favorites, and there were good reasons for this. Amelia was bright, always alert in my classes, and obviously interested in what was being discussed. She came to me after this class, and asked one simple question: Can one be an absolutist without being narrow-minded? What a profound question, and I knew enough about this girl to understand why she was asking it. She had come from a fairly liberal church background, but for some reason had attended a rather conservative Bible school in the prairies. She had already come to see me in my office several times, and had repeatedly told me about the seeming narrowness of the bible school that she had attended. And that is why she was enjoying taking my philosophy class now – she had the freedom to think. I met her parents later that summer, in downtown Medicine Hat, as Prince Andrew and Fergie were driving through the city, and they informed me jokingly that there was a shrine in their house, devoted to their daughter's favorite professor!

In one of my ethics classes in 1993, I was delighted to find students very much engaged in discussions in class. One student had been expressing very anti-religious feelings several times during class discussions. One time after he had raised another objection to Christianity, I replied, "I think you are being a little hard on God, Jack," which brought quite a few chuckles from the class. Then a little later, while I was winding down my introduction to ethics, he asked me very seriously, how one could be moral when it was so difficult. What a teachable moment! I explained that we needed forgiveness for failure and then help to try again. I then added that for me a belief in God was the only way in which to address these two needs in ethical living. His attitude after this was very different from previous times when he had raised sceptical doubts about religion.

In 1994 we were returning from our annual mountain biking trip in Kananaskis and were getting fuel at a Shell station in Calgary. Suddenly I was approached by one of my former students – I recognized his face but didn't remember his name. He informed me that when he saw me at the pumps, he just had to stop and tell me that of all the courses he took during his university years, he felt that my ethics course had been the most helpful. That was all he said. Someone was waiting for him, so he had to rush away after making me feel very good! Indeed, so good that I forgot to pay my bill at the gas station. A few weeks later I received an embarrassing letter from the Shell station manager informing me that I had not paid for my gas. I responded immediately, apologizing and explaining the reason for my unethical and untypical behaviour, and of course I enclosed a cheque for the gas that I had "stolen."

I had a series of conversations with another student who kept enrolling in more of my courses and who was writing some superb papers for me (1995-6). After I commented on one of her papers, she stayed back after class and asked me about philosophy, as she was enjoying it so much. Ardith had returned to school after years of work and was now thinking of preparing for a career in social work. At the beginning of a second semester with me, she stayed back again, and told me that she was having trouble deciding how angry she should be with me – she just didn't like any other courses anymore, except philosophy! Later she took my ethics course and in one of my lectures I reviewed the importance of story-telling in ethics. Each of us is in fact telling an ongoing story by the way in which we behave and live. After the lecture Ardith again stayed back and asked me how the notion of story-telling could help if one's past story was not a good one. I knew enough about her to know that this was a loaded question. I suggested that she needed to accept her past and then resolve to grow beyond it and reshape her story.

After a class a few weeks later, Ardith stayed back again and said she had some questions. She told me that she was sorting out her stance in ethics and was coming to see what she had to do, but she was having difficulty moving from theory to practice. "How do you act on what you believe to be right? I keep failing." I suggested that failure was a key problem in ethical living and that I had found that Christianity provided some answers to the problem of moral failure and the guilt that follows. "Why is it so hard to be moral?" Here I suggested that the problem was "the rottenness" in human nature, and perhaps the only solution was a religious and moral conversion. Maybe there was a God who could help one to be moral. This was not the last conversation I had with Ardith.

MATTHEW

Here is a longer story of one of my early students and a relationship that continued into my retirement. Matthew took his first class from me about ten years after my coming to MHC. At first I hardly took notice of him – he was a more mature student (about twenty-four years old), fairly quiet, serious, but I could tell that he was paying careful attention to my lectures and enjoying the class-discussions. After a while he came to see me in my office and this led to many more conversations. He had been in carpentry for a while, and was finding life somewhat meaningless. He loved the big questions that I liked to deal with in a first year course in philosophy. What is truth? Are we free? Are there moral absolutes? What is the meaning of life? He was also curious about my religious convictions, and we had many a conversation about God and Jesus. For a time, he and his partner, Mary, came to our home for "religious discussions," as he called them. At one point he even asked me what would be involved in becoming a Christian, and so I reviewed for him the story of Nicodemus in John 3. Matthew took an ethics class from me the following semester. This prompted questions about his live-in relationship with his girlfriend, Mary. My answer was quite simple – get married!

In the spring of 1984, I hired Matthew to help build a front deck on our house. It was a wonderful shift in roles and responsibilities – now he was the teacher and I the student, and not a very good one at that. He didn't even allow me to pound in the nails on the deck floor, because he didn't want any hammer marks on the flooring, and he knew my lack of skills in hammering all too well. We were always immensely proud of our deck – Matthew did a beautiful job, and we enjoyed many hours on this deck, barbequing, visiting, discussing ideas, reading, or just enjoying the outdoors during the spring, summer, and fall months.

Matthew went back to carpentry after his brief stint of studies at the College. Matthew and Mary got married in the spring of 1985, and I had the honor of being asked to give a little talk at their wedding. Given that both were the artistic type, I introduced my talk with the intriguing dialogue in "Fiddler on the Roof," between Tevye, a milkman and his wife Golde, on the nature of love after twenty-five years of marriage. I spoke about love and faithfulness, drawing on Proverbs 3:3, and closed my talk by referring to Jesus as God's gift of love to mankind, a story to inspire love and faithfulness in their marriage.

During our sabbatical at Oxford, I got a letter from Matthew. "Hello, Doc: I was just sitting, soaking in the bath, and thinking about how wonderful our marriage has been to date. Of course, not without its ups & downs, but nonetheless wonderful. It's taken me a long time to really relax and let myself love and be loved, and it is hard to express the joy that it gives me. The reason that I am writing is to thank you, as I feel that without your friendship and guidance I surely would have ended our relationship as I was stuck emotionally and could only see out as an answer. I thank God (however he manifests himself) that Mary is as patient as she is, or I would never have gotten to make a decision one way or the other."[4]

Sadly, this marriage did not last. Indeed, I didn't hear from Matthew for quite a few years after this. Finally we connected, and he confessed that the reason he had not bothered getting back in touch with me was that he and Mary had separated. It just didn't work out and he was too embarrassed to connect with me after this failure. I expressed my disappointment, but reassured him that this need not affect our relationship. After this Matthew moved to Salt Spring Island where he continued in carpentry (building some very exclusive houses) and getting into sculpture, finally setting up his own studio.

Meanwhile, we went to Lithuania and England for our sabbatical in 1993-4, and it is here where we exchanged some more letters. Here is part of a letter from Matthew: "Dear Elmer: Your trip sounds quite wonderful and full of a lifetime of stories, I'm sure. Your statement on your struggle for identity sort of shocked me. Perhaps we should spend more time asking the people around us who we are, as I'm sure we are always the last to know. You have been one of the most enjoyable, thought-provoking and entertaining teachers I have had the pleasure to know. I've never questioned who you are or your destiny. In my own case, acceptance of self has been a slow journey and it has no doubt been tied into my turning my back on God and community and vainly thinking that I was responsible for my life & subsequent choices (actually I wasn't that responsible). 'The hounds of God' have in fact got me. [I must have written Matthew about C.S. Lewis' lovely description of the hound of heaven eventually closing in on him.] I think that is such an adequate metaphor as I could always hear them and even feel them nipping at my butt a few times, but in all honesty, my rejection of God and occasional profession of atheism all lacked conviction, and certainly the time I spent in discourse with you helped me to a point where I could no longer (and gladly I might add) pretend that I did not believe in the existence of God. The next step for me has been one of breaking pride & ego (of which there seems to be no shortage) and truly submitting to the will of God, joining a community for support, and learning the joys of humility & daily prayer. I have a long way to go but feel good about being on the trail and not running from the hounds, but rather using them to guide the way. I've always liked dogs."[5] In this same letter and another written a short while later, Matthew described his exploration of the Bahai faith and his "leap of faith" into this religion which provided some of the comfort that he needed, particularly in facing the estrangement from his new partner and her children.

In the winter/spring of 2000, when we were on sabbatical in Victoria, Maggie and I made a visit to Salt Spring Island. I think we had tried to contact Matthew beforehand but were unsuccessful. Upon our arrival we took a taxi from the ferry terminal to the main town on the island – Ganges. We were looking for a restaurant, when suddenly, through the window, I spotted Matthew, who came dashing out to greet us. He introduced us to his charming new wife whom he had met at a square dancing event. We spent the entire afternoon with them, starting with a tour of the Ganges market and stores. After this tour they took us to their beautiful home deep in the woods. Matthew had just added a major addition to this house and of course there was his large and interesting studio. After a lovely meal Matthew took us back to the ferry.

Matthew invited me to return sometime for a ride in his sail-boat. So, later that semester, I took an early morning ferry to Salt Spring Island, but instead of sailing, we spent the day kayaking. (see picture in Chapter 6, p. 151) Matthew was a bit dubious about the abilities of this philosopher friend of his to manage a kayak on his own, but I proved him wrong. Indeed, I fell in love with the kayak and had an absolutely wonderful day, exploring the bays and smaller islands around Ganges, doing some crab fishing. I will never forget this marvelous experience with a wonderful friend.

At my retirement, the faculty association called Maggie to ask what I might want for a gift – they had a budget of $500 for retirement gifts for senior faculty. I had been thinking of a local painting when I suddenly thought of another possibility – a sculpture from a former student of mine. They contacted Matthew and he was delighted to be asked – indeed, when he returned their call, he had already picked out the sculpture that he wanted to send. In an email, he explained the sculpture which he titled "Inspiration." "I think this piece is well chosen. It is a play on the word spirit, breath, the place where God resides between the inhale and the exhale, a figure floating in tranquility inside an upper torso with the face of God sweeping past. It has been an honor. My best to you both."[6]

We continued to send Matthew our Christmas letters. In 2018 we got the sad news via Facebook, that Matthew was dying of cancer. We exchanged some notes via Facebook. His friends hosted a celebration of his life early in 2018 while he was still alive. He died on June 16, 2018. Here is part of his obituary: "Matthew's transformative journey brought him from struggle and pain to a sense of deep love and peace. Towards the end of his days, he said that he had hoped for a miracle but that on reflection, realized that the miracle had already happened. The miracle of healing for him was a profound sense of unconditional love, a love so profound, that it gave him the courage and grace he needed to leave this world and to journey into eternity in peace and dignity." I cherish this long-standing relationship with a former student of mine who became a dear friend. May he rest in peace.

SOME LATER STORIES

Leroy had been a student of mine many years earlier – rather strange, a hippy type, and very introspective. He went on to further studies but returned to Medicine Hat during the summers. Starting in the summer of 2000, he came to our church occasionally. One Thanksgiving weekend we had him down for a thanksgiving meal with some of Greg's other friends, and he ate and ate! I met him while biking one day, and we stopped and chatted, and I quickly came to realize that this was a providential encounter. I discovered that he was majoring in philosophy at the University of Saskatchewan. So here was a student in whom I had sparked an interest in philosophy without my knowing it. He wanted to go on to seminary and then go into street ministry. He was thinking of going to Three Hills graduate school, and when I raised some questions about this and suggested Regent, he said he felt that he was not bright enough for this. When I discovered that he was doing fairly well in philosophy, I pointed out that he was probably underestimating his abilities, sharing some of my own experiences in this regard. He too saw himself as a slow but deep thinker and so he resonated with my experiences. He was so thankful for my affirmation of him and the direction that he was taking – he realized he could never be a regular pastor. He also commented that he always appreciated it when I preached in church because it gave him something to think about.

Kurt had been a student of mine earlier – severely crippled and he never did look well. In class, he would often monopolize the conversation and thus become a bit of a nuisance. He was fairly bright and loved coming to my office to follow up on ideas raised in class. He was back in my class in the fall of 2001, after my sabbatical, and I had mixed feelings about seeing him again. Once again, he popped into my office after nearly every class. On one occasion I had to stop him from monopolizing the conversation in class as he did so often. He thanked me later in my office for doing so. A little while later he handed in a very weak essay and I was bold enough to add a comment at the end of his essay expressing my disappointment in his essay. He saw me in my office shortly afterward, and expressed his thanks at my making this comment. "It shows that you care. Of all my professors, you seem to be the only one that really cares about me," he said. Wow! Significant too, coming from a handicapped person, who no doubt seldom had people really challenge him. Interestingly, I had come to enjoy his visits – I guess it showed. Kurt phoned me in August of 2003, very concerned because he had heard that I had retired. He was relieved when I told him that this was my decision, because he was worried that I had been forced out. "You are the only person who made my college experience worthwhile," he said.

One of my students wrote this in the course evaluation of my introductory philosophy course in the fall of 2001: "This class has had a huge impact on me. I go to church regularly again." In the fall of 2002, one of my former massage therapy students stopped to talk to me on her way out of the chiropractor's office while I was waiting for my appointment. I remembered her as somewhat gruff and crude, and I thought she was quite resistant to my course. Now she told me that she often thought of what she learned in my course, and that it had really helped her. And she wished she could take another course from me. Ah yes, don't prejudge students – the more antagonistic ones may in fact be the most receptive to what you are saying.

Ron was a very bright student in my Philosophy 201 class in the fall of 2002. He was finishing up a degree in bio-chemistry by taking a few final elective courses at Medicine Hat College. He had already come to my office several times, to discuss issues with me, based on notes he was recording in a rapidly filling scribbler. He was an atheist. Towards the end of the semester he came to my office, scribbler in hand, and wanted to know why I believed in the spiritual domain. I proceeded to explain some "intimations" of the spiritual and the transcendent, drawing on Peter Berger's, *A Rumor of Angels* – truth, morality, the need for justice, forgiveness, and awe.[7] He was making notes all the while, and at the end commented that he had never heard this before. When he discussed these matters with Christians, they always pulled out the Bible and that didn't really help.

We met Shawn during a break at a College choir practice in March, 2004. I had taught him many years ago, and he was now vice-principal of a Christian School in Medicine Hat. He started commenting on my influence in his life. One comment he made struck me later, and so I called him back the next day to make sure that I had heard him correctly. He was most happy to expand and I made notes as he talked. "You taught me how to teach Christianly without being pushy or obvious," he told me. As he looked back on my course, he was now able to see more clearly the benefits of the course. There were flaws in his thinking at the time, he admitted. He was then an ethical relativist, and he was now most embarrassed about that. I had clearly and boldly exposed the flaws of that kind of thinking.

For him, coming to think Christianly had been a journey and I had been an important part of that journey, Shawn told me. The Lord had brought the truth to him slowly. No one in Sunday school or church or in the Christian schools he had attended had presented the alternatives regarding relativism and absolutism as clearly as I had done. "You taught with authority," he said. And yet, there was also openness in my teaching as I examined other viewpoints in class. He liked my being very upfront about my own position and my even trying to convince students about my position. My course had been a stepping-stone for him, not only intellectually, but also in his faith. And then this amazing statement, "Your course was more Christian than the courses that I took at a Christian college." While this might be a rather sad commentary on the Christian college he attended, it also says something about what is possible by way of a Christian teacher's influence within a secular college.

A story about a student I had at the end of my teaching career at Medicine Hat College will conclude this section. In the fall of 2006, I taught a formal logic course to a small class of nine students, many of whom were struggling with the abstract nature of the course. But the students got to know each other well and were usually chattering away with each other every time I entered the classroom. I too developed a very collegial relationship with them. At times I had to ask the class to focus, as they would be talking about personal things during the class. They kept expressing appreciation for what I was doing for them. And when they weren't working hard enough, they appreciated my putting some pressure on them. Several of the students mentioned that this was their favorite class. One student, however, said this was her least favorite class, but that I was her favorite teacher.

There was another student in this logic class, I will call her Cynthia, who I sensed didn't come from a very good background. Though she had a warm personality, she was a rather wild young woman, who liked to talk about drinking and her many boyfriends. As a class exercise, I had the class schematize a sentence which I invented on a spur of the moment: "All students who get A's in logic have loving parents." Cynthia responded out loud, and with some pathos, I felt, "Ouch, that hurts."

At the end of the semester, she announced that she would be taking another class from me the following semester, because she would miss me if she didn't do so. Then, on the day that I was proctoring the final exam for this class, Cynthia surprised me. After just one hour into a three-hour exam, I noticed that she was about to hand in her work and leave. I approached her, and in response to my query as to why she was leaving so early, she said she was having difficulty with the exam, but immediately went on to say that it was entirely her fault, as she had not been working enough on the course. I encouraged her to try a little more because she might still be able to get a passing grade in the course. She asked if she could go to the bathroom, and on her return, while I was busy marking papers, she planted a kiss on my cheek, in front of the entire class. A first for me!

The following semester, Cynthia took an ethics course from me and was obviously lapping it up, which I found interesting given her rough background. Mid-semester she missed a quiz because of a court appearance, so I let her write it late and in my office, while I was teaching. She wanted to give me her notes and textbook, but I said no, I trusted her. She responded, "Thanks." Then at the back of the quiz she wrote these words: "Thx again, Doc!! Geez, you're really a life saver!!" She missed a class towards the end of the semester and when I met her in the hallway later that day, I told her that I had missed her. She said she was running out of steam towards the end of the semester. I asked her if she needed a pep-talk. "No," she said, "but I sure could use a hug." So I gave her a fatherly hug, in front of students sitting on the bench nearby. She immediately went to the bathroom and came out a while later, and I had to wonder whether she had been crying. Ah yes, what a needy girl. I was thankful for the opportunity to be a little bit of a father figure for her, and also that I was able to point her in the right direction in terms of a good life style. Sadly, in today's hyper-sensitivity to sexual abuse, responding in this holistic way with students of the opposite sex would not be possible. We have lost something!

INSTITUTIONAL POLITICS

A teaching position at an institution of higher learning involves more than just teaching. There is membership in a department, in committees, in a faculty association, and even the possibility of becoming a member of a board of governors. And it is here, within the political dynamics of Medicine Hat College, that I encountered my most difficult trials. Early in my tenure at the College I was a member of the General Academic Council, and here I discovered first hand the high-handed political maneuvering of administrators at the College. Faculty were really thought to be obstacles that had to be circumvented somehow!

Early in my tenure at MHC I was appointed head of a committee to create a faculty handbook for the College. I even got workload relief for this job. But, as I have described in more detail in Chapter 3, this project was suddenly terminated in 1977 by our recently appointed Mormon President, Bob Sackley, who was not at all qualified to be President of an institution of higher education. I wonder how he got the job? In subsequent years I wrote letters to the administration and the Board of Governors and even the Department of Advanced Education regarding various issues that I felt needed to be addressed at the College. In retrospect I realize that I probably wrote too many letters. A colleague of mine once reminded me that I couldn't solve all the problems of the world or an institution. I think I cared too much and I was too idealistic. I will have more to say about this in the concluding chapter. But these letters and my political involvements also were costly in terms of my career. One example of this is my unsuccessful run for the chairmanship of my department which I have described in more detail in Chapter 4.

I also served the Faculty Association in a number of ways. I wrote a "Code of Professional Ethics and Professional Relationships" in 1976. I was President of the Faculty Association for one year (1984-5), during which time I commissioned a major survey of faculty morale, the very negative results of which were presented to the administration and the Board of Governors. It was not well received! In 1995 I was asked to serve on an ethics committee of the Faculty Association to deal with a faculty grievance and conflict between a faculty member and the Association President. This was a lot of work but I felt good about playing a mediating role here, though not everyone was pleased with the final report that I presented to the members involved, the Executive of the Faculty Association, and the Association at large.

My most significant political involvement occurred in 1988-89 when I took on the project of trying to get rid of the current President of the College, Chuck Meagher. Here was a man who was quite unqualified for the job and who had essentially appointed himself as President ten years earlier when he was Chair of the Board of Governors. He was of course a loyal member of the Conservative Party of Alberta and appointments to college boards were made by the government. He had astoundingly managed to get himself an unending contract, so termination would have to involve a political battle. Faculty morale was very low, hence the earlier survey I have already mentioned. I got myself elected as the faculty representative on the Board of Governors. There was a vote of non-confidence in the President by the Faculty Association – 78% in support, followed by 100% vote by the staff association (AUPE).

After these votes of non confidence I met with the President personally to discuss the underlying concerns suggested by these votes of non-confidence. He tried to get me onside to help him resolve the underlying issues, but when I indicated that there was no alternative but that he resign, he quickly ended the meeting. I then gave a formal report to the Board, stating my concerns and my reasons for believing that the President should resign. He attacked me personally at that meeting and at several future occasions. Later he unilaterally cancelled a course I was scheduled to teach at Hillcrest Christian College, even though this had been cleared by various levels of administration, and even though all these students would have been registered as students at MHC.

The Faculty Association President pressured me to give a report to the faculty association – this was probably a mistake, as it linked my role on the Board of Governors too closely to the Faculty Association. The Board then fired the Academic Vice-president, mainly out of spite, but also because they suspected he had been party to this uprising against the President. This was done very hastily and with no clear reasons given for the firing – in fact, they called it a resignation. This prompted me to write a lengthy letter to the Minister of Education in Alberta outlining the problems at the College as I saw them and encouraging the government to intervene as they had done during a crisis at another college in Alberta. At the Board level I suggested that we hire an outside consultant to do an evaluation of the President and the College as a whole, and amazingly, I was put on a Steering Committee which was given the task of finding a consultant. Somehow

I got in contact with Dr. John B. MacDonald, former President of the University of British Columbia and later CEO of the Council of Ontario Universities. Thankfully, he accepted the job.

Dr. MacDonald was a breath of fresh air on campus. He spent several weeks at the College, interviewing people and talking to whoever wanted to see him. Of course, I also made an appointment with him and he was very open with me about the problems he saw at the College. Indeed, after an initial meeting with the Board at which time the President once again attacked me verbally, MacDonald phoned to tell me that he found this most extraordinary and then empathized with the stress that I must be under. How therapeutic for me! I also managed to make arrangements for him to meet with the Vice-President who had been fired. After visiting the College several times, he wrote two reports, the first dealing only with the President. He recommended that the President's unending contract be terminated. This report was carefully guarded – we got to read it at a Board meeting, and all the copies of the report were collected afterward and destroyed. The Board decided to give the President a term-certain contract, extending his tenure for one more year, after which he would resign.

Then about a month later, Dr. MacDonald released his report on the College as a whole and sent it to all the bodies at the College (faculty, staff, and Board of Governors). The Board of Governors had forgotten to specify that he should send it only to them. Eventually the chair of the Board was forced to release the report to the Medicine Hat News so it became a very public document. It was a scathing analysis of all the administrative deficiencies at the College. The Board was furious, and one of the Board members even dared to call the report "chicken-shit." The report was of course also critical of them. But Dr. MacDonald calmly met with the Board after the report came out and skillfully managed to win their confidence, at least to some degree.

For me these reports were very reassuring. Finally I had someone who was highly qualified and for whom I had a high degree of respect, confirming my long-held conviction that there were indeed significant problems with the way in which the College was being run and with the administrators themselves. I was not wrong after all and so these reports were very therapeutic for me personally. Indeed, I was corresponding with Dr. MacDonald during this process and after it was all over. He wanted to be kept informed as to how the Board was responding to his reports. He was kind enough to provide me with some needed reassurance, encourage me to hang in there, and even give me some advice on occasion. In one of his letters he told me that he was not surprised at the Board's hostile reaction to his first report. "The need for change is so great that people will require time to change their perceptions. You should not be discouraged." Wise words from a seasoned administrator to an impatient political activist.

Nevertheless, the long process of addressing these problems was terribly hard on me, because I was pretty well at the center of it all, caught between the Board and the Faculty Association. The President and the Board were repeatedly attacking me, and I discovered later that they had in fact considered firing me as well. Clearly God protected me from this catastrophe. I concluded that I was not really thick-skinned enough to deal with high-drama politics. The emotional costs of this undertaking for me personally were huge and after it was all over I recall saying this will have shortened my life by five years. My yearly diary for 1988 begins with this statement: "This was a difficult year, probably the most difficult year of my academic career." But it was a learning experience, and I did survive. (See Chapter 4 for an analysis of lessons I learned from this experience.)

Was all this effort worth it? Not really. After all this, the Board did appoint a good man to be President – Dr. Fred Speckeen. But the person who replaced him a few years later, Ralph Weeks, left much to be desired and was in fact fired some years after I left the College. After my retirement I sometimes say that I have had the distinction of having worked at an institution that fired three Presidents and four Vice-Presidents during my tenure at Medicine Hat College (plus a few years). This is surely a sign of a very toxic political environment and I am surprised that I survived. There were periods of time when I adopted a closed office-door policy to somehow shut myself off from the poisonous political atmosphere of the College. I would explain this to my students and tell them to knock on my door if they wanted to see me! In retrospect, I have come to realize that I really had a very unpleasant working environment for most of my academic career. Coping with the poisonous political atmosphere at MHC was a challenge, and I am thankful to God for helping me survive. I want to believe that my presence at MHC played a small part in bringing the college a little closer to what God intended for educational institutions.

A final comment on what political involvement meant for me during my thirty-six years at Medicine Hat College. One of the academic vice–presidents of the College, Terry Cooper, sent me a note shortly after he had been appointed to that position and after I had written him a letter of congratulations, in which I also expressed some concerns over a few matters that I felt needed to be addressed at the College. He responded with a brief note: "I have always considered you to be the conscience of the college." Playing that role was not easy, and sadly sometimes I failed. But I believe being the conscience of whatever institutional setting we find ourselves in, is part of our Christian calling. Our job description as Christians always includes a bit more than is found in the official contract.

CALLING TO TEACH

In looking back over my career at Medicine Hat College, there is one significant disappointment that I should mention before I conclude – I got stuck teaching at a junior college. I began my career just as Canadian university positions in philosophy were drying up. Indeed, one of the major questions I faced when deciding to go on for a Ph.D. in philosophy had to do with the diminishing job market. When I accepted the position at MHC I was intending to stay for  just two years and then move on to a university. But there were very few job openings. In reviewing and cleaning up my job files after retirement I could not help but note how many applications for university positions I sent off over the years.

There were two other factors that played into my difficulty in finding a university position. One had to do with the way my career had unfolded. I had gotten a Ph.D. late in my career and by then already had many years of teaching experience behind me. Thus I was not an attractive candidate for universities who would rather hire a recent Ph.D. with only a few years of teaching experience.

I also believe that my Christian commitment played a role in my having difficulties in getting a university position. One incident stands out for me in this regard. While on sabbatical in Oxford in 1985-86, my first philosophy professor, T.Y Henderson, was also there and we met quite regularly for discussions. He had become chairman of the philosophy department and told me repeatedly about the hiring they had done in the previous year. There were 150 applicants for the position, half of them from the U.S.A. To his chagrin, he was unable to hire any of them because of a strong-minded immigration officer in Regina who simply refused to allow Americans into Saskatchewan universities. Henderson also told me about a well qualified applicant who had already published quite a few papers, but all of them involved a defense of a "fundamentalist" Christian position. The department wouldn't even consider this applicant, he informed me. He seemed to be oblivious to the fact that I had applied for that same position. I didn't bother to enlighten him on this. On second thought, perhaps I was the "fundamentalist" he was referring to, and he was quite deliberately bringing up this topic because he was trying to teach me some lessons about applying for jobs. Indeed, he told me that the only way to get a position in the philosophy of religion was to publish articles that took a more neutral position with regard to religion, citing John Hick and D.Z. Phillips as models to follow. So perhaps my defense of Christian education in my publications was also hurting me in getting a university position.

Ah yes, God had other plans for me. And in the end, the college setting was probably right for me. Teaching was after all my calling and the central focus of MHC was teaching. Fortunately, I could pursue my research and writing on my own. It took a lot of discipline, but I was allowed to do it, and was even given financial support for it. I attended conferences regularly. And the College gave me four sabbaticals – what more could I wish for!

Nonetheless, teaching at a college has its disadvantages. The teaching workload is much higher than at universities. One reason for my taking early retirement was my increasing frustration with the workload. Yes, there were the spring and summer months when I could work at a normal pace. But during the teaching semesters the pressures of work were nearly unbearable. During the final years at MHC I was teaching five courses per semester, with four different course preparations, and repeatedly marking over a hundred papers and other assignments throughout the semester. I was working ten to twelve hours per day and I had very little or no time for research and writing, which I needed for my own sanity. From time to time I wondered how I managed with such a heavy workload when I had children at home and when I was very involved in church. Perhaps it was simply due to my being a very disciplined person. On one occasion, when I talked to my Dean, Len Vandervaart, about the difficulties I was having with my workload, he told me that in order to survive the pressures of the heavy workload at MHC, I needed to look at teaching more as a job than as a vocation. Ah yes, that was a solution! But, it couldn't be my solution.

Despite these pressures, I am deeply grateful to God for a very satisfying career, most of which was spent teaching philosophy at a secular college. When I think of my earlier ambition to be a science teacher in high-school, I can only be thankful that I had the courage to switch to philosophy mid-way through my undergraduate university education. Clearly my preferences for dealing with big questions and engaging in abstract analytical thinking made me more suited to doing philosophy. As I kept reminding my students in the introductory lectures to my classes, philosophy is much more practical than the sciences, at least from an existential perspective. And the strength of my teaching, I believe, has always been my emphasis on working out the practical consequences of philosophical ideas. In this regard I repeatedly reminded my students of Richard Weaver's classic, *Ideas Have Consequences*.[8] Philosophical ideas are important. I am thankful for a career in which I could encourage students to reflect on the philosophical ideas that underlie all thought and action.

I have always seen my career in philosophy as a calling. Here I was encouraged by an essay that I used in my ethics course written by David Norton."[9] Norton is very critical of modern ethics. He argues that modern ethics is incapable of handling the ethics of vocational choice – indeed, modern ethics would classify such choice as non-moral. But Norton maintains that vocation should be seen as "a foundational form of generosity." Yes, indeed! And what more noble form of generosity and calling than to spend a lifetime shaping the minds of students. What could be more important than reflecting on the philosophical foundations of life, organizing ideas, and naming issues (compare the academic assignment given to Adam in Genesis 2:19-20). This was moreover a Christian calling. Doing philosophy was a way of worshipping my God. Paul reminds us repeatedly that whatever one does, should be done to the glory of God (Col 3:17). Work as a way to worship God – I enjoyed preaching a sermon based on these ideas during the year that I retired.

Further, as a Christian, I could think of no better mission field for myself than teaching philosophy in a secular context.[10] Here I am thankful that I did not make the mistake of accepting a position at the Mennonite Brethren Bible College when it was offered to me in 1977 and again in 1979. Later in my career I also received several invitations to consider administrative posts at Christian colleges.[11] Christian colleges were simply not where I belonged. What is rather odd here is that much of my earlier research and writing involved a defense of Christian schools and colleges. So, while I see their place in God's kingdom work, they are not where I belonged. Indeed, even my defense of Christian schools and colleges was geared mainly to a secular readership. God had called me to be a kingdom worker in the front lines. I can think of nothing more challenging than that. Daniel in the Old Testament has often inspired me and I have enjoyed teaching the book of Daniel several times in Sunday School over the years.

Beyond the challenge of teaching philosophy, I saw my work as a Christian philosophy teacher in a secular college in terms of doing pre-evangelism. I was breaking down the many artificial barriers that stopped students from considering the Christian faith. I was challenging their secular and materialistic presuppositions. I recall a student early on in my career at Waterloo Lutheran University (1969-70), who came to me and pointed out that I had shattered his worldview. He now felt adrift in a desert and didn't know where to turn. In my office, I could of course point him beyond the desert. Then later, when I was first entertaining the idea of retirement, a former mature student of mine met me at a downtown bookstore and expressed regret about hearing that I would soon be retiring. "Then who will teach Medicine Hat students about values?" she asked. This heartfelt question highlighted for me the very unique role that I had played at MHC. For thirty-six years I had the awesome privilege of pointing students in the right direction in the area of ethics. My replacement might very well be a skeptic or a relativist.

I love teaching, and consider myself to be a good teacher. In course evaluations, students would often comment about my enthusiasm for the course material, my encouragement of discussion in class, and my willingness to help them.[12] I always had an open-door policy with regard to office-hours. I wanted students to feel free to come and see me any time to get help with the courses they were taking from me. Often the conversations extended well beyond course-related matters, as students shared personal struggles or asked about the bigger questions they were facing about life and its meaning. Teaching for me wasn't just about philosophy – it involved mentoring and caring for the whole student. Invariably, there were a few students who would often engage with me after class, or whose visits to my office were more frequent, and I cherished these deeper relationships with what I called "my disciples." I was also able to counsel many students who were Christians and who after discovering that I was a Christian professor would share their struggles with the Christian faith and the integration of faith and reason.[13]

Another category of students I have influenced significantly is those students who were inspired to go on to further studies in philosophy. I counted eight of these, though there may be more from my early teaching years.[14] Two of these students went on to get a Ph.D. in philosophy – Ardis Alexander and Nathan Kowalsky. Ardis wrote this in the final paragraph of the acknowledgements page of her M.A. thesis at the University of Lethbridge: "And finally, I owe either thanks or vengeance (depending on the day), to Elmer Thiessen of Medicine Hat College, for infecting me with the virus of philosophy and derailing my academic and career goals, replacing them with the challenge of philosophic inquiry." Several of my students also went on to study religious studies, theology, and some went on to become pastors.[15]

How many students have I influenced in some way? I did some rough calculations and would estimate my total student count prior to retirement to be about 4,500.[16] Of these many students, there were always some each year who frequently came to see me after class or in my office. Over the years, I have made notes about significant conversations I have had with these students. I have kept these notes in my "ego-booster" file. Yes, I have such a file and am thankful for it because teaching can be discouraging at times. I have looked at this growing file from time to time when my fragile ego needed a boost. Upon retirement I looked at this file again. It brought back many memories of long student conversations, sometimes accompanied by tears, and sometimes ending with prayer in my office.

It is gratifying to know that by God's grace I have been able to help many students in a significant way. As a preface to this file, I added a note: "Only known students. God keeps a perfect record." Yes, indeed! But really, in the end, a tabulation of students I have helped is rather incidental. Success is not measured in terms of the number of people one has helped.

What matters is that one has tried to be faithful. I have often reflected on Jesus' words at the conclusion of his discourse on the end of the age: "Who then is the faithful and wise servant, whom the master has put in charge of the servants in his household to give them their food at the proper time? It will be good for that servant whose master finds him doing so when he returns" (Matt 24:45-6). That is how I view teaching – giving students the intellectual food they so desperately need.

Have I always been a faithful and wise servant in my role as a teacher? Sadly, no. The apostle James has some interesting things to say about teaching in the context of a discussion of the unruliness of the tongue. James begins by raising some cautions about becoming teachers because "we who teach will be judged more strictly" (James 3:1). Then comes a confession. "For we all stumble in many ways. If anyone does not stumble in what he says, he is a perfect man, able to reign in the whole body as well" (vs. 2, NASP). Of course, we as teachers are not perfect. We can at best only stumble towards perfection and wholeness in our teaching. Thankfully for us as Christians, there is in Jesus Christ abundant grace to cover our failures.

NOTES

1. I still have a summary of student evaluations for an introductory course I taught in Orillia during the summer of my first year of teaching. Of the twenty-nine students who completed the evaluation, nineteen rated me as excellent, eight rated me as good, and two above average. I was grateful for this endorsement of my teaching early in my teaching career.

2. See my *Teaching for Commitment: Liberal Education, Indoctrination, and Christian Nurture* (Montreal & Kingston: McGill-Queen's University Press and co-published by Gracewing, Leominster, U.K., 1993).

3. See my essay, "Evangelism in the Classroom," in the *Journal of Education and Christian Belief*, Vol.17, #2 (Fall, 2013), pp. 221-41, for a treatment of this problem. A condensed version of this essay appears in *Foundations of Education: A Christian Vision*, edited by Matthew Etherington (Wipf and Stock, 2014), pp. 104-118. See also Chapter 9, "Evangelism in Professional Life: The Academy," in my more recent book, *The Scandal of Evangelism: A Biblical Study of the Ethics of Evangelism* (Cascade Books, 2018).

4. Letter from Matthew dated February 24, 1986.

5. Letter from Matthew dated, January 1994.

6. In a later telephone conversation, Matthew suggested that the piece symbolized prayer. In a later email he explained the piece this way: "Spirit is what was meant to be used

in the middle, as the piece is about breath and meditation and that space between breaths, the pause. So it is a play between both inspire and spirit."

7. Peter Berger, *A Rumor of Angels: Modern Society and the Rediscovery of the Supernatural* (Doubleday, 1969).

8. Richard Weaver, *Ideas Have Consequences* (University of Chicago Press, 1948).

9. David L. Norton, "Moral Minimalism and the Development of Moral Character," in *Moral Philosophy: A Reader*, 2nd. ed. edited by Louis Pojman (Hackett Publishing Company, 1998), pp. 296-307.

10. Many years ago I found an essay that appeared in Christianity Today (Nov. 7, 1980), written by Charles Malik, to be most inspiring. In this essay entitled, "The Other Side of Evangelism," Malik argues against the anti-intellectualism of American evangelicalism and also highlights the university as an important domain for evangelism. "Save the university and Western civilization is saved, and therewith the world." Malik was the former ambassador to the U.S. from Lebanon, United Nations General Assembly president, and three times president of the UN Security Council. This article was adapted from his address on the occasion of the dedication of the Billy Graham Center at Wheaton College. A recent book also captures my sense of teaching philosophy as a mission. See Paul M. Gould, *The Outrageous Idea of the Missional Professor* (Wipf & Stock, 2014).

11. I rejected two invitations (1994, 1999) from Larry McKinney, President of Providence College, to apply for the position of Academic Dean at this Christian college in Manitoba. In 1999 I was also asked if I would consider an administrative post at Prairie Bible Institute. After teaching at Tyndale University College in 2008-9, I was asked by the President, Gary Nelson, if I would consider a position as interim Academic Dean. Again, I declined.

12. Here are just a few notable written expressions of appreciation from students.

Alvin, a student from my early days at Medicine Hat College, wrote to me after my retirement in 2011: "I asked the MHC Alumni Association for your contact information so that I could thank you for challenging me to engage in a life of wondering. You, more than any other educator I encountered as a student, inspired me to think about issues big and small. Thank you for your good work. You were/are a learner, willing to share and argue your thoughts, questions and beliefs. You have been a role model for me of healthy curiosity and gracious argument."

Occasionally I had students who did poorly in my classes, but would nevertheless tell me that they learned a lot. For example, Kelvin wrote: "Elmer, I have to say, that despite my best efforts I'm afraid I will only manage a "C" on any of your essays. However, I also feel that I got more out of your class than I have gotten from anything else in life . . . particularly this last class. . . . Even if no one else remembers you in ten years I will."

Of course, there invariably were one or two students in a class who would give me a negative evaluation. I found that I tended to focus more on these few negative evaluations than on the vast majority of students who were very positive in their evaluations. Over time, I learned not to be too upset with the occasional negative evaluation. You can't win them all.

13. Among these Christian students were students from Hillcrest Christian College who were also taking courses at MHC. In the fall of 1980 I had delightful group of fellows who were often in my office – Dallas Miller, Doug Ponto, Lloyd Raugust, Dale Schlenker. I recall conversations with some of them about the notion of vocation. They were feeling a

lot of pressure to go into full-time Christian ministry and I tried to help them understand that "secular" vocations were also a Christian calling.

14. Doug Ponto, Ardis Alexander, Lisa Brown, Angelina Dawes, Nathan Kowalsky, Dan Barbour, Dillon Derksen, and Lee van Westerborg.

15. Henry Schorr, Eric Muirhead, and Alvin Penner, are three students I know of who went on to become pastors.

16. I kept a fairly accurate student count at Medicine Hat College, though there are always some ambiguities because of students dropping mid-semester. I estimate that I taught over 3,800 students as of the final semester of full-time teaching at MHC (this is counting each semester separately). Then there are the students I taught early in my career at Waterloo Lutheran University, for which I don't have an exact student count. In addition there is the class I taught at the University of Waterloo during graduate school, the classes at Lithuania Christian College, and an education course for the University of Lethbridge.

Chapter 10
RESEARCH, WRITING, PUBLICATIONS, AND CONFERENCES

I was initially hoping to get a university press to publish my first book on the ethics of evangelism. In my ongoing search for an academic publisher I sent a letter of inquiry (via email) to Columbia University Press in December of 2006. I was pleasantly surprised to receive an email the very next day from the senior executive editor, thanking me for writing, and expressing interest in the manuscript, although she did have a query about my approach. "Our program takes a specifically religious-studies point of view; if you are taking a strong advocacy position, the book might be more appropriately published by a press with a theology list or a religious press with an academic division such as Eerdmans or Baker." She also had some concerns about the length of the manuscript. She ended her email, "I'll look forward to hearing from you."[1]

I wrote back the same day, thanking the editor for her quick reply and responding to her query with both a yes and a no answer. "Yes, I am defending the possibility of an ethical form of proselytizing. But is my style one of *strong* advocacy? No. My approach is one of careful analysis of arguments for and against, in the best of philosophical tradition. My hunch is that many academics in the religious studies field will be nervous about my defense of proselytizing because they tend to favor religious dialogue. In the manuscript I raise some problems with some of the assumptions underlying the supposed neutrality of religious dialogue. I also need to point out that I very much do not want to use a religious publisher. As with my previous books, my aim is to bridge the language barrier and the ideological gulf that often divides religious believers from unbelievers. My manuscript was very specifically written with both a secular and a religious readership in mind. So I really do want a university press to publish the book."

The editor seemed satisfied with my response to her query, and invited me to send her the manuscript. After forwarding the manuscript to two of her advisers in religion at Columbia, she wrote back a month later and said the book was not appropriate for their press. "This is not a reflection on its scholarship but rather, as I suspected on its advocacy (despite the philosophical arguments)."[2]

I was disappointed, but not entirely surprised. I believe advocacy in philosophical argument is inescapable. I suspect what she was really saying was that I was not advocating the *right* position. It also confirmed my growing suspicion that the underlying problem I was facing in finding an academic publisher for my manuscript was that it was being vetted by scholars in religious studies who tend to *advocate* dialogue and are opposed to proselytizing. Again, I found myself going against the stream of established opinion in academia, and hence my difficulties in finding a university press to publish my manuscript. Thankfully, McGill-Queen's University Press didn't object to my advocating a position when they chose to publish my earlier two books on indoctrination and religious schools.

Early in my teaching career I vowed that I would not adopt a "publish or perish" mentality that characterizes so much of the academic world. My focus would instead be on teaching. Research and writing would interfere with being a good teacher, I felt. In any case, research and publication were not priorities at the college level where I spent most of my career. Indeed, research and writing were looked at with some suspicion by many faculty at Medicine Hat College. Given all this, it is perhaps rather surprising to find that I need to devote a chapter of my life story to the topic of research, writing, publishing and giving papers at conferences.

In December of 2018, I took on the project of collecting everything that I had written or published – a good retirement project. There were several factors that inspired this endeavour. A good friend of mine, Graham Gladwell, a mathematician, died a year earlier. At his viewing, I took note of a table his family had set up on which they had displayed Graham's dissertations, books, and a binder of his publications. I rather liked the idea, because this display represented an important part of Graham's life. So I resolved to collect my publications at some point in time so that a similar display could be set up at my funeral. I was also trying to cut down on the shelf space devoted to books and journals spread throughout our entire house. One shelf in our spare bedroom was devoted to my journal publications. What better way to clear out this shelf than to cut out my articles from these journals and collect them in binders. So began a month-long project of collecting all my writings in journals, magazines, and newspapers.[3]

In completing this project, I was surprized to discover that my foray into writing began rather early. Already in 1962, while attending the Mennonite Brethren Bible College, I wrote a devotional "Have we been with Jesus?" for the student magazine, *The Companion*. A year later, students were debating the merits of Christian high schools and I wrote a piece for *The Companion* once again, an excerpt of which also appeared in the *Mennonite Brethren Herald*. Another early article of mine was printed in a broadsheet distributed by Inter-Varsity Christian Fellowship at the University of Saskatchewan, as a form of evangelistic outreach.[4] Most of my early writing was for the *Mennonite Brethren Herald,* which eventually led to my writing a regular "Opinion" column for the magazine in the early 1980s. During this same time a significant shift occurred in the venues for which I was writing. I now began writing for academic journals. In addition, I have written five books, of which I will say more later in this chapter.

THE HOW AND WHY OF WRITING

Clearly, I did not keep my vow of not getting into research and writing. But why did I break this early promise to myself? And why does one write and publish articles and books anyway? An honest answer to these questions must surely make reference to one's ego. It feels very good to have one's name on the cover of a book in bold and large print or at the beginning or end of a published article. This motivation isn't very Christian, of course, though here we must be careful not to be too hard on the motivation of ego-enhancement. There is such a thing as proper pride in what one does – a pride that admits that all that one accomplishes is finally a gift from God. More on this shortly.

There is an important qualification that needs to be made regarding the place of the ego in writing articles and books. Seeing one's name on a book will only stroke one's ego if in fact other people buy and read your book. Annie Dillard speaks to this issue in her short and funny book entitled, *The Writing Life*. "I cannot imagine a sorrier pursuit than struggling for years to write a book that attempts to appeal to people who do not read in the first place." Dillard's quote is an expression of the fear every writer has: "What if no one ever reads a word I write?"[5] Indeed, I recall wrestling with this very question before I wrote my first "real" book – *Teaching for Commitment*. As I was contemplating reworking my Ph.D. dissertation into a book, I met with a friend of mine, Stan Riegel, to discuss my motivation for doing so. We concluded that even if no one would ever read my book, I probably should still write it.

This brings me to the deeper motivation underlying all the time and energy I have devoted to writing and publishing articles and books. I need to write because this is in keeping with the gifts that God has given me. I like ideas. I get excited about the ideas of others and feel the urge to respond to these ideas. I love the college and university environment. I feel that God has called me to a life of the mind. Teaching is of course one important way to wrestle with ideas within the context of the classroom. Writing and publishing is another way. In fact writing and publishing invigorates teaching and *vice versa*. Writing and publishing is a lonelier exercise than teaching and there is always a delay in exchanges with readers. But exchanges do occur. And sometimes I have been asked to respond to readers' responses to what I have written. It is all very exciting. And that is why I keep writing and publishing and will do so until my faculties decline or God calls me to my eternal home.

How did I manage to do so much writing and publishing while teaching at the college level where my teaching load ranged from four to six classes per semester, and twelve to eighteen hours per week? Several aspects of my character help to answer this question. I am a workaholic. I can still recall a presentation made by someone at Medicine Hat College when I came to the realization that I am a workaholic, and that this really isn't a very healthy lifestyle. Retirement has been good for me in bringing about a better balance between work and play. I am also a very disciplined person, and have great powers of concentration. I recall many times when I was sitting in my basement office in our Medicine Hat house, quite able to read and write while the children were noisily playing in the basement. It is only when the noise reached a certain decibel level that I would be aroused from my academic preoccupations to intervene and calm things down so that I could return to my office and continue my work.

Another contributing factor to my productivity in writing has to do with the yearly cycle of the college and university setting. There is a two-week break at Christmas and then a four-month break in the spring and summer months. These were the times, when apart from taking holidays with the family, I could concentrate on my writing. It also needs to be kept in mind that much of my scholarly output occurred after our children became adolescents or had left home. I recall wanting to be careful not to be too ambitious with regard to my scholarly work while the children were young. Whether I was faithful in keeping this resolve is of course another question. I do sometimes wonder whether I should have spent more time with my young family and whether I should have had more dates with my wife.

MENNONITE BRETHREN HERALD

I have already drawn attention to my early writing for the *Mennonite Brethren Herald* (henceforth simply the *Herald*). The initial excerpt from a piece I had written for the MBBC *Companion* was followed by a letter to the editor, "A L'Abri Style of Bible Institute," responding to an earlier article by Hugo Jantz on the future of bible schools. I was then asked to write a review of two early books by Francis Schaeffer (1969) – we had visited L'Abri while we were in Europe on our honeymoon. I submitted an unsolicited essay, "A Personal Relationship with God," to the *Herald* in 1970. This essay was based on an extended biblical survey I had done on the meaning of this phrase in order to sort out my own thinking on this question. I believe my 1974 article, "For No Other Foundation," was similarly based on a personal study of what the New Testament says about the church. Then came a three-part series on "God – Yes or No: The Difference it Makes in Education" (1974), which I believe was solicited, as I was paid $50.00 for this series. The latter article explains how I changed my mind about

Christian schools and was already based on some work I was doing in my doctoral program.

Further book reviews and articles led to a surprise phone call from Harold Jantz, editor of the *Herald* at the time, asking if I would consider sharing the writing of the "Opinion" column with long-time writer, John Redekop.[6] What an honor! Harold obviously liked my writing.[7] In the end, John Redekop was not interested in sharing responsibilities for writing the "Opinion" column, and so Jim Pankratz was invited to come on board and the two of us alternated in writing this column. Interestingly, John Redekop was invited to return to the "Opinion" column a year later, while Jim and I were asked to write for a new column, "The Christian Mind." This led to an exciting and stimulating two years of writing a regular column for the *Herald* once a month (1980-82).

Harold was a wonderful editor, taking the time to personally respond to most of my columns with some evaluative comments. After my first column, "Personal Opinions and Opinionated Persons" (April 11, 1980), I wrote Harold a note: "Writing this was sheer delight. I can now appreciate why it was that I accepted the assignment so readily when you phoned. In retrospect, I was somewhat surprised and even a little embarrassed that I had accepted immediately. But it just seemed so right. I am coming to see that I really love writing, and that this is perhaps where God wants me to make a contribution. Thus, thanks for giving me this opportunity. I hope I won't let you down too much."[8] Harold responded to my note and my first column: "You had a nice way of starting off your columns, Elmer. I think people will discover that you enjoy clarifying ideas and defining terms. You can help us as you do." He also encouraged me to write on my own struggles with the faith as these would help young people as they faced their deep doubts.[9]

Of course, I was interested in how people would respond to my columns. So was my dear mother. In fact, writing these columns created considerable anxiety for her. She was very sensitive to the personal comments she received about my column, as well as the letters to the editor that were critical of my ideas. Some of my columns were more controversial. For example, "Jesus Christ vs. Alberta" (Nov. 21, 1980), dealt with some existing tensions between Edmonton and Ottawa, and prompted a number of angry personal letters, though some people liked it.[10] In another column entitled, "Fortune Obligates" (Dec. 19, 1980), I was criticized for quoting a non-christian writer, John Rawls. Indeed, the same letter accused me of being a Marxist! I was pleased to see this letter carefully critiqued in subsequent letter to the editor.[11]

After two years of writing these columns, I wrote a letter to the editors of the *Herald*, suggesting that they look for someone else to write this column, in part because I felt that a column like this should have a change of voice from time to time.[12] Harold wrote an "anniversary letter" a year later, thanking me for writing the columns and encouraging me to continue writing for the *Herald*. "I know you got under the skin of some readers in a way that probably pained you as much as it did those who were at the other end. You have a way of arguing from a Christian perspective which I like and I want to encourage you to continue doing it."[13] I am still grateful for the privilege of writing these columns for the *Herald*, in part because I acquired the discipline of conveying ideas in a succinct manner.

I did continue writing quite a few articles and book reviews for the *Herald* in subsequent years. I was very pleased to write a major essay for a new venture of the *Herald*, special quarterly issues that were intended to be used for outreach, under the title, *Encounter*. My essay was entitled "Truth in a Pluralist World" (Feb. 21, 1997). I say more about this essay in Chapter 12. A number of my later articles created considerable controversy.[14] Then there were a couple of essays that I submitted to the *Herald* that were accepted, and subsequently rejected due to political pressure or editorial squeamishness.[15]

Writing for a church magazine is an interesting exercise, especially if you as a writer are not entirely comfortable with the status quo and want to expand readers' horizons. I trust that some of my writing has influenced some leaders and members of the church in the right direction.[16] Am I now embarrassed about what I wrote many years ago? I believe my column on Fort McMurray, "O Great City" (February 12, 1982), which created a lot of negative feedback, would have been better left unwritten. There are times when I should have been more careful in how I said things, more gentle and more mediating between polarized positions. I certainly tried to do this with my article on "Contemporary Worship Culture" (May 3, 2002), but despite doing so, this article still garnered quite a bit of criticism. One indication that I am not too embarrassed about what I wrote for the *Herald* and how I wrote what I did, is the fact that I have posted many of my columns and articles as blogs since I started blogging in 2011, and I did so with very little revision.[17]

SECULAR MAGAZINES AND NEWSPAPERS

As with my teaching, I have also felt called to write within the "secular" domain. And here I have always been concerned to bridge the divide that often exists between the Christians and those who reject Christianity. I have already mentioned my early attempt to do so during my first year at the University of Saskatchewan, writing an apologetics piece for an IVCF broadsheet. While in Medicine Hat, I started writing op-ed pieces for the *Medicine Hat News* on such topics as religious schools (March 6, 1982), Sunday shopping (Jan. 15, 1987), and the controversial firing of Dr. David Swann, Regional Health Officer (Oct. 12, 2002). I was on the Ethics Committee of the Palliser Health Authority at the time I wrote the last-mentioned op-ed piece.

After we moved to Waterloo in 2007, I responded to an article inviting members of the community to apply for a one-year position on a sixteen-member Community Editorial Board of the *Waterloo Region Record*. Membership on this Board entailed writing an op-ed piece at least six times per year. Applications required a 500-word essay on a local subject. I submitted a piece about Ontario attitudes to religious schools which had become a wedge issue in the recent provincial election. My application was successful and so began a two-year stint of writing for the *Record* – they extended my term after the first year was up. I quite enjoyed writing these op-ed pieces, many of which focussed on ethical topics.[18] At the one-year anniversary of the election I submitted a revised version of my essay on Ontario attitudes to faith-based schools which I had written earlier as part of my application for this position (Nov. 7, 2008). Occasionally, members of the Community Editorial Board were also asked to submit additional short reflections on timely topics such as earth day, thanksgiving, and budget questions. As an Anabaptist pacifist, I agonized about what to write about remembrance day (November 11, 2008 & 2009).

Another effort at writing in the secular domain relates to events described in the previous chapter. I simply couldn't resist writing a response to a 2013 Calgary CBC News report, "Auditor general uncovers scandal at Medicine Hat College." My letter included this statement: "The politics of Medicine Hat College has been characterized by a pitiful parochialism for a long, long time."[19]

ACADEMIC PAPERS, CONFERENCES, AND SABBATICALS

I have already alluded to a shift in my writing which coincided with the completion of my Ph.D. in 1980.[20] My dissertation topic was on the concept of indoctrination, and this led to a number of subsequent publications. I still have a vivid memory of my excitement about the first major paper accepted by the prestigious *Journal of Philosophy of Education*, published by the Philosophy of Education Society of Great Britain. "Indoctrination and Doctrines" was based on a chapter in my dissertation, and was subsequently reprinted in an anthology, as were a good number of my papers.[21] Later articles and chapters in books that touch in some way on the topic of indoctrination number over thirty. Other topics that figure significantly in my academic writing include the following: parental rights in education; the possibility of a distinctively Christian curriculum; tolerance; educational pluralism; academic freedom; committed openness, and more recently, the ethics of evangelism.

I felt academically isolated at Medicine Hat College. So I made it a point to regularly attend the Learned Societies Conferences that met at a different Canadian university each summer. I was one of the few faculty at the College who did so. We had a professional development fund at the College (about $800 per year) which I used to attend these conventions. They were most often a highlight of the year and played an important role in connecting me to the broader academic and university community. One problem I encountered in attending these conventions was that I was torn between attending papers of the Philosophy Society and those in the in the philosophy division of the Education Society. Given that my research was in the area of philosophy of education, I presented papers mainly at meetings of the Education Society.

I did not feel secure in presenting these papers for quite some time. In part this was a result of my not being a quick thinker. I need time to digest any objections to what I have said, but the questions asked after a presentation require quick thinking. This feeling of insecurity was also part of a more general insecurity I felt about myself and my academic abilities.[22] In part my insecurity was also a result of the overall thrust of my writing. I was defending Christian nurture in the home and education in Christian schools. My position was very anti-establishment – objecting to a state system of education and defending educational pluralism. So I could expect that most scholars who heard my presentations would be strongly opposed to the arguments I was presenting.[23] And sometimes the hostility to what I was saying was palpable. At one of the first papers I presented at the Learned Societies meetings held in Ottawa in 1982 ("Indoctrination and Religious Education"), my first respondent started by saying, "I disagree with everything you say." Not exactly confidence boosting!

I also remember a paper, "Christian Nurture and the Ideal of Autonomy" that I presented at a branch meeting of the Philosophy of Education Society of Great Britain at Cambridge. This was during a short visit to England in the spring of 1990 to consult with a number of scholars, a visit that was funded by a Social Sciences and Humanities Research Council (SSHRC) grant. I discovered that Professor Paul Hirst, the guru of philosophy of education in England, was present at this meeting, dressed in a dark pin-striped suit. After my presentation, he gave a detailed and devastating critique of my paper. I was mortified and could only provide a weak response. Later in my college room, I wrote out a detailed response to Hirst, but it was too late! Interestingly, towards the end of his career, Paul Hirst changed some of his ideas about education so that they were in fact more in line with my own thinking. I like to think that my paper contributed to this change of mind!

I received a rather mixed response to a paper I gave at a conference in Saskatoon in 2003 – "The Future of Catholic Higher Education in Canada." The conference was sponsored by the Association of Catholic Colleges and Universities in Canada and was being organized by Rev. Dr. George Smith, President of St. Thomas More College in Saskatoon, and former President of St. Joseph's College in Edmonton as well as St. Michael's College in Toronto. When George called to invite me to this conference he informed me that he was reading my book, *In Defense of Religious Schools and Colleges*, and that he liked it and was in fact writing a review of my book.[24] He wanted me to present a paper defending Catholic Higher Education – a rather strange assignment given that I was not a Catholic, but he persisted because he felt that the presidents of Catholic colleges in Canada might discover things that might not be to their liking. Indeed, at the conference I was surprised to discover resistance to a statement on Catholic colleges and universities written by Pope John Paul II (*Ex Corde Ecclesia*, 1990). No wonder I encountered resistance to some of the ideas in my paper. After the conference, George Smith told me how pleased he was with my paper, and then informed me that some of the bishops present were ready to induct me into the Catholic church. The Secretary General of the International Federation of Catholic Universities, Prof. Guy-Réal Thivierge, approached me towards the end of the conference and complimented me on my paper, inviting me to visit him in Paris sometime. Gladly, though this never did happen! I was also pleased to sell a good number of my books, another measure of success, I discovered, when presenting papers at conferences.

I was invited to give a paper at a conference on "Religion, Spirituality and Character" to be held at St. Edmunds College in Cambridge, February 9-11, 2007. This was my last year at Medicine Hat College, though I was teaching on a contract-basis at this point in time.[25] I wrestled with the decision to go, given that I was struggling with anxiety and depression at the time, but with my doctor's encouragement, eventually decided in favor of going. Indeed, I saw this as a fitting conclusion to my career as a research scholar. However, I never did make it to Cambridge. After all my preparation, there was a severe snow storm in Medicine Hat on the day of my departure. My plane to Calgary was four hours late and so I didn't make the connection to the Heathrow flight. I tried again the next day and this time the Calgary to Heathrow flight was cancelled because of engine problems. I guess I was not meant to go, but it was most disappointing. However, my paper was still included in the book that grew out of that conference.[26]

I have always taken seriously the challenge that Alvin Plantinga gave to Christian philosophers, to the effect that we should always also be thinking of service to the church.[27] I was therefore happy to share my research conclusions at a number of church institutions and organizations. For example, in the spring of 2004 I was invited to be a plenary speaker at the annual Veritas Forum, sponsored by Lexington Christian Academy, near Boston. My biggest honorarium ever – $1,000. 00. More recently, my work on the ethics of evangelism has resulted in invitations to a number of international conferences which brought me to Switzerland, California, Albania, and Ghana. (See Chapter 7 for more on these conferences.)[28]

Other highlights of my time at Medicine Hat College were my sabbaticals. Given the academic isolation I felt at the College, sabbaticals were a way to connect to the larger academic world. What was somewhat surprising was that sabbaticals were being granted at the College even though it was in the main a teaching institution. I applied for a sabbatical every seven years and enjoyed four sabbaticals over my thirty-six year career at Medicine Hat College. The first sabbatical was spent back in Waterloo to finish my dissertation for my Ph.D. (1978-79). Then in 1985-6 we spent a delightful year at Oxford where I was a fellow at Mansfield College, arranged through John Wilson, a prominent British writer in the philosophy of education. I found the association with Mansfield College to be largely meaningless because their dinners were far too late for me and interfered with family time. What I enjoyed at Oxford was attending lectures, being part of the Christian Philosophers Association, having time to work on my first "real" book growing out of my dissertation, and enjoying a broadening experience with the family – described in Chapter 4.

My third sabbatical was spent in two places – teaching at Lithuania Christian College in the fall semester, and then spending time at the Stapleford Education Centre in England, working with Trevor Cooling and John Shortt (1993-4; see Chapter 5 for more details). Here I was working on my second book, *In Defense of Religious Schools and Colleges*. My final sabbatical was again spent in two places, first at the Centre for the Study of Religion, University of Toronto, and then the Centre for Studies in Religion and Society, at the University of Victoria (2000-1). This was a wonderful year, spending time with Geoff and Audrey and our grandchildren in Toronto in the fall, and then enjoying beautiful Victoria in the winter. This year was dedicated to working on my book, *The Ethics of Evangelism*. (See Chapter 6 for more details.)

BOOKS, GRANTS, AND AWARDS

I have already begun talking about the books I have published – five in total. It has been hard to separate the different elements of my academic career in this chapter. Describing the books I have published is of course closely linked to my sabbaticals. There were two other years that might be considered sabbaticals and that are closely tied to the writing of my books. Early in 1981 Harold Coward, head of the Humanities Institute at the University of Calgary, contacted me about a major grant he had received from the Alberta government to study the place of humanities in Alberta's thirteen colleges and technical institutes. I was ready for a change of pace and thought that accepting this assignment might open some other doors to get out of Medicine Hat College. So I was seconded to the University of Calgary for the 1981-82 academic year to work on this project. In retrospect, this year was a mistake, very stressful and hard on the family, and it didn't lead to any further academic opportunities. But it did result in a book co-authored with Harold Coward, *Humanities in Alberta Post-Secondary Technical and Vocational Education* (University of Calgary Press, 1985).

I had been thinking about converting my dissertation into a book for some time. Work on this project began in the spring of 1987. This project was given a significant boost a few years later when I was awarded a major Social Sciences and Humanities Research Council (SSHRC) grant.[29] For me, this grant had a double significance. It confirmed that God really wanted me to write this book, and it also gave me a year's leave from Medicine Hat College and a much needed relief from messy college politics. So in 1989-90 I spent a year at home writing my book, although I did visit the College once a week to keep up contacts. My schedule was therefore more relaxed and Maggie and I even took in a series of operas in Calgary during this year.

My SSHRC budget included a visit to England for research purposes and so I spent three weeks consulting with scholars and giving papers at conferences.[30] Maggie joined me a week after I arrived and so she was able to accompany me on some of these academic visits. We also enjoyed some holiday time together, including a return visit to Oxford where we met old friends at church and stayed at the Eddys. It was a good three weeks of academic contacts and travel – we put on a total of 1,600 miles in our rented car.

Writing continued over the summer. I hired Joy Chandler to edit the manuscript and discovered some deeply engrained grammatical and stylistic errors in my writing. Finally, on September 1, 1990, I was able to send the manuscript off to McGill-Queen's University Press by Greyhound Courier. Doing so felt very much like giving birth to a baby. Now began the long wait until my book would finally see the light of day. Here let

me interject two unique aspects of my getting this book into print. Publishing was very different at that time – you still sent a hard copy of a manuscript to a publisher and copy-editing also was done on hard copy. The second noteworthy feature of this writing project was that the first few chapters of this manuscript were written in long-hand. I purchased my first Abco computer and printer in the fall of 1987. I remember being very skittish about switching from long-hand writing to composing text on a computer. But making this switch was easier than I had anticipated and of course it was so much easier to make revisions on a word-processor. I am forever grateful for the invention of the computer and also that I learned to type in my early years at Medicine Hat College.

My choice of McGill-Queen's University Press for my book came after an unnecessarily prolonged search for a publisher.[31] In fact McGill-Queen's University Press expressed interest in my manuscript quite early in my search. My editor, Peter Blaney carefully walked me through the various steps in publishing a book.[32] I was somewhat humiliated with the copy-editing process – the manuscript came back with 100's of tabs on pages with corrections. Francis Rooney, my copy-editor, at one point inserted, "please" with a large question mark. Another sign of her frustration was her correction of my bad habit of using dangling pronouns, "many," "others," and "some." At one point she had a tab with another question, "rabbits?" After the copy-editing was done, she was kind enough to respond to my request for a list of common errors that I made in my writing. My editor also arranged to have the book co-published in the United Kingdom by a Catholic publisher, Gracewing.[33]

Finally, in January of 1993, upon our arrival in England from Lithuania, I got to see the first copy of my book with the bold title, *Teaching for Commitment: Liberal Education, Indoctrination and Christian Nurture*.[34] All told, it was a six-year process, not counting the work on the dissertation from which many of the ideas of this book were taken. In retrospect I realize that I had chosen a very timely topic for my dissertation and book that led to an array of published articles and papers presented at academic conferences. I also received a number of invitations to speak at Christian educators associations.[35]

I collected over twenty academic and ten non-academic reviews of my book, most of which were quite positive.[36] Brenda Watson from the UK wrote, "This is an important book which deserves to be widely read by educationalists. Formidable in its logic, it will be found difficult to refute its main thesis: the defence of religious nurture against any necessary charge of indoctrination."[37] I was delighted to read a review in the Canadian magazine, *Christian Week*, by Ron Richmond, Professor of Education at the University of Regina, who wrote: "So well executed within the scholarly tradition and so solidly and openly Christian in its approach, this work may well set a new standard for Christian apologetics by Canadian authors. . . . The book excels as a model for effective communication of our Christian worldview within the dynamic pluralism of contemporary life."[38] My friend, Trevor Cooling, rightly criticized the book for being too thorough and too long.[39] I would add that I quoted other writers too much and didn't let my own voice come through enough. But it was my first real book and thus I was still trying to prove myself in academia. I think I succeeded. The book sold fairly well for an academic book and I was pleased to find that it was used as a text in a few courses in philosophy of education at universities.[40] I promised the children each a car if the royalties on my book were high, but in the end I was only able to give them a dinky car that first Christmas after the book came out.[41]

My third book, *In Defence of Religious Schools and Colleges*, is in part a collection of essays that I had been writing over the years, though it is also a sustained argument against a monolithic state-maintained system of education and for a more pluralistic approach to schooling.[42] As with several of my books, my aim was to facilitate dialogue between religious and secular adherents of opposing positions, as stated in the Prologue to this book. "My approach aims specifically at bridging language and worldview barriers."[43] Work on this book began soon after my second book came out, during a sabbatical spent first in Lithuania and then at Stapleford Education Centre in the UK in 1993-4. I again attempted to get some outside funding for this project, but was unsuccessful.[44]

In the summer of 1994, I attended the Learned Society meetings in Calgary. While there I visited the booth of McGill-Queens University Press, where Peter Blaney, my former editor, asked me whether I was working on another book project. After my positive response he immediately expressed interest in my project. Given this interest and also given my satisfaction with McGill-Queen's publication of my previous book, it didn't take me long to decide that they would be my first choice for a publisher, even though there were a few presses which had expressed interest in this project.[45]

Reading proofs of my third book on the way to Victoria in 2000

In January of 1999 I sent two copies of the manuscript together with the registration form for the Aid to Scholarly Publishing Program (ASPP) grant to Aurele Parisien, my new editor at McGill-Queen's University Press.[46] I received a contract in December of that same year. I then hired Nora Harder to help me with macro-editing and we managed to condense the manuscript by 100 pages. The revised manuscript was submitted on May 23, 2000. An attempt was again made to co-publish this book with Gracewing in the UK, but they declined this time around. The book came out in the summer of 2001 – 2 ½ years after first submitting my manuscript to McGill-Queen's Press.[47] I collected about fifteen academic reviews of the book, most of them positive. Charles Glenn described the book as "the most comprehensive and systematic treatment" of criticisms of religious schools and colleges available at that time.[48] I could live with that, though I wish this would have translated into more sales.[49] One reviewer correctly pointed out that much of the material in this book had already appeared as published journal articles, and that the value of this book was that the arguments for and against religious schools were all brought together in one volume.[50]

My fourth book dealing with the ethics of evangelism, was begun during my fourth and final sabbatical which, as already noted, was spent in Toronto and Victoria in 2000-2001. I had a conversation with Roger Martin of McGill-Queen's University Press at the Congress meetings in 2003, and he expressed interest in my project. However, he felt I might be better off with an American publisher in terms of marketing such a book and encouraged me to pursue this avenue first. So I went on a long and rather fruitless search for an American publisher.[51] The introduction to this chapter gives one example of the difficulties I faced in getting a university press to publish my manuscript. Had this been my first book, I would have been very discouraged, but I never really doubted the merits of this project.

After a few years of searching for a publisher while still working on the project, I went back to Roger Martin at McGill-Queen's University Press who was surprised to hear about my difficulties and quite happy to take on the project himself. Unfortunately, our attempt to get a subvention to cover some of the publication costs from the Aid to Scholarly Publication Program was unsuccessful, and without this, MQUP did not feel it could publish my book. So, after two and one-half years of consideration by MQUP, I had to start once again searching for a publisher. Roger Martin was so disappointed that MQUP couldn't publish my book that he continued to work informally for me as a consultant in my ongoing search for a publisher.[52]

A colleague at the Evangelische Theologische Faculteit in Belgium where I was teaching in the winter of 2009 encouraged me to submit the manuscript to Paternoster Press in the United Kingdom. I did so and very quickly received an expression of interest from Robin Parry, the editor. However, he asked me to cut the manuscript by 40%. Reducing the manuscript by 40% seemed like a formidable challenge, but in the end I came to appreciate the request. Indeed, I believe my previous two books with McGill-Queen's University Press would have been improved considerably if my editors had been brave enough to demand cuts. In the end I only achieved a 25% cut, but Robin was satisfied with my revisions and accepted the manuscript for publication. Robin was also successful in finding a co-publisher for the book – InterVarsity Press in the USA. I was particularly pleased about this because over the years I have been very much influenced by the publications of InterVarsity Press. So finally, after a long search for a publisher, numerous consultations with scholars, and five major revisions of the manuscript, *The Ethics of Evangelism: A Philosophical Defense of Proselytizing and Persuasion* got to see the light of day, and with two publishers (2011).[53]

The Ethics of Evangelism can be seen as an extension of my previous two books. All of my books deal with the problem of religious influence and persuasion. My earlier books focused specifically on influence and persuasion in the educational context. In this book I am looking at the persuasion of individuals in relation to religious conversion. I had three basic objectives in mind when I wrote the book: to defend evangelism against a variety of objections, to defend evangelism more generally, and to develop criteria to distinguish between ethical and unethical forms of evangelism. This book was again written with two readerships in mind: skeptics who are opposed to religion and religious persuasion, and religious adherents, especially evangelical Christians, who are very much committed to evangelism.

I was very pleased with the response to this book. This has been my most popular book in terms of sales.[54] I was asked to do three radio interviews about the book.[55] From reviews and personal letters and phone calls I heard repeated comments to the effect that the book was being widely read, and even used in book clubs.[56] Reviews repeatedly made mention of the fact that I had written a well-argued and much needed treatment of the ethics of evangelism.[57] John Bowen, Director of the Institute of Evangelism at Wycliffe College, Toronto, wrote: "This book is a great gift to all who are reflective practitioners of mission and evangelism."[58] As might be expected, some Mennonite reviews were somewhat critical.[59]

I was somewhat hesitant about entering this book for The Word Guild's 2012 Canadian Christian Writing Awards, but in the end, submitted an application. Winners were announced at the Awards Gala at World Vision Headquarters in Mississauga on June 13, 2012. I was pleasantly surprised to discover that my book won awards in three categories: Apologetics/Evangelism, Culture, and an Award of Merit in the Academic category. I was further pleased when Medicine Hat College recognized me in a full-page interview in their alumni magazine in 2011, with a picture of me holding this book.[60] This would seem to have been a follow-up to my winning the Academic Achievement Award at Medicine Hat College in 1999.

It took me a while to get inspired to write my next book, which I had in fact already promised in my book on the ethics of evangelism.[61] Part of my hang-up in getting started on this project was that I was unclear as to my objectives, and at first was trying to include too much material in my projected table of contents.[62] I finally concluded that if I just did a biblical study of the ethics of evangelism and then applied the results of this study to some specific problems, this would be quite enough for a book. Another factor behind my hesitation in taking up this project was my feeling that this book would be better written by a biblical scholar. Then again, I've never been hesitant to study the bible on my own, and maybe there is some merit in having a philosopher try to discover what the bible has to say about the ethics of evangelism. My first task therefore was to read through the entire bible, noting any passages that might have some relevance to the topic.[63]

During our Mexico holiday in the winter of 2013 I wrote up a one-page description of the approach I wanted to take in writing this next book. I also reviewed some reasons as to why I needed to write the book, one being that I needed an ongoing project to give me purpose in life after retirement! Guidelines for this new book included a resolve to make it shorter than my previous books and that it be written at a more popular level. I also promised myself that this should not be an all-consuming project and that I would limit myself to two hours of writing per day – a promise I certainly didn't keep!

Serious writing on this project began in 2014. This time around I was more intentional about getting readers to give me feedback on the manuscript, with Maggie reading the entire manuscript several times.[64] In July of 2016, I submitted a proposal with some sample chapters of my manuscript to Paternoster who had first right of refusal on the next work that I might produce. They decided not to accept this manuscript and I was not entirely surprised or disappointed. I therefore wrote to Robin Barrow, who was my initial editor for the previous book, but who had since moved to Wipf & Stock. It took them only a few weeks to consider and accept my proposal, though Robin was encouraging me to condense the manuscript to under 100,000 words.[65] There were also a few more changes I wanted to make and so work continued on further revisions. I was able to send the completed manuscript to Wipf & Stock on September 6, 2017. We took a picture of the event because it seemed so anti-climactic to simply press the "Send" button on the computer. How very different from the process involved in submitting my first book.

I encountered a number of unnecessary hassles with the copy-editing process. Preparing indexes also took a considerable amount of time, this being the first book which needed a Scripture index. *The Scandal of Evangelism: A Biblical Study of the Ethics of Evangelism* was published in April of 2018, and I saw my first copies of the book a month later.[66] My first on-line review appeared in July of the same year and was written by Robin Brace, UK Apologetics. Very positive, in fact too positive. A review in *Themelios* credits this book with filling a gap in treatments of evangelism, and describes it as "both highly informed by academia and personal experience," and concludes by "highly" recommending it.[67]

Bob Robinson at Laidlaw College in New Zealand compared my book to some noteworthy classics: "not since Michael Green's *Evangelism in the Early Church*, and Walter Brueggemann's *Biblical Perspectives on Evangelism* – each now several decades old – has there been such a comprehensive and balanced account of the biblical foundations (of evangelism)."[68] I can handle such comparisons! However, Robinson did go on to critique the book for underplaying the "scandal" of evangelism highlighted in the title of the book, as well as not doing justice to the pluralist and postmodern context of the world in which evangelism is now practiced. Fair criticisms. Sales have so far been disappointing, perhaps because another book on the ethics of evangelism came out in the same year.[69]

SOME CONCLUDING REFLECTIONS

After collecting and organizing all my articles into binders and then writing this chapter, I was surprised to discover how much I had written. I obviously enjoy writing and in my retirement it has become a hobby – I don't seem to have any other hobbies that can fill my time. While I have researched and written on a wide variety of topics, a central focus of my writing has clearly been on the ethics of influence and persuasion in various contexts. I want to believe that I have made a bit of a contribution to the discussion of this topic, perhaps mainly in clarifying the language we use when talking about influence and persuasion.[70] I am after all an analytic philosopher.

I am also painfully aware of the limitations of my writing. I do not have an encyclopedic mind and so have not been able to do justice to drawing on the history of ideas in treating my topics. I have also tried very hard to write at a more popular level, but in the end, my books are all rather academic in nature. I think I have done better at writing on a more popular level when writing shorter pieces, columns for the *Mennonite Brethren Herald* and op-ed pieces for the *Waterloo Region Record*. I don't see myself as a brilliant scholar, but I make up for this in terms of discipline and careful research. I also don't see myself as very original in my thinking. I tend to feed off the ideas of others. My strength is in critique, and in bringing to light the presuppositions underlying arguments. I am thankful to all who have contributed to the development of my ideas.

Has there been some evolution in my thinking and writing in the areas of education and the ethics of influence? I certainly hope that my thinking has become more nuanced over time. Some convictions have remained the same. Others have changed or are still evolving. What follows are a few reflections on changing, unchanging, and evolving convictions of mine after several decades of research and writing about the ethics of influence and persuasion in the classroom and beyond. This is not the place to provide detailed explanations as to why I hold these ten convictions. For that the reader is encouraged to read what I have written over the years.

(1) First, I have come to the conclusion that we are not as free as we often assume. We are not completely autonomous as is so often assumed in educational and religious literature. All of us are born into a particular context that shapes who we are and what we think. We are also much more dependent on others in our thinking than we tend to realize.

(2) There is therefore a need for each of us to be more transparent with regard to the degree to which we have been influenced by others and by our social environment. Pretending that we are autonomous thinkers who are objective and completely rational is dishonest.

(3) Open-mindedness is therefore a key intellectual virtue. Open-mindedness is not the same as empty-mindedness. There are no empty minds. What is needed therefore is "committed openness." Genuine open-mindedness starts by acknowledging the commitments with which each of us begin in any conversation or debate. At the same time we need to be open to evaluating our commitments and this will require that we listen to the insights of others who might disagree with us. This also requires intellectual humility.

(4) I have found that much of our thinking with regard to indoctrination is and continues to be very muddled. I believe my early definition of indoctrination as the failure to foster growth towards normal autonomy is still correct. But it needs to be stressed that such growth presupposes that there is a starting point, that children are born into a primary culture, and there is nothing wrong with initiating a child into a primary culture. But parents and teachers must also foster the growth of children towards normal autonomy. Here the qualification of "normal" is very important. We are not aiming for complete autonomy because this is unattainable and undesirable for finite, fallible, and dependent human creatures.

(5) Given my emphasis on a developmental approach to defining indoctrination and describing a liberal education, I am increasingly questioning the need for Christian schools as students mature. This might be surprising given that I have written two books defending Christian schools and colleges. I still believe that a strong case can be made for Christian schools at the elementary levels of education. But surely at some point, students should be placed into an educational environment where they will encounter a plurality of worldviews and where they will be forced to grapple with challenges to the Christian worldview that they have been initiated into and that has been reinforced by their Christian upbringing and Christian education thus far.

(6) Of course, this begs an important question – at what point have Christian students matured enough to be released into the "world" and exposed to a Babel of values and beliefs without the security of a Christian educational environment? I believe this question needs more attention from Christian educationalists. Here let me be so bold as to suggest that when students begin their post-secondary education, there is no need for Christian colleges and universities. I have gradually come to believe that encouraging growth towards autonomy in Christian students is best accomplished within "secular" colleges or universities that are committed to plurality – a plurality of students and professors and worldviews. Here it needs to be stressed that the qualifier "secular" does not mean neutrality. Nor am I condoning higher education committed to a worldview of "secularism." As I have argued in many places, there is no such a thing as a neutral education.

(7) It needs to be stressed that my suggestion in the previous point would entail a fairly radical transformation of our "secular" colleges and universities. What is needed at each "public" college and university is an

educational environment that includes a genuine pluralism of worldviews. Thus more attention would need to be paid to ensuring that our colleges and universities hire professors representing a broad range of worldviews.[71] Professors would also need to be given the freedom to teach their courses from their particular worldview perspective. This would create an invigorating educational environment where all perspectives are welcomed and openly challenged.

(8) I do not expect that I will get too much support for my proposal in the previous point. So, for the sake of argument, let us assume that Christian colleges and universities continue to exist. Here let me share another growing conviction of mine that will no doubt also be met with a good deal of opposition. I am not at all sure that we need *denominational* institutions of Christian higher education. Why this growing conviction? In my writings, I have argued repeatedly for a distinctively Christian curriculum. I have also argued that recurring proposals for multiple models of Christian scholarship are unwarranted. I believe the Reformed model of integrating faith and learning (with perhaps some refinements) is in fact the best, and perhaps even the only valid way to approach Christian learning and scholarship. I believe the basic doctrines of creation, fall, and redemption, which all Christians share, are in fact central to defining what Christian scholarship and what a Christian curriculum should look like. Does it not follow that the plurality of denominational institutions of higher learning is therefore a mistake?[72] I therefore propose a more ecumenical approach when it comes to Christian higher education.

(9) I have also come to a greater appreciation of the importance of freedom of thought within a society, including the freedom of religious thought. My defense of Christian evangelism rests on the existence of genuine intellectual and religious freedom within a society. Such freedom must however be exercised in such a way that all influence and persuasion is done in an ethical manner. Hence the importance of guidelines for ethical evangelism and persuasion of any kind.

(10) Finally, I have been pleased to discover that since the writing of my first book on the ethics of evangelism, there has been a burgeoning of interest in evangelical circles of ensuring that evangelism is conducted in an ethical manner. The end does not justify any means. At the same time, I worry about the tendency in liberal and main-line churches to disregard the traditional notion of evangelism and to focus only on "embodied

witness" and a social agenda of working for justice.[73] We need both works and words. Jesus clearly taught us both to proclaim the good news and to work for peace and justice.

I turn now to some general reflections on research and the writing of articles and books. Writing is a lonely exercise, and thus I have found it very gratifying to be invited to conferences where I could share my ideas and interact with scholars working in the same field. Since the publication of my work on the ethics of evangelism, I have especially enjoyed the international conferences I could attend.[74]

Then there have been the surprise letters, emails, or phone calls that have affirmed me in the work I have done. For example, just a few years ago Jan Hábl, from the Department of Pedagogy at the Hradec Králové University, Czech Republic, wrote to me prefacing his request to write an endorsement for a book he was writing with this comment: "Many years ago your book *Teaching for Commitment* saved my intellectual life." Then in a subsequent letter: "Yes, your book on indoctrination was like revelation for me. So thorough and well argued. And liberating – in the process of educating my own children. Thank you again!"[75]

Early in 2017 I received a phone call from a complete stranger, someone from Brazil, visiting in Waterloo, who wanted to meet with me. We agreed to meet at Tim Hortons the following day. After a few pleasantries, I discovered that Alexandre Magno Fernandes Moreira was Catholic lawyer, working for parental rights in education in Brazil. He had run across my writings on-line, and so wanted to meet me in person and also purchase copies of my books which are hard to get in Brazil. His lovely wife and beautiful two-year-old twin daughters joined us later in our conversation. It was so good to meet this deeply pious Catholic Christian, working to build the kingdom of God in another country. It was also very encouraging for me – writing too is a ministry! Later Alexandre arranged for a Skype conversation with some of the people he meets with regularly in Brazil.

After the publication of my book on the ethics of evangelism, I received another email from Rachel Uthmann who introduced herself as working for the International Association for Refugees.[76] She is often a resource person trying to help churches think about the ethics of combining aid and evangelism. She had run across my paper from the Micah Network consultation in Switzerland and had also read my book, *The Ethics of Evangelism*. She went on to write: "Your work seems to be very unique and so very insightful for addressing the complexities of ministry in relief situations." She then asked if there was an updated version of the principles I had expounded at the Micah Network conference. Contacts like these make writing seem worthwhile and I am thankful for such encouragements.

In reviewing my files I came across a number of writing projects that never saw the light of day. In 1985, while on sabbatical in Oxford, I did some work on a bible study guide on epistemology. I sent a proposal to a few publishers but there was no interest in this project.[77] I still think the project has some merit. Who knows, I might take it up again. In 2008 Perry Glanzer and I began planning for a book that would work out the implication of a Christian worldview for education. As we proceeded, both of us found ourselves lacking motivation for the project, in part because we both had some misgivings about the focus of the anticipated book.[78]

I conclude with some comments about what has perhaps been the most difficult part of my career as a Christian academic, namely the call to suffer for the sake of Jesus Christ. For me this has come to the fore especially in an important part of academic life – applying for various kinds of research grants and fellowships. An essential part of this process is to have one's proposals for such awards vetted by referees. It is a good process, and generally it leads to helpful comments on one's work. But at times biases come to the fore as I have experienced on a number of occasions.[79]

In one case a referee chose to speak on behalf of other Canadian academics in my field, informing me that "some scholars, both in philosophy and in religious studies, regard [Thiessen] as dogmatic, inflexible, and narrow in training and perspective." He went on: "It is true that in certain ways Thiessen marches to the beat of a different drummer than most of his colleagues in Canadian philosophy of religion and religious studies." This same referee went on to encourage me "to adhere to a philosophical approach to [my] subject, and to avoid casual excursions into theology and other disciplines." Another referee expressed concern about my "consuming research interests and studies," which all seemed to focus on the defence of religion. And then this: "Could he overcome his own personal religious convictions and concentrate on developing philosophical arguments that could compel and stand against any critical inquiry simply because they represent philosophical thinking at its best." This very same comment appeared again in a later evaluation of an application for a SSHRC grant. I suspect it was the same person.

Well, I didn't get that grant, nor the earlier fellowship. While I would be the first to admit that there may be some good academic reasons as to why I didn't get them, and while I am also prepared to admit that some of the criticisms made in these reports may have some justification, I do have a problem with their cutting edge. There are anti-christian biases out there and they hurt. After reading these reports, I had to swallow hard a few times, pray a little, do some introspection, and ask myself the hard question as to whether there was some legitimacy to some of the criticisms. But, in the end I needed to move on, still marching to the beat of a different drummer, and still writing on topics that I felt called to write about. I also had to remind myself that insofar as these comments represented an anti-christian bias, I needed to accept them as inevitable consequences of my Christian commitment. After all, Christ has called us to share in His sufferings, and that includes philosophers who are followers of Jesus Christ (Matt 5:11; 1 Pet 2:21).

NOTES

1. Letter from Wendy Lochner, dated December 21, 2006.

2. Letter dated January 16, 2007.

3. My collection of short articles, letters to editors, academic articles, book reviews, and chapters of books fills four binders. The binder which contains all my articles in magazines and newspapers, both religious and secular, includes over 100 pieces as of January 2021. Another binder has over seventy-five book reviews that have appeared in religious magazines, academic journals, and my blogs. Two large binders collect my seventy-seven academic articles and chapters in anthologies (eight of these are longer critical reviews of books which are also included in the book reviews binder). Anyone wishing to have a list of all my publications should feel free to contact me. (See my contact information in the Preface.)

4. The article was entitled "The Historicity of the Bible," and was co-authored with Len Pauls (1964). Other titles in the broadsheet included, "Does God Exist?", "Is Morality Absolute?", and "A Chat with a Religious Leader," which was an excerpt from the Gospel of John, using the Phillips translation.

5. These reflections are found in a three-part *Convivium* series based on a workshop led by Canadian author, lawyer, and former MP, John Weston, at a meeting of the Christian Writers' Guild in Ottawa (May 7, 2018).

6. Letter dated February 16, 1980.

7. In fact while working on a piece for the *Mennonite Brethren Herald* which Harold Jantz had asked me to write, "The Church Facing the Eighties in a World of Shifting

Values" (1980), I asked Harold to edit a draft of this article because I was discovering "how bad a writer I really am," while in the process of writing my dissertation. He responded, "Don't under-rate your writing abilities (Letter dated November 29, 1979).

8. Letter dated March 22, 1980.

9. Harold also told me not to worry about my writing style. "My main concern is that you concentrate on saying what you want to say. If your idea gets through clearly – and I've no doubt that it will – the rest can easily be taken care of here." In fact he had done a little editing on this first column, and then came the reassurance: "As you can see, the changes are all minor, though I think they have the effect of making the writing seem lighter" (Letter dated April 25, 1980).

10. Harold Jantz liked this piece and encouraged me "to keep on tackling questions in such a forthright manner" (Letter dated Nov. 27, 1980). This piece was also reprinted in the *Catholic New Times*.

11. My later "Christian Mind" column, "Sports as Idolatry" (Sept. 25, 1981), also garnered a lot of criticism. I was informed that I was "honored" one day at Bethany Bible College in Hepburn, Saskatchewan, with students pinning my picture to their shirts as a way of sharing their dislike of Elmer Thiessen.

12. Letter dated April 30, 1982.

13. Letter dated August 25, 1983.

14. Controversial articles included: "Reflections on Natural Church Development" (Sept. 22, 2000); "Builders, Boomers and Busters" (Sept. 22, 2000 – I can't believe that they carried two of my essays in the same issue); "Contemporary Worship Culture" (May 3, 2002); "Laity and the Problem of Professionalism of the Pastoral Ministry" (Sept. 12, 2003).

15. Rejected essays include: "Ethnicity and Christianity: A Response to John Redekop's *A People Apart*," written in 1987; "The Idol of Newness," written in 2006.

16. My "Viewpoint" article, "A Response to the Confession of Faith" (March 20, 1996), was again controversial, though I did receive a response from Reuben Pauls thanking me for my critique of changes that were being proposed to our confession of faith. Reuben informed me that my article had been a touchstone for change, with many leaders referring to it and agreeing with my calls for change (Letter or phone call dated May 12, 1998).

17. Here are some interesting statistics on some of the blogs which duplicate material that I wrote for the *Herald*. The article on natural growth development received 2,111 views as of November, 2020 (i.e. in 9 ½ years); "Academic Arrogance," 2,080 views; "Sports as Idolatry," 539 views; "Contemporary Worship Culture," 138 views. I was told by Andrew Dick who wrote a D. Min. thesis on worship in Mennonite Brethren churches that my article was the last serious treatment of the worship wars in the M.B. church. Here are some further statistics on later original blogs: my review of James Smith's *Who's Afraid of Postmodernism*," 2,668 views; my review of Marcus Borg, *The Heart of Christianity*, 1,202 views; and my "Intellectual and Spiritual Journey," 852 views.

18. Some examples: the ethics of the pursuit of truth (Feb. 29, 2008); the ethics of advertising (Sept. 5, 2008); the ethics of Prime Minister Harper (Dec. 15, 2008); the ethics of consumption (Jan. 12, 2009); the ethics of persuasion (May 4, 2009 – this op-ed piece was reprinted in *The Guelph Mercury*); and the ethics of political attack ads (June 1, 2009).

19. Calgary CBC News, online reply, July 12, 2013.

20. I made a couple of attempts to write academic papers before this. The first was a paper on Immanuel Kant, based on my M.A. thesis, which I submitted to several Christian magazines in 1968 (the Inter-Varsity Christian magazines – *HIS* in the U.S.A. and *Inter-Varsity* in the U.K.; and Christianity Today). I received some very kind letters of rejection with suggestions on how to improve my writing. Then in the fall of 1977, I wrote an essay entitled, "Moral Dilemmas," but all efforts at presenting it at a conference or publishing it in a journal failed (Western Philosophical Association; *Canadian Journal of Philosophy*; *Journal of Educational Thought*; *Philosophy & Public Affairs*). Some first tries, but probably premature, with not too much philosophical depth.

21. "Indoctrination and Doctrines," *Journal of Philosophy of Education*, Vol. 16, #1, (1982), pp. 317. Reprinted in *Critical Perspectives on Christian Education*, edited by Jeff Astley and Leslie J. Francis (Leominster: Gracewing, 1994), pp. 376-96.

22. Madeleine L'Engle makes this astute comment about insecure artists which surely includes academics: "I think that all artists, regardless of degree of talent, are a painful paradoxical combination of certainty and uncertainty, constantly in need of reassurance and yet with a stubborn streak of faith in their validity, no matter what" (*A Circle of Quiet*, HarperSanFransisco, 1972), p. 38.

23. Later in my retirement I was encouraged when I read an excellent biography of Dallas Willard, a Christian philosopher, who is described as spending most of his academic career "swimming against the prevailing current of ideas and worldviews," and who therefore felt like an outsider and often came back from philosophy conferences depressed. Gary W. Moon, *Becoming Dallas Willard: The Formation of a Philosopher, Teacher and Christ Follower* (IVP Books, 2018), pp. 129-39.

24. The review appeared in the *Anglican Theological Review*, Vol. 85, #3, (Summer, 2003), pp. 568-9.

25. This conference was sponsored by the Von-Hugel Institute of St. Edmund's College in conjunction with the Center for Jewish Education of the University of Haifa in Israel, and was funded by the Templeton Foundation.

26. "Democratic Schooling and the Demands of Religion," in *Commitment, Character and Citizenship: Religious Schooling in Liberal Democracy*, edited by Hanan A. Alexander, and Ayman Agbaria (New York, NY: Routledge, 2012), pp. 161-178.

27. Plantinga, Alvin, "Advice to Christian Philosophers," *Faith and Philosophy* Vol.1, #3 (July, 1984).

28. The 5th. Global Triennial Consultation of the Micah Network, Thun, Switzerland, September 10-14, 2012; Loma Linda University School of Medicine, California, January 17-18, 2014; Orthodox-Evangelical Consultation, Lausanne-Orthodox Initiative, St. Vlash Monastery, Albania, September 15-19, 2014; and a Global Consultation on "Call to Mission, Perceptions of Proselytism," held in Accra, Ghana, June 8-11, 2017.

29. This grant was worth $33,220 and also contributed $27,000 to Medicine Hat College to hire a replacement for me.

30. I was in England from April 18 to May 10, 1990. Significant events here included attending a philosophy of education conference held at the Froebel Institute College in London; consultations at the Roehampton Institute with Nicola Slee and Leslie Francis; a visit with John Hull at the University of Birmingham; a paper at the North of England Institute for Christian Education in Durham, including an overnight visit with Jeff Astley who was the Director of the Institute; discussions with Trevor Cooling, including a paper

given to Christian educators connected with Stapleford Centre for Christian Education; a consultation with Terry McLaughlin at Cambridge, including a paper and a visit to Wittgenstein's grave; and a consultation with Mark Halstead in Exmouth.

31. I was quite aggressive in my search for the right publisher, agonizing about whether to choose a secular or religious publisher, and consulting with a number of scholars on the best choice. Already in 1985/86 I was sending out feelers for a publisher – SCM (UK), IVP (UK), and Wadsworth. In the spring of 1989, I sent out another set of inquiries, aiming rather high, but all these came back negative. In the fall of 1989, I sent out another batch of "more realistic" inquiries, with most of the responses indicating that they were not interested. Then in spring of 1990, I sent out another set of inquiries. The following publishers expressed some interest: Welch, Kruger, University of Ottawa Press, Wilfrid Laurier University Press, University Press of America, McGill-Queens University Press. All the religious publishers were uninterested (Eerdmans, Zondervan, Abingdon, IVP, SCM, Orbis, Crossroads, Twenty Third, and Religious Education Press). In retrospect, I realize that I did far too much work trying to find a publisher – another example of my being too meticulous in what I do!

32. First came the two referee reports, both of them quite positive, with a number of good suggestions for improvement. McGill-Queen's University Press made it a practice to apply for a subvention from the Aid to Scholarly Publishing Program, sponsored by the Canadian Federation of the Humanities. ASPP requested a third review before processing our application, and this review was by far the most thorough and thankfully again very positive. We were therefore successful in getting the $7,895 subvention. I also got an additional $1,500 grant from Medicine Hat College to help with publication costs.

33. McGill-Queen's University Press was at first wanting to start with just a hardback print run, but I protested. In the end, they printed 500 hardcover, 1,000 paperback, with Gracewing printing another 500 paperback.

34. Elmer John Thiessen, *Teaching for Commitment: Liberal Education, Indoctrination, and Christian Nurture* (Montreal & Kingston: McGill-Queen's University Press; co-published by Gracewing, Leominster, U.K. 1993). The main title of this book was suggested to me by John Franklin during a conversation at a restaurant while we were both attending a conference in Chicago in 1987.

35. For example, the annual meeting of the Association of Independent Schools of Alberta in 1988, and the Christian Principals Association of British Columbia in 1989.

36. In addition, my book was reviewed at a meet-the-author session organized by Ken Badley, held during the Learned Societies meetings in Calgary in 1994, and also at a "With Heart and Mind" conference in Toronto (1995).

37. *British Journal of Educational Studies*, Vol. 42, (Summer, 1994), p. 322. Alven Nieman wrote a full-length article reviewing my book for *Religious Education*, Vol. 94, #4, (Fall, 1999). In a reference letter for an application for a Fellowship at the Center for the Philosophy of Religion at the University of Notre Dame, I was rather flattered to be compared to Alvin Plantinga. Al Neiman wrote: "Thiessen's discussion of indoctrination was and remains the most judicious, creative and complete one to be found in the relevant literature. . . . In a sense Thiessen in this work does for the philosophy of education what much of Al Plantinga's work has done for the philosophy of religion and (more recently) epistemology." Sadly, he went on to say this: "He is a very bright man (no he isn't as bright as Al Plantinga but who is!), whose ability to refurbish perennial truths in the voice of our

rather secular profession makes him a scholar worth our greatest encouragement" (letter dated Oct. 30, 2002). I didn't get that fellowship.

38. *Christian Week*, Vol. 8, #1, (April 12, 1994).

39. *Journal of Christian Education*, Vol. 37, #3, (Sept. 1994), p. 53.

40. The book has sold an estimated 925 copies total, as of January, 2020, which isn't too bad for an academic book. I also saw my book listed in a number of course offerings. John Lang of Winnipeg told me that he had used my book as a text in a summer class a few years earlier (Congress, 1998). Walter Feinberg, at the University of Illinois at Urbana-Champaign, devoted three weeks to my book in a graduate course, "Religion and Education" in the spring of 2000. I was also pleased to see a good number of citations (see endnote #70).

41. My first royalty cheque in June, 1994, came to $234.88. The Canadian government sponsors a Public Lending Rights program in support of authors, librarians and publishers in Canada, handing out annual funding to each author, based on the number of times the book is found in a selection of Canadian libraries. This proved to be much more profitable for me – over $1,000 as of 2002, when I believe my book became ineligible for the annual grant.

42. Elmer John Thiessen, *In Defence of Religious Schools and Colleges* (Montreal & Kingston: McGill-Queen's University Press, 2001).

43. *In Defense of Religious Schools and Colleges*, p. 4. See also my *Teaching for Commitment*, pp. xi-xii, and *The Ethics of Evangelism*, p. xii.

44. In reviewing my files, I was surprised to see how aggressively I had applied for grants over the years of my writing. Already in 1977 and then again in the mid 1980s I was applying to various foundations. I kept applying for regular research grants from SSHRC, and in 1993 applied for a Strategic Grant which called for some collaboration with other scholars/institutions/organizations, and so I teamed up with the Association of Independent Schools and Colleges in Alberta and the Stapleford Education Centre for this application. Sadly, I didn't get this grant or another couple of regular SSHRC grant applications for work on this book.

45. Althouse Press at the University of Western Ontario and Irwin Publishing in Toronto both expressed interest in the project. Inter-Varsity Press (UK) and OISE Press in Toronto also both expressed some interest though they were dubious about the market.

46. My file was turned over to Aurele because Peter Blaney had left McGill-Queen's University Press. Reader's reports were positive, and so we were once again successful in getting a subvention from the ASPP for $7,000. McGill-Queen's once again asked for a $2,000 subvention from Medicine Hat College, but the College only contributed $1,300, expecting me to supplement this amount with my professional development fund of $750.

47. The print run was 300 cloth, 800 paperback.

48. *First Things*, (April 2002), pp. 57-8.

49. Sales were at first brisker than my previous book, but in the end I only sold an estimated 630 copies My first royalty cheque came to $245.18. Public Lending Right payments for this book and my earlier book have again proven to be much more profitable – $3,000 as of January, 2020. It would seem that a good number of professors were using parts of my books in courses, as Copibec payments for photocopying privileges for both of these books has come to just under $900 as of January, 2020.

50. Harro van Brummelen in *Journal of Education and Christian Belief*, Vol. 6, #1, (2002), p. 79-80; and in *Historical Studies in Education*, Vol. 154, #2, (Fall 2003), pp. 379-81.

51. I contacted over thirty academic/secular publishers and over fifteen religious publishers. I did have a few publishers expressing interest. The Catholic University Press of America processed my proposal and asked me to make some revisions to make the introduction more Catholic, but in the end weren't satisfied with my minor revisions. Hendricksen, a religious publisher, also expressed some interest, but for various reasons I didn't pursue them further.

52. See Chapter 6, p. 174 for some comments made by Roger Martin on the merits of the manuscript and his disappointment about not getting the ASPP subvention.

53. Elmer John Thiessen, *The Ethics of Evangelism: A Philosophical Defence of Proselytizing and Persuasion* (Crownhill, Milton Keynes: Paternoster Press, and Downers Grove, IL: IVP Academic, 2011). Paternoster had a print run of 1,050, and IVP a print run of 2,000. After my long search for a publisher, I felt generous and so sent Paternoster a subvention of $1,000 to help with publication costs. In the middle of processing my book, Paternoster went into receivership and were taken over by Koorong Publishers in Australia who quickly reassured me that they were still interested in publishing my book under the direction of Mike Parsons, the new Commissioning Editor at Paternoster – they still kept the old imprint. I received a revised contract from them on August 4, 2010.

54. I have sold over 2,000 books, including ebooks, as of January 1, 2021.

55. Premier Radio, London, UK; KSIV on their "Encounter program, St. Louis; and WGRC on their "The Matter at Hand," program, Pennsylvania. There was also an inquiry from Trans World Radio in the UK, but I am not sure whether this transpired.

56. Rod Reynar called me on January 25, 2013 saying that I had a fan club in Winnipeg and the book was making the rounds and was being used in a discussion group. Andrew Wright, in a review of the book in the *Journal of Belief and Values*, said my book "has already attracted considerable attention in both academic and Christian circles." He also highlighted a critical review of my book at a research seminar at King's College London, where the ensuing discussion suggested that "Thiessen has struck a major chord that resonated fortissimo in the minds of believer and unbeliever alike" (Vol. 33, #2, 2012), pp. 245-7.

57. I counted over twenty academic reviews in journals, plus another thirteen online. In addition there were nearly thirty short notices of the book published in magazines and online. Raymond Laird, from Australia, describes the book as "a well-argued and illuminating study of an issue that is vital to the future of the faith" (*Evangelical Review of Theology*, Vol. 36, #3, 2012), pp. 283-4. Stephen Bedard writes, "*The Ethics of Evangelism* is an important book, if for no other reason than that few scholars have looked at this subject. Thiessen does an excellent job of opening the path to further discussion" (*Studies in Religion*, Vol 4, #3, 2012), pp. 518-9.

58. *International Bulletin of Missionary Research*, Vol. 36, #1, (2012), p. 52.

59. Christina Reimer challenges my defense of exclusivism in the name of a "trans-cultural message of peace and inclusion" (*Conrad Grebel Review*, Vol. 30, #3, 2012), pp. 321-3. Ryan Dueck, who wrote a positive review of the book in the *Mennonite Brethren Herald*, nevertheless on his blog, affirms a "gut-level" resistance to proselytizing as

an "inescapably confrontative, obnoxious, and self righteous activity" ("Proselytism," and 'The Deep Slumber of a Decided Opinion" in Rumblings, Jan. 5, 2012). An exception to Mennonite failure to wholeheartedly endorse my work was written by Wilbert Shenk from Fuller, who wrote, "Elmer Thiessen makes an important contribution to this project by developing an ethical framework that ought to be incorporated into the theological and missiological curricula" (*Christian Scholars Review*, Vol. 41, #3, 2012), pp. 336-9.

60. *REAL People, Stories, Life*, Vol. 2, #3, (Aug. 8, 2011), p. 2.

61. In Chapter 9 of *The Ethics of Evangelism* I suggested, as one way of encouraging ethical proselytizing, that each religious tradition engaged in proselytizing, needed to develop ethical criteria for evangelism, drawing on their own sacred scriptures. In footnote #7 of that chapter, I made the following promise: "I intend to write a sequel to the present monograph in which I will deal with the ethics of evangelism from an explicitly Christian perspective" (p. 219).

62. I already had a table of contents prepared in the fall of 2000, revised it again in 2004, and then again in 2012 after the Micah Consultation in Switzerland. But all these outlines were far too broad in scope.

63. I began working on this bible survey in the fall of 2010 and finished this study in the fall of 2014, resulting in a twenty-page document listing relevant bible passages with some notes on each.

64. Philip Barnes from Ireland read an earlier draft of the entire manuscript, Robert Kruse read the chapters dealing with the biblical study of the topic, and a number of other people read a chapter or two – Daniel Hillion, Ron Mathies, Jennifer Cheek, Rachel Uthmann, Tim Grass, and David Armstrong.

65. I received a contract from Wipf & Stock on January 19, 2017.

66. Elmer John Thiessen, *The Scandal of Evangelism: A Biblical Study of the Ethics of Evangelism* (Eugene, Oregon: Cascade Books, an Imprint of Wipf & Stock, 2018).

67. *Themelios: An International Journal for Students of Theological and Religious Studies*, Vol. 43, #3, (Dec. 2018), pp. 538-9.

68. Stimulus: *The New Zealand Journal of Christian Thought and Practice*, Vol. 25, #2 (Dec. 20, 2018). https://hail.to/laidlaw-college/publication/kxn3N2S/article/jO8oxG7. Several reviewers have suggested that my book could be used as a text for undergraduate courses in Christian evangelism: Brad Penner in http://readingreligion.org/books/scandal-evangelicalism: A publication of the American Academy of Religion (Oct 23, 2018); and Robert G Tuttle, in *Witness: The Journal of the Academy for Evangelism in Theological Education*, Vol. 33, (2019). https://journals.sfu.ca/witness/index.php/witness/issue/view/35.

69. Bryan Stone, *Evangelism after Pluralism: The Ethics of Christian Witness* (Baker Academic, 2018). I have published a review essay of Stone's book: "The Reconstruction of Evangelism by Liberal Protestants: An Evangelical Response," in *Evangelical Review of Theology*, Vol. 44, #4, (2020), pp. 368-73.

70. One way to measure one's influence is to examine the number of times a book or an article is cited in other academic writings. I had never taken the time to review my citations until August of 2019, when I went to the Wilfrid Laurier University library and with a bit of help from a reference librarian and a search on "Google Scholar Citations," I got my numbers, which I updated in November of 2020. Total number of citations: 591.

Here are a few specific numbers on citations of my books: *Teaching for Commitment* – 201; *In Defence of Religious Schools and Colleges* – 121; *The Ethics of Evangelism* – 58. Another indicator of academic influence is the number of libraries carrying one's books. A search of WorldCat.org in August of 2019 gave the following world figures: *Teaching for Commitment* – 1,162 libraries; *In Defense of Religious Schools and Colleges* – 856; *The Ethics of Evangelism* – 735; *The Scandal of Evangelism* – 74 (but this is only 1 ½ half years after publication).

71. See Chapter 9, p. 272 for an example of a philosophy department that failed to satisfy this requirement with respect to my application for a position at the University of Saskatchewan.

72. I have raised this question in the conclusion of "Refining the Conversation," *The Evangelical Quarterly: An International Review of Bible And Theology*. Vol.79, #2, (2007), p. 152.

73. See for example Stone's *Evangelism after Pluralism*.

74. See endnote #28 for a list of these international conferences.

75. First email dated June 15, 2017; second dated June 16, 2017. Two other letters of note: Charles Glenn, a prolific writer in the field of education, when he discovered that we were both scheduled to speak at the Lexington Academy near Boston in the spring of 2004, expressed his delight about this and then added: "I have been talking up your books all over the place, and believe I have scarcely published anything in the last year or two – including several books – that does not give your work a plug" (Letter dated Jan. 27, 2004). Much earlier I received a welcome letter from Tom Sinclair-Faulkner, from the Department of Comparative Religion at Dalhousie University, telling me that he was reading my book, *Teaching for Commitment*, and finding it "enormously helpful." His letter concluded by saying how grateful he was "for the stimulation that your work has provided to all of us in religious studies" (Letter dated June 14, 1994). Earlier, I received a letter from Dr. Neil Snider, President of Trinity Western University, expressing his appreciation for an article I wrote for *Christian Week*, entitled, "Are Liberal Education and Faith Enemies?" (Sept. 8, 1992, p.7). He went on to encourage me to keep addressing these issues and asked if I could recommend articles or books on the integration of faith and liberal education (Letter dated Sept. 29, 1992).

76. Letter dated October 25, 2016. The website for the International Association for Refugees: www.iafr.org.

77. The tentative title: "Faith and Reason/Certainty and Doubt: A Bible Study Guide on Epistemological Questions." I sent the proposal to IVP in the U.S. and England, and also to NavPress.

78. A few other ideas for books that I found in my files: I did some initial planning on an anthology on indoctrination – obviously dropped. Evelina-y-Miranda Orteza, from the University of Calgary wanted to collaborate with me on a book. I wasn't too excited about this possibility as I didn't think our writing styles were compatible. I also planned a follow-up on my first two books, which was to be a more practical treatment of the problem of indoctrination, and would also explore the ideological connections of liberal education with liberalism. These aims are rather different and that is no doubt why this project evaporated. Another idea I toyed with was a book on teaching for commitment at Christian colleges and universities. Instead, I covered this theme in some of my later

articles. I also sent a proposal to IVP in the mid-1980s to write a book on the philosophy of education for their "Contours of Philosophy Series." Here I lost my bid to a proposal sent in by Michael Peterson who was the managing editor of *Faith and Philosophy*.

79. The following comments are taken from several referee reports on my application for a major SSHRC grant, as well as an earlier application to be a research scholar at the Centre of Studies in Religion and Society at the University of Victoria. Harold Coward was the director of the Centre at the time and requested five referee reports in March, 1993. My research proposal at the time: "Religious Schools in a Pluralistic Society: A Philosophical Defense."

Chapter 11
SPIRITUAL JOURNEY AND CHURCH EXPERIENCES

I loved my Grandpa Thiessen. Jacob George Thiessen (1876-1967) began his career in Russia (Ukraine) as a teacher, but after moving to the well-known Mennonite Brethren centre of Ruechenau, he was persuaded to become a "Reiseprediger," a travelling evangelist and bible teacher. Grandpa broke with custom and made it a point also to evangelize in the Slavic villages surrounding the Mennonite Molotschna Colony. The Orthodox Church was strongly opposed to any efforts at evangelism by non-Orthodox Christians and so my Grandpa experienced persecution. Attempts on his life failed because of the good will of his Russian neighbors. Often my grandmother and her eleven children were left to shift for themselves for weeks and even months without ever hearing from their father and husband. In the end, the family emigrated to Canada in 1923, in part out of fear for my grandfather's life.[1]

When the family came to Canada they settled in Dalmeny, Saskatchewan, where my Grandpa farmed and continued in the preaching ministry. Farming was clearly a secondary vocation, so after fifteen years in Saskatchewan, Grandpa moved his remaining family to Vancouver in 1938, where he became the pastor of the Vancouver Mennonite Brethren Church

(43rd. Ave). It is here where I got to know Grandma and Grandpa Thiessen during our family's yearly summer visits to British Columbia to pick raspberries and visit relatives.

What was my Grandpa like? D.B. Wiens describes how children – who sat quite passively during an English message – would suddenly perk up when my Grandpa stepped behind the pulpit. He had the gift of presenting sublime truth in simple speech, interspersed with interesting illustrations. His messages were usually short and to the point. If someone prayed too long in public, he began to sigh audibly. His own public prayers were brief, but his private prayer list was long.

Although Grandpa was a bit more flexible than other preachers of his time, he was still quite legalistic, resulting in the rebellion of many of his children. His ministry was characterized by a strong emphasis on prophetic teaching, following more or less the Plymouth Brethren dispensational outline. He firmly believed that Christ would come before he died. When he spoke about the love of Christ, he would often be moved to tears. His last sermon, preached on January 18, 1967 (my birthday), after some sixty-nine years in the ministry was based on Psalm 103:3 – emphasizing God's forgiveness of our sins.

I loved my Grandpa. But he was more than a Grandpa to me – he was my hero, my model, and my mentor. On one occasion an elderly gentleman from British Columbia, visiting his children in Waterloo, heard me preach and then told me that I sounded much like my grandfather.[2] I considered this a high compliment. However, Grandpa would not appreciate his grandson's radical departure from dispensational theology.

I resemble my Grandpa in some ways – hollow cheeks, a stooped posture, and a beard. I once heard Grandpa provide biblical justification for men having beards. I also inherited my Grandpa's ability to concentrate and his tendency towards absent-mindedness. Several stories (true stories, I believe) illustrate this. Grandpa would often practice his sermons while he was driving or walking. One Sunday he was walking to church with his wife, preaching his sermon as they walked, oblivious to everything around him. Upon arrival at church, his friends noticed that his wife was not with him and when they inquired about her, he was quite surprised. Some follow-up revealed that she had slipped and fallen on ice. On another occasion he drove his Model "T" Ford into the ditch. When a friend finally came to his rescue, he found my grandfather preaching a sermon with great gusto.

My Grandpa remained intellectually alert until the end. He died on February 25, 1967, thirty-seven days after his last sermon, and sixty-three days short of his ninety-first birthday. Several events in his later years stand out for me. My own father died eight years before my Grandpa died. Grandpa was with me at my father's bedside as he breathed his last. I remember Grandpa gathering his grandchildren around him and giving us some words of comfort. He reminded us that although we had lost our father, God has promised to be especially near to the fatherless and the widow. I have often been drawn to the Psalms which express this truth (10:14, 18; 68:5; 146:9), and have always prayed to God as Father. And I find it rather insensitive of Christians when they rob me of the comfort I still need by refusing to address God as Father. Sadly, there is also an arrogance that is all too often associated with this bowing to political correctness.

I visited Grandpa and Grandma in the summer of 1964. After my third year at the University of Saskatchewan, I took some holidays on my own, travelling to British Columbia by hitch-hiking and by bus. I recall Grandpa spending hours with me, giving me counsel and sharing from the Scriptures concerning Christ's second coming – a preoccupation of his. My last brief visit with my grandparents occurred in 1966 during one of my summer field trips for the Dominion Observatories when we were doing some seismic testing in southern B.C.

I loved my Grandpa. May he rest in peace.

RELIGIOUS UPBRINGING, CONVERSION, AND EARLY CHRISTIAN LIFE

The story of my Grandpa already gives some background to my spiritual journey. My father followed in his parents' footsteps, one of the few children who remained Mennonite Brethren in faith. My mother too grew up in a Mennonite Brethren home in Main Centre, Saskatchewan, her parents having emigrated to Canada earlier in 1904. Her home took the Christian faith seriously with daily morning devotions including singing, Bible reading and prayer, a practice that my parents continued. My parents were very committed to regular attendance at whichever Mennonite Brethren church was closest to the village where my Dad was teaching.

Early conversions were the norm in Mennonite Brethren churches and households at that time. I remember as a child sitting on the steps to the attic of our three-room teacherage in Rhineland, Saskatchewan, badgering my mother with questions as she was washing the dishes in the kitchen. I suspect all this questioning, including questions about the Christian faith, caused my poor mother to worry about me. But she patiently (and maybe sometimes not so patiently) answered my questions, including questions about hell. It was this fear of hell that eventually led me to see the need to be "born again." So in the summer of 1951, when I was nine years old, I told my mother I wanted to be saved. She took me into the attached school room and there she gave me John 3:16 as a verse on which I could base my salvation. I confessed my sins and accepted Jesus as my personal Saviour. In my yearly diary written some years later, I describe the feelings I had after my conversion: "I still remember the joy that flooded my heart as I went to do chores." Seven years later, while attending high school in Swift Current, I was baptized together with my sister, Ruth, and we joined the Swift Current Mennonite Brethren Church (September 14, 1958).

As a child I absorbed the rather conservative, pietistic, and even fundamentalist atmosphere of my home, my grandparents, some of my uncles and aunts, and the churches that we attended. Even now, a visit to a small country church will bring back memories of the Rheinfeld Mennonite Brethren Church which we attended while my father was teaching in Rhineland (1946-52). Somehow I still have a memory of the smell of that church and the sound of the booming voice of preacher Cornelius Penner. Mom and Dad felt free to attend other churches when necessary. For example, when the weather was inclement we would attend the local Mennonite church in Rhineland. I still remember the pastor of the Rhineland church, Mr. Friesen, coming to pray with us children when my sister Lottie, just one year old, became seriously ill and was taken to a hospital. In Pambrun (1952-55) we attended the church associated with the Millar Memorial Bible Institute. I enjoyed the Sunday School there and even won a bible memory verse contest. In my yearly diary I also make mention of coming home from an evening service with a missionary emphasis, and telling my Mom that I felt God might want me to be a missionary. In Gouldtown (1955-58) we once again often attended the local evangelical Mennonite church. My diary makes mention of my friendship with Don Gerbrandt, the pastor's son. We attended prayer meetings where we were encouraged to witness to others about Jesus Christ.

In the meantime, my parents bought their retirement house in Swift Current, thus enabling me to attend high school at the Swift Current Collegiate Institute for my final two years of schooling (1958-60). Here I became active with Inter-School Christian Fellowship where I was exposed to some vibrant Christians from other denominations, one of whom became my "first real close friend," Arnold Dyck, again a pastor's son. My diary records that I began to take notes during my devotional times of bible reading and prayer, so as to make these more meaningful. Clearly, I took my Christian faith seriously.

The final formative experience of my early life involved the death of my father when I was only seventeen years old. In March of my final year of high school (1959), my Dad got seriously ill and was eventually diagnosed with cancer. I can still remember the awkwardness of visiting Dad in the hospital, and wondering what to do. Often I would bring a book along to read. During one of my visits Dad spoke to me and left me with a final request, "Elmer, witness for God." That is quite a last testament to leave with a teen-age son, but I resolved, with God's help, to fulfil this last wish of my father. We were fortunate to have Grandma and Grandpa Thiessen with us in the final days of Dad's illness. They spent much time with my Dad, helping him with his doubts, reading God's word, praying and singing. I was at my Dad's bedside when he died on Aug. 14, 1959. Grandpa prayed, and I wondered about life and its meaning. And then began my journey without an earthly father, though very conscious of the fact that I still had a heavenly Father.

MATURING FAITH

That same fall I was off to the University of Saskatchewan (U of S). As I have already noted in earlier chapters, this was a difficult year for me. It was my first year away from home so I was lonely. I was rather young for university – just seventeen years old, and I was grieving my father's death. In my loneliness and grief I often cried to my heavenly Father. I noted the following in my diary written a few years later: "I can still remember the tremendous devotions I had in the morning, all alone in my room. This was one solid rock which did not vacillate." I was living in Qu'Appelle Hall, the male student residence on campus, and here I was supported by my friend and roommate, Arnold Dyck. Another key support was InterVarsity Christian Fellowship. One experience with IVCF stands out, although I'm not entirely sure exactly when it occurred. I believe it happened during my difficult first year at university, though it may have occurred during my fourth year at the university, when I was facing intense doubts about my faith, coupled with deep discouragement and a lack of motivation, even to the point of thinking about quitting university.

In any case, it was in one of these difficult years that I had what I can only describe as a mystical experience. Indeed, I may even have spoken in tongues. I was in the home of an IVCF staff member and must have been sharing the emotional turmoil I was going through. We all knelt down to pray and I kept on praying. I was so absorbed in prayer that eventually my hosts had to gently intervene, because they had to go to another appointment. I recall repeating the name of "Jesus" over and over again. While in this trance-like state, I experienced an overwhelming sense of peace. God, I am sure, was meeting some deeply felt needs of mine at the time. Over the years, this experience has served to temper my criticisms of the charismatic movement in Christianity. It has also helped me to understand that I am more than a rational animal and that a relationship with Jesus Christ is pretty central to the Christian life.

After one year at U of S, I attended the Mennonite Brethren Bible College. Although my initial intention was to study at MBBC for only one year, I ended up staying for three (1960-63).[3] These three years were significant in giving me time to mature, and also in helping me to get a better understanding of the bible. MBBC contributed to my faith development in other ways. Some close friendships with Nick Wiens, David Derksen, and Peter Klassen helped to give my faith a social dimension as we shared our struggles, wrestled with theological questions, and prayed together. Throughout these years I continued to struggle with an inferiority complex. Interestingly I came to associate this inferiority complex with pride as noted in a "Psychological Autobiography" that I wrote for Dr. F.C. Peters in his psychology course. I made this association once again in my graduation testimony given in chapel. I'm not sure this is an entirely fair analysis of my inferiority complex, as I clearly faced some obstacles to normal development given the physical defects I was born with. It took a long time for me to accept myself as God had created me. Social acceptance at MBBC certainly helped the process of overcoming this inferiority complex, which was brought to greater completion in later years as I got married, gained confidence in my profession, and ultimately as I came to accept myself in the light of God's love for me as a unique person.

In the fall of 1963 I returned to U of S to continue my "secular" studies in physics. I put "secular" in quotation marks to highlight a sharp sacred/secular divide in my thinking at the time. This is illustrated by the fact that I refused to transfer any course credits from MBBC to Waterloo Lutheran University (WLU) and then to the U of S. For some reason I wanted to keep these two worlds apart. This prolonged my education, but this was of little concern to me at the time. But upon returning to U of S I had clearly left MBBC and the secure Christian educational environment it provided for me. I was now in the "world" and had to face the challenges of living my Christian life within this secular environment. I will not dwell on my switch to philosophy here and how this affected my spiritual development as I have already dealt with this in Chapter 8.

InterVarsity Christian Fellowship continued to play a large role in my spiritual development. I can still remember the large weekly noon-hour meetings we had where guest speakers spoke on a variety of topics related to the Christian life. There must have been 100 Christian students gathering each week in a large lecture theatre. What an encouragement and what a stretching experience as I associated with Christians and heard speakers from other denominations. There were also multiple weekly bible studies and I was soon asked to lead one of these. At the end of my second year at U of S (1964) I was asked to take on the role of co-ordinating bible studies for IVCF in the following year. I'm not entirely sure whether I took on this task, since I was also getting more involved with reaching out to international students and had promised to help a friend of mine, Walter Regehr, with this work. In my final year at U of S (1965-66) I was asked to coordinate the work with international students, including the annual IVCF Banff Christmas. I found these coordinating roles taxing but I'm sure they served to develop my leadership skills.

SPIRITUAL AND PRACTICAL DISCIPLINES

Is there anything that stands out in my diary entries regarding my spiritual life during my student days? I have already made mention of my desperate clinging to God as my heavenly Father when my earthly father died, a charismatic experience during my first year at the U of S, and my desire to study the bible while at MBBC. More generally, I was very conscious of God's presence in my life throughout my student days. When I switched to U of S, I made it a practice to pray silently before each lecture, a recall of what was the norm at MBBC. Why not continue this practice in a "secular" environment? The evangelical notion of a personal relationship with Jesus was and continues to be an existential experience for me. With Paul I say, "For to me, to live is Christ . . . I want to know Christ," and I want to be like Christ (Phil 1:21, 3:10). Again and again in my diary there are notes about my times of bible study and prayer. During my first year back at U of S, I spent time translating the book of John from the Greek and then began a similar study of the book of Romans. "I felt this concentrated study of the Word was imperative in spite of my heavy course load." I also memorized the Sermon on the Mount that same year and made a resolve to recite it once a week for the rest of my life – a resolve which I have unfortunately not kept.

Over the years I have also from time to time reviewed (skimmed) the entire bible concerning some topic/issue that I was struggling with. For example, in 1969 while teaching at WLU, I made a study of the meaning of our relationship to Jesus Christ. This led to an article on this topic, published in the *Mennonite Brethren Herald* in 1970. In 1978, while teaching at Medicine Hat College I did a major study of the notion of the kingdom of God, wondering how this notion related to the church. In later years I have come to appreciate the significance of this study that I did much earlier in my life.

Another spiritual discipline that has played a significant role in my life began in 1964, after my first year back at the U of S. I took a holiday to British Columbia in April and stopped at Hope, booked a room in a hotel, and spent the day in prayer and fasting. I recorded the following objectives for that day: (a) to find God's will with respect to a life's partner; (b) to find God's will with respect to missions; (c) to find God's answer to my terrible inferiority complex; (d) to be sanctified and receive power in witnessing. My notes include an array of Scripture passages that I studied that relate to these objectives. I also made a resolve to repeat this spiritual discipline of setting aside a day of prayer and fasting each year. I kept up this practice for many years, though there was the occasional year where I did not observe this special day of prayer and "fasting." Why the quotation marks around "fasting"? Because fasting is difficult for me given my hypoglycaemia and so I would usually take along a light lunch and come home for a full meal after the day was over. I have not kept up this spiritual discipline since retirement because I now take more time for my daily ritual of bible study, meditation, and prayer.

Evangelism has been another preoccupation of mine, no doubt due to the church environment in which I was raised, but also due to my father's last wish for me as he lay dying. As noted earlier, already as a young student I was attending prayer meetings where we were encouraged to witness for Jesus Christ. In my diary I noted that during this time I felt God speaking to me about the need to witness to one of my classmates, but I refused to do so and felt badly as a result. While attending MBBC I attended weekly prayer meetings for missions and also was involved in counselling at a crusade.

I recall an incident at U of S where I was asked to help a friend of mine from IVCF who was witnessing to a fellow student who happened to be studying philosophy. My friend thought that I might be able to help this student, given that I was majoring in philosophy. So the three of us met in the cafeteria and I spent some time trying to explain the Christian faith to this student using the philosophical background that we had in common. My IVCF friend became increasingly unhappy with the language I was using and finally interrupted and explained the way of salvation using standard evangelical clichés. What he didn't realize was that this was not helping his friend to understand the Christian faith. I think I was on the right path, trying to communicate the good news of Jesus in ways that would appeal to a student who was studying philosophy.

In Chapter 9 I have described how teaching philosophy gave me natural opportunities to break down barriers to considering the Christian faith, a kind of pre-evangelism.[4] Sometimes my lectures would lead to further conversations with students in my office, and occasionally these would be followed up with evangelistic bible studies in our home. In 2003 I joined Henk Hak, a local doctor, in sponsoring some evangelistic bible studies with friends and colleagues that we invited. It is therefore perhaps not surprising that later in life I wrote two books on the ethics of evangelism. Over the years I have become less obsessed about doing evangelism, though quite happy to engage in "natural evangelism" that grows out of relationships and contexts where one earns the right to do evangelism.

I conclude this section with another spiritual discipline with practical overtones – tithing. I recall being inspired by some of my fellow students at MBBC who were generous in their giving. One student gave a unique interpretation of Paul's encouragement about giving in 2 Corinthians 9:7: "Each man should give as he has decided in his heart to give, not reluctantly or under compulsion, for God loves a cheerful giver." This fellow student suggested the following translation: "God loves an "hilarious giver." I also recall wondering what I should do at the end of one of my university years when I had some money left over. Should I not give this money to the Lord, given his generosity to me over this past year? And by doing so, would I not also show that I trusted God to provide for the next year? So I ended up giving away the money left in my bank account. Once I started receiving an annual salary we have made it a practice to tithe on our gross income as a minimum benchmark. Many years we have given over and above the tithe. We have tried to divide our giving into three equal parts – the local church, evangelistic efforts, and social aid/education. Since the arrival of our grandchildren, we have supported six needy children overseas through the Global Family Program of the Mennonite Central Committee. We have enjoyed giving hilariously even in retirement.

PHILOSOPHY, PRACTICAL DISCIPLESHIP, AND PIETY
Here let me interject some reflections on the integration of my love of philosophy and my love of God revealed in Jesus Christ. I love philosophy and the exchange of arguments with fellow philosophers. I love ideas and interacting with others about ideas. I love teaching and seeing students respond to new ideas. I love research and writing. But I have also come to see the dangers of a preoccupation with intellectual life and philosophy. An admonition of nineteenth century Danish Christian existentialist, Sören Kierkegaard has challenged me: "Christ did not appoint professors, but followers." So has Blaise Pascal, a seventeenth century French philosopher, mathematician, and physicist, who made this observation: "Pious scholars are rare." We are called to love God with our whole being – with heart, soul, strength, and mind. Then there is the call to love our neighbour as

ourselves (Matt 22:37-40). I have struggled with these calls to love and discipleship, and I don't think I am alone in this. I believe academics are generally not very good lovers – lovers of God, or lovers of our neighbours. The education we have received and the entire educational milieu seems to militate against love and old-fashioned piety.

We have received an education shaped by enlightenment ideals which have made us value being objective instead of committed; detached, instead of loving; rational, instead of passionate. We have come to enjoy questions, instead of answers. Answers would spoil everything. They might just carry with them a call to be committed. Or, to use Max Weber's prophetic description of the modern era, we have become specialists without spirit. We as academics seem to have difficulty blending academic excellence with piety, practical discipleship, commitment, and love.

This is not to say that academic life and being a philosopher are entirely unrelated to being a faithful follower of Jesus Christ. I feel called by God to be a philosopher. Wrestling with ideas is an expression of my being a follower of Jesus Christ. But there is more to the Christian life than this. We are also called to love God and our neighbour. We are called to become more like Christ, to display the fruits of the spirit – love, joy, peace, patience, kindness, goodness, faithfulness, gentleness and self-control (Gal 5:22). I have had to work at finding this balance in Christian discipleship – loving God with my mind, and loving God with my heart, soul and strength.

There is one particular dimension of this balance that deserves more comment. As already noted in this chapter, I grew up in a rather pietistic Christian environment. As I read my early diaries I discovered a strong pietistic strain in the expression of my early faith. Strangely, this was combined in my life with a strong bent towards asking questions and arguing. There is a tension here that I have had to work at resolving in my life. Again, I found my study of Kierkegaard while in graduate school helpful. Kierkegaard wrestled profoundly with the interrelation between objective and subjective ways of knowing the truth of Christianity. Here is his definition of truth: "the objective uncertainty, held fast in an appropriation process of the most passionate inwardness, is the truth, the highest truth available for an existing person."[5] There is something right about this. There is a deeper level of knowing, a knowing of the heart, as Pascal famously said.

I recall my time at MBBC, when for the first time I was reading the bible as part of my academic studies. And again, I loved it. I was hungry for a better understanding of the books of the bible, and I took every bible course that I could. But I also remember struggling with the relation of my studies to my times of quiet meditation, devotional reading of the bible, and prayer. In fact, were the latter even necessary, now that I was studying the bible as part of an academic program? I'm not sure I resolved this question entirely while I was at MBBC. Once I was back at a secular university, studying science and philosophy, the importance of a devotional life was again more obvious.

As I continued in my academic pursuits, I think I have come to a better integration of heart and mind. Most days I spend some time in the reading of Scripture, meditation and prayer. While teaching, I liked to begin my day with ten to fifteen minutes of devotional reading and prayer in my office – I felt it was important to "sanctify" the workplace. I have found it useful to combine the reading of a portion of Scripture with reading a good commentary on this passage of Scripture. As my mind is able to better comprehend the meaning of Scripture, I am led to worship, commitment, and prayer. So for me piety is very intimately bound up with the exercise of my intellect and I have become more comfortable with what I suspect is a rather unique kind of a blending of heart and mind.

As an academic it is all too easy to take a stance of sitting in judgment over the Word of God, critically analysing what is written. At some point it is necessary to let the Word of God judge me. This takes intellectual humility and a willingness to submit to authority. I hope and pray that these virtues continue to characterize my life with Jesus Christ.

DUALISM

There is one other dimension of integrating my love of philosophy and my love of Jesus Christ that deserves some comment. I grew up within a home and church environment that distinguished rather sharply between religious work and secular work. Religious work was important, and secular work merely necessary for survival. I have already drawn attention to one expression of this dualism in the sharp divide I drew between my religious studies at MBBC and my "secular" studies at U of S. A further expression of this dualism has to do with how one's secular work relates to evangelism. I was taught that work is only the context in which you fulfill your *real* calling which is to evangelize.[6] Paul is often cited as a positive example of someone who saw his tent-making job as an "avocation" to support his real calling of being a missionary.

It was only until I was well into my career that I was able to identify problems with this kind of dualism. The sacred/secular divide is simply not biblical. Work needs to be seen as one way of honoring God. It is a mistake to develop a theology of work and vocation based on the example of Paul. Paul may in fact just be a very special case of a "tent-making" missionary. For the beginnings of a theology of work we need to turn to the instructions that Paul gives to slaves, who were at that time the "professional" workers of the Roman Empire – teachers, doctors, accountants, and administrators. "Serve wholeheartedly, as if you were serving the Lord, not men, because you know that the Lord will reward everyone for whatever good he does, whether he is slave or free."[7] Here we have a robust theology of work, which in fact suggests that teaching philosophy can be a way of serving the Lord.

Thankfully, much has been written in the last while by way of advocating a healthier understanding of work as a calling or vocation.[8] Ideally, our work should be in line with the abilities and gifts that God has given us. Through our work each of us is able to do his or her part in building God's kingdom here on earth. I believe God has gifted me and called me to be a philosopher and an educator. Thankfully, I found a job as a college teacher where I could use these God-given gifts, doing my little part, in my small sphere of influence, to build God's kingdom. What a challenging mission![9]

Perhaps a note is in order on the focus of this chapter. I have titled it "Spiritual Journey and Church Experiences." This would seem to be an expression of dualism because I am separating my spiritual journey and church experiences from the rest of my life as an academic and a philosopher. But I believe that everything we do includes a spiritual or religious component. I reject a sharp compartmentalization of life into the sacred versus the secular. So a chapter devoted to my spiritual journey could cover all areas of my life. But this would become unmanageable. So for the purposes of these memoirs, I have had to make distinctions that I am not entirely comfortable with.

PREACHING AND BIBLE-TEACHING

If I had to choose the Christian ministry which I most enjoyed over my adult life it would clearly be bible-teaching and preaching. "September, 1962" is the date recorded on the notes of the first talk that I gave in a church (Sermon file #1). The title of this talk to the Swift Current Mennonite Brethren Church seems ungrammatical: "A Challenge to the Responsibility of the Church to the Student." I gave this talk before leaving for my third year at MBBC. I gave another talk in the church that same year at the Christmas young people's social on the topic, "Christian Characteristics."

Meanwhile at MBBC, I took a course on homiletics, and as part of that course, preached a sermon on the first beatitude, exploring the negative and positive connotations of what it means to be poor in spirit. Students in their final year at MBBC were at that time asked to preach a grad sermon, and I chose to speak on "Conditions for meeting challenges successfully," based on Joshua 1:1-9. I cannot help but see the influence of Professor David Ewert in my outline of this sermon: "a clear perception of the call of God; a claiming of the promises of God; a complete reliance on the Word of God." Ewert often outlined his lectures using alliteration at the start of each section. I preached two more sermons during the summer after graduation, when I was working in Swift Current (1963).[10] It is with some embarrassment that I read these early sermons written on half-sheets of paper in very small handwriting. But all preachers must start somewhere, and most of the time these early efforts at sermonizing are somewhat amateurish.

Of special significance for me was a sermon I preached in the Kitchener M.B. Church on October 12, 1969, at the invitation of Frank C. Peters who was the pastor of this church at the time, in addition to his job as Academic Dean and eventually President of Waterloo Lutheran University. My sermon title, "Not Ashamed of the Gospel," was based on Romans 1:1-4, 16-17 (Sermon file #18). It was an honour to be asked to preach in F. C. Peters' church because he had been my teacher at MBBC and he had also been very instrumental in my getting a teaching position at WLU. He also modelled combining a professional job with church ministry. The closest I got to this combination was doing pulpit supply for one year at the Seven Persons Community Church in 2001-2002, when the church was without a pastor. I shared this responsibility with Jake Penner and so I was usually preaching twice a month. While this made for a lot of extra work, I loved splitting my time between "secular" and church ministries.

Other signifi-
cant preaching assign-
ments have included
giving sermons at the
weddings of my stu-
dents, friends, my sons,
and a group of Greg's
close friends.[11] I also
preached my one and
only funeral sermon
for a student of mine,
Alvin Penner, and his

A pulpit in Europe from which I would have liked to preach - 2005

wife, Arlene, after their daughter, Alyssa, died soon after her birth.[12] From
the beginning I have numbered my sermons, and as of the date of working
on a third draft of this chapter (September, 2020), I am at Sermon #199. I
am not averse to using a good sermon over again when I preach in churches
other than my home church. So if I include repeat sermons I estimate that
I have preached over 320 sermons.

I have also had the privilege of doing a lot of teaching within the
church context. At the Crestwood M.B. Church I sometimes taught the
youth Sunday School class, though I didn't feel entirely comfortable doing
this. I often shared in the teaching of the adult Sunday School class with
Lorne Dick and Dave Rempel, and then for many years, I did long stretches
of teaching this class alone. I worked through many books of the bible in
Sunday School series, sometimes doing repeats in another church.[13] Then
there were topical series in Sunday School which allowed me to wrestle
with problems that I needed to think through.[14] For much of our church
life, Maggie and I have been leaders of Care Groups or Home Fellowship
Groups, and here again I did a lot of teaching. There were also occasional
invitations to give lectures or do a seminar series in other churches[15] or at
youth retreats.[16] I have also enjoyed giving lectures to Christian groups on
university campuses.[17]

How would I evaluate my preaching and teaching in the church context? I love preaching and teaching God's word. This is what God has called
me to do in the church. And I believe God has gifted me in the areas
of preaching and teaching and being a prophetic voice in the church. I
find preparations for sermons relatively easy. This doesn't mean that I don't

work at it. Indeed, I spend a lot of time carefully studying the biblical texts that have been assigned or that I have chosen. But out of this study, ideas for sermons most often come quickly. Indeed, I have several files of ideas for sermons that I have collected over the years as I have been reading the Scriptures. As I meditate on Scripture, I often find the "fire burning within me" as I get ideas that I would like to communicate via a sermon (Ps 39:3).

My sense of being called to preach and teach has also been affirmed by the church. Already while still a college and university student I was being asked to preach and teach in my home church and the churches in the cities where I was studying or working. When we moved to Medicine Hat the church very quickly got me involved in preaching and teaching – I preached over twenty sermons in the first six years we were at the Crestwood Church. My yearly diary notes a sermon I gave at Crestwood just before we left for my first full sabbatical in Waterloo in 1978. "What work is most important?" was the title. One of the older members of the church, dear Albert Lautermilch, approached me after the sermon and said, "You're in the wrong profession. You should have been a preacher." In fact, my diary goes on to say that this sermon grew out of a struggle I was facing at the time as to where God really wanted me to be. I was at the time wondering whether I should accept an invitation to teach at MBBC. Preaching is often autobiographical. I have preached that sermon in a number of different churches.

For me, the heart of good preaching and teaching is making the bible come alive for our time. This ideal is captured by Jesus in his description of a good teacher in the gospel of Matthew, a passage that I have often reflected on when preaching and teaching: "Therefore every teacher of the law who has been instructed about the kingdom of heaven is like the owner of a house who brings out of his storeroom new treasurers as well as old (Matt 13:52). I have tried hard to achieve this balance in my preaching and teaching.

All too many preachers stick very closely to an exposition of the biblical text. This is safe, but such sermons tend not to relate to the issues and problems that hearers are facing. Then there are preachers whose sermons are very relevant to current affairs but are not grounded in a biblical text. I cannot help but think that some of these preachers have been studying postmodernist Jacques Derrida in the seminaries they attended, and therefore feel at liberty to play with the text. The text has no objective meaning according to Derrida and therefore the biblical text for these preachers is just a launching pad for their own artificial creations. Hence their frequent tendency to get carried away with "secular" meditations and long stories which have nothing to do with the biblical text.[18] It is hard to avoid these extremes in preaching, but I believe that I have in the main been successful in steering a middle course.[19]

I try very hard to be faithful to the biblical text in my preaching and teaching. This is rooted in a conviction that God's word is powerful. "Is not my word like fire," declares the Lord, "and like a hammer that breaks a rock in pieces?" (Jer 23:29). The author of Hebrews echoes this description. "The word of God is living and active. Sharper than any double-edged sword, it penetrates even to dividing soul and spirit, joints and marrow, it judges the thoughts and attitudes of the heart" (Heb 4:12). Descriptions such as these give me courage to preach. As long as God's word is being faithfully taught, God has promised that "It will not return to me empty, but will accomplish what I desire" (Isa 55:11). Passages such as these have also made me very aware of the fact that ultimately it is God who makes his word effective, not my preaching and teaching.

Another emphasis of mine in preaching and bible-teaching is practical application. I like to ensure that each sermon and Sunday school lesson examines some practical implications of the biblical text under consideration. I have frequently quoted the title of Richard Weaver's book, *Ideas Have Consequences* (1948). Theological ideas too have practical consequences and it is incumbent on the preacher or teacher to spend some time showing how a biblical text intersects with the cultural norms of our day. I recall a psychologist who worked in Medicine Hat for a few years and who happened to come to our church. I think she was from a United Church background. She enjoyed the preaching in our church as well as my Sunday School classes, and at one point said that she couldn't get over how quickly I moved from the text to practical application.

The most frequent comment I get after I have preached a sermon – "It made me think." Wonderful! People also comment about my having helped them to see the text in new ways. I also try hard to avoid clichés and familiar language. Sometimes of course I disturb. That too is inescapable in faithful preaching, though I have realized in retrospect that sometimes I disturbed people unnecessarily. I recall one sermon I preached where I tried to highlight the fact that our believing is not entirely under our own control.[20] I tried to couple this idea with an emphasis on God's grace, even in our coming to believe. But one couple only heard my philosophical musings and actually left the church as a result of what they thought was heresy. I now realize, regretfully, that I went too far in delving into philosophical issues that are important, but probably better treated in the context of a philosophy seminar!

LEADERSHIP IN THE CHURCH CONTEXT

My early church-related activities beyond preaching and teaching began in the summer after I graduated from MBBC. I was asked to be the director of a daily vacation bible school at the South-side Chapel which was being supported by the Swift Current Mennonite Brethren Church. I was then cajoled into also being the director of the church DVBS. At the same time I was teaching a group of intermediate boys at the Chapel. I was also serving on the young people's committee at the church. In my diary I noted that "All this work was enriching and helped to pass the time away." A somewhat mixed endorsement! In the summer of the following year (1964), I was asked by Menno Martens to be the church and choir pianist. Here I have a distinct memory of Menno complimenting me after I had played through a hymn before the choir began singing. Compliments mean something when we are young! I have already mentioned other early leadership roles like leading a bible study and coordinating the work with international students for IVCF during my student days at U of S.

Soon after we arrived in Medicine Hat in 1971, Maggie and I were immersed in a variety of activities in the Crestwood Gospel Chapel. I was soon appointed secretary of the church board. It is perhaps symbolic that it didn't take  very long for me to be immersed in a difficult church situation. The church had just hired a new pastor when we arrived, and it quickly became apparent that there were some significant problems with his ministry. Dave Rempel was the chair of the church board and together we realized that something needed to be done, and so we agreed that each of us should meet with the pastor and try to help him face his shortcomings. These meetings did not go well, with the pastor seeking to put the blame on everyone one else, including me. At one point in the process he tried to get me to side with him, hoping that together we could face the opposition, but I had the wisdom to reject this offer. This was a difficult time for me, given that I was young and had so little church experience. Sadly, my experience at Crestwood ended some thirty years later with me facing another very difficult church situation.

Soon I was involved in helping our church become a model of inter-Mennonite co-operation. The closure of a small "General Conference" Mennonite Church in the nearby hamlet of Seven Persons resulted in a number of these people attending and becoming very involved in the Crestwood Church. The idea of "associate membership" for these people was explored and rejected, as this seemed to make them "second class citizens." So we developed a constitution that allowed people to become members of the Crestwood Church while retaining their membership in another Mennonite denomination. Thus on October 19, 1975 , we held a special Thanksgiving and Missions Festival, during which time Lorne and Kay Dick, Ernie and Irma Nickel, Rudy and Irma Neufeld, and Art and Nettie Thiessen became full members of our church. Although there was some resistance to this change, a spirit of harmony eventually prevailed. Soon thereafter it was agreed that our denominational affiliation should once more be included in the church name and so we changed our name from "Crestwood Gospel Chapel" to "Crestwood Mennonite Brethren Church."

The early difficulties we faced at Crestwood, together with the fact that there were a number of capable leaders in the church, led the church to move towards a leadership model that included significant involvement of lay leaders. Thus, on April 20, 1975, we had a dedication service of four lay-ministers – two M.B.'s (Dave Rempel and Elmer Thiessen), and two G.C.'s (Lorne Dick and Elmer Regier). We helped the church when it had weak pastors, and carried the church through times when it was without a pastor. Our wives (Martha Rempel, Kay Dyck, Agnes Regier, and Maggie Thiessen) were very much involved in supporting us and also in providing leadership in areas of worship, hospitality, and church fellowship. We tried our best to be supportive of our pastors. Yes, sometimes there were tensions – a group of four seasoned leaders in the church can seem threatening to a young pastor. But in the end, I think we as lay-ministers contributed to the stability of the Crestwood Church.

I very much cherish a plaque that was given to each of us in June of 1984, when the church was without a pastor. The text reads thus:

> *The mantel of leadership seems to fall so naturally onto the shoulders of those men most able to bear it. We have been blessed with four such men who have, for the past years, worn this mantel most dutifully and admirably.*
>
> *Alas, when affairs are run so smoothly, we the led, too often forget that this mantel of leadership sometimes wears heavily, no matter how willing and able the bearer.*
>
> *We, the worshippers of the Crestwood M.B. Church, wish hereby to express our gratitude, Elmer and Maggie Thiessen*
> *For your dedication to keeping the fire of our fellowship,*
> *For your inspiration and words of experience and learning,*
> *For your guidance, advice and teaching,*
> *For the unnumbered, unnoticed hours given selflessly to planning, praying, meeting, writing, worrying.*
> *May God occasionally make us mindful of each other's burdens.*

What a wonderful encouragement this was to each of us to continue to be faithful in serving the church. Yes, at times the mantel of leadership became a little heavy. But God was good. He gave strength when we were weary. He restored to health and wholeness when we were sick. We gave thanks to God for the privilege of being leaders at the Crestwood Church. And I want to believe the church was stronger and healthier as a result of our leadership.

Over time, I became increasingly involved in the administrative leadership of the church. I believe I held every position on the church council except that of treasurer. There were many periods when I was chair of the church council and moderator of the church, interrupted by my sabbaticals at Medicine Hat College. Some of these years were good years, especially when we had strong pastoral leadership.[21] I enjoyed providing leadership in the church, though I did not enjoy leading the church through a building program in 1993-1994.

I was also involved in the Alberta M.B. Conference leadership – first serving as member and then chair of the Alberta Higher Education Committee (1974-77). Later I was appointed as an Alberta representative on a Higher Education Commission of the Canadian M.B. Conference (1990-91). I was then elected to the MBBC Board of Governors just as it was making the transition to becoming Concord College (1991-93). Towards the end of our stay in Medicine Hat, I was even invited to consider becoming Moderator of the Alberta M.B. Conference (2002). In the end I declined, as I wasn't sure I had the necessary background and qualifications for the position. Besides, this would have interfered with my writing projects.

TENSIONS IN THE CHURCH

Belonging to a specific church is not always easy. Churches are not perfect because they consist of imperfect individuals whose basic credential for belonging to a church is the unmerited grace they can claim in Jesus Christ. Most often I was the only philosopher in the church, and there were always some in the church who were suspicious of academics, and more specifically of philosophers. As has been documented by scholars, anti-intellectualism has been very pervasive among North American evangelicals over the years, and this includes the Mennonite Brethren church.[22] Indeed, I have had to listen to sermons where Paul's seeming attack against scholars and philosophers in 1 Corinthians 1-3 was used to criticize philosophy and philosophers, and I couldn't help but feel that these sermons were very pointed, because I was the only philosopher in the church. So I have had to work at continuing to relate to those who were not academically inclined, and to love those who looked at me with suspicion. I have also felt called to counter the narrowness and dogmatism that is all-too-often present in evangelical churches and to offer critique where I have felt this was necessary.

Sadly, the story of my church involvement in Medicine Hat had a rather difficult ending. After some twenty-five years of leadership in the church, some of the later pastors and a few of the younger leaders in the church felt it was time to move the church in "new" directions. Now I have always been all for moving the church in new directions as long as that is in the direction of greater faithfulness to Jesus Christ. But I was seen as a traditionalist, holding the church back from being relevant to our contemporary world. I wrestled with what to do about this resistance to my leadership and concluded that I needed to bow out of leadership as gracefully as I could. I didn't want to engage in a power struggle and felt Christ calling me to continue to influence the church but from a position of powerlessness.

Unfortunately, the church experienced a slow and eventually a serious decline, and in the end I was asked to return to leadership in 2003. I discovered too late that I could do little to help the church. My authority had by then been thoroughly undermined in the church. It is not easy to face failure, together with the vicious attacks that accompany a full-blown church fight. Thankfully, God led us to move away from Medicine Hat. The healing of painful memories of being unjustly treated took a long time. Over the years, God has given me the assurance that I was acting in good faith and trying my best to solve a no-win situation. God asks us to be faithful, not necessarily successful. I am learning to be satisfied with that.

What are some other lessons I learned from this very painful experience? The church is imperfect. I am imperfect. God still loves the church and wants us to continue to love the church. Jesus is the head of the church, even of an imperfect church. One needs to be patient in bringing about change in the church. One also needs to be gentle when disagreeing or confronting someone.[23] It is very difficult to sort things out when one is in the midst of a crisis. I also learned that some critics should simply be ignored. Academics don't necessarily make the best church leaders. I have a tendency to think that problems can be solved by putting things on paper, or writing up a policy, and this just isn't enough.[24] I also learned that leadership is costly and revolts against leaders happen, as Moses experienced a number of times.[25]

I am still not clear about what I should have done about the frequently made criticism that I had too much influence in the church, even after bowing out of leadership. I continue to remain puzzled about the proper use of authority and positions of power in the church. I am also still unclear as to how far one should go in defending oneself when one is under attack. I learned that a good reputation can disappear rather quickly, and that providing leadership in church will sometimes entail suffering. I took some comfort in 1 Peter 3:13, while in the midst of this church crisis: "Who is going to harm you if you are eager to do good?" But I learned that people do harm you even if you are eager to do the right thing. Interestingly, the verse goes on: "But even if you should suffer for what is right, you are blessed." I have taken comfort in that promise. Another lesson I learned was that reconciliation requires genuine repentance. In retrospect, I believe it was probably a mistake on my part to return to leadership in 2003, given the complexities of my relation to the church and its leadership at the time.

These difficulties in the church played a major role in contributing to a psychological crisis in my life which I have described in more detail in Chapter 6. Yes there were a number of other factors contributing to my fairly rapid descent into high levels of anxiety and depression – my loss of identity in retirement, my turning sixty-five, a very difficult semester at Lithuania Christian College in 2006 and the resulting shift in retirement plans, and the stresses connected with deciding where we should live after my full retirement. But the stresses surrounding my experiences at the Crestwood M.B. Church were clearly front and center in my declining mental health.

So here was another significant episode in my life that shaped my spiritual development. Experiencing anxiety and panic attacks was frightening. I had to learn the lesson of human vulnerability in a new way. I appealed to God again and again for help. I spent many hours reading and meditating on the Psalms and other comforting passages of Scripture. I also had a good physician, who gently persuaded me to accept the fact that I needed some anti-depressants. I am thankful to a former student of mine, now a dear friend, who provided external counsel, and of course, the faithful support of a loving wife. I got through this period somehow and after a few years recovered full mental health. God is good.

One final observation regarding my relation to the church. After moving to Waterloo, Ontario in 2007, we spent several months visiting various Mennonite churches in Kitchener/Waterloo. In the end we decided that there was no Mennonite Brethren church in the area in which we would feel entirely comfortable. So we joined the Waterloo North Mennonite Church (WNMC). In part this choice was dictated by our desire to find a church that was close to where we had bought a house. We quickly felt very much at home at WNMC whose membership includes a good number of academics and professionals. We have also enjoyed a vibrant seniors group in the church and even provided two years of leadership to this group. There are however some tendencies towards liberal theology in the church and learning to navigate these has again been an interesting learning experience. While in Medicine Hat I was considered too liberal, at WNMC I am viewed as too conservative. Perhaps that is exactly where I want to be theologically, somewhere in the middle! But again I have found myself trying to challenge the status-quo in the church, trying to stretch people's thinking, trying once again gently to urge people to be faithful to orthodox belief and praxis. Taking this kind of a stance has led to my feeling somewhat theologically isolated in the church.[26] Then again, perhaps this is what we as Christians should expect given that we are always longing for a better home (Heb 11:13-16).

I conclude with some more general reflections on my spiritual journey and my church experiences, highlighting what has remained the same and what has changed. I am deeply grateful for my rather conservative Mennonite Brethren upbringing. Clearly there has been some evolution in my understanding of the Christian faith and what it entails. But, I look upon my conservative religious upbringing as a foundation upon which I have been able to build. As one writer with a similar background puts it, "the fundamentalist beliefs of my early years gave me something tough to chew on, something to cut my teeth on intellectually.[27] That has been my experience as well.

What has remained the same for me is my deep appreciation for God's revelation in the Scriptures and in Jesus Christ. I love reading the bible. I love Psalm 119, a long and carefully constructed poem extolling the word of God. I continue to find comfort in God's word as suggested in this Psalm (vs. 57). God's word continues to be a lamp to my feet and a light for my path (vs. 105). I find it deeply distressing when those who reject God ignore or disobey God's word (vss. 51-3). My distress is only exacerbated when I find Christians themselves ignoring or distorting God's word. But for me, God's statutes have been my song wherever I have made my home (vs. 54). With Jeremiah, I say, "When your words came, I ate them; they were my joy and my heart's delight (Jer 15:16).

However, my view of Scripture has changed over time. Earlier in my life I had a rather simplistic view of the bible. I once believed in the inerrancy of Scripture. I now believe inerrancy fails to do justice to the complexity of language generally and the language of the bible more specifically. Also, there are errors in the bible and as a writer, I am forced to admit there are portions of the bible that could stand some editing! And it simply will not do to appeal to a speculative ideal of a perfect bible in the original manuscripts. But I still have a very high view of the authority of the bible.

Indeed, I like to say that my view of Scripture is even higher than that of inerrancy. With Paul I still affirm that Scripture is inspired by God (2 Tim 3:15). Jesus clearly accepted the Old Testament as the word of God, and so do I. I believe there is a significant historical core to the gospel accounts of Jesus and that is sufficient for me. I don't need "historical exactitude." I recognize that the writers of the gospels are giving us their interpretations of what they heard and saw. "Truthful narratives are possible without exact words or exactly accurate accounts."[28] I still believe that the bible is God's true and living Word.

I continue to spend some time meditating and studying Scripture nearly every day. God continues to speak to me, and I continue to speak to God. I continue to find God's word to be "a sure foundation" for my life and for understanding the world around me, "a precious cornerstone" that never disappoints (Isa 28:16). The apostle Peter applies this same imagery to Jesus, "the living Stone" (1 Pet 2:4). My relationship to Jesus Christ is very real. I am frequently comforted by the fact that Jesus Christ is in heaven interceding for me (Heb 7:25). I continue to find the Holy Spirit re-assuring me that I am a child of God (Rom 8:16). Praise to God the Father, God the Son, and God the Holy Spirit.

Another way in which I have changed relates to my approach to in-terpreting Scripture. In the past I tended towards a literalist approach to Scripture, though as with most conservatives, I am sure I recognized that parts of Scripture were poetry, metaphor, and parable. I am embarrassed to discover that there was a time when I challenged a proposed building pro-gram at the Waterloo M.B. Church (1970-71) by arguing that the concept of a "church building" was foreign to the New Testament. Rather naïve, I admit. I now have a greater appreciation of the complexities of hermeneu-tics. I now realize that each of the books of the bible were written for a very specific context, and great care must be taken in applying Scripture to the contemporary world we live in. However, I believe some parts of Scripture still need to be taken literally, for example, the eye-witness accounts of the life of Jesus. Indeed, as should be apparent from what I have already writ-ten, I still believe that Jesus died and rose again in real space and time, and that he is the Son of God, the Messiah, and therefore must be the center of Christian faith and life.

I have also come to appreciate the importance of looking at the overall narrative of the bible, the big picture, and the Christian worldview that emerges when the bible is read in this way. Here my thinking has been shaped by Reformed theology with its emphasis on the central themes of Scripture – creation, fall, and redemption. Whereas I once interpreted redemption in very personalistic terms, I now see redemption as much bigger than this. The cosmic Christ wants to redeem all of creation to himself (Col 1:15-20). But this all-encompassing view of redemption must not be seen as eliminating the need for personal redemption. I still believe that human beings are alienated from God and can only be freed from their captivity to Sin through faith in the death and resurrection of Jesus Christ. It is here where I part company with the strain of liberal theology arising in the early 1900s and famously characterized by H. Richard Niebuhr in the sentence: "A God without wrath brought men without sin into a kingdom without judgment through the ministrations of a Christ without a cross." Sadly, this is all too accurate an account of liberal theology even today.

For me probably the most challenging part of the Christian life has been my relationship with the church. Yes, I know the church cannot be perfect, but does it have to be so terribly imperfect? I struggle with disillusionment about the church. But then I am reminded of the early church at Corinth, a church with a lot of problems, and a church that I would not want to join if given a choice. Yet Paul dares to describe this very same church as "the body of Christ," as consisting of "those sanctified in Christ and called to be holy" (1 Cor 12:27; 1:2). If Christ does not give up on the Corinthian church, who am I to be so cynical about the church? So, I carry on, convinced that Jesus Christ does not give up on the church, and neither should I. Jesus Christ is the head of the church, "his body of which he is the Savior," and so as a follower of Jesus, I too must continue to love and serve the church, even if it is imperfect (Eph 5:23).

Another dimension of my struggles with the church has been with liberal expressions of the Christian faith. I took a course on liberal theology while I was studying in Germany in 1967-78. Later I experienced a year-long immersion in liberal theology while we were at Oxford in 1985-86 where we attended the Wesley Memorial Church, a Methodist church that had departed considerably from the theology of John Wesley. More recently, we have attended Mennonite churches in Toronto and Waterloo where the theology of many members is more liberal than my own. Out of love for my brothers and sisters at Waterloo North Mennonite Church, where we have now been attending for some thirteen years, I have felt obliged to read the literature that seems to sustain many of them. Thus I have read books by Marcus Borg and Peter Enns, as well as books that defend homosexuality and gay marriage.[29] But my exposure to and study of liberal theology has only served to reinforce my commitment to orthodox Christianity.

Sadly, I meet too many liberal Mennonites who are still reacting and over-reacting to their conservative backgrounds. And the result is a narrow "liberalism" that loves to question but is forever insecure, "tossed back and forth by the waves, and blown here and there by every wind of teaching" (Eph 4:14). The inability of liberal-minded Mennonites to question their foundational assumptions continues to baffle me. As already mentioned earlier in this section, I cherish my narrow background. I have moved beyond it, to be sure, but it gave me a foundation upon which to build. "Honor your father and mother – which is the first commandment with a promise – that it may go well with you and that you may enjoy long life on the earth" (Eph 6:2; Deut 5:16). I suggest that honoring our parents includes honoring the beliefs they held, not necessarily agreeing with the beliefs they taught us, but nevertheless still respecting them and building on them in a positive and constructive manner.

I will admit that after years of attending a conservative Mennonite Brethren church, it was refreshing to hear the Christian faith expressed in language that was new and creative. But after sustained immersion in liberal churches, I have found that the language in these churches is as prone to the use of tired clichés as in conservative churches. God is put into a box, certainly a different box than that of conservative churches, but nevertheless the language about God is tightly constrained in a liberal straightjacket. I have further been disappointed to discover that the overall church culture of liberal churches tends to be narrow despite frequent claims to be very liberal in outlook. Topics that are obviously debatable are treated as though they are beyond discussion. There are frequent appeals to "a consensus of scholarship," when there is no such consensus. There is an unwillingness to listen to conservative voices. Indeed, I have found as much dogmatism among the liberal-minded as there is among those who are conservative. I also worry about a hyper-critical spirit that I find present in liberal churches. This translates into a "hermeneutic of suspicion" when interpreting the bible.[30] While I would be the first acknowledge the importance of critical thinking in theology, we must never forget that criticism can only come after one has first been initiated into a tradition.[31] A healthy religious tradition is therefore one in which there is both continuity and critical thinking.[32]

I also find that liberal theology has been tarnished by the Enlightenment faith in progress. The assumption is that liberal expressions of Christian theology are somehow an advance on conservative dogma. But a dominant theme of Scripture is that the people of God and the Christian church are always in danger of regressing and falling away from the truth. In the Old Testament the people of God are frequently described as "rebellious," "not loyal," and "not faithful." There are warnings that God's people will "stumble" and "turn from the way" and "wander" like lost sheep. Before Moses dies God gives him the pessimistic prognosis that His people "will forsake me and break the covenant I made with them," and this betrayal is rooted in something even more basic – "I know what they are disposed to" or "I know which way their thoughts incline already" (NEB). Then there is the prophet Amos who describes a people who have strayed so far from God that they are "searching for the word of the LORD, but they will not find it." Hence young men and women who "faint because of thirst."[33] I fear for the next generation.

This same dire prognosis is found in the New Testament. Jesus foresees a time when "many will turn away from the faith." Paul talks about a time "when men will not put up with sound doctrine" and "will turn their ears away from the truth and turn aside to myths." John warns about "false prophets" and urges us to "test the spirits." And the author of Hebrews urges us to "pay more careful attention . . . to what we have heard so that we do not drift away." There are also repeated encouragements to "hold fast" to the teachings of the apostles.[34] So, regress, not progress would seem to be the normal pattern for the people of God and the church. There is therefore a need for more intellectual humility on the part of those who are inclined towards liberal theology in the church, although I would be the first to admit that the need for intellectual humility also applies to those on the conservative end of the theological spectrum. Given our tendency to forsake God and stray from the truth, there is also a need for an ongoing process of evaluation, renewal, and reformation in the church.[35]

So how do we navigate the differences between liberal and conservative Christian theology? I would suggest that a first step in overcoming theological differences is a proper respect for the intelligence of persons on each end of the conservative/liberal spectrum. What I find most hurtful is to be viewed as naïve and narrow-minded simply because I am fairly conservative in my theological outlook. I suggest that liberals have much to learn about respecting those who are conservative. Of course conservatives also need to respect liberals. I have further come to believe there is a desperate need for greater understanding of what lies behind the deep differences between liberals and conservatives in theology. All too often, debates between liberals and conservatives occur at a surface level. There needs to be an honest and frank discussion of deeper differences.[36] Here I have especially appreciated the dialogue between Marcus Borg and N.T. Wright in *The Meaning of Jesus* (1999) which I have reviewed elsewhere.[37] What is missing in the Borg/Wright exchange is any attempt to try to resolve the differences between these two eminent theologians. These are some of the issues I am hoping to research and write about in my final years.

NOTES

1. These details have been gleaned from the life-story of my uncle, Jacob Thiessen, "We are Pilgrims," written in 1974, but unpublished. See esp. pp. 29–30, 45, 94.

2. This comment was made by a Doris Redekop's father, Mr. Nickel, when he heard me preach in the Waterloo M.B. Church in 1979 when I was on sabbatical writing my dissertation.

3. For a fuller description of my three years at MBBC, see Chapter 8, pp. 224-6.

4. See also Chapter 9 of my book, *The Scandal of Evangelism: A Biblical Study of the Ethics of Evangelism* (Eugene, Oregon: Cascade Books, 2018).

5. Soren Kierkegaard, *Concluding Unscientific Postscript*, trans. by D.F. Swenson & W. Lowrie (Princeton University Press, 1974), p. 182.

6. I still have in my files an article by Frank C. Peters entitled, "Your Work is not Your Calling," *Mennonite Brethren Herald*, (Aug. 27, 1971), pp. 2-3.

7. Ephesians 6:7; cf. Colossians 3:23. Paul generalizes: "And whatever you do, whether in word or deed, do it all in the name of the Lord Jesus, giving thanks to God the Father through him" (Col 3:17).

8. See, for example, Os Guinness, *The Call: Finding and Fulfilling the Central Purpose of your Life* (Nashville W Group, 2003). Timothy Keller, *Every Good Endeavor: Connecting your Work to God's Work* (New York, Riverhead, 2012). Amy Sherman, *Kingdom Calling: Vocational Stewardship for the Common Good* (InterVarsity Press, 2011).

9. I believe it is appropriate to talk about the "mission" of a Christian philosophy professor at a college or a university. See Paul Gould, *The Outrageous Idea of the Missional Professor* (Wipf & Stock, 2014).

10. In August of 1963 I gave a sermon in the Swift Current M.B. Church, "Redemption from the Tyranny of Things," using of all things, the difficult story of Abraham nearly

sacrificing his son Isaac. Then in September, I spoke at the South-side Chapel on "The Path to Humility," based on Deuteronomy 7:6-8, 9:4-7. Other early efforts at preaching were at the Mountview Mennonite Brethren Church in Stoney Creek, which I was attending while at McMaster University (January, 1967), as well as at the Hamilton Rescue Mission that same year.

11. Wedding sermons: Mike and Susan Page, 1973; Bob and Trudy Nickel, 1980; Ray and Young-Soon Benoit, 1984; Morley and Margo Myers, 1985; Andrew and Rachel Thiessen, 1998; Nathan and Stephanie Kowalsky, 2000; Dan and Renae Barbour, 2003; Greg and Laura Thiessen, 2004; Richard and Bre'el Nickel, 2008. Nathan Kowalsky told me at one point that my sermons at these weddings were having a significant impact on his non-Christian friends.

12. The funeral was held on August 10, 1988, in Brooks. (Sermon file #88)

13. Books of the bible I have taught: Exodus, Isaiah, Jeremiah, Hosea, Amos, Habakkuk, Malachi, Daniel, Acts, 1 & 2 Corinthians, Romans, Philippians, Ephesians, Colossians, I John, 1 Peter, James.

14. Topics covered in Sunday School series and in other contexts: basic Christianity, eschatology, ethics, bio-medical ethics, technology, theology of work, apologetics, Christian mind, spiritual disciplines, prayers of the bible, Christian worldview, and intellectual virtues and vices.

15. Seminars in other churches: Alvin Penner invited me to do a series in the Duchess Mennonite Church (Sept. 2002), on the topic: "Following Jesus: from Damascus to Danzig to Duchess. More recently, I did a series on Christian ethics at the Leamington United Mennonite Church (Nov. 2018).

16. Lectures and seminars at youth retreats: M.B. College and Career Camp, Fairhavens, 1969 ("Christian Involvement Academically"); Grad Camp, 1970 ("The Case for Pacifism"); I gave two presentations at the M.B. Youth Convention at Banff in 1977 ("From Doubt to Faith," and "Philosophy and Christianity"); a series of three lectures at the Ontario M.B. Youth Retreat, 1978 ("Place of the Mind in Christian Discipleship, in apologetics and in epistemology"); M.B. National Youth Convention in Calgary, 2002 ("Philosopher's Stone: A Christian Philosopher's Journey").

17. Lectures to Christian groups on university campuses: "A Faith that Risks," WLU, 1971; "Knowledge, Doubt and Faith," University of Lethbridge, 1977; Contemporary Ethical Relativism, University of Lethbridge, 1983. I also gave a lecture on "Worldviews and the Christian Mind," for Power2Change at WLU and U of W, as well as four-part series on the same topic at U of W in 2018.

18. The prophet Jeremiah warns about prophets who "speak visions from their own minds, not from the mouth of the LORD" (23:16).

19. Here I have been helped by Richard B. Hays' treatment of the task of hermeneutics (*The Moral Vision of the New Testament*, New York: HarperSanFrancisco, 1996). Hays argues that we need some imaginative creativity in applying the biblical story to our times. He describes the challenge in this way: "the use of the New Testament in normative ethics requires *an integrative act of the imagination*, a discernment about how our lives, despite their historical dissimilarity to the lives narrated in the New Testament, might fitly answer to that narration and participate in the truth that it tells" (p. 298). I also deal with this problem in my book *The Scandal of Evangelism*, Chapter 2.

20. Sermon title: "Faith and Doubt." (Sermon file #104)

21. Pastors at the Crestwood M.B. Church while we were attending: Walter Epp (1971-3); Walter Wiens (1973-77); Dave Rempel and Lay-ministers (1977-78); Jake Penner (1978- 82); Lay-ministers (1982-4); David Funk (1984-9); Mark Jantzen (1989-98); Murray Schmidt (1998-2004); Jim Miller, Interim (2004-7).

22. See for example, *The Scandal of the Evangelical Mind*, by Mark A. Noll (Eerdmans, 1994).

23. I have certainly tried to be gentle when arguing in the church, but probably not always sufficiently so. My good church friend, Dave Rempel, once told me, "You are a formidable opponent in opposition" (1988). This is probably one of the liabilities of being a philosopher.

24. This doesn't mean that policies aren't important in the church. I am still proud of my work on a Guidelines Manual for the Crestwood M.B. Church that I worked on in 1992, and was pleased when other churches called me because they had heard about the Guidelines we had developed in hiring and evaluating pastors.

25. This truth was hammered home to me while working on a second draft of this chapter when I happened to be reading the Torah for my daily devotions. The Israelites repeatedly challenged Moses and even suggested that they would have been better off still being in Egypt (Exod 16:2-3; Num 11:1-3; 14:1-4; 16:1-3; 16:41). At one point Moses and Aaron even suggest that it isn't really against them that the Israelites were complaining, but against God (Exod 16:7-8). Even Aaron and Miriam revolt against Moses and it is in this context that Moses is described as being "the most humble man on earth (Num 12:1-3). See also Samuel's experience of rejection and God's comforting reminder to Samuel that "it is not you they have rejected as their king, but me" (1 Sam 8:7). I found these passages very relevant to reviewing my experiences at the Crestwood Church. Perhaps I should have taken all the criticism more in stride.

26. For some comments on how I have coped with this theological isolation, see Chapter 7, p. 208.

27. Raymond D. Bradley, "From Fundamentalist to Freethinker," in *Religious Upbringing and the Costs of Freedom: Personal and Philosophical Essays*, edited by Peter Caws & Stefani Jones (Pennsylvania State University Press, 2010), p. 50. My review of this book is found in *Studies in Religion*, Vol. 42, (June, 2013), pp. 262-4, and on my blog https://elmerjohnthiessen.wordpress.com/2014/09/05/some-stories-about-religious-upbringing-and-the-costs-of-freedom/

28. I am drawing here from Donald A. Hagner, "Faith, Historical Criticism and the Grace of God," in *I (Still) Believe*, edited by John Byron and Joel N. Lohr (Grand Rapids, MI: Zondervan, 2015), pp. 105-116.

29. For my review of Borg's *The Heart of Christianity* (2003), see https://elmerjohnthiessen.wordpress.com/2012/09/27/a-philosopher-examines-marcus-borg/ For my review of *The Bible Tells Me So ...: Why Defending Scripture Has Made Us Unable To Read It*, by Peter Enns (2014), see *The Evangelical Quarterly* Vol. 88, #2, (2016/17), pp. 63-7; and also https://elmerjohnthiessen.wordpress.com/2018/05/ For my review of Peter Enns' *The Sin of Certainty* (2016), see https://elmerjohnthiessen.wordpress.com/2018/05/

30. For an argument against a "hermeneutic of suspicion" see my blog, https://elmerjohnthiessen.wordpress.com/2017/11/

31. See Chapter 6 of my *Teaching for Commitment* (McGill-Queen's University Press, 1993). As Ludwig Wittgenstein puts it, "The child learns by believing the adult. Doubt

comes after belief." Ludwig Wittgenstein, *On Certainty*, edited by G.E.M. Anscombe and G.H. von Wright; trans. G.E.M. Anscombe (New York: Harper & Row, 1969/1972), para. 160.

32. Alistair MacIntyre describes vital traditions and the institutions that bear these traditions as being constituted by a "continuous argument," and as embodying "continuities of conflict." "A living tradition then is an historically extended, socially embodied argument." In *After Virtue*. 2nd ed. (Notre Dame, IN: University of Notre Dame Press, 1984), p. 222.

33. Deut 11:28; 28:14; 31:16-17, 21, 29; Judg 2:16-23; Pss 78:8; 95:10; Jer 5:23; 11:10; 13:10, 18:15; Amos 8:11-13.

34. Matt 24:10-13; 1 Cor 15:2; Eph. 4:14; 6:14; II Tim. 4:3-4; 2 Thess 2:15; Titus 1:9; 2 Pet 1:12; I John 4:1-6; Heb 2:2; 3:14; Rev 3:3.

35. My thinking here has been shaped by the works of Richard Lovelace which I read many years ago. *Dynamics of Spiritual Life: An Evangelical Theology of Renewal* (InterVarsity Press, 1979); *Renewal as a Way of Life: A Guidebook for Spiritual Growth* (InterVarsity Press, 1985).

36. I once made these suggestions to a prominent church leader who was very much a liberal theologically and who was having trouble understanding the differences between conservatives and liberals on the issue of gay marriage. Sadly, I received a very caustic response, which misrepresented what I was saying, and was sarcastic and demeaning. Of course this put a stop to any further conversations.

37. For my review of Borg and Wright's *The Meaning of Jesus*, see https://elmerjohnthiessen.wordpress.com/2018/09/

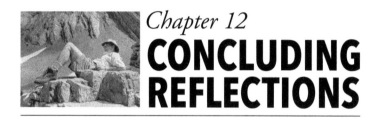

Chapter 12
CONCLUDING REFLECTIONS

Writing one's autobiography or memoirs is a strange exercise. It is impossible to describe everything that has happened in one's life. One has to select what is thought to be important. But such selection is of necessity subjective and even biased. Then there is the problem of trying to remember what one has experienced. Our memories too are faulty and biased. And then there is the question of why one even bothers writing about one's life. Is it to make oneself feel important? Or is one trying to satisfy the curiosity of others who will read one's story?[1]

These are the questions that Augustine asks towards the end of his famous *Confessions*. "What am I, then, O my God? What is my nature? It is teeming life of every conceivable kind, and exceedingly vast." Augustine confesses that he has tried "to penetrate as deeply as I can" into the mysteries of his life, but he has discovered that there are "no boundaries anywhere." And then after some comments on memory, some irony: "So great is the faculty of memory, so great the power of life in a person whose life is tending towards death!"[2]

How does Augustine solve the problem of accurately remembering the inexhaustible complexity of his life? He appeals to God who knows his life so much better than he himself does. "O my God, profound, infinite complexity . . . Let me, then, confess what I know about myself, and confess too what I do not know, because what I know of myself I know only because you shed light on me, and what I do not know I shall remain ignorant about until my darkness becomes like bright noon before your face."[3] And then follows adoration and worship of the God who knows him completely. "I love you, Lord, with no doubtful mind but with absolute certainty. You pierced my heart with your Word, and I fell in love with you."[4] With Augustine, I too worship my Lord after my incomplete and inadequate attempt at summarizing my life. Only God knows me perfectly. And contrasting the complexity of my life with the infinite complexity of my Lord helps to make me properly humble. My story is incomplete and biased. But I offer it to the reader hoping and praying that it might in some way be an encouragement to readers as they stumble towards the new heaven and the new earth when everything will be made new, including ourselves.[5]

FAILURES AND FLAWS

There is another problem with my autobiography that needs to be identified. I don't think I have been honest enough about my flaws and failures. Augustine was more transparent. But I do want the reader to know that I am very much aware of my failures and flaws and sinful nature. With the Psalmist I say, "Surely I have been a sinner from birth, sinful from the time my mother conceived me" (Ps 51:5). But even here, I am probably not as aware of my sinful nature as I should be. That is why the Psalmist also talks of God knowing our "secret sins" (Ps 90:8). "Who can discern his errors? Forgive my hidden faults" (Ps 19:12). So one reason why I haven't been more transparent about my sins in this recounting of my life is that some of them are hidden from me. I couldn't describe them even if I wanted to. But there is more. While I have from time to time tried to describe some flaws and failures that I am aware of, I have by no means described all of them. Why? Because to describe some of them is simply too embarrassing and even painful. Further, to describe all of my flaws and failures would be repetitious and boring. There just are so many. So my story is incomplete and biased in terms of glossing over many of my mistakes, failures, flaws and sins. The reader will therefore have to be satisfied with a more general treatment of this subject.

But I will say this. Later in my life I was made aware of a prayer that was frequently on the lips of the patristic fathers, and I have often prayed with them: "Lord Jesus Christ, be merciful to me a sinner." And praise God, there is abundant mercy to be found in our Lord Jesus Christ. It is further significant that in the same Psalm where David confesses that he has been a sinner from birth, he repeatedly throws himself on the mercy of God. "Have mercy on me, O God, according to your unfailing love; according to your great compassion. . . . Cleanse me with hyssop, and I will be clean; wash me, and I will be whiter than snow. . . . Create in me a pure heart, O God and renew a steadfast spirit within me" (Ps 51:1, 7, 10). I thank my Lord that he has forgiven all my sins, even the sin of not confessing all my sins in telling my story. Lord Jesus Christ, be merciful to me a sinner.

As will be apparent from my comments thus far, these memoirs could have been very different from what I have in fact written. Julian Barnes, in his novel, *The Sense of an Ending*, has his main character tell his story twice, and each story is very different.[6] So it is with my own story. I could have written a very different story. But the one I have written is already too long and I am content to stick with the story I have written. Besides, while my children will no doubt be able to correct some things I have written, there are few who can challenge the overall narrative. "The longer one lives," Tony reflects in Barnes' novel, "the fewer those around to challenge our account, to remind us that our life is not our life, merely the story we have told about our life. Told to others, but-mainly-to ourselves."[7]

There is some truth to this assessment though I would counter the rather postmodernist interpretation of reality implicit in Tony's account of story-telling. Our lives are more than the story we tell. There is after all a God who can recount our stories more accurately. Indeed it is God who has "the last word."[8] Or, as Paul puts it, summarizing a theme that runs throughout the bible, "For we must all appear before the judgment seat of Christ, that each one may receive what is due him for the things done while in the body, whether good or bad" (2 Cor 5:10). The books will finally be opened at the end of time, John, the apostle and poet, tells us in the last book of the bible, and then we will be given an accurate account of all that we have done (Rev 20:11-15). So my full story will have to wait until the day of judgment. And I am content with that, because I know the One who will tell my full story is also longsuffering and gracious. My hope and prayer is that my Master will be able to say about at least some of my life, "Well done, good and faithful servant" (Matt 25:21). The rest will need to be covered by grace.

GOOD TIMES AND BAD TIMES

There is another sense in which I have in fact told two stories in this autobiography. There is a story of difficult times and there is a story of times of contentment and joy. In Chapter 1, I have told the story of my difficult beginnings, times spent in the hospital undergoing a number of surgeries to repair my deformities. But the difficulties didn't end there. My father died when I was only a teenager. There were also times when the challenges of raising a family seemed burdensome, when I felt trapped with my responsibilities. Then there were the crises in my life, challenging times, when I tried to correct injustices at the college where I spent most of my teaching career, the feeling of abandonment and the loss of reputation after years of devoted service in a church, and months of anxiety, mental depression, and panic attacks that are scary because they are completely beyond one's control.

I have also told the story of good times, times when I was contented and filled with deep joy. I thank God for finding a wife who has loved me and has been faithful to me throughout all these years, and who has also provided the stability I so much needed to do anything constructive. I thank God for the many joys brought to me by my children, times of playful laughter, times of contentedly reading a book to them as part of their bed-time routines, and times when they would wrap their arms around me and tell me that they loved me. Then there were the joys of watching them grow into adults who continued to love me despite my not always being the father they needed me to be. Weddings were highlights, as also the gift of grandchildren. I thank God for many years in a challenging and meaningful career where I could use my gifts in teaching and writing. I am thankful for the many student affirmations of my teaching, sometimes coming many years after I taught these students.

Then there are the experiences of a deep sense of contentment that comes in knowing that one has tried to do that which is right and good. I thank my Lord and Saviour, Jesus Christ, for opportunities to preach and teach and lead in the church which he founded and continues to love. I thank God for long-lasting friendships and also for those that are not so long because life has carried us to different places or because friendships have been formed later in life. Either way, I am thankful for times where both the joys and the burdens of life could be shared with these friends without any hesitation. I thank God for the many wonderful times in His bounteous creation – times in campgrounds with my family, times climbing mountains with my friends and family, times canoeing rivers in northern Ontario with my son, and times alone in prayer and meditation, feeling God's presence in some quiet spot in nature.

Yes, life is a mixture of the good and the bad. I resonate with Job's friend Eliphaz who makes the astute comment that "man is born to trouble as surely as sparks fly upward" (Job 5:7). Then there is the prayer of Moses in Psalm 90 where he describes the length of our years as seventy or eighty (or ninety in our time), "if we have the strength; yet their span is but trouble and sorrow, for they quickly pass, and we fly away (Ps 90:10). But the Psalms also describe happier times. "[M]ay the righteous be glad and rejoice before God, may they be happy and joyful" (Ps 68:3). "How abundant are the good things that you have stored up for those who fear you, that you bestow in the sight of all, on those who take refuge in you" (Ps 31:19 – NIV-UK).

The writer of Ecclesiastes captures the balance: "When times are good, be happy; but when times are bad, consider: God has made the one as well as the other" (Ecc 7:14). The epistle of James too addresses both the good times and the bad times of life: "Is any one of you in trouble? He should pray. Is anyone happy? Let him sing songs of praise" (James 5:13). So, on balance I can only say that life has been good. Even the bad times have a good side to them.

It would be a mistake, however, to assess one's life simply on the basis of a calculation of good times and bad times. Such an approach is not only too subjective, but also too earthly, too this-worldly. Finally, we need to rely on a more transcendent perspective, and here I am thinking of God's evaluation of our efforts here on earth in the here and now. Surely this is finally the most important measure of the significance of what we do with our lives here on earth. Hence Paul's conclusion after a brilliant analysis of the implications of the resurrection of Jesus Christ: "Therefore, my dear brothers, stand firm. Let nothing move you. Always give yourselves fully to the work of the Lord, because you know that your labor in the Lord is not in vain" (1 Cor 15:56). There have been times when my work at the college or in the church has seemed to be in vain, with no evident positive results, and even without meaning. And then I have had to remind myself that insofar as my work has been done in obedience to Jesus Christ, my work is not in vain. Even a cup of cold water given to those who are unimportant is acknowledged and given importance by our Lord (Matt 10:42).

CARING AND NOT CARING

How to assess the significance of one's life and work? That is a question that I have wrestled with throughout my life. There is a danger of seeing life as meaningless and hence also seeing one's work as insignificant. But there is also a danger of placing too much importance on one's life and one's work. I think I have been especially prone to the latter danger. I am by nature a serious person. I think deeply about things. I feel deeply about my experiences. I am passionate about what I do. I am an idealist and a perfectionist, and therefore I care deeply about that which is not ideal or not perfect. The teacher and writer of Ecclesiastes, one of my favorite books of the bible, says this: "For dreams come with many cares" (Ecc 5:3). How true! And how very true for me.

I remember a sermon I preached many years ago entitled, "The Cost of Caring and the Cost of not Caring."[9] In reading it over once again while writing this chapter I was somewhat surprised (and perhaps also pleased) at the depth of insight in this sermon. The sermon begins with an illustration borrowed from Calvin Miller's *The Table of Inwardness*. Miller tells the sad story of a physician he knew who eventually committed suicide. He had spent his life caring for children with leukemia. As he grew older he never adjusted to the seeming riddle of a God who loved children and yet created a world with diseases that killed them. Finally after seeing so many children die he could no longer face his inadequacy and his inability to heal. Taped to the gun he used to kill himself was this short note, "It hurts too much to care, and it hurts too much not to care"[10] Miller adds, "His grieving life issued in a grieving death."

In my sermon I shifted the focus of the above quotation slightly – "It hurts to care, and it hurts not to care." What an accurate description of the human condition. Really caring about what one does causes a lot of pain and heartache. But being apathetic about life has its own problems. So how do we resolve this seeming dilemma? I went on in my sermon to review the overall narrative of the bible where we find God caring deeply about mankind and where God is often described as grieving about people who spurned his love. We are made in the image of God and therefore we too are made to care about our endeavors, even as we realize that the cost of caring will often create agony and grief. But this grief is bearable if we keep before us the example of Jesus, God's only begotten Son. Jesus shows us how costly caring is. Indeed, it would seem that Jesus himself was tempted not to care when he prays in the Garden of Gethsemane, "My Father, if it is possible, may this cup be taken from me." But in the end Jesus went on to pray: "Yet not as I will, but as you will" (Matt 26:36-39). And God sustained him and ultimately glorified him, though it involved suffering even unto death.

What is further interesting about my sermon is that it was given in 1988, a year which I have described as "one of the most difficult years of my academic career." It was in fact the year in which I took on the project of getting the president of Medicine Hat College removed, a project that I now realize was probably a mistake. I believe I cared too much about this venture. In the end removing the president didn't solve the deeply-rooted problems of Medicine Hat College. Indeed, it is impossible to eliminate all the problems of any institution. There will always be a crack in everything. So we need to care but in measured amounts. And we must never think that we can create utopia here on earth. This kind of idealism brings about despair and even suicide.[11] But all this has been a difficult lesson for me to learn.

Interestingly, my yearly diaries reveal that a few decades earlier I was wrestling with the related notion of "idealistic realism" – a phrase that appears in the title of another sermon I first preached in 1976.[12] It has been well said that all preaching is in part autobiography. This notion of idealistic realism is really another expression of the tension between caring and not caring. Long after I preached these earlier sermons I have come to a greater appreciation of the nature of Christian hope – we await the consummation of the kingdom of God when all things will be put right, but we live at a time when the kingdom of God on earth is not fully realized. So we continue to pray, "Your kingdom come, your will be done on earth as it is in heaven," and we work towards that end, realizing that only partial healing and restoration is possible in the present time. The word "partial" is important here. Perfect healing and restoration is not possible in the present time. Christian hope means "that we trust in what is coming but is not yet with us in its fulness. We live between the times, after the inauguration of the kingdom but before its final consummation."[13]

There is another indicator of my early struggles with idealism and realism, and the tension between caring and not caring. In 1976 I wrote a review of Jacques Ellul's *The Ethics of Freedom*.[14] Towards the end of his book Ellul has a chapter on being pilgrims and strangers here on earth. He wrestles with the tension of being deeply immersed in this world while at the same time drawing on our Christian vision of what is possible. Ellul talks about the need to relativize our projects. While our projects are important, we must not become obsessed with them, he argues. There is a danger that we see our tasks as too significant. If we see them as temporal, we will be able to view them in proper perspective. The absolute must wait for the eschaton.

Finding the right balance between idealism and realism, or between caring too much and caring too little, is not easy. As I look back on my life I realize that I cared too much and have been too serious about many things. I took my studies at university too seriously. I have taken argumentation and critical analysis too seriously. My writing has been described as too serious.[15] I was too serious about finding a life's partner. I cared too much about solving the problems at Medicine Hat College. I was too serious about rescuing the Crestwood Mennonite Brethren Church from its problems. I have gradually come to realize that I can't solve all the problems of this world. The Psalmist repeatedly warns us not to put our trust in the human effort of mere mortals, mere people of the dust.[16] And this also applies to my own efforts to make things right. What I have gradually learned is that I need to be patient and trust that God will ultimately make all things right, if not in this world, then in the next.

I have often found solace in one of Jesus' beatitudes: "How blest are those who hunger and thirst to see right prevail; they shall be satisfied" (Matt 5:6 - NEB). Jesus is here commending those who passionately yearn for that which is right and just. There is realism here because the longing for righteousness is unending. Not until we reach heaven will we "hunger no more, and thirst no more" for only then will Christ our Shepherd lead us "to springs of the water of life" (Rev 7:16-17 - NRSV). In the meantime, we are still declared blessed and happy, because we know that our present deepest longings are in line with the kingdom of God, and we also know that ultimately righteousness and justice will prevail. I often call to mind Jesus' words, "Come to me all you who are weary and burdened, and I will give you rest" (Matt 11:28). I think Jesus' words also apply to the burden of wanting to make all things right.[17] And so I need to relax more.[18] I need to learn to live in an imperfect world, and enjoy the good that still keeps shining through despite all the evil and injustice around me. I am a slow learner, but I like to think that in my old age I have arrived at a better balance between caring too much and caring too little. Praise to you, O Christ.

TRUTH

It is perhaps appropriate to conclude the memoirs of a philosopher with a brief treatment of a philosophical topic. What is truth? This was the question that Pilate asked Jesus during his trial (John 18:28-40). It is a question that has also haunted me throughout my life and my philosophical career. And it seems that my life's vocation has increasingly been one of defending the very notion of truth. The impact of postmodernism has made this task increasingly difficult. But I soldier on, and will, to my dying day, continue to argue that there is such a thing as Truth with a capital "T".

I wrote an article on truth in 1997 for *Encounter,* a special issue of the *Mennonite Brethren Herald.*[19] I quote from the first paragraph of this article entitled, "Truth in a Pluralist World." "The notion of truth is under siege today. In my twenty-seven years of teaching philosophy at colleges and universities, there is perhaps no other topic which sparks as much debate as the question of the existence of truth. And any time I dare to suggest that there just might be such a thing as Truth with a capital "T", I invariably encounter a battery of standard objections, outright disbelief, and even indignation. It is as though I had suggested that the earth is flat!"[20]

In my ongoing deliberations on this topic, I have come to realize that much of the opposition to the notion of truth is based on a failure to make an important distinction between Truth as an ideal concept which is in some way absolute, and the human search for truth which is in fact relative. I have tried to illustrate this distinction with a philosophical diagram which I have labelled "The Ladder of Truth."[21]

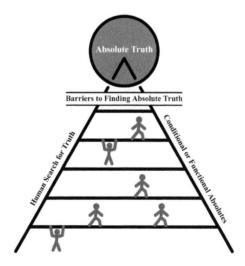

In this diagram, you find Truth with a capital "T" placed above a barrier. Below the barrier you find human figures desperately trying to climb the ladder in order to get closer to the Truth. Already as children, we are trying to discover the truth about things. An ongoing search for truth would seem to be an essential aspect of human nature. In fact we also have a tendency to think that we have arrived at the truth. As William James puts it, all of us instinctively "dogmatize like infallible popes."[22] This very tendency is itself a pointer to the ideal of Absolute Truth. We long for Truth with a capital "T". But we often find that we get it wrong. This again points to an ideal of Truth which serves as a standard by which we measure our mistaken convictions. The concept of error presupposes the concept of Truth.

Now I quite agree that we can never presume to have actually arrived at the Absolute Truth. Hence the barrier in the diagram. Here it needs to be stressed that we as human beings can never cross this barrier. Why? As finite creatures we are stuck with having a limited perspective. "We don't yet see things clearly," as the apostle Paul puts it in his famous discourse on love (1 Cor. 13:12 – *The Message*). We are fallible and sinful creatures. And so we remain on the ladder of truth below the barrier, trying hard to arrive at Truth. If we are honest, we will be very aware of the fact that we can never arrive at absolute certainty regarding our convictions about what we believe to be true. Hence the notion of "conditional or functional absolutes" found below the barrier. Our certainties are at best provisional. Our claims to truth are always tentative. We can at best only stumble towards the Truth.

One of my favorite quotes that I have often used when discussing this diagram is taken from American pragmatist, William James, who describes the notion of Absolute Truth in this way: "The 'absolutely' true, meaning what no further experience will ever alter, is that ideal vanishing-point towards which we imagine that all our temporary truths will someday converge."[23] I believe James has got it exactly right. We cannot do away with the notion of truth with a capital "T". That is what we all aspire to, but there are significant barriers to our ever saying with absolute confidence that we have got the Truth. We are therefore stuck with "temporary truths," and humility demands that we admit the same, though we never give up on our continuing search for Truth. Without an ideal of Truth, without a goal in our search for Truth, we are left with aimless floundering in a sea of relativism.

More recently I have written three reviews of books dealing with postmodernism, relativism and truth.[24] In 2012 I posted on my blog a review essay of James Smith's book, *Who's Afraid of Postmodernism? Taking Derrida, Lyotard, and Foucault to Church*. This blog has received the highest number of views of any of my blogs.[25] This review essay was also published in *The Evangelical Quarterly* in 2011, and I don't know how many people have read the printed version of this essay. But it is clear that my critique of Smith's flirtation with postmodern relativism is being read and I trust those reading it are duly warned about the dangers of denying truth.

At the time of writing a first draft of this chapter, I was reading an anthology of Michel Foucault's writings, trying to get a better understanding of this French postmodernist's treatment of truth.[26] The focus of Foucault's writings is on discovering the "genealogy" of claims to truth. What are the conditions under which truth claims are made? Here are Foucault's own words in *Truth and Method*: "'Truth' is linked in a circular relation with systems of power which produce and sustain it, and to effects of power which it induces and which extends it. A 'regime' of truth."[27] It is not easy to interpret Foucault's writings. On the one hand, Foucault can be interpreted as giving us a prescriptive analysis of truth. In other words he is defending the idea of truth as a power construct and therefore he is saying that it is wrong to believe in Truth with a capital "T." The problem with this prescriptive analysis of truth is that it is self-refuting. If truth is merely a power construct, then Foucault's own genealogy of truth is itself simply a product of powerful contextual forces. So, why bother listening to him?

There is however another way to interpret Foucault. Rather than giving us a prescriptive definition of truth, perhaps Foucault is trying to give us a description of how the nature truth claims is changing. Perhaps the real thrust of his genealogy of claims to truth is to show how truth has in fact become linked to power. And there is something to be said for interpreting Foucault as giving us a prophetic analysis of what is happening to truth in the modern world. "Post-truth" has become one of the defining words of our time. Disinformation, half-truths, falsehoods, and conspiracy theories are being disseminated at such a volume that this phenomenon has been appropriated dubbed "the firehose of falsehood." And the result is an escalating power struggle for the right to define "truth" whatever that might mean.

What is the solution? Unfortunately, Foucault is not clear on this. I would suggest that the only way to overcome these problems is to rehabilitate the abstract ideal of truth. We need to move beyond power struggles for the right to define truth. It is only if we unite in a common search for Truth that we will be able to overcome the problems of disagreement, diatribe, disinformation, divisiveness and power struggles, problems that are tearing our societies apart. Sadly, Foucault has little to contribute in resolving these problems. Instead, he contributes to these problems by failing to defend Truth with a capital "T."

My ongoing wrestling with these issues has led me in the last while to focus on intellectual virtues and vices. The search for truth is often considered to be foundational to all the intellectual virtues. I taught a six-week course entitled, "Dogmatism, Open-mindedness and Other Intellectual Virtues and Vices," in the life-long learning program at Wilfrid Laurier University in the fall of 2018. Not only was there a lot of interest in the topic – I had a full class of twenty-nine students with another twenty on a waiting list – but discussions were lively. I also taught a two-part series in the adult Sunday School program at Waterloo North Mennonite Church in the fall of 2019, and again there was a keen interest in the topic and a lively discussion.[28] These are just two indicators that there is hunger for clarity about truth in our day. Perhaps the prophet Amos is speaking to our time when he describes a famine throughout the land, "not a famine of food or a thirst for water, but a famine of hearing the words of the LORD" (Amos 8:11). Indeed, Amos goes on to provide a vivid description of relativism: "Men will stagger from sea to sea and wander from north to east, searching for the word of the LORD, but they will not find it" (vs. 12). And sadly, it is particularly young women and men who are fainting because of our loss of Truth (vs. 13).

My "Ladder of Truth" diagram does, however, acknowledge one important contribution that postmodernism has made to epistemology, namely the recognition that our search for truth is always situated in "the present and the particular."[29] Our starting point is therefore always quite subjective. But our aim is to move beyond our subjective starting point. We therefore find ourselves on different rungs on the ladder of truth, recognizing always that we ourselves don't have "the last word," to quote from another book that I often refer to in discussions of this topic.[30] Hence the importance of intellectual virtues like humility, open-mindedness, and the love of truth. They are a key to getting closer to the truth.[31]

So here is a philosophical puzzle that continues to fascinate me. The Psalmist's description of aging philosophers has been an inspiration for me: "They will still bear fruit in old age, they will stay fresh and green" (Ps 92:14). I hope to continue my philosophical explorations until the day I die. I may even write a book on intellectual virtues and vices.

My favourite hike, Ptarmigan Cirque, Kananaskis, 1997. Photo Peter Mah

I conclude my story with some final reflections on aging. I am getting older. Psalm 71 has been called a Psalm of old age. The Psalm is somewhat disorganized, which might be one indicator that it was written by an old man. Perhaps my memoirs are similarly disorganized! The Psalm also makes repeated references to old age. "Do not cast me away when I am old; do not forsake me when my strength is gone" (vs.9). "Even when I am old and gray, do not forsake me, O God" (vs. 18). There is also a keen awareness of the stages of life. The Psalmist acknowledges his dependence on God at his birth (vs. 6), and also in his youth (vss. 5). Indeed, his life has been one long journey of learning. "Since my youth, O God, you have taught me" (vs. 17). And he is very much aware of his responsibility as an old man to "declare . . . to the next generation," God's "power" and "might" (vs. 18).

How does the writer of this Psalm sum up his life? "Though you have made me see troubles, many and bitter, you will restore my life again; from the depths of the earth you will again bring me up" (vs. 20). Indeed, the

Psalmist seems to facing a host of troubles even in his old age. He feels insecure and so he clings to God as a refuge (vs. 1). He feels abandoned in old age (vs. 9). He is facing accusations and even attacks from enemies (vss. 4, 11, 13, 24). Not exactly an upbeat account of old age, but it is realistic. Thankfully the Psalm includes some words of reorientation.

> *In you, O LORD, I have taken refuge;*
> *let me never be put to shame.*
> *Rescue me and deliver me in your righteousness;*
> *turn your ear to me and save me.*
> *Be my rock of refuge,*
> *to which I can always go;*
> *give the command to save me,*
> *for you are my rock and my fortress. (vss. 1-3)*

> *For you have been my hope, O Sovereign LORD,*
> *my confidence since my youth.*
> *From birth I have relied on you;*
> *you brought me forth from my mother's womb.*
> *I will ever praise you. (vss. 5-6)*

> *But as for me, I will always have hope;*
> *I will praise you more and more.*
> *My mouth will tell of your righteousness,*
> *of your salvation all day long,*
> *though I know not its measure.*
> *I will come and proclaim your mighty acts,*
> *O Sovereign LORD;*
> *I will proclaim your righteousness, yours alone.*
> *Since my youth, O God, you have taught me,*
> *and to this day I declare your marvelous deeds. (vss. 14-17)*

I trust these memoirs will be similarly read as an expression of praise to my Sovereign LORD. The Psalmist also captures the purpose in writing these memoirs. "Even when I am old and gray, do not forsake me, O God, till I declare your power to the next generation, your might to all who are to come" (vs. 18).

My journey as a philosopher has been challenging, but deeply satisfying, intellectually and spiritually and practically. I wouldn't exchange it for anything. Praise be to God. My journey isn't over yet. But the telling of my story has to end before my journey has ended. Dead men can't write memoirs. So my story ends here, though my journey with my Savior and my God continues. I conclude with one of my favorite lines from the apostle Paul, lines which have inspired the title of these memoirs. "Not that I have already obtained all this, or have already been made perfect, but I press on to take hold of that for which Christ Jesus took hold of me. Brothers (and Sisters) I do not consider myself yet to have taken hold of it. But one thing I do: Forgetting what is behind and straining toward what is ahead, I press on towards the goal to win the prize for which God has called me heavenward in Christ Jesus" (Phil 3:12-14).

NOTES

1. Paul Griffiths provides a telling description of these problems in his review of a novel by Julian Barnes which tells two stories of the same person. "You're not the person you take yourself to be. That's because the person you take yourself to be is a creature of narrative, and narratives are inevitably fabulous and fabricated, which is at least to say that they are opaque, partial, unreliable, and embroidered" ("Our Stories and God's," *First Things*, March 2012), pp. 53-4.

2. Saint Augustine, *The Confessions,* trans. by Maria Boulding (New York: Vintage Spiritual Classics, Random House, 1997), pp. 213-14.

3. Ibid., pp. 213, 201.

4. Ibid., p. 201.

5. While writing the first draft of this chapter, I was reading J. Richard Middleton's excellent book, *A New Heaven and a New Earth: Reclaiming a Biblical Eschatology* (Grand Rapids, MI: BakerAcademic, 2014).

6. Julian Barnes, *The Sense of an Ending* (Knopf, 2011).

7. Quoted in Paul Griffiths, "Our Stories and God's," p. 54.

8. This phrase comes from a book by Thomas Nagel, who is probably not a Christian, but who nevertheless counters postmodern subjectivism. See details in endnote #30 of this chapter.

9. Sermon #87 in my files.

10. Calvin Miller, *The Table of Inwardness* (Inter-Varsity Press, 1984), p. 108.

11. Rebecca Konyndyk DeYoung, in her insightful analysis of the seven deadly sins, including the vice of anger, identifies another consequence of idealism and caring too much about righting the wrongs of this world. "When we take for ourselves the responsibility for

making everything right, and rely on our own power and plans for effecting justice, our anger becomes excessive, aroused too quickly and too easily and smoldering too long when unassuaged." What is needed is patience to trust God to ultimately make things right, if not in this world, then in the next. (*Glittering Vices: A New Look at the Seven Deadly Sins and their Remedies* (Grand Rapids, MI: Brazos Press, 2009), p. 132.

12. Sermon #35 in my files.

13. Middleton, *A New Heaven and a New Earth*, p. 272.

14. Jacques Ellul, *The Ethics of Freedom* (Grand Rapids, MI: Wm. B. Eerdmans, 1976). This review is found in the *Mennonite Brethren Herald* (Oct. 15, 1976), pp. 26-7. I also wrote an opinion piece in the *Mennonite Brethren Herald*, entitled, "Realistic Idealism," (Oct. 24, 1980), p. 17.

15. A referee report on a research proposal for a SSHRC grant described my writing as "a bit solemn, lacking in wit and irony," though he went on to compare me to another scholar whose wit and irony sometimes became sarcasm, and so "perhaps a little solemnity is not a bad thing" (March, 2000).

16. Psalms 20:7; 118:9; 146:3. See also Isaiah 31:1.

17. Here again I find it significant that I gave a sermon later in my life based on this text "Bearing the Burden of Christian Discipleship" (Sermon #143 in my files, dated, Jan. 11, 2004).

18. T.S. Eliot, seems to capture this balance in her poem, Ash Wednesday: "Teach us to care and not to care. Teach us to be still."

19. *Encounter* was a new venture of the *M.B. Herald*, in which the editors were trying to create issues that could be distributed to non-Christian friends, The article in question was entitled, "Truth in a Pluralist World." *Encounter: A Mennonite Brethren Herald Special* (Feb. 21, 1997), pp. 14-18.

20. I have often referred to Allan Bloom, *The Closing of the American Mind*, where he begins his masterpiece with this commentary on today's students: "There is one thing a professor can be absolutely certain of: almost every student entering the university believes, or say he believes, that truth is relative. If this belief is put to the test, one can count on the students' reaction: they will be uncomprehending" (New York, NY: Simon and Schuster, 1987), p. 25.

21. This diagram was designed by my son Greg, and appears in two of my books: *In Defence of Religious Schools and Colleges* (Montreal & Kingston: McGill-Queen's University Press, 2001), p. 214; and T*he Ethics of Evangelism: A Philosophical Defence of Proselytizing and Persuasion* (Crownhill, Milton Keynes: Paternoster Press and Downers Grove, IL: IVP Academic, 2011), p. 69.

22. William James, *Essays in Pragmatism*, edited by Alburey Castell (New York: Hafner, 1968), p. 97.

23. Ibid., p. 170.

24. Review essay of James K.A. Smith, *Who's Afraid of Postmodernism? Taking Derrida, Lyotard, and Foucault to Church*, (Baker Academic, 2006), in *The Evangelical Quarterly*, Vol. 83, #4, (2011), pp. 347-51; Review Article: *Who's Afraid of Relativism: Community, Contingency, and Creaturehood*, by James K.A. Smith (Baker Academic, 2014) in *The Evangelical Quarterly*, Vol. 87, #2, (2015), pp.169-75; On-line review of Richard Rorty and Pascal Engel. *What's the Use of Truth?* (New York: Columbia University Press,

2007) in *Dialogue: Canadian Philosophical Review*, published January 8, 2018. https://doi.org/10.1017/S001221731700110X

25. As of June 2021, this blog has received 2,738 views.

26. *The Foucault Reader*, edited by Paul Rabinow (New York: Pantheon Books, 1984). Commenting on Nietzsche, Foucault writes, "Truth is undoubtedly the sort of error that cannot be refuted because it was hardened into an unalterable form in the long baking process of history" (Ibid., p. 79).

27. Ibid., p. 74.

28. See also a blog on this topic, https://elmerjohnthiessen.wordpress.com/2019/04/

29. This expression is found in Charles Bailey's, *Beyond the Present and the Particular: A Theory of Liberal Education* (London: Routledge and Kegan Paul, 1984).

30. Thomas Nagel describes absolute truth as "the view from nowhere." Although we cannot get a view from nowhere, according to Nagel, there is within each of us an impulse to transcend our particular personal point of view. This occurs because we recognize that it is merely a point of view, a perspective, and not simply an account of the way things really are. "The recognition that this is so," he writes, "creates pressure on the imagination to recast our picture of the world so that it is no longer the view from here" (*The View from Nowhere*, Oxford University Press, 1986, p. 70). In other words, each of us is aware of the possibility that our particular perspective might be wrong, and so we aspire to "the view from nowhere," to a view uncontaminated by any perspectival factors. Or, as Nagel puts it in his more recent work, the last word is not that this is justified "for me" or "for us." Instead, it is an affirmation of objective truth that any reasoner is obliged to recognize. The last word does not belong to human nature. "The idea of reason, by contrast, refers to nonlocal and nonrelative methods of justification – methods that distinguish universally legitimate from illegitimate inferences and that aim at reaching the truth in a nonrelative manner" (*The Last Word*, Oxford University Press, 1997, p. 5).

31. See Chapter 8, p. 241 for some more comments on intellectual virtues.

Lightning Source UK Ltd.
Milton Keynes UK
UKHW021825151021
392281UK00009B/2006